The Sport Psych Handbook

Shane Murphy, Editor

Human Kinetics

Library of Congress Cataloging-in-Publication Data

The sport psych handbook / Shane Murphy, editor.
  p. cm.
 Includes bibliographical references and index.
 ISBN 0-7360-4904-5 (soft cover)
 1. Sports--Psychological aspects--Handbooks, manuals, etc. I. Murphy,
Shane M., 1957-
GV706.4.S667 2004
796.01--dc22

                              2004015224

ISBN: 0-7360-4904-5

The Web addresses cited in this text were current as of August 2004, unless otherwise noted.

Developmental Editor: Jennifer L. Walker; **Assistant Editor:** Mandy Maiden; **Copyeditor:** Cheryl Ossola; **Proofreader:** Anne Rogers; **Indexer:** Bobbi Swanson; **Permission Manager:** Toni Harte; **Graphic Designer:** Nancy Rasmus; **Graphic Artist:** Tara Welsch; **Photo Manager:** Dan Wendt; **Cover Designer:** Keith Blomberg; **Photographer (cover):** Frank Perry/Getty Images; **Art Manager and Illustrator:** Kareema McLendon; **Printer:** United Graphics

Human Kinetics books are available at special discounts for bulk purchase. Special editions or book excerpts can also be created to specification. For details, contact the Special Sales Manager at Human Kinetics.

Printed in the United States of America   10 9 8 7 6 5 4 3 2 1

Human Kinetics
Web site: www.HumanKinetics.com

United States: Human Kinetics
P.O. Box 5076
Champaign, IL 61825-5076
800-747-4457
e-mail: humank@hkusa.com

Canada: Human Kinetics
475 Devonshire Road Unit 100
Windsor, ON N8Y 2L5
800-465-7301 (in Canada only)
e-mail: orders@hkcanada.com

Europe: Human Kinetics
107 Bradford Road
Stanningley
Leeds LS28 6AT, United Kingdom
+44 (0) 113 255 5665
e-mail: hk@hkeurope.com

Australia: Human Kinetics
57A Price Avenue
Lower Mitcham, South Australia 5062
08 8277 1555
e-mail: liaw@hkaustralia.com

New Zealand: Human Kinetics
Division of Sports Distributors NZ Ltd.
P.O. Box 300 226 Albany
North Shore City
Auckland
0064 9 448 1207
e-mail: blairc@hknewz.com

To Annemarie, Bryan, and Theresa.
I love you.

Contents

Preface   vii

Acknowledgments   ix

Introduction   xi

Part I

Inner Drive

| Chapter 1 | Motivation: The Need to Achieve | 3 |
John F. Eliot

| Chapter 2 | Goals: More Than Just the Score | 19 |
Chris Harwood

| Chapter 3 | Competitive Drive: Embracing Positive Rivalries | 37 |
Cal Botterill

| Chapter 4 | Overtraining: Balancing Practice and Performance | 49 |
Kirsten Peterson

Part II

Emotional and Mental Control

| Chapter 5 | Anxiety: From Pumped to Panicked | 73 |
Gloria Balague

| Chapter 6 | Anger: How to Moderate Hot Buttons | 93 |
Mitch Abrams and Bruce Hale

| Chapter 7 | Concentration: Focus Under Pressure | 113 |
Clark Perry

| Chapter 8 | Imagery: Inner Theater Becomes Reality | 127 |
Shane Murphy

Part III

Interactive Skills

Chapter 9	Leadership: Full Engagement for Success	155
	Jim Loehr	
Chapter 10	Teamwork: For the Good of the Whole	171
	Tracy L. Veach and Jerry R. May	
Chapter 11	Coaching: An Effective Communication System	191
	Charles J. Hardy, Kevin L. Burke, and R. Kelly Crace	

Part IV

Potential Pitfalls

Chapter 12	Injuries: The Psychology of Recovery and Rehab	215
	Charles Brown	
Chapter 13	Eating Disorders: When Rations Become Irrational	237
	Karen D. Cogan	
Chapter 14	Substance Use: Chemical Roulette in Sport	255
	Mark H. Anshel	

Part V

The Educated Consumer

Chapter 15	Roles: The Sport Psychologist	279
	Sean McCann	
Chapter 16	Qualifications: Education and Experience	293
	Bradley Hack	
Chapter 17	Success in Sport Psych: Effective Sport Psychologists	305
	David Tod and Mark Andersen	

Notes	315
Index	336
About the Editor	343
About the Contributors	345

Preface

We are not on earth to live up to someone else's expectations. To make
our unique contributions to the world, we each need to prize our individual worth and pursue our dreams.

California Task Force to Promote Self-Esteem and Personal and
Social Responsibility Toward a State of Esteem, 1990

All of us who worked on *The Sport Psych Handbook* are excited to bring this
resource to you. Sport psychology is a vibrant and stimulating field to work
in, and tremendous progress has been made in research and application during
the past 25 years. But for too many coaches and athletes, sport psychology is
a mystery, and the relationship between the mind and athletic performance is
not well understood. A big problem for sport psychology is that research has
not been widely disseminated. Original research is hard to read and new theories are often difficult to understand. What has been needed is a resource for
coaches and athletes that takes sport psychology research and makes it easy to
understand and apply to real-life competition. Now that resource is here! Every
chapter in *The Sport Psych Handbook* was written by experts in the field. All the
latest research is summarized in a simple but comprehensive manner, and each
chapter focuses on applying the knowledge gained from years of research to
the world of modern sport. For the first time, athletes and coaches have a fun,
easy-to-read resource that brings them up to date with the latest findings in
sport psychology. No wonder we're excited to bring this book to you!

After 20 years as a sport psychologist, I'm still surprised at how little most
people know about the field. At a conference last year in a lovely resort town in
the Hudson River Valley in New York State, I had just finished a presentation on
how sport psychology interventions can be used in many areas of life when one
of the conference attendees approached me. He was kind and generous in his
praise of my presentation, but then he said something I have heard often: "You
must enjoy working in such a brand-new field as sport psychology." Actually, the
roots of sport psychology go back to research carried out at the end of the 19th
century, and one of the forefathers of our field, Coleman Roberts Griffith, carried out most of his work in the 1920s and 1930s, publishing *Psychology of Coaching* in 1926 and *Psychology and Athletics* in 1928. He was even hired away from
academia by the Wrigley family to help and do research with the Chicago Cubs
baseball team (which, as we sport psychologists like to say, no doubt explains
the enormous success of the Cubs ever since!). Although I always chuckle when
people tell me that I work in a brand-new area of psychology, the reality is that

we need to do a much better job of making our knowledge widely available so that sport psychology is no longer one of the best-kept secrets in sport.

The organization of *The Sport Psych Handbook* is straightforward. There are five sections in the book, each of which contains several chapters covering that topic. Part I is "Inner Drive," which focuses on the motivational issues that are essential for athletic success. Why do athletes work so hard for so long to achieve goals that are often far off? What happens when an athlete hits a slump or seems burned out? What can coaches do to keep workouts interesting and motivating? Is competition among teammates a good thing, and if so, how much should be encouraged? What happens to an athlete who trains harder and harder but whose performances keep getting worse and worse? All these questions, and many more, are answered in part I.

Part II deals with the fundamental psychological processes that determine success and failure in competition. One of the great contributions of sport psychology in the past 20 years has been the increased understanding of how thoughts and emotions govern sport behaviors. Emotions, such as anxiety and anger, and cognitive processes, such as concentration and imagery, are vital parts of the competitive experience for every athlete. The role these issues play in sports competition is explored thoroughly in part II, "Emotional and Mental Control."

All athletes know that success in sports is not a solo undertaking. Good coaching, inspiring leadership, and sound teamwork are essential for victory in all sports. These social aspects of sport are covered in part III, "Interactive Skills." Coaches and team leaders will find a wealth of useful suggestions in these chapters, but all athletes will find the information on communication and leadership helpful.

One of the fundamental themes of *The Sport Psych Handbook* is that athletic success comes only when individuals balance all aspects of their lives, not just their sport participation. Anyone who has been involved in high-level sports competition knows that a variety of problems complicate the lives of many athletes and can make success difficult to obtain. These life problems are the focus of part IV, "Potential Pitfalls."

The book's final section is immensely practical; it helps coaches, athletes, and parents wishing to work with a sport psychologist know how to find one and how to work with them when they do. Part V, "The Educated Consumer," takes the mystery out of sport psychology consulting and shows what it is, how it's done, and what one should know in order to make it work.

Sport psychology is a fascinating and important topic to study and understand. I have always believed that our knowledge should be shared and disseminated as widely as possible in an effort to get the information to those who can most benefit from it. My thanks to all the wonderful individuals who have helped put the information in this book together—I hope you enjoy and benefit from our hard work.

Acknowledgments

Just as a sports team requires a great supporting cast to be successful, an edited book requires many people working together to make the vision a reality. For making our shared vision come true, I wish to thank:

Jim Brown—for getting the ball rolling.

Ted Miller—for your ideas and energy.

All the contributors—a fantastic team to work with. I asked so much from you and you delivered!

All the athletes and coaches I have ever had the pleasure to work with—your ideas and experiences, and those of your colleagues who worked with the other authors, formed the basis for the accumulated wisdom collected on these pages.

Jennifer Walker—I am surely the only one who knows just how hard you worked to make this book successful.

Mandy Maiden and Cheryl Ossola—I thought I was a good editor! Your attention to detail was exemplary.

Aidan Moran—for sharing your insights that made this book so much better.

To everyone at Human Kinetics—thanks for all the hard work and the professionalism.

There are three people to whom I owe everything. They know how much I love them. Perhaps they don't know how much I appreciate them putting up with me and all the interruptions, deadlines, phone calls, faxes, trips, and the hassles that go along with writing and editing. Annemarie, my wife; Bryan, my son; and Theresa, my daughter. Thanks.

Introduction

The mind is the athlete; the body is simply the means it uses to run faster or longer, jump higher, shoot straighter, kick better, swim harder, hit further, or box better.

Bryce Courtney, The Power of One, *1992*

Over the past 80 years, sport psychology has evolved from a research discipline that studies the effects of mental factors on performance to a broad field that incorporates such diverse disciplines as psychology, counseling, kinesiology, and sport and exercise science. Today sport psychology encompasses professional and active research communities that are committed to enhancing the performance and well-being of athletes through a variety of psychological interventions.

Coaches and athletes have always understood the importance of the mental aspects of sport; writings about this topic can be found as far back as the days of ancient Greece, when sports celebrations were pivotal parts of community experience. A scientific approach to the study of performance psychology began to emerge during the 20th century with the work of such sport psychologists as Coleman Roberts Griffith, but sport psychology began to flourish as a separate discipline during the 1970s and 1980s. By the mid-1980s, the field was cohesive enough to support the emergence of such organizing bodies as the International Society of Sport Psychology (ISSP), the Association for the Advancement of Applied Sport Psychology (AAASP), and the Division of Exercise and Sport Psychology of the American Psychological Association (Division 47). These professional organizations served as focal points for the many people interested in the science of sport psychology, and they are all active in promoting the field today.

Vigorous debate within the sport psychology community, as in any emerging field, surrounds its goals, scope, and background. However, a broad consensus has emerged on a variety of issues. In *The Sport Psych Handbook*, we have tried to emphasize these areas of consensus while alerting the reader to those areas that remain controversial. Several themes define sport psychology today, and they are central to the approach taken by the authors. These themes include the following.

New Insights and Applications in Sport Psych

The central theme of sport psychology over the past 80 years has been the search for the truth about how the mind and body interact to produce a skilled sport performance. This search has been undertaken via the application of the scientific method, which emphasizes that we should pose sound questions and carefully collect evidence before we begin to address how emotions and thoughts influence sport performance. Sport today is a big business throughout the world, as evidenced by the tremendous popularity of events such as the FIFA World Cup and the Olympic Games, but unfortunately some people try to take advantage of coaches and athletes by selling gimmicks and shortcuts to success. Some try to "sell" athletes unsubstantiated "mental success" programs; in this book, we emphasize that serious athletes and coaches should always seek out the evidence behind intervention techniques and never rely on testimonials, gurus, or guarantees of success. There are no guarantees in sport, but the systematic application of scientific approaches such as exercise physiology and sport psychology does give athletes the best opportunity to succeed.

The guiding force in sport psychology is a theoretical approach called "cognitive–behavioral psychology." The term comes from a focus on both the thinking you cannot see (cognition) and the actions you can see (behavior). The cognitive–behavioral approach theorizes that by changing people's thinking, you can change their behaviors. As a straightforward example, take the concept of goal setting. Evidence is overwhelming that setting specific goals for a behavior greatly increases the likelihood that the behavior will occur (see chapter 2). If you have ever found that making a "to-do" list on a Saturday at home resulted in getting a lot of errands or projects finished, then you understand the value of goal setting. Goal setting is an example of cognitive behaviorism. Simply by changing your thinking (through the organization process of creating a list, then by the visual reminder it provides throughout the day), your behavior also changes (more tasks get done).

In sport, an example of the cognitive–behavioral approach is using imagery exercises to train the thought processes during difficult times in competition. For instance, if a rugby player who responds to his own mistakes by trying too hard, getting angry, and subsequently earning stupid penalties practices a relaxed, problem-solving approach to game mistakes in his *imagination*, his *actual* game behavior is more likely to be relaxed and solution oriented (see chapter 8). Changing the athlete's pregame thinking changes his game behavior.

Thus, although sport psychology began by emphasizing the relationship between mental processes and physical performance, it has expanded over the years to include many important areas. Today's sport psychologists help athletes lead well-balanced, productive lives and assist those who have serious clinical problems such as drug abuse or depression. They study motivation in order to understand how people become active exercisers and athletes, and examine how the organization and processes of sports teams and clubs influence the behavior of athletes, coaches, and fans.

One of my greatest challenges as editor of *The Sport Psych Handbook* was to capture the field's diversity and illustrate its holistic approach in a single volume. I challenged the contributing authors to present the most widely applicable information they could find, and I believe the results are outstanding. Never before has one book captured the whole range of sport psychology and made the information so accessible for everyone.

Be an Educated Sport Psych Consumer

One of my chief goals for this book is that it will help readers become informed and educated consumers of sport psychology. Each chapter will help you apply the knowledge of experts to your own sporting situation. In addition, should you ever choose to work with a sport psychologist, this book will help you understand the key aspects of the consulting process and identify the type of consultant you wish to work with.

One extensively discussed area within the field of sport psychology concerns the training and experience needed to ensure that consultants are competent and effective. Although discussion continues, sport psychologists and organizations around the world have arrived at several conclusions, which are illustrated by the variations among the certification, or registration, processes in countries such as Australia, Great Britain, New Zealand, and the United States (see chapter 16). These processes establish the minimum training and experiences needed for competent practice. If coaches and athletes know about the certification requirements in their countries, then they will be able to identify qualified consultants. However, certification does not guarantee that a consultant will be helpful.

The issues of certification and effectiveness are explored thoroughly, and for the first time, in part V of this book. Let me point out briefly that because of the wide variety of issues within sport psychology, consultants often have diverse backgrounds and training and can provide excellent assistance to coaches and athletes. But to be an educated consumer, you need to know which type of help you want (Sean McCann provides many useful suggestions in chapter 15), which types of training and qualifications consultants are likely to have (Bradley Hack makes them clear in chapter 16), and which qualities you seek in a consultant (David Tod and Mark Andersen describe the main characteristics of effective consultants in chapter 17).

I suggest that you look for someone who endorses the scientific and holistic approach to sport psychology. The scientific approach means that your consultant should be able to provide a sound rationale for the approaches or interventions suggested. Even when current research offers no firm answers to your questions, the consultant should proceed using an empirical, client-centered approach. And you should expect to see progress in a reasonable amount of time. The sport psychology consultant should be able to suggest a system to monitor progress, whether for tracking competitive performance, behavior modification, or changes in mood and emotion. The chapters that follow offer many examples of sport psychology assessment.

The holistic approach means that your consultant should be comfortable looking at the big picture of your life. As all athletes and coaches know, what happens off the court can affect what happens on the court, and vice versa. No matter what your concerns, issues, or problems are, a sport psychology consultant should be comfortable listening to you and working with you to find possible solutions. Sometimes the recommended course of action will be beyond that person's expertise; in that case, you should expect a referral to others who might be better qualified to deal with your particular needs. In general, a professional known as a "psychologist" has a doctorate in psychology and is licensed by the state they practice in. Many other consultants in sport psychology have different backgrounds in exercise science, sport psychology, kinesiology, etc., and have different sets of skills. These issues are clarified in chapter 16.

Expanding Horizons for Sport Psych

Sport psychologists have worked with athletes in every professional and Olympic sport. Sport psychology training is included in the majority of grassroots and elite coach-education workshops and conferences. Athletes' public comments about their work with various sport psychologists are regular occurrences at news conferences and in newspaper and magazine articles. With increasing awareness of the work that sport psychologists do, athletes and coaches are becoming more sophisticated consumers of their services. Frequently, sport psychologists who work with elite athletes or their coaches discover that the athlete has worked with multiple sport psychologists over the years.

Over the past 25 years, sport psychology has moved from an "outside of the box" concept to a standard part of the high-performance sports team. In modern sport programs, sport psychology has become well integrated into athletic preparation as has strength and conditioning, sports medicine, and sports nutrition. Today, a number of college campuses have sport psychologists in their counseling centers and athletic departments. High schools around the country now include sport psychology training in team-building, communication, and crisis management as part of their mandatory coaching education programs. Many professional sports teams have sport psychologists on staff. And at the 2002 Olympic Games in Salt Lake City, 12 sport psychologists were given coaching credentials so that they could work with U.S. Olympic teams. More and more, sport psychology is regarded as a "normal" resource for any team that takes performance seriously.

I expect this trend to continue for the foreseeable future. Gains in research in cognitive science and neuropsychology are helping us understand the workings of the brain at a deeper level than ever before. These breakthroughs help us better understand important processes such as concentration, motivation, stress, and imagery, and this increased knowledge can be passed along to coaches and athletes to help them manage their performances. I believe the work of sport psychologists will become increasingly relevant to other important fields of human endeavor. Through most of its history, sport psychology imported applied techniques from other areas in psychology, but now its concepts are being exported to other areas such as executive coaching and the development of high-performance skills in business, the military, the performing arts, and other high-stress fields.

Sport psychology is about winning, because it focuses on understanding how athletes succeed and assisting athletes and coaches in achieving their best performance. But it is about much more than that. It is about learning how good you are and discovering how far you can go; it is about the joys of teamwork and striving for a team goal that is greater than any individual goal; it is about enjoying each moment because neither success nor failure is permanent, so if the journey isn't worthwhile, the destination isn't worth reaching. And it is about the wonders of self-discovery, learning to understand how you respond to pressure, and how you can make yourself better every day by learning from your experience. Let the voyage begin.

Inner Drive

The first of the most important lessons I've learned in 22 years of competition is that success will come if you work hard and believe. The second is that failure isn't fatal. All the setbacks I've had, although heartbreaking at the time, were only temporary. The important thing is to learn from adversity and walk away as a better man. The third lesson is that success isn't final. Past performance is forgotten in every new competition.

Don Shula, coach of the Miami Dolphins NFL team

A young soccer player wakes up in darkness as the alarm buzzes. It's 4:30 A.M. and he has 30 minutes to dress and eat before catching a bus for the hour-long drive to the regional club training facility where he will join other talented young players for a two-hour dawn training session. School begins at 8:30 A.M. and ends at 1:00 P.M. for this player and for others on the club's Under-17 team. The program is for only the most talented players, and a place on the team is highly coveted. His afternoon includes more training, strength and conditioning workouts, and a skills drill session with the club's professional team coach. After the long ride home, his mother helps him with homework in the evening. By 9:00 P.M., exhausted, he is ready for bed. In a few hours, the whole cycle will start anew. The young player is looking forward to several more years of this schedule and then for the opportunity to sign a long-term contract in the professional league.

This sort of dedication is not unique. In all sports, similar scenarios are repeated every day. Whether the goal is representing one's country, achieving a professional career in sports, or being able to play for a college team, athletes the world over display tremendous motivation as they strive to make their dreams come true. In part I of *The Sport Psych Handbook*, we explore how that motivation develops and what keeps athletes going in the face of such daunting requirements of commitment and persistence. What is motivation, how can it be promoted and encouraged, and what role does setting goals play in developing this motivation? We also explore what happens when motivation fails and athletes burn out. Why do some athletes lose their natural love of the game and leave sports before they have had a chance to achieve their goals? What can be done to prevent such problems?

After all the hard work and sacrifice, the final test for every athlete is competition. When an athlete accepts the challenge of competition, he or she seeks answers to the questions of "How good am I?" and "How well will I handle pressure?" In part I, we also take a fresh look at the topic of competition in sports and seek to understand how athletes and coaches can develop a healthy, effective attitude toward competition that helps them perform at their best without succumbing to the pressures of public scrutiny.

Four chapters make up part I, "Inner Drive." The first two deal with the intertwined topics of motivation and goal setting. In chapter 1, "Motivation: The Need to Achieve," John F. Eliot explores where motivation to excel comes from and how it can be nurtured. In chapter 2, "Goals: More Than Just the Score," Chris Harwood looks at the goals that athletes set and how goals motivate or sometimes distract athletes. In chapter 3, "Competitive Drive: Embracing Positive Rivalries," Cal Botterill takes a fresh look at the topic of competition and explores how positive rivalries in sport can lead all participants to excel. Finally, in chapter 4, "Overtraining: Balancing Practice and Performance," Kirsten Peterson shows us some of the ways motivation can go bad and looks at modern approaches to preventing and overcoming overtraining.

Motivation: The Need to Achieve

John F. Eliot

The subject of motivation is a complex one—in short, it's an intangible variable that can ebb and flow widely in short periods of time. Athletes with seemingly unparalleled drive lose it. Loafers show up to practice one day with a fire lit inside them. From week to week, teams, athletes, and coaches fluctuate in their intensity and level of dedication. This chapter focuses on understanding how we create and sustain motivation, and, specifically, how we can win with it. Along the way, we'll give you tips on how to apply motivation effectively in competition and answer some of the following tough questions.

Why are some of the biggest, most readily available motivators—money, fame, trophies, and other accolades—ineffective over the long haul? Why does motivation come and go? Why do people enter into sport or the quest for a particular goal in the first place? How do they persevere in the face of adversity? Why do they discontinue prematurely?

The Mental Edge of Intensity and Drive

Norman Triplett is generally credited with the first formal experiment in sport motivation psychology. A psychologist at Indiana University, Triplett was a bicycle enthusiast who had noticed that racers seem to ride faster in pairs than alone. In 1889, he tested his hypothesis by asking children to reel in fishing line in a number of competitive conditions. As predicted, the children reeled in more line when they performed next to another child. The same held true when Triplett examined racing times—cyclists rode faster when paced or pitted against others than when they rode by themselves.

Triplett's motivation discovery—now referred to as social facilitation—was not fully utilized for roughly half a century. In the early 1900s, leading psychologists took a deterministic approach to human behavior. Psychoanalyst Sigmund Freud argued that motivation was a product of the subconscious instincts of sex and aggression. Our behavior, he said, is largely shaped by our instincts. Similarly, C.L. Hull's drive theory posited all motivation to be a function of basic physiological needs, such as hunger, thirst, and fatigue. Behaviorist B.F. Skinner was on the other end of the nature–nurture continuum. He didn't believe in the subconscious. To explain motivation, Skinner put forth stimulus–response psychology, claiming that all behavior is controlled by external reinforcements. We are essentially a black box, Skinner said; what goes in determines what comes out.

Although their beliefs were radically different, these psychologists agreed on one thing: Motivation is not up to the individual. They professed humans to be, essentially, products of genetics or the environment. The argument at the time laid groundwork for the nature-versus-nurture debate that still continues today: Is our behavior dictated by our biological makeup or is it a product of what our experiences have taught us? The answer is both.

Drive theory, also called "instinct theory," explains why a hockey player tends to strike back when hit—aggression is an innate human impulse. Recruiters and scouts tend to rely heavily on drive theory. In addition to physical genet-

© Empics

Hockey players' aggression is explained by drive theory as an innate human impulse, inclining them to challenges of aggressiveness, high pain tolerance, and initiative.

ics, they look for athletes whose "mental genetics" suggest a greater natural inclination toward aggressiveness, high pain tolerance, initiative, attraction to challenge, and so forth. Before the draft in every sport, athletes are bombarded with psychological inventories that try to quantify these drives, or psychological *traits*. From a motivational standpoint, the search is for those with the inner determination to stand up to the challenges of sport.

Reinforcement theory, on the other hand, explains why many athletes cut back their exertion at the end of a contest. The satisfaction of reducing fatigue or quenching thirst pushes our systems to prioritize those goals. Likewise, the reward of feeling safe and secure can inhibit the inclination to tackle challenges, and it can impair one's efforts in the face of adversity. In a similar manner, a pat on the back can make one feel secure. A positive word of encouragement can go a long way in manipulating future effort. Just as we are driven by biological needs, we are driven by the need to feel pleasure, acceptance, and competence (called "need achievement" in sport psychology literature). We are naturally motivated by activities that reward us with such feelings.

Thus, the environment, both internal and external, is a strong motivator, often one we fail to consciously attend to. Coaches are wise to create checklists of environmental stimuli that will pull and push at athletes' attention, desire, and direction of perseverance. But motivation is more than the forces acting on an individual. I'm sure you can think of occasions when you deliberately acted counter to your biological drives or chose to ignore external incentives. Perhaps you skipped lunch to get in a workout. You cranked out a few more sets of crunches despite the pain. Maybe you turned down a stack of hot pancakes on the pregame breakfast table even though your mouth was watering at the sight of melting butter and glistening syrup. Hopefully the notion that motivation is predetermined doesn't sit well with you. It wasn't acceptable for cognitive psychologists, either.

Performance From the Inside Out

By the midpoint of the 20th century, determinism was rapidly being replaced by a new branch of psychology, based largely on the writings of William James. James championed the notion that humans have free will. We are free to think whatever thoughts we want, he insisted. Regardless of the influences bombarding us, we can choose our actions, interpretations, focus, and attitude.

Enter cognitive sport psychology, the current trend to examine performance based on conscious, controllable thoughts. According to cognitive psychologists, motivation is a decision; it's up to the athlete. Does this mean that drive, reinforcement, and need-achievement theories are no longer of use in sport? Not at all. For example, when structuring practice, an effective coach will set up the schedule so that hunger and thirst do not interfere with motivation, and so that athletes will have the opportunity to experience pleasure and

© Empics

Lance Armstrong is a great example of how the power of the mind can propel an individual to overcome tremendous obstacles.

competence during practice. But cognitive psychology also teaches us that motivation is as much a matter of personal choice as it is affected by what coaches say and do. It is misguided to think that players' efforts are the result of selecting the right stick and the right carrot. It's equally misguided to believe that pencil-and-paper tests will reveal who "has it" and who doesn't. We can all recall an athlete whose enormous heart allowed him to surpass physical limitations, or one who was given every indication that it was time to hang it up yet succeeded anyway. Lance Armstrong and Rudy Ruettiger come immediately to mind, as do countless others. The power of the mind is exceptional; coaches cannot overlook it when deciding how to motivate or when selecting individuals.

Great coaches like Tom Landry, Red Auerbach, Phil Jackson, and Joe Torre attend to influences coming from biological and environmental conditions and manipulate them as best they can, but they don't assume that they can ultimately control motivation. They don't let external forces dictate their athletes' drives. They tap the power of free will; they learn how their players view tough situations and help them make choices that lead to greater personal enthusiasm, desire, and effort. Athletes who embrace their controllable ability to alter commitment outperform those who leave motivation up to drives and reinforcements.

A fascinating, "accidental" piece of research shed light on the differences in performance when motivation is primarily deterministic versus controlled by free will. Ohio State University Professor Emeritus of Physical Education, Daryl Siedentop, tells the story of an eccentric old man who came home one day to discover that his flower garden had been trampled. He was exceptionally fond of gardening and distraught that someone or something would ruin his masterpiece and show such complete disregard for his dedication. He proceeded to stake vigil until the culprit returned.

Expecting a neighborhood stray, he was surprised the next afternoon when a group of four adolescents showed up toting a football and began playing two-on-two in his backyard. His flower garden was the end zone! As the old man watched, he noticed that the boys took immense joy in diving into the end zone to make spectacular catches. The flowers were not something to be vandalized; rather, they were the goal of great play, respected almost. The old man was now more curious than irate. Though he still wanted to halt the destruction of his flowers, he decided he would conduct an experiment. He went outside and called the youngsters over. He explained that he too loved the flower garden and wished to reward the boys for their play. He would provide them each with a dollar every day that they came to his lawn. At first, it was a marvelous treat—the kids felt like professional athletes being paid to play sports. But interestingly, as the old man reduced his remuneration in the following weeks, the boys showed up with less frequency. In fact, they became agitated that they were no longer being paid what they were worth. As a moral to the story, Siedentop concludes that the elder gentleman had altered the young people's motivation from the love of diving into the end zone and catching touchdown passes to the chore of making money.

Characteristics Influencing Your Potential

Although the Siedentop story is not a controlled work of research, numerous studies have replicated its finding in laboratory situations. Motivation to engage in physical tasks can be appreciably modulated by what's called the "locus of causality." When participation in a sport is inherently pleasurable, when effort is based on enjoyment of competition, excitement, or the desire to learn and improve, athletes are said to have *intrinsic* motivation. On the other hand, when sport involvement is steered by trophies, ribbons, salaries or scholarships, or the approval of others, athletes are *extrinsically* motivated. Internal and external rewards can both improve motivation; they can also affect one another.

The most significant finding along this line of research is that athletes who are motivated intrinsically lose some of their enthusiasm when extrinsic incentives are added, just like with the young football players in the flower garden. The variable at work turns out to be athletes' perception of which force controls their efforts. This force is the locus of causality. If athletes view the cause of their behavior as external to themselves—someone else is "pulling the strings"—they feel a reduced sense of self-determination and motivation declines. However, if they believe *they* are the cause of their behavior, they feel greater autonomy and motivation rises.

The locus of causality is a perception of the individual. Athletes can deem certain external rewards as having a high degree of personal value and therefore see striving for them as an individual choice; they feel an internal locus of causality. Motivation remains high despite the incorporation of outside rewards. College scholarships, for example, can be associated with the opportunity for education and gaining knowledge; in such a case, chasing dollars is internalized as personal growth, and commitment grows.

Sport psychologists have learned that intrinsic feelings—perceptions of autonomy and competence—are the most powerful motivators, while the promise of a pot of gold actually has potential to generate *amotivation*. The best way to ensure steady motivation is for an athlete to identify effort with something personally satisfying and meaningful. A sense of purpose carries an athlete the farthest and helps him weather the worst storms.

Extrinsic encouragement is not necessarily negative, though. In circumstances in which athletes lack inner drive—for unpleasant modes of training, such as weightlifting or wind sprints, or maybe for dietary change—motivation can be increased by artificial incentives, be they marks on a locker room progress chart or release time from certain drills. One needs to take caution, however, not to squelch potential inner enjoyment by assuming it's not there simply because it's not obvious. Likewise, an overreliance on prizes, player-of-the-week honors, and time off can impede the development of intrinsic motivation. Just because it's missing or low doesn't mean it can't be built or encouraged: Your most fundamental motivational goal should be to locate inner meaning and enjoyment.

Identifying a sense of purpose, an intrinsic value to training and competition, is at least half the battle in building and sustaining high-level motivation. But what about athletes who don't engage to begin with? Without attempting it, they can't know the fun of a new sport. Without loading on the resistance in the weight room, they can't experience the sense of accomplishment from a hard workout.

Self-Efficacy

The reasons why athletes want to compete depend on the contrast between internal and external rewards as well as an athlete's preperformance assessment. In other words, if an athlete believes he or she can be successful, he or she is more likely to participate. In sport psychology, this is generally referred to as self-confidence or self-efficacy. High self-efficacy is a judgment about one's capability to perform a particular task (1) at an elevated level, (2) with certainty, and (3) repeatedly over time. Motivationally, athletes with higher self-efficacy tend to try harder, persist longer, choose greater challenges, experience effort more positively, and feel less anxious. NHL players who can picture winning a Stanley Cup, for example, will bust their butts come playoff time (and year-round, for that matter), but a minor-league rookie who is enticed by a call-up for the postseason, yet thinks of himself as unready and cannot see himself competing with the "big boys," may be afraid to put his all on the line and may end up slacking off in practice.

The value of self-efficacy is often overlooked or downplayed in traditional sport thinking. Many coaches caution against overconfidence because they think that by assuming he or she will be successful, an athlete will take his or her opponents too lightly (i.e., he or she won't log in enough preparation). Simply put, the supposition is that confidence can impair motivation. But it's incorrect;

the opposite is the case. Without feelings of self-efficacy, there is little reason for athletes to believe that their efforts will pay off. Therefore, why bother?

High self-efficacy, in fact, can overcome what would otherwise be very significant motivation killers. When an athlete envisions a successful future, his or her belief can outweigh "realistic" probabilities. This power of belief—faith—goes a long way to explain the extremes of motivation we witness in some individuals. For example, the most driven Division III college athletes spend four or five years notching 40-hour training weeks without so much as a dime in scholarship or a single call from a scout. And despite low odds for repeating as Super Bowl champions, NFL players will go to extraordinary lengths in off-season training and preparation. Similarly, on the strength of earning a PGA Tour card, professional golfers will play thousands of rounds, over many years, without ever winning a tournament. Spending time envisioning yourself as successful—seeing your efforts pay off—is sometimes all that is needed to maintain consistently high motivation.

Self-efficacy, however, should not be confused with self-esteem. Self-esteem pertains to a person's generalized feelings of worth, whereas self-efficacy concerns specific skills, abilities, or opportunities. Merely feeling good about oneself may prompt action but will not sustain the sort of demanding commitment necessary for elite performance.

Goal Orientation

The inclination to give something a shot is one distinct kind of motivation—moving from inaction to action, changing inertia. Sticking with a sport or fitness activity, however, takes an entirely different kind of motivation: sustainability. Experiencing feelings of self-efficacy on a regular basis is critical to sustainability, as are feelings of autonomy and purpose; athletes continue to participate because it's their choice and it fulfills the interests they value.

Katie

Katie is a successful high school point guard in a top program who one day decides to quit. In her junior year, she had nearly single-handedly led her team to the state semifinals. She had worked with a personal trainer all summer to increase her strength and stamina, and she gave up playing soccer to devote herself to basketball. During fall preseason, her team practiced twice a day and was projected to win it all. Scouts from the WNBA even came to the gym to watch Katie play. Yet right before the first game—usually the part of the season second in excitement only to the playoffs—Katie lost interest. Why? Workouts were tapering off in difficulty; applause from fans and recruiters was growing; motivation should have been peaking. But

(continued)

(continued)

the coach assigned captainship to another guard, a girl who'd contributed little but led in popularity rather than on-the-court production. It was no longer Katie's team. While there were plenty of strong motivators—from trophies and a championship to potential college and professional playing opportunities—the ones that mattered to Katie centered around leadership. Without that, there went her dedication. Ask yourself, If you were Katie's coach, what would you have done to maintain her drive? If it was in the best interest of the team to appoint a captain other than Katie, how could you help her to maintain autonomy and a sense of purpose?

As you consider Katie's situation, take into account that sustained motivation also hinges on something called "goal orientation." Sport participants are said to have a *task-mastery orientation* when they take pride in the progressive improvement of their knowledge and ability relative to their own past performances. The marathon runner who judges her success according to her PR (personal record) is task involved, while the runner who evaluates his time compared to the other members of the field is ego involved. Individuals with an *ego orientation* are intent on demonstrating superiority over others; they are motivated by social comparison and desire statistics in the win column. Those with a mastery orientation are motivated to see how well they can execute a set of tasks. In other words, task mastery centers on the process of improvement while ego involvement targets the outcome of competition. Goal orientations are discussed in detail in chapter 2.

When a sport situation—also called a "motivational climate"—does not match a participant's goal orientation, interest dissipates. For instance, a mastery-oriented gymnast may relish practice time in an empty gym, while his ego-oriented peer looks for an excuse to go home early. An ego-involved pitcher performs better after studying how to lower the batting averages of opponents; a task-involved hurler would rather analyze game tapes of himself. The key as a coach or athlete is to identify feedback mechanisms that correspond to motivational orientation. Every practice and game is replete with both types of information; one must hone in on the sort that matches individual perspective.

Interestingly, many critics warn against the downside of maintaining too great an ego orientation, claiming that athletes who are ego involved often feel incompetent and lose motivation when they don't win. These critics believe that when social status is involved, athletes try to protect themselves from being viewed as inferior. They avoid challenges, put out minimal effort, and make excuses, all of which sabotage motivation.

But the world we live in demands social comparison. It is all around us: who signed for how large a bonus, which college teams have the lowest RPI, who scored the most points? The solution is to develop *both* task and ego orientations. While task mastery or social comparison may be a predisposition, it is not a performance variable akin to height. Athletes should strive to become motivated dually, to perfect their skills while also using them under competitive circumstances. To this end, they should enjoy the thrill of both getting better and of producing results at precise moments of pressure.

Taking another look at Katie's situation, we can see that she was juiced by the thrill of leading her team. She was also an extremely hard worker, enjoying grueling, late workouts in the gymnasium. Unfortunately, the publicity of the captain's position, along with the manner in which the coach handled it, pushed the two types of goal orientations apart—leadership and basketball performance became separated. What Katie needed to maintain dedication was for her task motives and ego motives to contribute to one another.

Performance Feedback and Interpretation

A person's beliefs can easily override urges or instincts; confidence, as we've discussed, is a valuable motivational asset. Accomplishment doesn't always generate feelings of confidence, and failure doesn't always diminish them. And we can't merely wait for success in order to build self-efficacy. Enter attributions. Where self-efficacy explains the transition from expectation to effort, attribution addresses the *causes* of expectancy beliefs and how success and failure affect continued motivation. According to Bernard Weiner, who mainstreamed the burgeoning research on attributions, winning and losing by themselves are meaningless in incentive terms. Competitor A can view a loss as a victory: She played well, improved her performance, and gained the experience she needed to win the next time. Competitor B, on the other hand, might see a complete failure: "I must always win," or "I must always execute correctly."

What matters is how an athlete *interprets* positive or negative outcomes. Winning a racquetball match, for instance, could be the result of your superior skill, your opponent's lack of sleep, lucky bounces, your new equipment, calls in your favor, or a whole host of reasons. Your belief in future successful outcomes hinges on which explanation you choose—and that choice is not always rational or accurate!

Three critical characteristics underlie attributions: (1) locus of causality (perceiving an outcome to have resulted from either internal or external factors); (2) stability (perceiving the likelihood of the same outcome recurring); and (3) locus of control (the perception of whether an outcome can be manipulated). Examples of attributions along each dimension are shown in table 1.1.

As you can see, there is plenty of room for the causes of performance to be pinned to more than one attribution category. For example, luck can be both a stability and a controllability factor; effort could be placed in any of the three loci. What matters is that attributions are perceptions, not facts. And exceptional coaches and athletes take the time to assess their perceptions. Coaches want to know, for instance, whether an athlete sees their abilitiy as unchangeable. Those who do tend to give up much more easily in the face of failure than those

Table 1.1 Characteristics of Attributions

Locus of causality	Internal	Effort An injury
	External	Field conditions Equipment
Stability	Stable	Your talent
	Unstable	Weather Luck
Locus of control	Controllable	Your game plan Pregame meal
	Uncontrollable	Referees' calls Opponents' mistakes

who believe they can change. Athletes who perceive their ability to be unstable, thinking "Some days I have it; some days I don't," may leave performance up to circumstance; they then turn in subpar effort on occasions when things don't naturally fall into place. Similarly, evaluating where an athlete focuses is valuable. Research suggests that those who put their focus on controllable, or process-oriented, performance factors generally exhibit more tenacious effort.

Internal, stable, and controllable success attributions are considered ego-enhancing. However, some athletes are turned off by the perception that success is a stable commodity. Research shows that the most elite performers tend to show excitement and energy when uncertainty exists. Right after winning a Super Bowl, for example, the most motivated athletes will wonder, "Gosh, can I pull off back-to-back Super Bowl wins?" If the answer was forseeably negative, they would be less likely to train voraciously in the off-season.

Elite athletes also tend to be quite passionate about their failures, internalizing losses even when they couldn't have done anything about them, looking forward to making personal adjustments, and taking the blame off teammates' shoulders. For them, motivation springs from efforts to boost their future self rather than protect their current ego; the latter occurs when one attributes failures to external, unstable, and uncontrollable causes in an effort to avoid shame, frustration, anger, or other ego-damaging emotions that mitigate motivation.

The take-home message is that athletes need help and encouragement to look inside themselves for answers, see improvements they can make for the future, and enjoy what they're doing rather than trying to manipulate or manage unstable and uncontrollable performance factors.

Higher Performance Consciousness

To this point, we've considered motivation as a collection of cognitions about the resolve of future effort that occur primarily before engaging in participation or between contests or training bouts. The most recent research takes a different approach. In the 1960s, Mihaly Csikszentmihalyi began scrutinizing how engrossed painters and other artists became in their work. What he discovered was an effect similar to being on automatic pilot while driving down the interstate: The conscious mind shuts off when one becomes absorbed in a task. This state of *flow*, as Csikszentmihalyi coined it, is so intrinsically pleasing that people in it lose track of time; their perception of reality is distorted.

Csikszentmihalyi delineated the experience as a balance between external demands and internal skills. When there is essentially a one-to-one relationship between difficulty and ability, the door is open for athletes to get into flow. But it is recorded as a rare and fleeting experience. When challenges exceed aptitude, anxiety is typically the result. At the other end of the spectrum, when talent outpaces one's performance load, boredom ensues (see figure 1.1).

When athletes talk about their best-ever performances or being in the "zone," they use language similar to the description of flow: effortless movement, transformation of time, clarity of vision, distortion of objects, loss of sense of self, and so forth. Flow is a change in consciousness. The elimination of excess thoughts, doubt, and evaluation combined with a sense of effortless, timeless performance

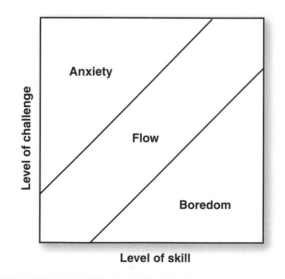

Figure 1.1 Csikszentmihalyi's chart of flow.

make for an incredibly pleasing experience—it's so intrinsic that athletes will chase flow independently of any other motivational variable. Certainly cognition plays an important role in commitment and dedication; however, it appears that in the highest order of motivation, choices and actions are instinctive but driven by the pure, rhythmic experience of sport rather than the basal instincts of homeostasis or reproduction.

In terms of sustaining and enhancing motivation, flow itself can be the goal, rather than statistical performance outputs. To maximize its chances of occurrence, coaches and athletes should do the following:

1. Balance challenges with skills.
2. Perform in the present (think of what is happening in the immediate term without concern for past or future outcomes).
3. Concentrate on a small, specific target.
4. Concentrate only on the aspects of performance that are controllable.
5. Have a well-thought-out game plan so that decision making during performance is simplified.
6. Eliminate in-game evaluation and self-judgment.
7. Enjoy the rhythm and feel of performance rather than focusing on technical aspects of a particular sport.
8. Have fun!

Building and Sustaining High-Level Motivation

By now you're armed with a thorough psychological conceptualization of motivation. But how do you put these principles to work, practically and effectively?

First, discard the notion of a pregame pep talk. Immediately before the gun, kickoff, first pitch, or puck drop is not the time to address motivation. The potential performance enhancement that comes from being in a state of flow clues us in to the need for decreased self-consciousness at game time. That means trusting oneself, not thinking about motivational issues. If a coach plans on a pregame locker-room session, he or she should use the time to help athletes clarify goals, reduce self-awareness, generate a sense of control, get absorbed in the task at hand, and leave rewards behind. And he or she should do so in a manner that gives each athlete responsibility for his or her own motivational state as he or she enters competition. Instructions to the team as a whole should be minimized in favor of providing resources that allow each athlete to execute an individualized game plan (such as narrowing focus, listening to rhythmic music, or absorbing themselves in film).

The proper time to work on sustaining motivation is outside of competition. Again, a unilateral approach will fail to do the job. Assessment of individual differences is mandatory since motivation is perceptual, the result of interaction between an athlete and his or her training environment. It is a must to create multifaceted performance climates that promote individualized, personally meaningful feedback and rewards.

A great leader is someone who knows his or her charges distinctively and takes the time to get to know them one on one. In the same vein, a great team motivator will know the following about each player:

- Remember, motivation starts with a sense of purpose. If you ask "Why?" often enough, you should be able to get to athletes' inner values, past what they want to have hanging on the wall.

- Do they get excited to flat-out beat another competitor, or are they elated to make personal improvements? If you have trouble gleaning goal orientation from conversation and observation, chapter 2 provides useful suggestions. A sport psychology consultant can also help you assess athlete goal orientations.

- Naturally, individual-sport athletes and team-sport athletes have different perspectives on group work. However, even within a squad, some members are juiced by the team's performance while others are concerned with their individual contribution. Knowing which athlete sees it which way will aid in short-term motivation as well as long-term efforts to develop a healthy balance of both.

- When giving feedback, distinguish between information (critiques, statistics) and rewards (pats on the back, verbal praise). Motivation will become hamstrung if an athlete's primary reason for hard work becomes extrinsic rewards. Coaches or parents should know what each athlete values and frame their feedback to be informative with respect to those values. Further, if an athlete feels his or her behavior is being controlled, motivation will suffer drastically.

If this seems like too much to remember, especially for large teams (such as a football lineup of 65 players), keep a detailed chart that lists each athlete's internal motivators and motivational orientations. Laminate it on the back of your clipboard so you can refer to it in the middle of practice. The intrinsic reward of getting to know your athletes this well makes it surprisingly easy, before long, to recall individual motivation styles and provide cues, feedback, and expectations accordingly.

Evaluating Motivational Approaches

As important as it is to know which athletes are motivated by external and intrinsic outcomes and who is into the process, so too is it critical to gather information about attribution patterns following wins and losses. Of greatest pertinence are trends, or habits, an athlete develops along the three dimensions of attribution: controllability or locus of control, stability, and locus of causality. The Causal Dimension Scales 1 and 2 (CDS and CDSII) are pencil-and-paper methods of collecting this data, which can then be incorporated into postperformance evaluation sessions with the help of a sport psychology consultant.

If a consultant is not available, athletes can examine trends by keeping a log or diary in which they record their reasons for success and failure across a season, periodically assessing how their attributions fall on the table illustrated earlier in this chapter (see table 1.1 on page 12). Or they can have regular conversations with a coach, who might ask specific questions about winning and losing, such as "What were the five key determinants of the outcome?" or "Which elements of the contest were within your control?" or "Which components of the competition will remain fixed and which are changeable?"

Repeated and regular collection of attributions can help a coach and athlete improve accountability (focusing on what they can and can't control), hope (viewing failures as unstable), and self-confidence (augmenting internal reasons for success). At the same time, it can reduce instances of learned helplessness (viewing failures as stable), low self-confidence (not taking personal credit for successes), and excuse-making (constantly associating failures with external causes).

Long-Term Motivational Strategies

The most robust motivation—the sort that can push through four years of grueling training for the Olympic Games, or six years of maneuvering the frustrating politics of minor league administrators and scouts, or dealing with a coach who doesn't believe in you—is rooted in the heart and the soul. Motivation strategies should foster autonomy, competence, and connectedness. Examples include:

Push the edge   Find a weakness or hole in your game and get excited about where your game will be after you change it. Similarly, be creative. Think up something no one in your sport has dared or perfected.

Experience success   When learning new skills and strategies, go step-by-step. Start with an easy piece, master it, and then move on to the next-easiest piece. Or begin by modifying the skill to something you can do well. Let yourself experience success. Keep track of your PRs and how many times you can break them.

Change your thinking   The old adage about learning from your mistakes is well and good, but over time you should have a short-term memory for failures and a long-term memory for success. Keep a vivid mental catalog of your greatest performances.

Get involved   Autonomy directly improves motivation, and perhaps the greatest contributor to autonomy is having input on decisions that affect you.

In both individual- and team-sport settings, athletes should feel ownership of training rules, competition choices, and strategy decisions. Interestingly, on the professional level, many head coaches comment that their success depends entirely on their players' belief in the "system" or playbook. The easiest way to ensure this is to get them involved!

Praise others   If you can't see positive or exciting things in the athletes and coaches around you, how can you do the same for yourself? Moreover, a sense of connectedness depends on everyone's awareness of the contributions that others make.

Vary training   An imbalance between high competence and low task difficulty can result in boredom. So too can constant hammering at one task. A significant portion of training—just as much as is reserved for skill advancement—should be devoted to play for the sake of play, without rules or evaluation.

Put yourself first   Human beings are most productive at homeostasis since in that state they are not distracted by conflicting basal drives. Make sure to eat properly, stay hydrated, and get ample rest.

Find motivated peers   Both on and off the playing surface, spend your time with people who want to accomplish great things, aren't afraid to talk about it, and get revved up by other people's dreams. An effective support system is vital to motivation, especially during difficult times. Conversely, motivational "black holes" are people who always criticize the coach, moan about bad calls, loaf in practices and workouts, and generally focus on obstacles, frustrations, and what can't be achieved.

Think positively   What conversation goes on in the back of your head? It's with you all day, but how much of it do you pay attention to? Actually, all of it, subconsciously. You'd better start paying conscious attention. Is it positive or negative? Is it about what you *can* do or what you *can't* do? Is it hung up on difficulties or engaged in a search for solutions?

Remember your dream   Don't make revisiting your dream a rare event. Spend time frequently reconnecting with the *real* reason why you perform—once again the heart, soul, and will of it all.

Future Directions

Historically, psychology has been associated with understanding, dysfunction, and abnormality. Inspired by the works of Martin Seligman, who coined "learned optimism" as an antonym for "learned helplessness," and Mihaly Csikszentmihalyi, who evolved the study of optimum experience, more and more psychologists are now investigating the most positive end of the human continuum: what's right rather than what's wrong, success and happiness instead of merely the alleviation of pain and suffering.

What does this trend mean for athletes and coaches? First, more practitioners are looking at performance through an "enhancement" lens as opposed to a "rehabilitation" lens. That means more psychologists are interested in working on the assessment and implementation of motivation, which is great news for the growth of the field. Coaches and athletes, though, must correspondingly raise their standards for consultation service and be aware of the most relevant markers of an effective sport psychologist: (1) experience working with elite populations, particularly a concrete track record of improving performance; (2) advanced education and extensive supervision with leading *applied* consultants; and (3) a working emphasis on education rather than therapy, advising the successful rather than treating head cases. What to look for in a good consultant is discussed thoroughly in chapter 17.

Second, more learning will concentrate on the top 1 percent of the top 1 percent. Athletes intuitively look to role models, such as Michael Jordan, Mia Hamm, or Tiger Woods. Many books have been written about their success; however, more formalized study will allow us to move past clichés, distinguishing effective motivational tools from sporting myths and "old school" notions. For example, many coaches used to believe that drinking water during practice was a sign of weakness, a distraction, or a lack of dedication. We now know better. And the more we systematically study great performers, the more we'll learn how to most effectively and healthily sustain motivation.

Third, as we learn more about the psychology of success, we shift more toward the knowledge that peak happiness comes from engagement—the process of performance—rather than material rewards, outcomes, or quantitative sport measures. As we move forward in our understanding of motivation, we'll need to address the growing clash between enjoyment, optimal experience, and cultural materialistic pressures. We'll also need to ditch our overreliance on statistics. Coaches and scouts lean heavily on performance numbers. In doing so, athletes' true motivations are overlooked, or worse, discouraged. This must change. So too must our emphasis on motivation in the short term—quick-fix, have-it-now solutions (such as performance-enhancing drug use) over steady, sustainable growth. Sustainable growth is what positively affects the future.

Our lottery-ticket buying, pill-popping, plastic-surgery, instant-success society presents enormous challenges for motivation, particularly across generations, and particularly for the kind of intrinsic, uninterrupted effort that leads to the zone. We know that flow is the pinnacle of motivation. As coaches and athletes we must, now more than ever, stay aware of how cultural trends affect motivation and understand the ways in which motivation can be influenced.

Goals: More Than Just the Score

Chris Harwood

Coaches and athletes have all witnessed occasions when two athletes have achieved exactly the same score or distance—and one athlete celebrates while the other appears disbelieving, anguished, and defeated. These postcompetition reactions show us that success to one person can mean failure to another depending on their achievement goals. This chapter focuses on defining achievement goals and addresses the critical difference goals can make in performance and sport participation.

Defining Success or Failure Through Achievement Goals

Psychologist John Nicholls was the first to argue that success and failure are not concrete events but instead depend on an athlete's perception of whether he or she has reached his or her personal goals. In other words, whether an athlete perceives an outcome as a success or failure depends on how he or she defines success or failure in the first place. It's fairly obvious that this perception has implications for an athlete's confidence, interest, effort, and persistence—all factors that ultimately determine how well he or she performs and how long he or she stays in the sport.

We know through research into achievement goal theory that an athlete's main motive for engaging in sports is to demonstrate physical ability and feel competent. However, athletes can formulate their sense of competence or achievement in two ways, as chapter 1 explains: a *task-involved* manner and an *ego-involved* manner. For example, an athlete may try hard, stay focused, learn a new skill, and begin to understand a move or improve a particular shot under pressure. To him, all of these achievements are criteria that determine his perception of ability or competence. By meeting such criteria in training or competition, he is likely to feel a positive sense of achievement, a healthy perception about his ability, and a continuing motivation to participate. When an athlete views success in these terms he is said to be task involved.

Task-involved athletes   A task-involved athlete is concerned with the development of his or her competence and uses levels of effort and task completion to assess his or her competence in a self-reflective manner. He or she views ability as something that is improvable; therefore, he or she is satisfied if he or she performs at a level that extracts the best of his or her current ability by mastering a particular technique, increasing tactical awareness, or making personal improvements in a given skill.

In contrast, another athlete may view success purely in terms of comparisons with others; his or her criteria for a high perception of ability and achievement is beating the opposition or achieving a similar result at the expense of observably less effort. In other words, to feel successful and competent, this athlete has to demonstrate ability superior to somebody else, regardless of personal improvements or developments that may have occurred in the process. In this case, the athlete is ego involved.

Ego-involved athletes   Ego-involved athletes view their ability as stable and fixed, thereby limiting the effect that high levels of effort could have on their performance. Their priority is to show ability, often at the expense of effort. Naturally, they judge themselves relative to others and have to demonstrate superior ability in order to gain a positive perception of themselves. The next few pages should give you a feel for why this area of sport psychology is so fundamental to coaches and athletes.

Luke

In 1994, at age 14, Luke was viewed as one of the most promising players in British tennis. He was ranked number one in the Under-14 age group and had won back-to-back national titles in the Under-12 and Under-14 age groups. He began to court constant attention at tournaments as the top-seeded player and had already signed a number of clothing and racket deals. He liked the attention and was a target for the media as the next great British "hope." Life was looking very good for the player who had been nothing but a success story since age 8, when he entered his first competition and reached the final against a boy two years his senior.

From ages 9 to 12, Luke physically dominated his age group, although he played few tournaments against older peers. By the time he was 11, the national governing body had offered him a place on an elite junior academy squad as recognition for his ranking and tournament successes. Luke lost very few matches during this phase of his life.

As a player, Luke worked hard in training but did tend to be flashy in matches when he knew he was in a winning position. The public attention was shaping him into a player who wanted to impress others with his skills. Nobody questioned these flashy tendencies because they showed others that he was a talented player without needing to try too hard. When he did lose a match, his parents, who doted on him, would find various reasons to explain away the defeat. They would tell him, "You can't expect to beat older players all the time," or "You've had a tiring week—take a break and you'll beat him next time." To further protect Luke's self-confidence, his young coach also used external reasons to "help" Luke come to terms with why he hadn't won.

When Luke entered the Under-16 age group, the psychological dynamics of his involvement and progression in tennis began to change for the worse. Until that point his physicality and technical skills had served him well. However, his peers were catching up physically and technically, and now Luke was in an age group in which high levels of strength, speed, and stamina were the rule, not the exception.

Luke's coach and parents did not spend any systematic time helping him understand *why he had won* particular matches and *what he had learned* from each experience. Since his effort levels and the quality of his technical skills, tactical decision-making, physical movement, and mental skills (e.g., concentration, self-control) were not the bases for his sense of achievement and success, they were always secondary to the discussion.

As his self-esteem came under more and more pressure, Luke experienced a variety of emotions that didn't help the quality of his on-court game. He began to feel very anxious before his matches, particularly against those players he had beaten previously and was expected to beat. He became an angry and frustrated player whose on-court body language and behavior deteriorated in the presence of unforced errors. He also began to give bad line calls on important points, earning him the reputation of being a bit of a cheat among his peers.

Luke began to hate playing tournaments, and after two years in the Under-16 age group he dropped out of international and national junior tennis for good. Having invested so much in the sport, he felt ashamed that he hadn't made it big as well as perplexed about what else he might do with his life.

At its simplest level, Luke's story is one of extreme ego involvement and minimal task involvement. However, many other factors contributed to Luke's development as an ego-involved player, leading him into a downward spiral and eventually causing him to drop out. To fully understand the significance of achievement goals, you must appreciate what research tells us about the causes and the consequences of task- and ego-involved goals.

Due to extensive research conducted on achievement goal theory in the 1990s and beyond, sport psychologists have a much clearer understanding of two central issues:

1. How an athlete becomes task or ego involved in the first place
2. What repercussions are associated with task and ego involvement in sport

An understanding of achievement goal theory helps prevent negative psychological outcomes like Luke's, and helps athletes to think and feel positively and show the best responses to competitive sport.

Links Between Goals and Our Thoughts, Feelings, and Actions

Achievement situations in which athletes have an opportunity to display physical competence (i.e., in training or competition) activate their task- or ego-involved goals. They might be either highly task involved or ego involved in that situation, or they might even switch between the two, because their perception of what they need to feel could change from moment to moment. For example, imagine yourself as a young soccer player in a knockout match. You've felt great during the game because you've worked hard, made some great tackles and accurate passes, and your work on your concentration skills has paid off by allowing you to refocus quickly. You've spent most of the game in a highly task-involved state of mind and have received praise from your teammates. The game is tied and goes to a penalty shoot-out. You are the last player of five selected, and the score is 4-4. As you make that long walk to the penalty spot, how does the situation and its potential consequences affect your view of success and competence? Will your feelings of competence depend entirely on scoring or missing? And, if you do become ego involved, how might it affect your chances of scoring?

All athletes have an innate preference for task- or ego-involved goals in sport. These predispositions, referred to as *task and ego goal orientations*, are believed to develop throughout childhood largely due to the types of people the athletes come in contact with and the situations they are placed in. If children consistently receive parental praise that's contingent on their effort and recognition for personal improvement from their coaches, and are encouraged to learn from their mistakes, then they are likely to foster a task orientation. It becomes natural for them to believe that success is associated with mastery, effort, understanding, and personal responsibility. The behavior of their role models in sport also affects this development. Such an environment is far different from one where children are shaped by rewards for winning (alone), praise for the best grades, criticism or non-selection despite making their best effort, or coaches whose style is to hand out unequal recognition. This kind of environment helps an ego orientation to flourish, along with the belief that ability and talent, not effort and personal endeavor, earn success.

Goal orientations are believed to be relatively stable and enduring characteristics that are largely formed by mid- to late adolescence. Hence, coaches and parents should attempt to shape a child's development as early as possible during the 6- to 14-year-old phase. In this developmental period, children's cognitive abilities start working overtime as they begin to understand that effort isn't the sole reason for success at a task. At about 11 or 12 years of age, they begin to realize that regardless of effort, some kids simply have more ability than others. That's when the fantasy of being the next Michael Jordan comes under obvious pressure for some children.

The strength of a goal orientation influences whether an athlete will adopt a task- or ego-involved goal in a specific sport situation. It is also perfectly feasible for growing athletes to develop both high task and ego orientations if they have been exposed to an assortment of task- and ego-oriented situations and people. However, never underestimate the power of a particular situation. The adolescent athlete might be quite high in task orientation, but in a competition with a high degree of public evaluation, judgment, criticism, or comparison based on who's best, with rewards and benefits for winners and negative consequences for losers, he or she might become ego involved. Competitions accompanied by high perceived expectations and consequences arguably form the natural spine of sport. Factors such as the stage of the event (e.g., final or qualifying match), whether selection is at stake, previous head-to-heads, financial rewards, age of the opponent (e.g., playing a talented younger player), representing the team or country for the first time, and the hostility of the audience can make competition a natural ego-involving laboratory. Nevertheless, not all sport is like that; in fact, some sport situations offset the natural importance of superiority by emphasizing participation and publicly reinforcing or rewarding personal effort, improvement, and problem solving rather than focusing on comparisons. An example is a swimming club that encourages all standards of swimmer, with a coach who gives recognition solely based on individual improvements in time or technique. These situations increase the importance and number of task-involving cues. The key message here is that the availability of task-involving cues in sports that are naturally ego involving allows the athlete to develop a more task-involved approach to competition.

The behavior of coaches, parents, peers, and teammates has a powerful effect on the athlete's understanding of what achievement means. These individuals create an environment around the athlete that's known as the *motivational climate*. If, in a team situation, everybody (including the coach) reinforces high effort, constant cooperation, the importance of learning, and shared contributions, then athletes are likely to perceive a task-involving motivational climate. In contrast, if the team is characterized by players, and coaches, giving punishment or

The behavior of influential people like coaches, parents, peers, and teammates has a powerful effect on the athlete's understanding of what achievement means.

negative feedback for mistakes, rivalry among teammates, or special treatment for star players, then a more ego-involving motivational climate is likely to prevail in the eyes of the individual athlete. Carole Ames, one of the first researchers in this area, notes that coaches and parents make important choices in the way they present information to the athlete. A rather casual ego-involving prematch comment, such as "He's not as highly ranked as you—you should have no problem beating him," sends a clear message to a tennis player about what success means to his parents or coach and what is expected of him. Contrast this with the task-involving direction in a statement such as "Work hard for every point, and concentrate on finding a bit more depth on your backhand like you have practiced well all week." Equally, a fellow athlete who comes up to you after a match asking, "How come you lost to him? He's not that well ranked," reveals how ego involved some peers can be. Compare them to those who ask how you played and which areas of your game need to get better and you can see how easily significant others can contribute to an ego-involving or task-involving state of mind.

Our research consistently suggests that parents and coaches can influence the achievement goals adopted by children. Whether it is something that is said, not said, or a noticeable reaction to an event (e.g., an error), the effect on the athlete can be immediate. For this reason, a great deal of research has investigated what happens to athletes if they perceive the prevailing motivational climate in a task- or ego-involving manner. Overall, the message to coaches, athletes, and parents is to spend some time understanding the athlete's goal orientations and appreciating the prevailing motivational climate.

Specifically, of the immense amount of research conducted on achievement goal theory since the late 1980s, the majority has focused on understanding the *implications* of adopting task and ego goals in sport. Of prime interest to coaches and athletes are the the links between achievement goals and the thoughts, feelings, and behaviors reported by athletes. Factors such as effort; the tendency to take personal responsibility, make excuses, or cheat; effective use of thinking and planning strategies; anxiety; and enjoyment of sport have all been linked to task and ego goals. This research reinforces the advantages enjoyed by athletes who possess a high task orientation. It also suggests that although athletes with a high ego/low task orientation are most at risk of negative thoughts, feelings, and experiences in sport, athletes with a high task/high ego orientation are potentially the highest achievers. The first key factor here is the role played by an athlete's perception of his or her ability.

The Role of Perceived Ability

Athletes high in task orientation believe that learning, improvement, and mastery are associated with success, so it is not surprising that such orientations tend to be associated with high perceived ability. A high or low ability for a particular skill or task is not the key issue; if the athlete is task involved, then there is always room for improvement. In contrast, perceived ability is much more fragile for athletes high in ego orientation. Personal judgments of their ability depend on comparing well to others. Therefore, *as long as they are winning*, there is likely to be a positive association between ego orientation and perceptions of ability. One expects to see a similar pattern of behavior in ego-oriented athletes with high perceived ability and those who are highly task oriented. They will work hard to ensure that they achieve their "superiority" goals, face up to challenging tasks, and take responsibility for themselves. The double-edged sword, however, is brandished when the ego-involved athlete succumbs to a succession of losses and begins to pay the price for equating achievement with not losing. We don't know exactly how long highly ego-involved athletes with high perceptions of ability can suffer those losses before they begin to crumble, but when they do, the pattern of behavior changes entirely. The expectation of feeling incompetent causes athletes to engage in competitive situations that are either too easy or too difficult for them so that they can take responsibility for achieving the easy tasks but blame external factors for failing at the difficult ones. If they do risk (or have to face) moderately challenging confrontations in which failure to win heightens incompetence, then they are likely to feel high levels of anxiety that can impair their performance.

To further protect themselves, ego-involved athletes carefully choose how much effort to invest in order to avoid looking incompetent or, in many cases, to look cool. They also tend to withdraw effort if failure is imminent (i.e., withdrawal acts as the scapegoat). This pattern of effort investment is easy to spot in highly ego-involved teenage tennis players like Luke. When they are confident of winning, they try to "showboat" and play with ease, as if to tell the crowd that they have so much ability they don't even need to work hard to win. However, if such a player had lost the first set of a match and was under pressure in the second, then he'd be likely to "tank" the second set, mentally throw in the towel, or conveniently feign an injury. Ego-involved athletes reduce effort to maximize ability when winning, and reduce effort or involvement to protect ability when losing. Their strategy is to make others think that they are blameless and that injury, illness, or another external factor caused the loss, and that on another day, they'd be likely to win. To pull this off effectively is quite difficult in individual sports where there is no place to hide, but it's seen in team sports in players who don't want the ball and hide for the rest of the game. It's one of those fascinating spectacles that you see in mentally weak athletes when the heat is on.

The Thoughts-Feelings Connection

Research into the relationships between goal orientations and the thoughts and emotions experienced by athletes is very relevant to coaches. A high task orientation has been associated with enjoyment, reported satisfaction, and intrinsic interest in sport, as well as the frequency of experiencing a state of flow. Researchers find a positive relationship between ego orientation and levels of enjoyment only when athletes also have a high task orientation. Most studies have found either no relationship or a negative one between an ego orientation and enjoyment, intrinsic interest, and satisfaction.

Researchers have also pinpointed the fact that athletes with a high ego orientation and low self-confidence tend to experience the highest levels of anxiety before competition, including disrupted concentration and negative thinking. Generally, the opposite is true of those athletes with a task orientation, although when they do experience stress, they tend to deal with it quite functionally by working harder, seeking social support, and curtailing competing activities. Athletes with a high ego orientation, however, tend to cope with stress by venting their emotions more, getting upset, and losing their cool. These findings help explain Luke's anxiety and tensions, as well as his frustration during matches when opponents weren't giving him his own way.

Differences in Information Processing

Some of the most innovative research I've come across suggests that task-oriented athletes value practice and commit to it, whereas ego-oriented athletes are more likely to take the easy route and prefer simply to compete. Those who have a high task orientation seek personal feedback and use it to develop their skills, while those high in ego orientation don't care for feedback about the quality of their performance; they only want to know if they've won. Ego-involved athletes might come across as not that interested in learning, even if the information and support is available to help them improve. Even if they lose, they may still reject the information and coaching that could help them to perform better.

Research also shows that athletes with a task orientation use the feedback they get and consistently process information that will help them perform better in the next few seconds or minutes of a task or contest. They appear to spend that time thinking in a proactive and task-focused manner. On the other hand, ego-oriented athletes simply think about how they compare to others and the consequences of winning or losing, leaving little mental capacity to process information about how to improve the task and learn. Luke spent very little time focusing on feedback that would help him become a better tennis player. In fact, he did not develop any sort of routine "self-debriefing" at all!

Finally, new research shows how young athletes who are moderately high in both task and ego orientation report using more imagery and mental rehearsal than athletes with lower levels of both goal orientations. As preparation for competition, they visualize both mastering skills and winning—reasons closely associated with their goal orientations. These studies shed light on the cognitive functioning of individuals who are higher in task and ego orientation, and they generally support the proactive qualities of a task orientation with respect to long-term development and optimal performance.

Reactions to Peers and Feedback

Our preoccupation with high-level competitive sport sometimes prevents us from recognizing that achievement goals matter for anyone, at any skill level, who picks up a racket or kicks a ball. An area of research that applies to everybody who plays sports explores how achievement goals relate to moral behaviors such as being a good sport, taking unfair advantage, breaking the rules or cheating, promoting aggression, and intentionally injuring an opponent. The majority of this research does conclude that, like our poor friend Luke and his unfortunate habit of selective eyesight (bad line-calling), athletes with a high ego orientation and low task orientation are more likely to be unsportsmanlike and take any advantage to ensure that they win. The reverse tends to be true for athletes high in task orientation and low in ego orientation.

Creating Goals That Get Results

Coaches, parents, and athletes must be aware of achievement goals and understand their implications to sport performance and participation. Sport psychology practitioners might be quick to support the development of a high task/low ego-oriented profile in athletes; however, the reality of competitive sport does not make this an easy proposition for coaches or athletes. The athlete is consistently bombarded by ego-involving criteria, which makes suppressing the development of an ego orientation a difficult, complex task. Also, an ego orientation may be beneficial as long as a high task orientation accompanies it and the athlete's perceptions of ability are solid. Indeed, most of the recent research in sport reports several psychological advantages of possessing a complementary balance of both high task and high ego orientations. At high levels of sport, many coaches are reluctant to compromise the winning mentality or "killer instinct" that they want to see in their athletes, particularly in a competitive sport society. Coaches must recognize, however, that without a task-oriented mentality, their athletes will never be competitive in the truest sense of the word. They are unlikely to see any of their athletes win over the long haul because they, like Luke, will never grow. Further, although a high ego orientation may be useful for performance, it may have side effects in moral terms or in longer-term participation. Coaches and athletes to whom these observations apply face three challenges when working together.

First, a high ego/low task orientation places the effort, persistence, performance, and participation of a young athlete (particularly one with low perceptions of ability) in jeopardy. Implementing strategies that build up a higher task orientation or activate a state of task involvement as early as possible is critical. In fact, if you believe in inclusive participation and keeping all levels of athletes interested, motivated, moral, and feeling competent in sport, then everything you do should be geared toward enhancing task orientation and suppressing ego orientation.

Second, you'll probably find that talented teenage athletes who are involved in more exclusive, competitive, and high-level sport programs are capable of viewing their competence in both ways. If they have developed both task and ego orientations, then maximizing task-involving activities and keeping ego orientation in check is probably the best method to maintain a healthy balance between the two. Your role in helping adolescent athletes to *understand* their task and ego orientations is invaluable. For example, educated athletes can use their ego orientation to their benefit and not allow themselves to succumb to some of its maladaptive side effects. Encouraging athletes to use self-talk of the correct achievement mind-set for a given situation is one way to put this education into practice.

Finally, an effective coach recognizes ego-involving situations before they happen and ensures that athletes are equipped with task-involving strategies and appropriate social support to combat excessively ego-involved motivational climates. Coaches want a high task/high ego-oriented athlete who is heading into competition to "enter the fire" with a clear mind that's focused on staying in the here and now, and who is able to commit appropriate levels of effort to optimize personal skills and strategies. Such a task-involved state is easily undermined in a context that's highly ego involving and prompts the athlete to overthink about the consequences of winning and losing, either before or during the match.

Research that informs us how to practically influence the achievement goals of an athlete is limited, which is why my colleague Austin Swain and I did several studies that investigated the factors that tennis players believed influenced their achievement goals. This data helped us design exercises, tasks, and strategies for coaches, players, and their parents. After we had worked with them over a whole tournament season, the players felt more task involved before their matches and felt less threatened and more challenged by each match. They also felt that although they were still highly competitive and loved winning, they approached their matches with less fear of failure or need to prove themselves to others. They wanted to win because that was the test or challenge, not because of the social consequences of losing.

Let's focus on how coaches can help athletes develop skills to enhance their task orientation, stimulate task involvement, and manage their ego orientations. Table 2.1 introduces a series of objectives that focus on integrating the principles of achievement goal theory into coaching technique. Each objective has a number of goals that lead to specific activities for coaches and athletes.

Table 2.1 Coaching Techniques Using the Achievement Goal Theory

Coaching objective	Goals	Activities
Assess athlete's achievement goals	Understand the levels of an athlete's task and ego orientations and which goal orientation is perhaps most dominant. Understand how achievement goals may influence thoughts, feelings, and behaviors in an athlete. Establish any pattern of responses that you see in an athlete prior to or during certain types of competition.	Interview the athlete using questions from the Task and Ego Orientation in Sport Questionnaire (TEOSQ) or Perceptions of Success Questionnaire (POSQ) (e.g., "When do you feel most successful in sport?" "How much success do you feel when you beat others?" "What about when you try really hard but don't win?" "Do you feel successful if you learn something new?") Study the athlete's thoughts and feelings prior to competition. Try to establish his or her levels of anxiety prior to different types of events; his or her behavior in response to winning and losing; his or her emotions during competition and reasons he or she gives for success and failure.
Assess the *sources* of athlete's achievement goals	Explore the most important influences on the athlete's achievement goals. Understand the "who or what" criteria the athlete is using as the sources of information to tell him or her that he or she is good or not.	Talk to the athlete about "what" or "who and why" he or she focuses on most in order to feel a sense of achievement. "What" responses might include "Winning," "Improving a skill," "A personal best time," or "Beating my opponents easily." "Who and why" responses can include "Mom because she expects me to win all the time," "My coach because he'll praise me if I try hard," "My team because I don't want to let them down," or "My opponent because if I win, then I will get selected for the team."

(continued)

Table 2.1 *(continued)*

Coaching objective	Goals	Activities
Educate the athlete about achievement goals	Help an athlete understand his or her sport and how different achievement goals exist for him or her. Help an athlete understand the advantages and disadvantages of task and ego orientations. Teach an athlete about the Competitive Performance Mentality (CPM).	Work with the athlete to explore the psychological demands of the sport and discuss with him or her what makes his or her sport psychologically tough. Use quotes to help the athlete understand that he or she is not alone in what success can mean to him or her: "Tennis is just about winning…no more, no less…no one looks at how well you played." (high ego/low task example) "I just go out and play, I don't really care if I win or lose." (high task/low ego example) "It's about performing to the best of your ability, being competitive and hungry, and learning about why you might have won or lost on that particular day." (high task/high ego example) Ask the athlete about which attitude he or she feels is the best one and why. Use role models to help the athlete understand and justify the most appropriate ways to view success. Introduce the athlete to the fact that two challenges are made of them in all competitive situations: 1. The self-challenge: to maximize, improve, and maintain current standards of effort and personal skills in the physical, technical, tactical, and mental components of that sport. 2. The game challenge: to use the self-challenge to overcome the test or opponent set for them on that day.

Coaching objective	Goals	Activities
Help the athlete to develop an achievement system including the identification and review of key performance qualities and responses	Work with the athlete on identifying specific qualities and skills to be reviewed in training and in competition. Develop an achievement log with the athlete in order to facilitate a task-oriented approach to each day or week. Help the athlete develop a system for task-involved goal setting and reviewing in competition. Score the development and performance of the athlete in a task-involving manner.	Work with the athlete, identifying important technical, physical, and mental skills and qualities that need to be maintained or developed within him or her over the short, mid-, or longer term. For example, mental qualities might include concentration span, positive self-talk, self-control, body language and posture, and routines. Develop a coaching system where he or she is encouraged to set a performance goal for these skills in training or competition, and consistently reflect on the attainment of the goal. Help an athlete to construct an achievement logbook where a score on a 1- to-10 scale can be assigned daily or weekly to qualities, skills, or activities that are relevant to performance (e.g., consistency of effort, communication, diet, rest and recovery). The athlete can calculate an average score for his or her achievements in each quality weekly or monthly, allowing them to set higher personal goals for the following period. Ask the athlete to record up to three "self-challenge" goals for the upcoming competition. These can be rated by both coach and athlete after competition. Ask the athlete to review the competition fully, with such questions as: 1. Describe the course and the flow of the match or competition. 2. Which of your skills were "on form"? 3. How positive were your thoughts, feelings, and behavior throughout the match? 4. What skills of the opposition tested you out? 5. What are your areas for improvement, and what did you learn from the self-challenge and game challenge today? Help the athlete develop a scoring system (e.g., a percentage) for his or her overall development and performance in that competition. This percent should be based on how they performed or improved in the range of qualities or goals that were important in that event.

One of a coach's first steps is to clearly establish the achievement-goal profiles of his or her athletes. Using statements based on the Task and Ego Orientation in Sport Questionaire (TEOSQ) and Perceptions of Success Questionaire (POSQ) (see figure 2.1) in a casual interview, you can explore what achievement and success mean to them. He or she can then continue to explore the thoughts and feelings of the athletes before, during, and after each competition.

Assessing the sources of the athlete's achievement goals helps coaches ascertain whether the sources that generate feeling of competence (or incompetence) are task or ego involving (or both). A coach may find that an athlete's mother is desperately ego involved, puts pressure on her child to win, and needs to be educated about the appropriate ways to behave as a sport parent in helping her child to develop.

If asked, "When do you feel most successful in your sport," an athlete's level of ego orientation would depend upon how strongly they agreed with this type and range of statements:

- When I'm the only one who can do a certain skill
- When I can do better than my friends
- When the others can't do as well as me
- When others mess up and I don't
- When I score the most points/goals
- When I outperform my opponents
- When I'm the best
- When I beat other people
- When I'm clearly superior
- When I accomplish something others can't do
- When I show other people I am the best

An athlete's level of task orientation would depend upon how strongly they agreed with this type and range of statements:

- When I learn a new skill and it makes me want to train more
- When I learn something that is fun to do
- When I learn a new skill by trying hard
- When I work really hard
- When something I learn makes me want to go and practice more
- When a skill that I learn really feels right
- When I do my very best
- When I show clear personal improvement
- When I reach a goal
- When I overcome difficulties
- When I master something I couldn't do before
- When I perform to the best of my ability

Figure 2.1 Statements based upon the TEOSQ and the POSQ.

Helping athletes understand their achievement goals is a critical role for a coach. Information is power, and young athletes can feel very liberated if they understand their motives and why they feel, think, and behave in certain ways in certain situations. Using quotes and role models is useful; however, introducing them to a task-oriented approach to competition (e.g., the "competitive performance mentality") guides the development of their attitudes as competitors. A Competitive Performance Mentality is essentially a mind-set that reflects both task- and ego-involved goals, but it does so in a way that doesn't excessively pressure or coerce athletes to prove themselves to other people. Possessing a CPM reflects how the athlete deals with two simple tests, the self-challenge and the game challenge, that sport will always provide. The *self-challenge* reflects the opportunity to strive to the best of your current ability in sport and, as the foundation for feelings of personal success, must be the primary focus. However, the sport also challenges the athlete to be competitive with the opposition and the *game challenge* reflects this competitive test set by the sport. The two challenges exist in every competition, whatever the situation or level of opposition, and either, both, or neither of the challenges may be met successfully. After *every competition*, it is critical to review and appraise the self-challenge first (i.e., the level of individual skills and efforts relative to personal expectations), and then review the game challenge by reflecting on the skills of the opponent, aspects that tested the athlete's resources in competition, and what he or she learned about their opponent.

The development of a CPM is facilitated when athletes identify important skills or qualities that are relevant to the self-challenge and the game challenge. The self-challenge is based on the self-reflection of qualities or processes that are fundamentally important to personal performance in a particular sport. Therefore, an athlete who consistently reflects on the execution of these qualities will develop a higher task orientation.

In my experience, one of the most practical methods to promote task orientation is for athletes to complete a daily or weekly achievement log, which is perfect for goal setting. This system encourages athletes to set maintenance or improvement goals for the following week in particular areas. Note that many athletes find that rating themselves is quite a difficult task at first and may need guidance. In addition, many athletes benefit from recording their thoughts, feelings, and events during the day, which give context and reasoning to the scores they have given themselves. The achievement log is a great vehicle for enhancing task orientation and getting athletes to take greater responsibility for evaluating themselves on controllable behaviors that are keys to success in sport. Coaches and parents can make an even stronger task-involving impact on the athlete if they sign off in the log each day and include a comment about how hard the athlete worked and what would be important to focus on the next day. Of course, if athletes want to keep certain aspects of their logs private, then parents and coaches must respect this. However, when coaches or parents show that they value the achievement log, they reinforce the importance of achieving its components. This is how athletes begin to perceive a task-involving climate around them.

Setting self-challenge goals in certain targeted areas should help athletes maintain a task-involved state of mind in competition. After competition, a full performance review aided by the statements in figure 2.1 on page 32 allows them to understand appropriate levels of personal responsibility and what can be learned from the competition process and outcome.

Finally, to round off a complete assessment of what the athlete has achieved, I encourage coaches to develop a scoring system or percentage that shows achievement in a number of areas. This score gives players a personal and competitive achievement standard, akin to a personal time in swimming or track and field, that they are responsible for maintaining or improving. This is the final component in an overall system that positively encourages players to reflect on individual performance and self-regulation of thoughts, feelings, and behavior, and take personal responsibility while appreciating what the game challenge (i.e., opponent) had to offer. The information gained can then be channeled into training or preparation for the next competitive event.

Advanced Strategies for Coaches

The strategies and exercises presented so far are comprehensive and useful for all coaches. However, those who work with higher-level athletes may choose to consider more advanced techniques.

Develop a script   The Newspaper Article, an exercise that is done the day before competition, projects the athlete to *the day after the competition*, when he or she reads what the local newspaper said about him or her. The article talks about the task-involved qualities that he or she showed and how he or she was able to overcome ego-involving pressures to stay focused and make significant progress. (A good way to help the athlete prepare for a very ego-involving competition is to rehearse a mental-imagery script that includes instructions for staying calm and focused. Coaches have had more experience with such competitions and can help the athlete develop a realistic imagery script. It should contain descriptions of the situations and cues that prompt the athlete to experience feelings and physiological arousal, as discussed in chapter 8.) Another option for this exercise is an audio commentary given by the coach in the role of a local news reporter commentating on the athlete's qualities after the fact—but before the event! The athlete can listen to this piece during the build-up to the event in order to allow the relevant information to filter in and produce highly motivational effects.

Create a supportive climate   Coaches might not always find it easy to implement training logs and competition review systems with all athletes in order to shape their goal orientations from the *inside out*. For younger athletes, it is imperative that the climate shape them from the *outside in*. Coaches, parents, peers, and teachers are the significant influencing agents in the development of a young athlete's attitude about and confidence in competition. Coaches and parents in particular need to play a *united role* in what they say to young athletes and how they physically and visually respond to them before, during, and after competition. After the match, they should make observations and ask questions that relate to technical, physical, tactical, or mental skill areas, such as "How did your shots feel today?" or "You looked fast around the court and seemed composed before shooting." They could ask, "How was your passing that you've been working on?" or "How effective were your tactics—did you stick to your plan?" or "I thought your reaction could have been better after that point. What do you think?" None of these examples are ego involving; instead, all ask for self-reflection on a personal skill.

Using the right verbal and body language to transmit task-involving values and emphasize mastery, effort, and personal responsibility (rather than the expectation of winning) is a valuable skill for coaches and parents. It is a skill to be used at home, in the car, prematch, during performance, postmatch, and in the car again. Each of these contexts is a motivational climate in its own right and an opportunity to nurture the best attitude for competition.

To help parents and coaches become skilled at this type of communication, I like the idea of using a "language logbook" in which they note times when they have purposely used task-involving comments and questions in various situations with the athlete. Parents in particular find this a useful way to improve the quality of what they say and their reactions to their children when they play sports.

I also encourage coaches of individual and team sports to check their delivery style and treatment of athletes, particularly the quality of information and the context of why, when, and how it is transmitted. For example, do you make the purpose of specific drills clear and relevant so that the athletes are able to explain why they are done? Do you set goals with the athlete to direct behavior in the session? Do you give feedback to everybody in a consistent manner, and is it individualized and relevant to their goals or focused on comparisons? Are athletes encouraged to self-evaluate their performance in a drill? Is public and private recognition given for personal improvement and high levels of mental and physical effort, or is public humiliation and embarrassment part of your climate? Do you make off-the-cuff remarks to athletes publicly that can cause perceptions of favoritism or intrateam rivalries? Are athletes encouraged to praise and support each other? Is a positive climate in place with equal treatment for all athletes? The answers to these questions may inject some new approaches into your coaching.

Seek input Environments that are most effective in shaping the achievement goals of young athletes are ones in which coaches, parents, and athletes work together with similar agendas. Unless systems that foster this kind of environment are put in place, it is unlikely that the athlete will experience the benefits of such cohesion. The coach should back up the parent, the parent should back up the coach, and both should reinforce each other's activities and discussions with the athlete. Together, they develop an understanding and awareness of what is required from each party and discuss it in an open and honest manner.

To aid this unified approach, I encourage each coach, parent, and athlete to construct a *sport-involvement contract* that consists of expectations and acceptable behaviors to which they are committed. They then read through the others' contracts, discuss the task-involving expectations and behaviors, and revise them, if necessary, before agreeing to adhere to their own contract and each signing one. Periodically, the coach-parent-athlete team meets, and each member presents a brief, personal progress report. (The athlete should act as chair of the meeting to increase his or her sense of responsibility.) This can also be a useful exercise for a team coach to do, with each player presenting a report to the group.

The ideas presented here are designed to encourage athletes to accept appropriate levels of personal responsibility, ownership, and motivation toward improvements. In sum, the coach, parent, and athlete are not isolated units in helping the athlete develop a task-oriented, healthy, competitive approach to sport. Successful development comes through integrating task-involving attitudes and behaviors of those individuals who have the most influence on the athlete.

Future Directions

Luke, our tennis player, had quite an eventful adolescence, and ultimately a psychologically painful one in many respects. I believe that the nature of a young athlete's achievement goals is critical to their enjoyment, participation, and excellence in sport. This is why the practical suggestions have been described here in detail and involve the explicit and dedicated roles of coaches and parents, as well as commitment by athletes.

We have much to understand about achievement goals and how to balance a high task orientation with a healthy level of competitiveness. The most significant advancements in this research, in my opinion, lie with what the educated coach tells us about what works and what doesn't work in practice. Practitioners need to learn from the coaches, athletes, and parents, because it is these people who work with thoughts and feelings about achievement on a daily basis. Within the next 5 to 10 years, I'd like to see this expanding practical knowledge base provide coaches, athletes, and parents with tried and tested means to help everyone reach their potential.

chapter 3

Competitive Drive: Embracing Positive Rivalries

Cal Botterill

Competition has the potential to bring out the very best—or the very worst—in us. Historically, competition played a role in evolution, and it continues to do so in a wide range of fields around the world. Sport is a great way to explore the potential and limitations of competition. It has also helped us identify effective and ineffective approaches to competition.

At its best, competition can trigger the drive to excel—to realize our human potential. Excellence is competition's best ally! But in the absence of an open striving for excellence, competition can produce problems.

The comparative nature of competition can easily make us self-centered, judgmental, envious, and negative in our rivalries. These effects can interfere with our focus and ability to perform optimally. A shift from a "want to" to a "have to" perspective occurs easily in competition, which often complicates focus and performance.

Understanding Competitive Pressure for Better or Worse

A closer look at how competition affects performance reveals several factors that explain the poor results sometimes associated with competition pressure. Most important is the inability to fully focus on the task at hand.

Initially, desire for a competitive outcome may help athletes focus on a field of endeavor, set aside distractions, and apply themselves. But difficulties with focus often start when athletes begin to define themselves by competitive outcomes. When this happens, a healthy "want to" approach to excellence and competition often becomes a pressured, "have to" approach, to which perceived pressure, insecurity, and a focus on outcomes all contribute.

Athletes who focus on outcomes and irrational pressures often find it impossible to focus fully on the process of performing. But we can't force it; if we are busy telling ourselves to focus, our total attention is not on the task. We need to prepare, allow it to happen, and enjoy the process. The ideal performance, or "flow," state allows total focus (see chapter 1 for more information on flow and its relationship to performance). Overemphasis on outcomes can interfere with chances of achieving that state; too much competitive pressure can cause tension or stress, interfere with focus, and limit our ability to anticipate and "read" the field of play. Concern about outcomes can also lead to overanalysis, which also interferes with focus and performance.

Even more problematic than the acute effects of competitive pressure are the chronic effects. Long-term preoccupation with competitive consequences can interfere with rest and recovery as well as with performance. The cycle can lead to physical, mental, and emotional fatigue or exhaustion—and health as well as performance problems! Figure 3.1 outlines how our physical, mental, and emotional capacities can be masked if we are not in a recovered state. Physical, mental, and emotional fatigue can dramatically affect the ability to perform and compete, and lack of recovery in any area can affect the others. Emotional

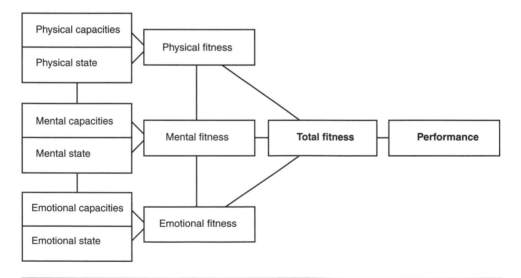

Figure 3.1 Total fitness model.

Reprinted, by permission, from Cal Botterill and Clare Wilson, 2002, Overtraining: Emotional and inter-disciplinary dimensions. In *Enhancing recovery: Preventing underperformance in athletes,* edited by Michael Kellmann (Champaign, IL: Human Kinetics), 145.

fatigue can be especially debilitating. Regular debriefings, processing of feelings, and identifying lessons from experiences can play a huge role in emotional and total fitness.

Irrational beliefs in sport that are commonly part of a developing obsession regarding competitive results are as follows:

1. My self-worth is on the line in the next few moments.
2. I must perform for others.
3. I must be perfect.
4. The world must always be fair.

Variations of the underlying irrational beliefs can easily interfere with focus and cause problematic short- and long-term stress effects. Some authors such as Albert Ellis suggest that rational emotive therapy is what athletes need to overcome these irrational beliefs. Replacing these beliefs with a rational perspective on competition and life can make a big difference to health, performance, and happiness.

Throughout my career, I have seen irrational beliefs interfere with health and performance; sometimes parents unintentionally contribute to these problematic perspectives. Because parents often invest so much time and money in their children's sport activities, it is easy for children to feel that their self-worth is on the line or that they *must* perform for others. These perceptions can create tremendous pressure and hurt the child's ability to compete. Perfectionism is common in gymnastics, figure skating, and goal-tending, but excellence should be the goal; perfection by definition is impossible. Finally, because many sport performers have not had the benefit of adversity training or experiences, they often have limited coping skills and persistence. They naively feel that the world should always be fair. At times it clearly isn't—ask a child who has leukemia—and expecting it to always be fair is irrational.

Intrinsic Motivation for a Competitive Edge

Why are some people more prone to problems with competition than others? Simply stated, because the challenge of maintaining focus on the task at hand is so critical, those who are *intrinsically* (internally) motivated have a huge advantage. Because they love what they do for its own sake, they are more likely to stay focused on personal excellence and thrive on competition. People who are more *extrinsically* (externally) motivated are more likely to be distracted and affected by competitive conditions and outcomes. Top performers and competitors almost always love the process of what they do. Connecting with their personal destiny helps prevent competition from becoming a problem—it helps ensure that they do things for the right reason. Developing intrinsic motivation can have many payoffs, including a task-relevant focus, less fluctuation in motivation, and decreased stress and distraction.

Coaches and parents should nurture a love of the activity in the performer. It's unlikely that many athletes will invest the hours necessary to excel and compete at the top level if they don't intrinsically love what they are doing. On the other hand, we can easily undermine or destroy intrinsic motivation by emphasizing extrinsic rewards. Kept in perspective, extrinsic rewards can add to motivation, but they also have the potential to distract and destroy great competitors.

Process goal setting can help prevent problems with competition. Great coaches like John Wooden (UCLA basketball) and Vince Lombardi (Green Bay football) are tremendous examples of how to make personal and team development the keys to success. For example, Wooden's pyramid of success is an impressive tribute to personal-development, process goal setting. When players took care of what was in the pyramid, winning took care of itself. Lombardi encouraged players to take care of faith, family, fitness, and fundamentals first. Those who knew him best suggest his original quote was, "Winning isn't everything; it's the only thing left to do."

People who have learned to approach success with a process focus, a daily development approach, and team goals are much less prone to problems with competition. They have learned that if you take care of the process, the outcomes will take care of themselves. This discipline also helps them live in the moment, perform well, and get the most out of life.

Insecurity also makes us prone to difficulty with competition. A preoccupation with self-esteem makes us too self-centered, fearful, and worrisome. The result is too much focus on ourselves, competitive outcomes, and comparisons rather than on the performance task. It seems that *self-acceptance* may be more important than *self-esteem* in athletes. People who are happy with themselves and their identity are less affected by competitive pressure; many top performers are humble and respectful (indicators of self-acceptance). Maintaining high self-esteem can be an ever-escalating, ego-based competitive need. Knowing who we are and what we love to do can make us much less prone to problems with competition.

Setting the Mental Stage for Competition

It often isn't easy to get past our egos and basic needs so that we can enjoy positive rivalries and thrive on competition. It is great when teams and performers show us the maturity and perspective that make a huge difference. Once we realize the difference, we want it to be a way of life! The positive approach is reinforcing for focus and energy—and we want to avoid the problems that are commonly part of negative rivalries and competition.

Canadian Speed-Skating

I had the privilege of working with the Canadian national speed-skating team during its preparation for the 1998 Olympics in Nagano, Japan. My initial observations and interviews in 1996 revealed that an emphasis on teamwork and positive rivalries could probably help with both internal and external dynamics and competition.

Susan Auch, the senior Canadian female skater, had previously enjoyed a great positive, supportive rivalry with American competitor Bonnie Blair, which had brought out the best in both of them. Ironically, it is often easier to enjoy a positive rivalry internationally than on your own team. Ego needs (the need to belong or succeed) can often be greatest close to home! Nevertheless, Auch (the decorated veteran), Catriona Le May Doan (the emerging star), and all their teammates acknowledged that it would be a good idea to embrace positive rivalry and teamwork ideas.

In order to get the best coaching and make a "real team" model work, Doan had to trust that coach Derrick Auch, Susan's brother, would treat her fairly and that her teammates would help prevent any bias. Doan and Auch had to embrace their top competitor—each other—as a teammate. They had to trust and support one another (and their teammates) toward excellence. Ethical dilemmas in high-performance environments can be a real challenge, but once solved they promote trust and a supportive training and competitive environment. The emotional maturity that results makes for a stronger athlete later.

It took a team approach to make this sensitive competitive situation work. Teammates regularly provided support and monitoring for fellow competitors and staff and ensured that everyone's needs were given priority. Periodic team meetings and daily monitoring fostered a strong respect for those needs. It became a great high-performance group: The stress and static of negative rivalries and competitive sensitivities disappeared, and the quality of training and interaction improved dramatically.

During the Olympic 500-meter final race between Auch and Doan, I had never felt more confident in two performers. They had faced the rivalry demons many times before and were totally focused on their task. Auch started with the fastest 100-meter opener in speed-skating history, and Doan responded to the challenge to come from behind to win the gold medal. With their teammates and a healthy approach to competition, they had indeed pushed one another to the top of the world!

In 1998, the Canadian Olympic speed-skating team finished with its best results and most medals ever. Many skaters and staff contributed to this impressive show. It was an exceptional demonstration of the potential of a positive approach to competition and rivalries.

Fear of losing or feeling one's self-worth is on the line brings added performance pressure in high-profile sporting events.

As the speed-skating story shows, feelings and focus can change easily and dramatically in the middle of competition. The underdog usually believes he or she has nothing to lose and everything to gain if he or she performs well; it's a psychologically attractive position. However, if an underdog gets out to an early lead, he or she may experience some of the fear of failure that is part of being a contender or a favorite. Favorites often fall into the trap of playing to "not lose," which is not an effective response to competition. Basketball coach Pat Riley points out that when his teams "play to win" versus "play to not lose," their focus and performance improve greatly.

Fear of failure may be useful to trigger preparation, but it is not a good perspective to perform with. In order to compete and perform well, a favorite must respond to fear of failure with a positive game plan and a process focus. The favorite learns how vulnerable he or she is (with everyone challenging him or her) and how critical emotional preparation is to maintaining a good response to competition. Competition dynamics confirm the adage that "it's hard to get on top, but even harder to stay there."

When Doan, from our speed-skating story, used positive rivalries and "real team" dynamics to help her become the top skater in the world, the pressure and expectations of being a favorite were never greater. Fortunately, she realized that regardless of how good she was, she could always work on her race plan to improve. When media and competitors drew attention to the pressure she was under, she focused on her game plan and personal excellence. This focus, along with her ability to maintain a strong, healthy perspective, probably helped her to repeat as a gold-medal champion in the Salt Lake City Olympics in 2002. The dynamics of being the defending champion and favorite for four years made repeating the feat difficult, but staying rational and responding to fear of failure with a *process* performance plan seemed an important part of the story.

Dr. Doug Newburg, author of *Resonance* from the University of Virginia Medical School, describes the *essence* of the competitive challenge in life as learning ways to "keep one's desires greater than one's fears." The astute competitor who embraces competition learns to manage this challenge in two ways. First, as suggested earlier, he or she responds to fear with strong desire, a plan, and a focus to face the challenge and perform well, growing in the process.

The astute competitor also explores ways to reduce or eliminate irrational fears so that he or she can optimize positive energy, recovery, and performance. Managing this fear–desire relationship effectively can greatly improve one's response to competition.

Another dynamic that can change dramatically in sport is the concept of the home-field advantage, in which perceived demands and resources seem to play a role. Under normal circumstances, the home venue would appear to provide greater perceived resources (fans, home field, and so on). However, researchers Roy Baumeister and Andrew Steinhilber were among the first to point out that these competitive factors can change; for example, the success percentage for home teams in the final games of a playoff or World Series seems to drop. Fans can become part of the perceived demands rather than resources under those circumstances. This change in perception can also explain why a team that's struggling at the start of the year will often welcome a road trip to reduce perceived demands and pressures.

The athletes who have learned to enjoy challenges and focus on what is within their control are less prone to these kinds of competitive effects. Those whose perspective enables them to respond more effectively to pressure have a huge advantage. When asked how he handled pressure, NBA Hall of Famer Magic Johnson responded with "What pressure? I'm just glad so many are interested!" His comment is a great sensitizer. We create most of the pressure in life with our perceptions and perspective. If we have a rational personal perspective, pressure can be defused and put in its place.

Focusing on what's within our control can help us with competition and life. In a study of Canada's top character athletes, researcher Matt Brown and his colleagues identified three key components of effective *perspective* in sport. The best performers knew who they were—they had a diverse identity (and strong self-acceptance). They also knew where their support was—they had strong, meaningful relationships with people who were unconditionally supportive. Finally, they knew how they wanted to live and compete—they were humble, grateful, and had strong personal values and attitudes.

Working on these three components appears to allow people to see the "big picture" more clearly and openly. A great perspective can put pressure in its place and make a big difference in how we handle competitive dynamics.

Competition Skills That Enhance Performance

Evidence has been building regarding the importance of "win–win" perspectives on competition. Positive rivalries demonstrate the potential of positive approaches to competition and life. The "win–lose" approach to competition and life seems to have real limitations. In the long run, a "win–lose" perspective may very well turn out to be "lose–lose." A return to the pickup games most of us played as children shows us how. If a "win–lose" approach dominates in a pickup game and respect and appreciation of competitors drops off, it is not long before the game breaks down. The so-called winners lose over time when they have no one to play or compete with.

Often the dynamics of how cooperation and competition complement each other are not taught very well. In order to be a great competitor, a performer needs to be a great team person (cooperator). Life is a team game, and the skills of cooperation and collaboration play a big role in realizing one's potential. Rather than being polar opposites, competition and cooperation involve complementary skills and values. An appreciation of both is part of a healthy perspective on sport and life.

Even the argument that competition automatically leads to excellence is lost if lack of cooperation results in no strong opponent to compete against. Global and environmental challenges demonstrate the limitations of competition without cooperation in a deadly way. Competitive corporations and governments that use up natural resources without concern for the environment or the future contribute to a serious problem. Winning won't matter if there is no sustainable world to live in. Once again, the situation becomes "lose–lose" without some cooperation and perspective.

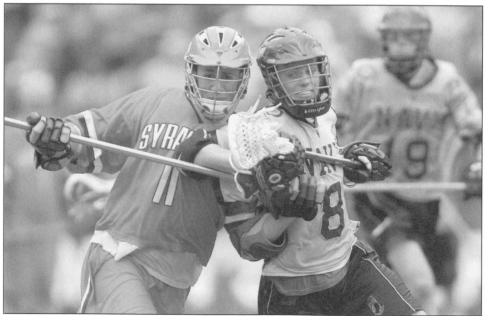

Competition and cooperation are linked by complementary skills and values. To be a professional at the top of your game, an appreciation of these concepts both on and off the field is a must.

Perhaps the ultimate example that competition alone won't work is the threat of nuclear war. The consequences of overcompetitiveness with nuclear weapons would clearly be "lose–lose." A planet that is damaged so badly that it may no longer sustain life is hardly much of a prize.

By studying peak performers, we begin to appreciate their balanced skills, attributes, and perspective. Charles Garfield, a noted performance expert, identified six attributes, which relate to both competition and cooperation, that are common in people achieving excellence:

1. A sense of mission: This, along with the feeling that you are fulfilling your destiny, can play a big role in both competition and cooperation. Motivation for people who have a sense of mission is very natural because they are engaged in something that they enjoy and believe is important.

2. A tremendous work ethic: This is the desire to be action-oriented. Excellence requires persistence. Top performers' love of what they do seems to fuel their drive and effort.

3. Use of resources: Peak performers invest in their health, development, and recovery because they know it is necessary to help them optimize their potential and to help others.

4. A strong "preparation ethic": Superior preparation enables top performers to appreciate the big picture and be much more creative, open, and focused under pressure.

5. A love of challenge and change: Enjoying challenge is a huge attribute. Looking forward to the process of succeeding rather than fearing failure is dramatically more effective, and helpful to others as well.

6. Great "team people": Great performers recognize the importance of working with others and relating effectively.

So it turns out that top performers are an exciting blend of competition and cooperation. Those who have or develop these attributes are likely to have the perspective and skills to enjoy health, happiness, and high performance. Also, when we look closely at the challenge of competition and cooperation, we see that the pursuit of excellence is something top performers have in common. Perhaps, as Garfield discovered when he was part of the 1969 mission that first put a man on the moon, our best performances come when we focus on the pursuit of excellence.

The skills that are part of cooperating and competing effectively need to be taught and shared so that more people can realize their individual and collective potential for excellence. Perhaps most important, we need to understand how the concepts of competition and cooperation relate, in both the big and little pictures.

Teaching Effective Competition Skills

As we have discovered, the key to having more people embrace competition in an effective way is developing *perspective*. People who have self-acceptance, support, and strong values are much more likely to appreciate the big picture. As Abraham Maslow suggested, a strong, open perspective gets us past basic human needs and enables us to function at a higher level. It allows us to embrace positive rivalries, healthy competition, and big-picture responsibilities.

Groundwork on perspective should probably be followed by development of and experience with competitive and cooperative skills. Activities and challenges that reinforce the complementary importance of these skills should be regularly experienced and followed by a discussion of their value.

Wrestling with "real" team-building and collaborative approaches to excellence are important growth and development challenges. The component skills of respect, trust, empathy, communication, vision, preparation, and focus need to be explored and developed because they play key roles in the ability to embrace competition and cooperation.

Teaching *emotional management* and *emotional preparation* can also enhance people's ability to respond to competitive and cooperative challenges. We need to understand and learn to manage effectively the seven basic human emotions. Fear, anger, guilt or embarrassment, surprise, sadness, happiness, and interest can all produce strong personal reactions. If we understand how these emotions affect us, good preparation and management can keep them functional rather than dysfunctional. Emotional preparation, or the anticipation of possible feelings in competition and rehearsal of effective responses ahead of time (inoculation), can help people maintain focus in competitive and cooperative situations. Emotional inoculation should be part of the preparation for every important event because of its positive effect on readiness, coping skills, and focus. Emotional management—the acceptance and processing of feelings—can help us stay emotionally healthy and more responsive. It also helps prevent repression and denial of feelings, which can lead to latent, immediate, or subconscious complications. Thorough postcompetition debriefing can help with processing emotions and identifying lessons learned. Parents and teammates can also help by supporting loved ones and encouraging them to honestly accept, share, and process emotions. Everyone can contribute to facilitating emotional health.

In addition to building perspective in youth and performers, perhaps adults also need to regain perspective in sport in many settings. Countless incidents over the past 40 years (especially in youth sport) suggest that some people have lost perspective. Abuse and deaths among parents of youth in sport provide evidence of how competition can sometimes bring out the worst in people. Perhaps many of us involved in sport need to be reminded of the following quote:

> The great thing about sport is that it enables us to care passionately about something that really doesn't matter!
>
> *Scott Taylor, Winnipeg Free Press, 1996*

Clearly, when we compare sport to other community and global priorities, we should regain perspective. Yet as the quote suggests, sport is a great way to learn how to care passionately and manage our responses. Perhaps the raison d'etre of sport is character development, but unfortunately we often let irrational hypercompetitiveness (and a win-at-all-costs outlook) destroy this potential. Regaining our perspective may be every bit as important as trying to develop it in youth performers.

Team-building can be an important intervention to overcome individual differences and clarify roles and strengths. It can help us appreciate others and big-picture challenges and priorities, and mobilize the power of belief and collective effort. The world often seems full of "pseudo" versus "real" teams. There are many differences, but a real team has dealt with its ego needs and competitive dynamics. Its members get past the "disease of me" and acknowledge their vulnerability, need for support, and commitment. They have embraced competition and positive rivalries and have committed to open, caring, genuine communication. In this superior climate, teammates feel supported, have complete focus, and experience less-troubled recoveries.

One activity that has proven an excellent "real" team builder involves asking each group member, "What do you need from the team to have a great year?" and "What can you bring to the team?" The exercise quickly demonstrates vulnerability (and need for one another) and identifies important roles that members can play. Through the sharing, trust and respect begin to develop along with a "real" team environment. These kinds of activities help us develop cooperative and competitive skills and demonstrate how interrelated and complementary competition and cooperation are. We need one another in order to pursue excellence and compete at the highest level.

Team-building can be every bit as important in individual sports as with teams. We all need support to handle competition and the pressure around us. Individual sports can foster negative rivalries and limelight pressure. The performer's support team may be smaller but it may be even more important than in a team sport. Coaches, parents, siblings, clubmates, support staff, and fellow competitors are often key team members; to be optimally effective, they need to form a "real" team where support is unconditional, perspective is strong, and static, politics, and petty jealousies are minimized. When asked to describe the difference between a "real" team and a "pseudo" team, performers who had experienced both said, "A *real* team has no B.S." They have clearly noticed the tremendous difference an authentic, trusting team can make.

"Real" team-building can do a lot to help people grow and learn to handle internal (within one's team) and external (beyond one's team) competition. As well, their collaborative and interactive skills and experience are part of an enhanced perspective. Perhaps the most important payoff is experience with the concept of collective belief. Our ability to believe under pressure is often related to the beliefs of those who matter to us. National junior hockey team captain Nolan Baumgartner, between periods of a World Championship gold-medal game, told his team: "I looked in their eyes, boys—they are hoping and we are believing!" Few would argue that this is the key to most competitions. Once we have experienced "real" team dynamics and collective belief, we realize how much closer it can take us to our potential. When we truly realize that life is a team game, we compete and excel much better. We realize how important it is to believe in others, and feel others' belief in us—it's "higher-order" functioning with huge implications in sport and life.

Future Directions

Embracing competition in the way outlined in this chapter will result in many benefits to athletes, coaches, and citizens when widely adopted. First and foremost is an improved ability to compete and excel in sport or in life—an enhanced capability to thrive on and survive life's demands and opportunities.

In the process of embracing competition, hopefully we become happier with our perspective, health, and performance. Competition can bring out the best in us, but we shouldn't let it destroy our focus and perspective. With the right approach, we can improve our focus in every setting, from grassroots to elite.

Sport, performing arts, business, politics, education, health, and social work are all fields that would benefit from an enhanced perspective and a mature approach to competition and teamwork. Global, community, and family challenges all need fresh vision and new collaborative skills and effort. Often, our greatest competition in life is with *ourselves*. Being the better person, as well as performer, is a start on the world's challenges. Remember:

> As we are liberated from our own fear, our presence automatically liberates others.
>
> *Nelson Mandela, 1994*

Overtraining: Balancing Practice and Performance

Kirsten Peterson

In today's "no pain, no gain" culture of sport, many athletes at all levels are pushing the training envelope with the goal of improving performance. Nowhere is this more evident than in the ranks of elite sport, where winning margins are measured in tenths or even hundredths of seconds. In my work as a sport psychologist at the Olympic Training Center (OTC), I frequently hear athletes talk about how doing more than their competitors is the key that separates them from the pack and gives them confidence. And small wonder: Sport science researchers suggest that training loads are increasing by some estimates at a rate of 10 to 20 percent every five years. Mark Spitz, for example, won his seven gold medals in the 1972 Olympics by swimming 9,000 meters per day. Within 20 years, however, average college swimmers were surpassing this mark, and by 1995, Olympic swimmers were putting in over 36,000 meters per day.

The pressure that this continuous focus on getting better and better evokes can be intense. At the same time, however, athletes and sport scientists alike are discovering that performance improvement is not as simple as "more is better." The law of use and disuse, for example, suggests that athletes who apply the same type of training load over and over again are in effect going from use to disuse of critical physiological systems, leading to eventual performance stagnation as opposed to improvement. The experience of some returning veteran athletes to Olympic-level competition also belies the idea that training loads must increase for better performance. These athletes report that they have experienced international success with dramatically reduced training loads. Joan Benoit Samuelson notes a similar sentiment: "When you don't feel right, back off. [In

Sport science researchers estimate that training loads are increasing by 10 to 20 percent every five years. Olympic-level swimmers frequently log 36,000 meters per day compared with a typical 9,000 meters in the 1970s.

marathon training] it is all too easy to fall victim to the idea that you must run a certain number of 20-milers. When you're tired, it's better to run less."

Despite these examples and others like them, however, it is becoming increasingly common for athletes of all levels to attempt to push the optimal-training envelope, with the result that they shoot out of their ideal training zones into the realm of overtraining.

This chapter first outlines the basics of overtraining: who is at risk, how the syndrome is defined, and what symptoms to look for. Next, it discusses ways to assess both the physical and psychological symptoms of overtraining. Finally, it addresses the available interventions, including recovery techniques that coaches and athletes can use to minimize this syndrome's effects and speed recuperation.

The Trend Toward Increased Training Intensity

Overtraining, defined by the U.S. Olympic Committee (USOC) in 1999 as "the syndrome that results when an excessive, usually physical, overload on an athlete occurs without adequate rest, resulting in decreased performance and the inability to train," is on the rise. Differences in how overtraining is defined have made a true estimation difficult, but researchers suggest that, on average, 10 percent of athletes are overtrained at any given time. Endurance-sport athletes are usually more hard hit; by some estimates, 60 percent of elite competitive runners and 33 percent of nonelite runners are or have been overtrained. For elite athletes searching for the elusive "edge" over their opponents, overtraining has fast become something of an occupational hazard. The USOC sponsored a research project conducted by sport psychology consultant Dan Gould of Greensboro, North Carolina, to determine the factors that differentiated Olympians' successes and failures at the 1996 and 1998 Games. Embedded in the findings were some surprising statistics about overtraining. Twenty-eight percent of 1996 summer Olympians and 10 percent of 1998 winter Olympians reported overtraining as a significant reason for their competitive difficulties.

While we might argue that overtraining is an almost inevitable by-product of elite athletes being willing to do anything to "get the edge," this phenomenon is spreading to other levels of sport as well. Researchers are noting an increased incidence of overtraining among even the youngest athletes, who appear all too ready to absorb our culture's messages about "more is better" and "no pain, no gain." Jay Coakley, a sport sociologist who has studied the effects of overtraining on these younger athletes, notes that the side effects can be especially devastating for this group, often leading to athlete burnout and dropout. He attributes part of this problem to tightly organized youth sport programs that structure out fun by restricting free-play opportunities and limiting athletes' abilities to control the action. Children generally enter sport in order to have fun, gain competence, and be with their friends—needs that are at odds with programs that emphasize beating one's opponent and limit opportunities for social interaction and fun. Youth sport experts agree that when children's values are not met in a particular program, they are at greater risk for burnout when they try to fit into the more competitive environment—or they will simply leave the situation altogether.

Josh

Josh is a nationally ranked wrestler, a resident athlete at the Olympic Training Center who is preparing for Nationals. With his sights set on the competition date a month away, Josh sets out not only to attend his team's twice-a-day practices and semiweekly weightlifting sessions, but also to do more than any other wrestler every day. He comes to practice early in order to drill and stays afterward to ride the exercise bike. He's up early each morning to get in an extra run. After week one, Josh is tired but confident that he will be in far superior condition than his competitors.

Week two brings on increasing fatigue and difficulty sleeping, which begins to worry Josh. He decides he needs some advice, which brings him to my door since I am the sport psychology consultant who works with wrestlers at the OTC. Josh tells me, "I need to learn how to relax or something—I can't seem to get myself ready for practice." After learning more about his symptoms of hard training and fatigue, I broach the subject of overtraining,

(continued)

(continued)

but Josh isn't interested in hearing about it. He acknowledges the symptoms as we check them off but can't think about backing off anything at this point—he has Nationals in two weeks! He eventually agrees that he could try to work on some relaxation techniques as long as he does not have to back off anything else. I teach him some things he can work on and provide some materials on meditation as well.

Meanwhile, Josh pushes on with his training regimen, hanging onto his belief that he is distancing himself from his competition in terms of preparation. Week three brings a tune-up competition that Josh just manages to win, even though he does not think he wrestled well or with his usual fast pace. He had to lose 16 pounds to get to his competition weight and felt completely unmotivated to wrestle. The victory is a hollow one, and Josh's worry about Nationals increases.

The competition is now but a week away, and Josh returns to see me, hoping there is something I can tell him or teach him that will get him back on track. He nods ruefully as I repeat myself about overtraining and admits he didn't think he had the time to work on his relaxation. He decides to try to integrate more rest into his schedule and recommits himself to his relaxation exercises, but it is a case of too little, too late. Josh's lack of competitive motivation continues; he is uninterested in eating and lethargic, and he becomes increasingly anxious about his prospects at Nationals. At the competition, he wrestles poorly and finishes seventh.

Josh's case is all too common—an athlete who seeks to put distance between themselves and their competition by doing more, and then more again. Josh's opposition to acknowledging that he might be overtraining is a frequently observed feature of this syndrome. Resistance to the concept of overtraining and the ensuing treatment—training less—is so widespread among athletes that it has fostered a movement to intervene on the other end of the spectrum. That is, rather than trying to encourage less training, coaches can help at-risk athletes by emphasizing more recovery activities. This active approach has shown promise, particularly for those athletes who will not risk doing less of anything in their quest for competitive excellence.

Optimal Training vs. Overtraining

What is overtraining, and how can you tell when you or an athlete you coach is overtrained? One of the major difficulties in answering this question is the lack of a reliable way to assess whether an athlete is training at the optimal level versus entering the negative realm of overtraining. Integral to modern concepts of training is the notion that athletes need to be exposed to successively more difficult training regimens, called "training overload," with fatigue as a natural by-product of this process. The goal is to displace the athletes' baseline level of fitness by forcing their physiological systems to adapt to increasing stressors. Accurately defining what constitutes an optimal training-load increase, however, is difficult. Factors that influence the process to varying degrees include baseline fitness levels and individual differences between athletes, as well as the specific demands of various sports. The end result is a complex equation, the success of which depends on a vast number of highly individualized variables. What works for one athlete is unlikely to be ideal for another.

Enmeshed within the debate about how to assess overtraining is the lack of standardized criteria and the absence of a way to diagnose when a particular athlete is overtrained versus merely tired. Recent research and theorizing in this area conducted by Michael Kellmann and colleagues suggest that we need to distinguish between the process and the outcome of overtraining. This confusing state of affairs was introduced when you consider that the original meaning of the term "overtraining" meant the process involved in a progressively more difficult training regime, with the desired outcome being the later physiological adaptation to that increased training load. More recently, of course, overtraining has come to mean something very different—an undesirable outcome of too much training that actually prohibits positive adaptations. For the sake of this discussion, I will limit the term to refer to an undesired outcome of fatigue and performance decrements, the constellation of the syndrome's symptoms rather than the process of reaching the overtrained state. Some researchers use the terms "staleness" and "overtraining" synonymously; however, I use only the term "overtraining" in this chapter.

Both terms should also be distinguished from "burnout," a condition experienced by athletes who lose the motivation to maintain their training regimens. Burnout sometimes leads to the athlete dropping out from sport altogether. The central struggle for overtrained athletes, on the other hand, is balancing their continuing drive to train hard with their reduced ability to do so. Thus, overtraining and burnout are different but related issues. To make it even more complex, becoming overtrained is not an all-or-nothing process. Sport scientists have come to differentiate between short- and longer-term effects of training; consequently, they now limit the meaning of overtraining to a negative training effect that lasts three weeks or more. A milder form of the syndrome is now called "overreaching," which includes effects that can be reversed in two or three weeks and that sometimes does lead to increased performance.

Causes of Overtraining

Stressors related to training and nontraining can cause overreaching and overtraining. In the training realm, an overtraining effect can be elicited in several ways: sessions that are too long or too intense, progressions of training increases that are too steep, and too little time devoted to recovery between sessions, to name a few. Although training volumes and intensities and competition frequency are important factors in this equation, athletes and coaches need to be aware of nontraining stresses that can contribute to overtraining, including nutrition, general health, lifestyle issues such as sleep behavior, and environmental stresses caused by juggling life areas such as school or family. When a number of these stressors combine, they can lead to emotional distress and an increased susceptibility to overtraining. So just as all athletes may react differently to the same training load, they may also react differently to other life elements that interact with their training and lead to overtraining. Good coaches and self-aware athletes pay attention to such outside stressors and adjust the training accordingly. If an athlete, for example, knows that she needs a lot of time to study in order to feel prepared for her final exams at school, she is likely to do herself a favor by reducing her training load or increasing her recovery time between workouts during finals.

According to physiological research, we cannot define the exact point at which training goes from being effective to negative for all athletes. In fact, our understanding of the interaction of physical and psychological stress shows that such a point cannot exist, since overtraining is an individualized response. The good news is that this understanding points to a direction for intervention. Although simply reducing the training load is not a guarantee against overtraining, careful and individual tailoring of the training load, with a simultaneous awareness of the effects of other life stresses, helps to optimize training plans. How coaches and athletes can more effectively accomplish this task is the focus of the remainder of this chapter.

Periodized Training As Prevention

With all the confusion in terminology and the inability to accurately assess overtraining, coaches and athletes may wonder if reasonable criteria for safe yet effective training exist. Training theory, which originated more than 2,000 years ago in the ancient cultures of Greece and Rome, has evolved into a discipline with components that involve science, medicine, and technique. Central to modern training is the concept of periodization, which is a framework for formulating an individualized training program.

A periodized training program begins with an overall design based on the long-term program for the season. Coaches need to plan for the entire season or even the year, not just for one week. Within this long-term program, they create shorter-term, sequential training plans (generally planned around specific competitions) with loads that increase progressively and cyclically. These plans follow a logical sequence; that is, training loads are not suddenly increased after a break, and there are taper phases before competitions. Each phase should build on the one before it.

Optimally, these programs are supported by monitoring in all areas of sport science (i.e., physiology, biomechanics, psychology, and sports medicine). This focus on training is balanced by the inclusion of recovery techniques that are used intensively throughout the program. Emphasizing skill development and refinement while also developing strength and conditioning also helps to maintain balance. Figure 4.1 shows an example of what a periodized training program might look like over the course of a season.

Periodization centers on the concept of overload and adaptation. At each periodized training level, the training load is designed to cause an initial performance decline with accompanying fatigue as it challenges the athlete's physiological system. As the body recovers from the stress of training, it also adapts to meet the challenge, resulting in later performance increases. Figure 4.2 illustrates how this would work for a single athlete after one workout. Figure 4.3 shows how the overload and adaptation concepts work in the context of a periodized, seasonal training program.

Coaches typically make two types of errors when applying periodization programs. The first problem is doing too much, too soon. Coaches tend to increase training demands too rapidly for optimal adaptation, maintain an overall training volume that is too high, or program an excessive amount of high-volume or high-intensity training. Other mistakes include giving athletes too much high-complexity technique at the expense of less-intense practice time, or packing in too many higher-pressure competitions without the necessary support training in between. Alternatively, they may make the mistake of offering too much at the wrong time; for example, some coaches insert too much intense training during periods when endurance training would be more appropriate. Sometimes they inadvertently pressure athletes too much by setting inappropriately high competition goals, which can lead to repeated failure and discouragement. Finally, some coaches err by attempting to return athletes to full training too quickly after illness or injury.

Yearly Training Plan					
Phases of training	Prepatory		Competitive		Transition
Subphases	General preparation	Specific preparation	Pre-competitive	Competitive	Transition
Macrocycles					
Microcycles					

Figure 4.1 Periodization/planning template.

Adapted, by permission, from T.O. Bompa, 1999, *Periodization theory and methodology of training* (Champaign, IL: Human Kinetics), 195.

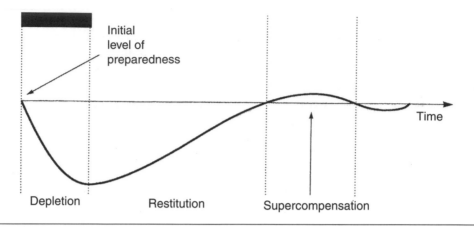

Figure 4.2 Theoretical model of time course of athlete preparedness after a workout.

Adapted from V.M. Zatsiorsky, 1995, Basic concept of training theory. In *Science and practice of strength training,* edited by V.M. Zatsiorsky (Champaign, IL: Human Kinetics), 13.

Reprinted, by permission, from Vladimir Zatsiorsky, 1995, *Science and practice of strength training* (Champaign, IL: Human Kinetics), 13.

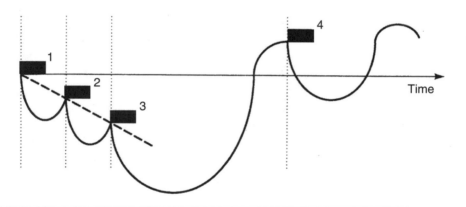

Figure 4.3 Theoretical model of time course of athlete preparedness after a cycle of training.

Adapted from V.M. Zatsiorsky, 1995, Basic concept of training theory. In *Science and practice of strength training,* edited by V.M. Zatsiorsky (Champaign, IL: Human Kinetics), 15.

Reprinted, by permission, from Vladimir Zatsiorsky, 1995, *Science and practice of strength training* (Champaign, IL: Human Kinetics), 15.

The second problem area in training-program design is one of "not enough." Coaches sometimes neglect to build in specific, planned recovery activities to offset the demands of training. Often it's not a conscious omission; rather, it's the result of assuming that athletes know how to recover on their own or a lack of familiarity with how or when to best apply recovery techniques.

Understanding training-program basics is a first step, but how do you recognize when a specific athlete is experiencing difficulties with his or her training? Good coaches have ways to "read" their athletes so that they can quickly adjust training loads before the players go from merely tired to overtrained. Keeping in mind the notion of catching the signs of overtraining early, let's examine what we do know about the indicators and symptoms of overtraining syndrome in athletes.

Detecting Overtraining

As a syndrome, overtraining is a mix of physical and psychological symptoms, some, all, or none of which may show up in a particular athlete. Table 4.1 contains some of the most commonly reported overtraining symptoms. Virtually all of these symptoms can be signs of numerous other problems, so rather than relying on them to determine whether a particular athlete is overtrained, think as holistically as possible. If you or your athletes show some of these symptoms, think about why that might be true:

- What is going on in your life or the athlete's life?
- Which symptoms are evident?
- When did the symptoms start, and what was going on when they did?

A lack of confidence, disinterest in training, and depression could be signs of overtraining—but they might also be due to trouble with a romantic relationship or difficulties in school.

Table 4.1 Physical and Psychological Symptoms of Overtraining

Physical	Psychological
Elevated heart rate	Loss of self-confidence
Weight loss	Drowsiness and apathy
Muscle pain or soreness	Irritability
Elevated resting blood pressure	Emotional/motivational changes
Gastrointestinal disturbance	Sadness
Delayed recovery from exertion	Anxiety
Loss or decrease in appetite	Anger/hostility
Severe fatigue	Confusion
Overuse injuries	Concentration difficulties
Disturbed sleep patterns	Boredom
Immune system deficits	

I cannot overemphasize that the overtraining syndrome is a highly individualized one. A training load that might bring on symptoms of overtraining in one athlete may be perfectly adequate or even light for another. Life stress may be the "straw that breaks the camel's back" in one case, but another athlete with a similar situation may remain unaffected. To illustrate this individuality, here are two athletes whose training and life situations affect them in distinctly different ways:

Jesse and Brad

Jesse, a triathlete, recently switched to this sport from distance running. Her triathlon coaches are impressed with her work ethic and speed, particularly on the road. She has a harder time with her swimming and cycling because she is technically less skilled in these areas, so she puts in extra time in the pool and on the bike, trying, as she notes, to "make up for lost time." Her coaches are delighted with her willingness to work on her weaknesses but note that she becomes frustrated when she makes mistakes or when she progresses more slowly than she thinks she should. As Jesse continues to learn the triathlon, she becomes increasingly irritable and negative because her progress does not match her expectations. Her answer is to train harder in the pool and on the bike—more focus with various coaches on technique, as well as more laps and miles.

Her primary coaches are at first unaware of this extra training, but they soon realize that at least some of what Jesse is doing is counterproductive to other aspects of her training. Jesse, desperate to catch up with her teammates, dismisses the concerns of her coaches and continues to train on her own. She starts to develop nagging injuries—muscle pulls, a sore right shoulder—which she initially dismisses. Within a few weeks, however, her right shoulder soreness has spread to both shoulders, making it difficult and finally, impossible to train in the pool.

Another athlete, Brad, decides to try out for his high school football team because his father encourages him, several friends are on the team, and it seems like something fun to do. He comes to the sport somewhat overweight and not in good shape, but he figures he can train himself into shape through practice. A willing student of the game, Brad pushes himself through practices in the late-summer heat but finds after several weeks that he is less and less interested in the sport. He broaches the subject of leaving the team with his father, who is adamant that Brad complete a season on the team before deciding it is not for him. Brad knows that his dad is proud that he has a son on the team and decides that he'll do his best to stick it out for his father's sake.

At first, Brad makes steady gains in his strength and skill, but after a month he finds himself at a plateau. Nevertheless, he continues to participate at every practice, following the coaches' philosophy that "tough training makes for tough players." He is tagged as a starter at the defensive linesman position because of his size, but as the season goes on, Brad finds himself losing weight, which makes him progressively more disadvantaged on the field. Making matters worse, he discovers that his appetite is not what it used to be. Brad renews his focus in practice, but the harder he tries, the slower and weaker he seems to become. He begins to feel down and has trouble sleeping. He awakens hours before anyone else in his family and finds himself unable to go back to sleep. He remains tired and irritable all day.

The similarities between the two athletes illustrate some of the factors we must account for in assessing overtraining. Both Jesse and Brad initially behaved in ways that any coach would desire—pushing themselves, overcoming adversity, and training hard. Yet both athletes showed performance decrements and emotional distress despite their adherence to this hard training ethic. On the other hand, there are important differences: Jesse's symptoms appear to be a function of her hard-driving, perfectionist personality, while Brad's problems seem to be a function of outside factors—namely the pressure he feels to succeed in his sport to please his father and his coaches. Jesse responded to her situation with anger, while Brad became depressed. So despite the similarities, the differences in these situations demonstrate the individualized nature of the overtraining syndrome.

Coaches and athletes are interested in finding ways to detect overtraining in its earliest stages before it negatively affects performance, mood, or results in injuries. Given the progressive nature of the overtraining syndrome, early detection makes good sense. If at-risk athletes are identified when they first display symptoms of overtraining, coaches can make adjustments and increase recovery strategies before the onset of more serious, chronic symptoms. Because the constellation of symptoms is broad and can be taken for symptoms of a number of other issues in an athlete's life, researchers interested in overtraining look for key variables that discriminate between an overtrained and a non-overtrained state. Physiologists note that several such variables have been identified, including changes in blood lactate levels, elevations in serum creatine kinease, depletion of muscle glycogen, altered testosterone and cortisol levels, and depressed hypothalamic functioning.

Such laboratory-based findings, however, may not be practical for the coach or athlete who doesn't have access to this level of service. The good news is that less-invasive methods to assess for overtraining may be used outside the laboratory.

Resting heart rate   As athletes increase their fitness, conventional wisdom and experience suggest that their resting heart rates will decrease over time. A paradoxical effect has been noted, however, in some athletes whose resting heart rates increase as a result of an overly intense training load. These athletes, who report that they are fatigued and unable to recover from workout to workout, may be in the early stages of overtraining. Coaches and athletes should monitor morning resting heart rate on a regular (preferably daily) basis; those whose heart rates increase by 10 or more beats per minute over baseline may have extended themselves beyond their ability to adapt to the training load and are therefore at risk for the effects of overtraining.

When measuring morning resting heart rate, the athletes must truly be at rest. They should be instructed to take their heart rates as soon as they wake up in the morning, before they get out of bed.

A variation of this method, used by elite athletes, is called the Rusko orthostatic heart rate test. In this method, athletes lie down for 10 minutes at the same time each day and record their resting heart rates for the last two minutes of the rest. Then they stand up, wait two minutes, and record their heart rates again. A change of more than 10 beats per minute between the resting and standing heart rates indicates that the athlete may be fatigued and on the verge of reduced performance. As a final note, keep in mind that an increased resting heart rate may indicate other problems, including nutritional deficiencies, dehydration, infection, or emotional difficulties, all of which should be examined as possible causes before assuming overtraining is an issue.

Monitoring training intensity   A truism in sport is that it isn't what you say you do, it's what you do—which is particularly accurate when assessing for overtraining. Athletes often have misconceptions about training loads or their intensity, which can pose difficulties when assessing for overtraining. The first line of defense, then, is to help athletes become self-aware enough to be able to perform their training at appropriate levels, and then to recognize its effects on them, positive or negative.

- Rating of perceived exertion. Athletes can rate themselves on an objective scale such as Borg's Rating of Perceived Exertion (RPE). This simple 10-point scale has descriptors associated with each number, ranging from 0 (very, very light) to 10 (very, very heavy). Athletes can easily rate themselves during or immediately after each workout. With time and experience, they get better at recognizing the differences between workout intensities. Of course, a workout that rates a 10 from one athlete may elicit a very different response from another. The goal in using this scale should be to help each athlete develop a personal internal monitoring system and learn which perceived intensity levels correspond with desired training intensities.

- Exercise heart rate. Another behavioral monitoring method is to measure the heart rate during exercise. It's particularly useful in sports in which the goal is to attain and maintain a specific level of exertion during a workout. Manually checking the heart rate immediately after a workout has limited value for longer-duration workouts when a specific effort must be maintained over time. In these situations, commercially available heart rate monitors work well by providing instant, continuous feedback.

- Training logs. Measuring RPE and heart rate are useful tools that provide immediate data, but they don't provide a picture of an athlete's reaction to training over time, which is necessary in identifying longer-term trends that could lead to overtraining. An invaluable solution to this problem, which is used by elite athletes across all sports, is a training log. It needn't be complicated, but it does have to be maintained regularly if the athlete is to get maximum benefit from it. Essentially, it is a record of the variables that the athlete decides are important to track in training, and it can be kept in whatever way works best for the individual. Commercially produced training logs are available, but they can also be as simple as a blank notebook.

In monitoring for overtraining, athletes should record their resting heart rates and the type, length, and intensity of their workouts, including their ratings of perceived exertion and exercise heart rate when appropriate. In addition to these training details, documenting other life issues that have been shown to put athletes at further risk of overtraining (e.g., school exams, problems at home or with important relationships) is useful. Finally, it is important to keep track of the major physical and psychological symptoms that correlate with a possible overtrained condition, such as length and quality of sleep, energy level, mood, nutrition, and muscle soreness. Again, the degree of documentation can range in complexity depending on what's being measured as well as on the particular athlete's preferences. Some athletes are minimalists, preferring to use a number scale, such as a 0-to-10 scale, while others prefer to create a more elaborate written record. Figure 4.4 and table 4.2 on page 63 illustrate some examples of different ways athletes can document their daily experiences.

Pencil-and-paper assessments　Because overtraining has so many potential causes and symptoms, researchers in this area advocate for regular, broad-based assessments of athletes on a variety of physiological and psychological markers. Given how difficult it is to assess for reliable physiological markers, researchers have focused more on athletes' self-reports of their physical and psychological symptoms.

- Profile of Mood States (POMS). One assessment method that has been used and researched extensively is the *Profile of Mood States*, a pencil-and-paper questionnaire that measures levels of disturbance on six emotional states: tension, depression, anger, vigor, confusion, and fatigue. William Morgan and his colleagues from the University of Wisconsin spearheaded the use of POMS in the 1980s as a way to differentiate between the emotional states of overtrained and non-overtrained athletes. Mentally healthy athletes tended to have relatively lower scores on tension, depression, anger, fatigue, and confusion and higher than average scores on vigor. POMS results for overtrained athletes, on the other hand, revealed the exact opposite pattern: high scores on tension, depression, anger, fatigue, and confusion, along with a low vigor score. These opposing results led researchers to use POMS as a way to predict when overtraining might be a potential threat. Later work in this area, however, suggests that POMS may not be sensitive enough to distinguish between high-intensity training that is actually productive and one that constitutes an overload. Use of POMS with athletes has also come under fire because it was originally developed for use with non-athlete populations and emphasizes negative mood states, the lack of which can't be interpreted to imply more positive emotions. Other critics have pointed out that although it may be a general indicator of overtraining, it is not specific enough to direct athletes to the most appropriate recovery strategies.

- Recovery-Stress Questionnaire for Athletes (REST-Q). More recently, the *Recovery-Stress Questionnaire for Athletes*, developed in 2000, has been used

Logbook Page Example A

Date _____

Hours of sleep _____

Sleep quality _____

Resting pulse _____

Appetite _____

Feel of muscles _____

Nap? Y_____ N_____ How long? _____

Energy: How much energy did I have?

1	2	3	4	5
Very low energy				Very high energy

Why? _____

Mood: How am I feeling?

1	2	3	4	5
Negative (down, irritable, angry)				Positive (up, happy)

Why? _____

Attitude: How motivated am I?

1	2	3	4	5
Don't want to practice		Average motivation		Can't wait to get training

Why? _____

Training plan

Type _____

Desired intensity level: Easy   Moderate   Hard

Specific training goals

1. _____

2. _____

Training evaluation

Actual intensity level: Easy   Moderate   Hard

If different from desired, why? _____

Did I accomplish my specific training goals?

1	2	3	4	5
Met no goals		50% met goals		100% met goals

Issues at school/work/home?

_____

_____

_____

Figure 4.4   Training questionnaire.

Table 4.2 Logbook Page Example B

Date	3/1 Sun	3/2 Mon	3/3 Tues	3/4 Wed	3/5 Thurs	3/6 Fri	3/7 Sat
Sleep (#hrs)	7	6					
Sleep quality (0 - 10)	8	9					
Rest HR (bpm)	68	65					
Nap (Y/N and # hrs)	Y .75	Y 1.5					
Energy (0 - 10)	5	5					
Eating quality (0 - 10)	6	9					
Muscular comfort (0 - 10)	8	6					
Mood (0 - 10)	5	6					
Motivation to train (0 - 10)	8.5	7					
Training intensity (low/med/high)	med	high					
Training focus (0 - 10)	7	6					
Training evaluation (0 - 10)	8	6					
Life balance (0 - 10)	6	7					

0 = Not good

5 = Average quality

10 = Great, best it could be

Comments: _____

as an alternative to other written assessments, such as POMS. This paper-and-pencil assessment measures athletes' stress and recovery states—the extent to which they experience physical or mental stress—and their use of recovery strategies. The rationale is that the combination of life and sport stressors as well as a weakened potential for recovery lead to performance difficulties, including overtraining. The REST-Q has 76 items that form 12 general stress-and-recovery scales: general stress, emotional stress, and social stress as well as conflicts/pressure, fatigue and lack of energy, physical complaints, success, social recovery, physical recovery, general well-being, and sleep quality. Six additional sport-specific scales include disturbed breaks, burnout/emotional exhaustion, fitness/being in shape, personal accomplishment, self-efficacy, and self-regulation. This assessment has been tested with European and American athletes and proves able to pick up differences in stress levels and use of recovery strategies to combat those stresses. It is more useful than POMS in that it not only assesses the athlete's current emotional state with increased detail but also provides more concrete directions for possible interventions.

• Recovery-Cue. Since not all coaches and athletes have the time or desire to fill out and interpret a multi-item test such as the REST-Q, researchers developed the *Recovery-Cue* as a more succinct measure of stress and recovery. It can be completed quickly and provides more immediate feedback for athletes and coaches. Because of its simplicity, it can be administered more frequently than the REST-Q, in order to maintain a more immediate measure of an athlete's risk for overtraining. For maximum comparative benefits, the athlete using the Recovery-Cue should take the test at the same time each training day, such as after each morning workout, and think about what information is desired and take the test accordingly. For example, if a coach wants to know about the effects of each day's training on her athletes, she should have them take the test at the end of each day. On the other hand, if she's interested in learning if her athletes are optimally ready for training each day, she should administer the test before each day's training session.

Winning Tips for Optimum Recovery

Overtraining, as we have seen, is a complex syndrome with no guaranteed solutions. However, certain interventions show promise for prevention and treatment. A key concept is recovery, the antithesis of overtraining. One of the biggest difficulties in dealing with motivated but overtrained athletes is that the interventions generally consist of asking them to do *less:* "Take a day off from training." "Take it easier on those intervals." "Don't do that workout." "You're hurting yourself by training too much." The idea of doing less presents a dilemma to athletes who likely became good through tough training and pushing through the bad days and who are seduced by "if this much training is good, more must be better" thinking. They overtrain by simply doing more of what made them good. The message of doing less is therefore extremely difficult for these athletes to hear and goes against most training philosophies. A typical reaction: "What do you mean, do less? My competitors aren't taking a day off."

Recent developments in research on overtraining have shifted focus from overtraining to the idea of underrecovery. This shift has had important implications in how we work with athletes at the OTC; it takes away the problem of doing less and instead focuses the athletes' efforts on what they can do more of to help themselves recover more effectively. Instead of telling an athlete to cease some aspect of training, we can instead channel their need for action toward recovery activities. Indeed, the concept of effective, regular, and varied recovery activities has become part of the language of today's smart, professional athlete, which is also the best way to sell it. Statements like "You're not doing everything you can to succeed if you're not taking care of your recovery" challenge athletes to tackle recovery (and decrease susceptibility to overtraining) in a way that telling them to reduce their training regimen never could.

As compelling as the case for increasing recovery activities to mitigate overtraining appears to be, our understanding of this concept is still developing. There is no science of recovery that mirrors the science of training in terms of which specific activities are optimal for each situation of hard training, muscle

©Empics

Many athletes overtrain by doing more of what makes them good at their sport. It is often hard for elite athletes to understand the importance of recovery in enhancing their performance.

soreness, or overreaching. Despite this lack, a number of recovery principles are worth mentioning. This emphasis on enhancing recovery and the development of recovery principles has been led by a group of European sport scientists including Michael Kellmann, whose book, *Enhancing Recovery: Preventing Underperformance in Athletes,* is important reading for coaches and athletes who are interested in the latest information from a variety of perspectives.

If we understand recovery to be an active process, then we must put to rest its old definition as simply a lack of stress. Kellmann and his colleagues suggest that recovery consists instead of a proactive, individualized process to replenish one's psychological and physical resources. Our work with Olympic athletes supports this notion. Some important principles have emerged:

• Recovery is gradual and cumulative; that is, recovery from higher training volumes will require more time than recovery during the taper phase of training.

• Recovery depends on a reduction of, change of, or break from stress, which suggests that athletes can substitute other activities rather than merely doing less of something in order to recover. Also note the general use of the word "stress," which implies the importance of recovery from any kind of stress, be it training or other life situations. So not only do we need to tailor recovery programs to the intensity of athletes' training, we also must be aware of other stresses in their lives that can add to the need for recovery in a given situation.

- Recovery is specific to the individual and depends on his or her appraisal or perspective on the situation. An activity that helps one athlete recover may be stressful for another—not everyone likes getting a massage, for example. In addition, every athlete should have multiple recovery strategies to choose from.

- Recovery can be described on a variety of levels, including psychological, physical, social, and environmental. We speak of physical recovery strategies such as eating a balanced diet to regain lost nutrients, but athletes also report the importance of psychological recovery—their need to feel relaxed, re-energized, and motivated to get back to training. Social recovery includes the quality of relationships with significant others, as well as social activities that are relaxing and rejuvenating. Environmental recovery may mean a change of locale; for athletes at the OTC, it sometimes means going somewhere else to train for a change of pace or going home to recharge through a visit with family. A hike in the mountains may not come to mind as a recovery activity, but for some athletes it can be a welcome change of environment, leading to psychological and environmental recovery.

- Effective recovery strategies can take several forms: passive, active, and proactive. For example, moderate exercise is better than passive rest for recovery after training since it maintains higher blood flow, which aids in the flushing of lactic acid from muscles. To be proactive in recovery means to anticipate one's likely recovery needs, plan to meet those needs through appropriate activities, and adhere to those plans. This might mean scheduling in a trip home or another relaxing break prior to a heavy period of training. Athletes who make a highly detailed training plan often neglect to put in the same effort when planning their breaks from training.

How can coaches and athletes apply these recovery principles to enhance training and decrease the chance of overtraining? Individualization is key. The first step is to incorporate recovery systematically into training. If a periodized training program is used, it's important to incorporate more recovery activities into the higher-volume and more-intensive training periods. And just as good coaches adjust training on a daily or weekly basis to account for differences in their athletes' responses, they must do the same for recovery. Regular use and review of behavioral monitoring, logbooks, and assessments such as the Recovery-Cue may provide the critical feedback needed to make those changes.

Coaches, particularly those who have succeeded with the "more is better" philosophy of training, sometimes have difficulty embracing the concept of recovery. As a result, it's easy for them to subtly undermine athletes' motivation to engage in these activities. Questions for coaches to ponder include the following:

- Do you know the basics of recovery so that you feel as comfortable talking about it to your athletes as you do training techniques? Are you familiar with a variety of passive and active recovery techniques?

- How do you approach the concept of recovery with your athletes? Are recovery periods built into your training cycles? Do you refer to them in the same tone of voice and with the same sense of reverence you reserve for your athletes' most difficult workouts?

- What kind of training environment do you foster for your athletes? Athletes who come from training programs that expose them to high levels of competitive situations, for example, tend to experience higher levels of stress and a greater potential for overtraining than those who come from more supportive environments.

- Do your athletes feel "safe" enough to discuss honestly their physical or emotional training states with you? Clearly this requires a great deal of trust, communication, and knowledge between coach and athlete.

- Do you model good recovery strategies in the context of your own lifestyle?

In addition to being good role models, coaches must be good teachers and enforcers of recovery principles with their athletes. For example, an active rest day at the swimming pool shouldn't turn into a water polo game if rest was the goal. Particularly at the elite level of sport, athletes need to learn that appropriate recovery is as much a part of their job as is their training regimen, diet, or sleep.

An ideal training program that incorporates passive and active recovery activities should include a variety of techniques. Just as there are numerous ways to work on endurance training (hill running, strength and conditioning programs, sustained skill practice), and good coaches mix things up to maintain motivation, there are many ways to enhance recovery. Coaches and athletes should keep this aspect of their training programs as fresh and interesting as the rest of their training.

Passive and Active Recovery Techniques

Passive recovery activities that require the least amount of active involvement include sleeping, lying down, watching TV, and treatments such as massage, hot or cold baths, and saunas. These activities are what athletes typically think of when asked to name recovery strategies, but they are only part of the picture. Active recovery strategies include stretching, yoga, relaxation techniques, easy swimming or running, spinning on an exercise bike, or other low-key group athletic activities such as basketball or Frisbee. Group activities incorporate both active and social aspects of recovery, as long as the emphasis is on fun over intense or competitive activity. An additional benefit of active recovery is that it maximizes a sense of control over the recovery process; that is, the athlete is proactive, initiating and actively engaging in the recovery strategy rather than sitting and doing nothing, which can actually add stress for some athletes.

Relaxation might not seem like an active recovery technique, but we need to differentiate between passive "couch potato" techniques and active relaxation strategies. Active relaxation can bring on both physical and psychological benefits. By learning how to actively "untense" their muscles, athletes (and coaches, too) can hasten the recovery process by easing muscle tension and soreness. Research on stress management shows that regular use of an active relaxation program has demonstrable health benefits. People who master and make regular use of active relaxation are more flexible and less tense, and therefore better able to cope with future stressors. These techniques also help calm the mind, which enhances relaxation benefits. It is extremely difficult, for example, for someone to be actively engaged in a relaxation program while also thinking about stress-inducing ideas or events. Regular use of active relaxation techniques may allow athletes to engage in more intense training without the negative effects of overtraining, in effect extending that invisible line between good training and overtraining.

Progressive relaxation　Active relaxation techniques include progressive relaxation, in which the individual learns to relax each body part by first tensing it, then letting go of the tenseness. For most people, this "letting go" sensation is instructive from a biofeedback perspective, giving them cues about what true relaxation (or, more accurately, the absence of muscle tenseness) feels like. Athletes who use this technique sequentially tense and relax specific muscle groups, moving from their feet, up the legs (calves, quads), through the core (abdomen, low back), to the arms, shoulders, and face.

Autogenic relaxation or autogenics　Autogenics is another relaxation technique that works through self-suggestion. You repeat to yourself statements about what you want to happen and the relaxation effect you want to feel. You focus on the body parts you want to relax and repeat statements such as "My arms feel heavy and warm," until you begin to experience the desired sensation. Athletes use key phrases or images to facilitate feelings of relaxation and calmness, usually focusing on feelings of heaviness, warmth, or calm within the desired body parts or functions (typically arms, legs, heart rate, breathing).

Guided imagery　Some coaches and athletes use guided imagery to increase the relaxation effect. This technique works by having the athlete create or remember a relaxing scene or memory, deepening the effect by using all of the senses. That is, the athlete imagines the sounds, smells, and kinesthetic features of the scene so as to make it appear as vivid as possible. At the same time, relaxation cues are introduced to remind the athlete to focus on physically relaxing while also imagining the pleasant, calming scene. Once relaxed, the athlete can be directed to imagine a successful competition situation while simultaneously maintaining the desired energy levels.

Biofeedback　Biofeedback teaches athletes how to manage their energy or tension levels more effectively. The term refers to the idea of obtaining feedback from the body's biological systems in order to control them. Athletes can use biofeedback mechanisms such as heart rate or galvanic skin response to learn to control their autonomic nervous systems and thus manage energy or emotions more effectively. Heart rate monitors are a type of biofeedback system. An athlete can watch the monitor to determine his or her heart rate, then use relaxation techniques to see if it can be slowed. The instant feedback of an increase or decrease in heart rate lets the athlete know immediately if what he or she is doing is effective.

The following checklists summarize what athletes and coaches can do to minimize and even avoid overtraining.

Athletes can help themselves by doing the following:

- Developing self-awareness of how training and other life stresses are likely to affect them
- Proactively learning strategies to deal with sport and non-sport stressors
- Recognizing the symptoms of overtraining
- Regularly using training logs and other behavioral monitoring techniques to assess optimal training levels
- Learning and properly using recovery techniques
- Striving for balance between sport, school, work, family, social aspects, and other life elements
- Choosing the right coach, who
  - balances support and challenge in training situations;
  - is a good communicator;
  - encourages recovery, and
  - helps other athletes thrive.

Coaches can help themselves by doing the following:

- Understanding the causes of overtraining, including the fact that it can be brought on by numerous sport as well as non-sport factors
- Taking time to know their athletes, understanding how all kinds of stress may affect them and how vulnerable they are to overtraining
- Creating a supportive and challenging coaching environment that allows athletes to honestly share their thoughts and feelings about their training
- Incorporating regular monitoring of training intensities for each athlete by using logbooks, heart rate assessment, and pencil-and-paper tests
- Adding recovery strategies as a regular part of training, and using good training/recovery principles
- Keeping hard training fun

Future Directions

The overtraining phenomenon is still in a relatively early stage of conceptual development. There is no universally accepted set of symptoms for overtraining, much less agreement on anything resembling a cure. Researchers continue to define the syndrome at a physiological and even biochemical level. We have learned that overtraining encompasses the fields of physiology, nutrition, psychology, and chemistry, and it requires interdisciplinary collaboration for progress to be made. Future research and practice will need more complex models to encompass this interdisciplinary aspect of the problem.

Quicker and more reliable methods of determining if an athlete is overtrained will be developed over the next 10 years, hopefully identifying overtrained athletes earlier in the process. Another area that will see growth is the study of training recovery. The current body of knowledge in this area is rudimentary and anecdotal. Future research directions include determining which recovery techniques correlate most strongly with improved health, training, and competitive outcomes.

If this chapter has a principal message, it is that overtraining is a complex process that requires individualized and proactive planning in order to be avoided. Coaches and athletes who seek to reach their athletic potential often push the line that separates optimized training and overtraining. The good news is that there are ways to help keep athletes on the performance side of that line. Effective training is a necessary first step, and smart coaches and athletes plan carefully, using periodization as well as good communication and recognition of individual differences. At the same time, they need to learn to recognize and treat early symptoms of overtraining. Smart athletes also recognize the importance of recovery; they understand its principles and how best to apply specific techniques. Coaches who learn more about the athletes they coach will do a better job of coaching and of avoiding overtraining. Similarly, athletes who learn to better "read" their psychological, emotional, and physical selves and who incorporate recovery and balance into their lives will increase their chances of competitive success.

Emotional and Mental Control

I go into the locker room and find a corner by myself and just sit there. I try to achieve a peaceful state of nothingness that will carry over onto the golf course. If I get that feeling of quiet and obliviousness within myself, I feel I can't lose.

Jane Blalock, LPGA golfer

I'm sitting in the stands at the figure skating venue of the 1992 Winter Olympic Games in Albertville, France. Around me people are clapping and cheering for their favorite skaters as they take the ice, but I feel as if I am about to throw up. Along with the sport science team of the United States Olympic Committee (USOC), I've been working with the USA figure skating program for four years. In a few moments, the U.S. team members will compete and we'll find out if all that hard work and sacrifice has paid off. I try to remember my own advice to the skaters a few hours ago, and I take some deep breaths and consciously relax my muscles. It only helps a little—I still feel as if I'm in an airless room and there's not enough oxygen for me to breathe. Then the athletes appear and I feel the pressure build even more. I look down and find myself clutching the metal edge of my seat so hard that red marks have appeared on my palm. And then I laugh. My goodness, I'm just here to support the athletes. I don't really have anything to do anymore except cheer. The athletes are out there right now looking at four minutes of competition that will decide their place in Olympic history. How do they feel?

Many similar experiences with Olympic, professional, and collegiate sports have taught me that pressure and anxiety are infectious—the players feel it, the coaches feel it, and the fans feel it. Many athletes have been publicly berated for failing when the pressure was great—"choking," as it is called in sports—but some of the worst mistakes I have seen committed in intense competition have come from coaches who let the pressure get to them. One of the worst mistakes coaches and athletes can make when the pressure rises is to stop playing "their" game and to change their approach and tactics. This usually leads to disaster. But it requires excellent preparation and mental focus to stay with your game plan when you are losing a critical competition. The natural temptation is to try something different, perhaps even something you haven't practiced.

The issues that arise from the pressure of performing at one's best when the stakes are high are the focus of the four chapters in part II. These chapters deal with the mental and emotional skills that athletes and coaches need in order to keep their focus and play naturally, without excessive tension and anxiety. In chapter 5, "Anxiety: From Pumped to Panicked," Gloria Balague brings her extensive experience with world-class athletes to bear on the topic of anxiety. The often-ignored but crucial topic of anger in sports is explained by Mitch Abrams and Bruce Hale in chapter 6. Australian sport psychologist Clark Perry sheds new light on the intriguing process of concentration in chapter 7. And in chapter 8, I continue my 20-year journey into the understanding and practical applications of the mental process we call imagery, one of the most remarkable functions of the human brain.

Anxiety: From Pumped to Panicked

Gloria Balague

Anxiety is present in competitive sports, and the good news is that its presence is not always negative. One of the positive consequences of anxiety is an increase in effort and preparation. Fear of failing an exam is often a good source of motivation to study, and fear of failing to make the traveling squad tends to result in more intense workouts. So anxiety has a function of preparedness and planning, making the person more vigilant about possible negative consequences in the future. According to David H. Barlow, the capacity to experience anxiety and the capacity to plan are two sides of the same coin.

Too much anxiety will likely interfere with preparation efforts and result in changes in muscle tension, inefficient activity, difficulty making decisions, negative focus, and, ultimately, reduced enjoyment and self-confidence. (John's case following seems to fit this scenario.) Too little anxiety will result in reduced intensity and less consistent effort and motivation. As many coaches know, the game against a very easy opponent, or a competition seen as easy, can be easy to lose if the team or the individual athlete is too relaxed about it. The issue can be seen as one of balance: the right amount of anxiety to feel challenged and to prepare adequately but not so much that too much energy is spent in worrying, success is seen as unlikely, and the result is decreased performance.

John

John knew what he wanted: a chance to play pro ball. Since very early on, when he showed promise as a baseball player, he kept sight of his dream. During his four years in college, John had struggled with consistency, usually putting too much pressure on himself. He had very high standards and a sharp, critical eye. He excelled at finding what should have been better and what he needed to do to improve his performance. If things were going well, he dominated; but if he had a couple of mistakes or bad outcomes in a row, his confidence would plummet and it was hard for him to recover. He worked on minimizing his negative self-talk and had a consistent senior year. A smart, hard-working man, he graduated on time with high marks. And he got his chance: John was drafted and joined a minor league team right after the end of his collegiate season. Everything seemed great, but John started worrying constantly about demonstrating that he belonged there, putting lots of pressure on himself. An old injury flared up and he played through it, afraid that he would be seen as unable to handle that level of performance. He started having trouble sleeping and he isolated himself further from his teammates and family, and his negative thinking increased. Even with the injury, he managed to get good numbers and was moved up a level. In the airport going to his next destination he experienced a massive anxiety episode and changed his flight to go home instead, unable to face the mounting pressure.

Framing the question in terms of balance makes the actual issue seem deceptively simple: What is the right amount of anxiety for this particular athlete, in this particular sport, and at this particular moment? These are the questions that sport psychology tries to address. This chapter discusses the meaning of anxiety and distinguishes it from other related terms. Symptoms and consequences of anxiety are also discussed. Individual and situational elements associated with variations in anxiety are also reviewed. Finally, this chapter addresses how to detect and measure anxiety and techniques and interventions available to modify and regulate anxiety.

Competitive Anxiety: A Double-Edged Sword

Anxiety is a topic particularly relevant to sport: The threat of a negative evaluation or negative performance can manifest itself in all aspects of competition from beginning to end. Let's look at some of the ways that anxiety manifests itself in the athlete in two key areas—precompetition and competition.

In an anxious athlete preparing for competition, the biological preparedness function of anxiety causes a number of physical changes that have a direct

Striking a balance between effective mental preparation before performance while not hurting the competitive edge by worrying too much is difficult for many professional athletes.

©Sport The Library

impact on sport performance. These changes include increased muscle tension, heart rate, and respiration rate. Anxiety can also cause narrowed attention and perception and diminished cognitive flexibility. The anxious athlete before competition is likely to worry about what can go wrong or review in his or her mind images of past bad performances against this opponent or in this field. The lack of cognitive flexibility makes it difficult to take a balanced look at the situation, and the anxious athlete often confuses something "possible" with something "likely to happen." The movement pattern of an anxious athlete and his or her timing, reaction time, and decision-making style are also different from the habitual, low-anxiety movement patterns. An athlete who has a smooth, long stride pattern when running relaxed will look choppy and rigid when anxious. A baseball player who has good mechanics when relaxed will tighten, shorten his swing, and have poor timing, going to the ball rather than waiting for it, when anxious.

Coaches often notice these changes but are not always able to intervene. Sometimes because they do not know what to do, they resort to telling athletes, "Relax!" Other times coaches know how to teach athletes to relax, but, appropriately, do not want to try anything new right before a competition. Finally, each coach has his or her own level of anxiety to deal with before a competition, making it harder to deal calmly with someone else's tension.

One of the most common presentation problems for sport psychologists has to do with athletes who train well but do not perform at the same level in competition. The golfer who, in practice rounds, enjoys being on the course and is relaxed and confident changes his or her focus when anxious. Instead, the anxious golfer is likely to play to avoid mistakes, which is a very different approach. The goal of avoiding mistakes forces one to keep those mistakes in the forefront of the mind, and the result is a defensive approach, with increased muscle tension, narrower focus of attention, and, ultimately, less confidence, thus more mistakes. Anxiety is often the common denominator of these inconsistent performances.

The following section defines the main terms used when talking about anxiety and describes the research-based understanding of anxiety and its manifestations.

Labeling Anxious Feelings and Responses

One of the main problems in the study of anxiety is the variety of terms used to label it. Some of the terms represent different phenomena, whereas others imply only a slight distinction. The result is the use of the same words meaning different things—in other words, confusion

Anxiety   Apprehension occurs when one perceives a threat to some value considered essential. The threat may be physical (injury), psychological (shame), or interpersonal (loss of prestige). John clearly saw a major threat resulting from poor performance, and every opportunity to perform became another chance to fail.

Fear   Traditionally, the distinction has been made between anxiety and fear on the basis of the presence or absence of a specific, observable danger. Fear would be the reaction to a specific danger, whereas anxiety is seen as a diffuse apprehension. In many instances the distinction between the two terms becomes blurred, and it is impossible to tell them apart.

Arousal   This refers to the physical level of activation of the person and the intensity of behavior. The confusion stems from the fact that anxiety has physiological manifestations of increased arousal, and sometimes these terms are used interchangeably, describing anxiety by its physiological symptoms. John used many arousal descriptors: He talked about being tight, jumpy, on edge.

Stress   This is the result of the cognitive perception that one does not have the necessary resources to cope with the demands of a specific situation. The definition of anxiety given earlier overlaps with this definition of stress; these two terms are probably the ones most often used as synonyms, not only in the popular vocabulary, but also in research texts. The definition of stress fits John's situation well; He felt that now that he had been drafted he had to produce perfect performances and clearly did not think he had the resources to do so.

In addition to mere definitions, anxiety has physiological manifestations, indicative of the involvement of the autonomic nervous system, as well as cognitive and behavioral manifestations. The physiological symptoms are as follows:

- Palpitations, accelerated heart rate
- Sweating
- Trembling or shaking
- Shortness of breath
- Feeling of choking
- Chest pain or discomfort
- Nausea or abdominal distress
- Feeling dizzy, lightheaded
- Chills or hot flashes
- Paresthesia (numbness or tingling sensations)
- Restlessness, feeling keyed up or on edge
- Feeling easily fatigued
- Increased muscle tension
- Sleep disturbance

The cognitive symptoms of anxiety include the following:

- Uncontrollable worry, apprehensive expectation about activities (such as sport performance and injuries)
- Difficulty concentrating
- Difficulty making decisions

The following are the emotional symptoms of anxiety:

- Irritability
- Negative-affect apprehension
- Emotional outbursts such as crying and anger

The behavioral symptoms of anxiety are as follows:

- Withdrawal, isolation
- Rumination
- Shifting of activity, difficulty staying on a plan or course of action

It is easy to see how anxiety symptoms would be particularly disruptive in sport performance. Looking at the lists helps us understand how the timing of movement changes when an athlete becomes anxious. The movements become less fluid and coordinated compared to the movements seen in practice or in relaxed conditions. A look at the symptoms also helps us see the effects of poor decision making during a competition. Anxious athletes have great difficulty with decision making and will likely resort to impulsive decisions just to "get it over" or will ponder too long, searching for the perfect decision. By the time they make a move, it is too late.

The Basis of Anxiety

Numerous theories have suggested that anxiety has a strong neurobiological basis. There is evidence that the brains of anxious people show different levels of activity. They have high resting levels of cortical arousal and high reactivity from the autonomic nervous system.

Current trends in the research on temperament have shown many connections between temperament in children (a highly heritable component) and the development of anxiety disorders. Biology can account for only a part of the puzzle, and it is clear that biology must interface with a certain environment to result in anxiety behaviors. Some of the examples used traditionally to describe an anxiety-generating environment are households with very high levels of achievement, where achievement is highly valued; critical parenting styles with an emphasis on what was missing or what should have been better; and climates that offer "conditional approval," that is, acceptance as long as performance or outcomes are good. Often parents are not aware or do not intend to convey that message, but the child perceives it as such and therefore responds to it with anxiety. One wonders if John's parents would have described him as a worrier from a young age or more high strung than other children.

While environment and biology do play a role, most of the intervention models for anxiety focus on the role of cognition. One of the most widely accepted theories is Charles Spielberger's State-Trait Model. Spielberger sees anxiety as a personal characteristic (a trait, not unlike the traits of sociability or introversion) that makes some people more likely to perceive more situations as threatening and see dangers looming ahead. He makes the distinction between that trait and the state of anxiety resulting when anyone perceives a specific situation as threatening. Some people get anxious before a test, when they have to speak in public, or before a competition. These would be considered state anxiety. Trait anxiety means that someone is more vulnerable to anxiety and therefore likely to consider many situations as anxiety provoking. John's cognitive style was consistent with that of trait anxiety: He was a perfectionist, looking always at what he should have done better. He tended to discount positive feedback and focus on the negative, and he saw many situations as threatening.

When an athlete gets anxious, his or her focus of attention changes and so does his or her intellectual functioning. This means differences in *what* information is processed and *how* it is processed. Let's review some of the ways in which anxiety interferes with attention, memory, and other information-processing skills and how that affects performance.

Of particular relevance to sport is the connection between cognitive anxiety (worry) and attention. A threat results in a narrowing of attention (to maximize efficiency in a dangerous situation). In sport, the threat of failure or the threat of pain, the most common, focus the attention internally. The result is a narrow, internal focus of attention, where the player contemplates how badly he or she is doing or feeling. This in turn increases self-monitoring and the awareness of physiological sensations. The increase in proprioceptive information is likely to result in increased emotional intensity. Because the main emotion here is anxiety, the narrowing of attention has the effect of making the person feel even more anxious.

Another theory links the presence of attentional bias and hypervigilance in anxious athletes toward threatening cues. At the same time, memory for threatening thoughts or events is more readily available and easily accessible. For example, an athlete who got injured making a specific move is more likely to remember the one time when he got injured doing it than the numerous times when he did it and was safe.

Finally, there is evidence that anxious patients interpret ambiguous material as threatening. The anxious athlete who faces a new situation is likely to think of it in terms of possible danger or threat. The negative thoughts act as a filter, scanning the environment for evidence of what can go wrong, making the athlete perceive only the negative or possibly negative elements of his or her environment. Perhaps the situation that best illustrates this scenario is that of a player coming back from an injury. A player who is anxious about reinjury is likely to pay extraordinary attention to her internal cues, but only the negative ones, looking for any sign of malfunction. She may remember vividly the situations that lead to her injury and is likely to construe any ambiguous sensation as a threatening one. A full return to performance is not possible until she manages her anxiety, even if physical functioning is fully restored.

From an intellectual standpoint, one of the main activities of anxious subjects is *worry*, which is the continuous consideration of possible negative events and adverse consequences. The fact that worry may be seen as having a protective function provides a false sense of control and may help explain its self-reinforcing nature. Unfortunately, worrying hardly ever results in finding solutions or active problem solving, making it a very ineffective coping mechanism. John was a first-class worrier; as soon as a game was over, he would start worrying about the next one. He interpreted the past in an idiosyncratic way: If his performance was good, he evaluated it as bad because it had not felt good. He reconstructed the situation not as having played well but as having narrowly escaped catastrophe, which meant his predictions for the future were negative as well.

The Strong Relationship Between Anxiety and Performance

We know that the anxious athlete worries more and focuses his or her attention on negative elements. What is the actual effect of anxiety on performance? Can we predict when worrying is helpful and when it is too much? Are there some types of worries that are worse than others at performance time? Stephen J. Bull and colleagues, in their book *The Mental Game Plan*, describe the three main types of worries experienced by anxious athletes in precompetition: worries about the task ("This is a very difficult course" or "These guys look huge"), about their own ability or readiness ("I do not have my best stuff today" or "I feel slow" or "My ankle hurts"), and about consequences ("If I miss this shot, we won't have a chance at conference" or "If I fall, my parents will be furious"). The thoughts are often combined with images; for example, the thought "These guys look huge" may be accompanied by an image of oneself as weak and small. The thoughts are multilayered, and addressing the underlying feeling is important. For example, the thought "If I miss the shot, we won't have a chance at conference" may have the following unspoken fear attached: ". . . and my teammates will blame me, and it will all be my fault."

Later on we address how to intervene with these thoughts, but for now let's examine the relationship between anxiety and performance. Since different theories have come up with different explanations for their relationship, we will review the main ones.

The Inverted U

One of the first theories addressing the relationship between arousal and performance was the inverted-U hypothesis (see figure 5.1). The theory states that optimal performance occurs at an intermediate level of arousal and that both very low and very high levels of arousal will result in impaired performance. Sport psychology embraced the theory, and the terms "arousal," "anxiety," and "stress" became interchangeable in many of the theory's descriptions. The explanations offered by the theory had a commonsense appeal: An athlete (or a team) who is not aroused sufficiently is unlikely to exert great effort or persevere. The typical example is that of the athlete or team who faces a less-skilled opponent. If the competition is labeled as easy and the resulting arousal is too low, this athlete or team risks losing the contest because the performance is expected to be subpar under these conditions. At the other end of the continuum we have the competitor who faces a must-win situation that results in a very high level of arousal. Decision making is impaired, and the rhythm and mechanics of his movement are disturbed, partially because of excess muscle tension. Arousal activates both flexor and extensor muscles so that it literally results in the athlete "putting the brakes on himself" while he is trying to go as fast as possible. Most people agree that the inverted-U theory is familiar to everyone in sport.

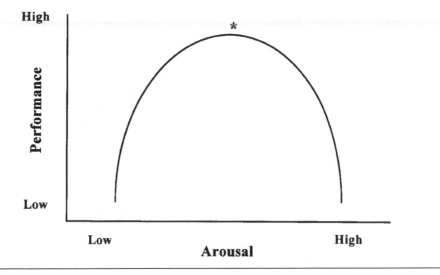

Figure 5.1 Inverted U.

Reprinted, by permission, from D. Kirk, M. Kiss, L. Lahey, D. Penney, and R. Burgess-Limerick, 1999, *Senior physical education: An integrated approach,* 2nd ed. (Champaign, IL: Human Kinetics), 30.

However, a theory should allow us to predict outcomes, and this one allows for explanations only after the fact: If someone does not perform well, we will assume that their level of arousal was not adequate. How do we know the level of arousal was not adequate? Because the athlete did not perform well—a circular argument that explains itself. Another problem is that the theory does not explain *how* arousal affects performance. Arousal, understood as physiological activation, can be interpreted by one athlete as anxiety and by another as readiness or energy. The theory does not take into account the fact that different cognitive interpretations of arousal affect the performance. Finally, the symmetrical curve of the U used to describe the relationship would seem to predict a gradual deterioration of performance with increased arousal, but in most performers' experience, that extra level of arousal tends to result in dramatic and rapid decreases in performance.

Individual Zones of Optimal Functioning

Another model is the one proposed by a Russian scientist now settled in Finland, Yuri Hanin. He developed an idiographic model that proposes that an athlete's individual optimal zone of functioning (or optimal activation level) can be identified, and as long as the athlete remains within that optimal level, his or her performance can be expected to be optimal.

Individual Zones of Optimal Functioning (IZOF) allow for a description of a variety of emotional states classified as helpful or unhelpful. The old distinction between positive and negative emotions was replaced by the profile of helpful or unhelpful emotions. Some athletes, for example, would indicate that feeling happy was not conducive to performing well, while others would state that feeling moderately angry helped them reach the optimal state.

Balague

Research that utilizes IZOF supports its applicability in analyzing athletic performance. The main criticism of IZOF is that it is not a theory but a descriptive model; thus it does not explain why some people function better when in certain emotional states and others do not. However, IZOF may be a helpful tool because of the impact it has on the athlete's self-awareness and because it gives coaches important information about the emotional readiness of an athlete. To develop an IZOF profile (see figure 5.2 for two sample profiles), an athlete must learn to identify which emotions were present and with what intensity before and during successful and unsuccessful performances. Then the athlete must learn to replicate the desired emotional profile. The coach who works with IZOF profiles can

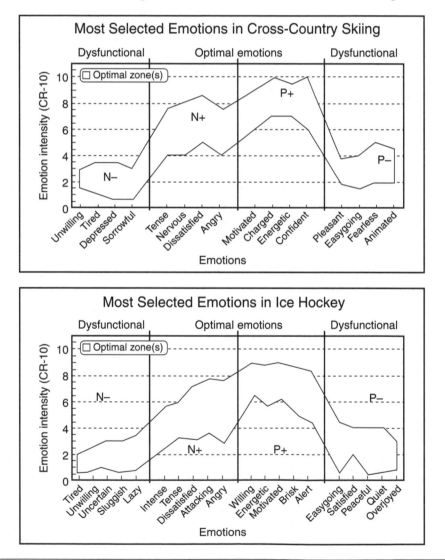

Figure 5.2 IZOF profiles.

Reprinted, by permission, from Yuri L. Hanin, 2000, Successful and poor performance and emotions. In *Emotions in sport,* edited by Yuri L. Hanin (Champaign, IL: Human Kinetics), 185.

82

detect problems with emotional readiness before a competition and take preventive action. Some coaches have an intuitive understanding of what their athletes need and are able to intervene by joking with one athlete in order to get him or her in a good mood before an event, while chastising another one so that he or she gets angry before the same event. IZOF offers a more systematic alternative to the trial-and-error approach. What IZOF does not do is advance our knowledge of how emotions facilitate or interfere with performance in different individuals.

Reversal Theory

Reversal theory, developed by Michael Apter, proposes that the level of arousal is filtered by the perception one has of it: A low level of arousal, for the same person, can at one time be perceived as pleasant when the person says he or she is relaxed; at another time it can be perceived as unpleasant when the person then says that he or she is bored. At the high end of the arousal spectrum we can perceive the same level of physiological activation as anxiety (unpleasant) or as excitement (pleasant). The theory also states that individuals can alternate between these states at any moment. These changes are called "reversals."

The application of the reversal theory in the field of sport has focused on the four states mentioned: relaxed, bored, excited, and anxious. John Kerr states that one of the main elements that explains the switch, or reversal, from one state to another is the presence or absence of evaluation, which pushes for a negative interpretation when the outcome is not the desired one. Sport offers many examples of the effect that evaluation has on the emotional climate experienced by some athletes. A typical case is the "practice athlete," who enjoys training but gets very anxious, does not enjoy competition, and cannot repeat his practice performances. Another typical case is the recreational athlete, who only wants to hit balls and avoids keeping score. Even within a single competition, we can find examples of quick reversals: An athlete feels anxious, evaluates her performance negatively, and feels exhausted and drained, and then suddenly may reverse to a state of excitement and euphoria if she comes across a competitor who is doing worse than she is. The only thing that changes is the evaluation, and with it the interpretation of the sensations.

With the exception of the work by Kerr, research on applying reversal theory to sport is limited and its results are unclear. The theory does not offer a good rationale for predicting what prompts the reversals in a situation like competitive sport, in which evaluation is always present, nor is it clear why a positive feeling should lead to better performances. But it opens the door to a number of interventions from cognitive therapy aimed at changing the interpretation of symptoms. If we could teach athletes to interpret butterflies in the stomach as a sign of readiness rather than fear, we would greatly reduce the number of fearful, anxious competitors, but would the changes be stable enough to last an entire competition? According to reversal theory, probably not.

All of the models reviewed to this point looked at anxiety as a unidimensional emotion. Multidimensional models consider a number of components in anxiety.

The first distinction is made between *somatic* anxiety (that is, the anxiety that is experienced as physical symptoms of nervousness and tension) and *cognitive* anxiety (defined as worry, preoccupation, and negative expectations). This distinction is relevant because one of the suggestions made by the proponents of this approach is that of "matching" the intervention to the predominant type of anxiety reported by the athlete. So for someone who experiences mainly physiological symptoms, relaxation training would probably be the best intervention, while it may be ineffective with someone who experiences cognitive symptoms of anxiety. In fact, people high on cognitive anxiety tend to have a hard time relaxing precisely because their negative thinking patterns interfere too much.

Traditionally, research has measured only the *intensity* of the anxiety (that is, how much of it the athlete experiences), but other dimensions are emerging as important. *Frequency*, defined as the number of anxiety thoughts in a given time, is one of the important dimensions. There is some evidence that the frequency of the worries increases in the week before a competition, but the intensity of the anxiety remains stable. That is, the athletes' degree of worry does not change, but they think about it much more often.

Another, more-controversial dimension of anxiety is *direction*, which refers to how athletes label the symptoms on a debilitative–facilitative axis. Some people argue that anxiety cannot be perceived as facilitative, but some athletes appear to equate moderate anxiety with readiness and might feel less ready to perform if they do not experience anticipatory tension. Some performers describe anticipatory anxiety in terms of an adrenaline rush. Perhaps the direction dimension is more relevant to experienced competitors, who know that feeling nervous is part of the process of gearing up for an important event. Inexperienced competitors may attribute feelings of anxiety to their lack of experience, which makes these feelings more debilitating.

Recent studies demonstrate that the direction of both cognitive and somatic anxiety is a better predictor of basketball performance than their intensity. This means that it is no longer enough to compile a list of anxiety symptoms and ask athletes how many of them they experience if we want to understand their emotional readiness before competition. We must include in our assessment the athlete's labeling of the symptoms. Research in this model is still very scarce, but it raises important questions and merits further study.

Catastrophe Theory

The last multidimensional theory of anxiety and performance we cover is the application of catastrophe models to sport performance. This theory states that as arousal increases beyond an optimal level, performance drops rapidly and dramatically to lower levels. This fits with the experience of many coaches and athletes who have seen performers go from competing evenly against the opponent to suddenly being overtaken and losing the match in a matter of seconds. According to Lew Hardy, one of the main proponents of the theory, the catastrophe model has three variables: physiological arousal, cognitive anxiety, and performance. The model predicts that when cognitive anxiety is low, the relationship between physiological arousal and performance follows the inverted-U curve (that is, performance will be better under moderate arousal conditions). When cognitive anxiety is high, performance improves as physiological arousal increases until a point, after which there is a catastrophic drop in performance. When physiological arousal is high, higher cognitive anxiety results in lower performance. When physiological arousal is low, higher cognitive anxiety results in improved performance. The model originally did not allow for subjective interpretation of anxiety symptoms, but recently Hardy has included other moderating variables, such as self-confidence and task difficulty. The catastrophe theory model is very difficult to test and translate into practical applications. From a research standpoint, it is a great challenge that should be met. The relationship of anxiety, emotions, and performance is complex; it makes sense that no simple model will accurately explain it.

Measuring Anxiety

As we have learned, numerous views of anxiety are prevalent, and they often involve different measurements and instruments. Do we need tests to measure anxiety? Is this something we could simply observe? Research conducted by Dan Gould on coaches indicates that they are not good at reading the emotional states of their players, but they are confident that they are accurate in their perceptions. In defense of coaches, athletes have many reasons to hide anxiety from their coaches. They may fear it will affect their chances of playing or starting. Having some easy way to measure anxiety seems helpful.

Self-report questionnaires are the primary form of anxiety assessment. Some count the number of symptoms experienced, while others ask about the intensity of the experience. Almost all instruments have some questions about physical symptoms, thoughts, and emotions.

In sport, the questionnaire most often used for research purposes is the Competitive State Anxiety Inventory-2 (CSAI-2) developed by Rainer Martens, a pioneer in using sport-specific instruments. The inventory measures somatic anxiety, cognitive anxiety, and what the author considers the opposite pole of anxiety, self-confidence (see figure 5.3).

Numerous concerns have been raised about the validity of this and other questionnaires. First, the questions can be interpreted in more than one way. For example, the item "I am concerned about this competition" can be understood as "I am worried about doing poorly in my event" or as "I am aware that my event is important and I want to be ready." Second, some items may have different relevance to different sports: "My hands are clammy" may not be worrisome to a swimmer but can interfere with a tennis player's performance. Finally, the issue of when to administer a questionnaire is also unresolved: Does the score obtained two hours before the competition predict what will happen once the

Illinois Self-Evaluation Questionnaire

Name _____ Sex M F   Date _____

Directions: A number of statements that athletes have used to describe their feelings before competition are given below. Read each statement and then circle the appropriate nember to the right of the statement to indicate *how you feel right now*—at this moment. There are no right or wrong answers. Do *not* spend too much time on any one statement, but choose the answer which describes your feelings *right now*.

	Not at all	Somewhat	Moderately so	Very much so
1. I am concerned about this competition	1	2	3	4
2. I feel nervous	1	2	3	4
3. I feel at ease	1	2	3	4
4. I have self-doubts	1	2	3	4
5. I feel jittery	1	2	3	4
6. I feel comfortable	1	2	3	4
7. I am concerned that I may not do as well in this competition as I could	1	2	3	4
8. My body feels tense	1	2	3	4
9. I feel self-confident	1	2	3	4
10. I am concerned about losing	1	2	3	4
11. I feel tense in my stomach	1	2	3	4
12. I feel secure	1	2	3	4
13. I am concerned about choking under pressure	1	2	3	4
14. My body feels relaxed	1	2	3	4
15. I'm confident I can meet the challenge	1	2	3	4
16. I'm concerned about performing well	1	2	3	4
17. My heart is racing	1	2	3	4
18. I'm confident about performing	1	2	3	4
19. I'm concerned about reaching my goal	1	2	3	4
20. I feel my stomach sinking	1	2	3	4
21. I feel mentally relaxed	1	2	3	4
22. I'm concerned that others will be disappointed with my performance	1	2	3	4
23. My hands are clammy	1	2	3	4
24. I'm confident because I mentally picture myself reaching my goal	1	2	3	4
25. I'm concerned I won't be able to concentrate	1	2	3	4
26. My body feels tight	1	2	3	4
27. I'm confident of coming through under pressure	1	2	3	4

Figure 5.3 CSAI-2.

Reprinted, by permission, from R. Martens, R. Vealey, & D. Burton, 1990, *Competitive anxiety in sport,* (Champaign, IL: Human Kinetics), 177.

competition starts? Will answering the questionnaire before a competition make these thoughts more salient and thus make the athlete more likely to get anxious? Even researching these questions has become difficult because many coaches and athletes do not want to risk increasing the probability that someone will become anxious after being made to think about anxiety by answering the questionnaire.

Other authors report good success using the Profile of Mood States, which is a non-sport-specific questionnaire that assesses several mood states: tension, depression, anger, vigor, mental confusion, and fatigue. (See chapter 4 for more details.)

Pencil-and-paper questionnaires are used to measure cognitive anxiety and the perception of somatic anxiety, which some authors argue is unlikely to coincide with actual somatic anxiety. Proponents of better physiological measures argue for actual measurements, not merely awareness of the sensations by the performer. The advances in telemetry now allow for measurements of heart rate, respiratory rate, and other physiological functions that can be done in the field. Some athletes and teams have also purchased equipment to teach relaxation to their athletes by monitoring brain waves. Measuring heart rate or breathing rate during sports is likely to give mixed results, because those rates will increase because of the physical effort. There is also the issue of specificity of response; that is, different people respond to anxiety with changes in different systems. Some respond with increases in heart rate, others with changes in muscle tension, and others with digestive-tract distress. Unless the response style of each athlete has already been identified, a biofeedback system may not be equally helpful for all athletes.

Summarizing, we have different views of what anxiety is and how it interferes with athletic performance. The issue of measuring anxiety in a way that is helpful for athletes and coaches has not been fully resolved from a research standpoint, but it is possible to develop a descriptive model of the best emotional performing state for any given athlete. Increasing the awareness of both athlete and coach about the elements present during a good performance and a bad one is important. Encouraging the athlete to examine physical symptoms, thoughts, and focus of attention after both good and bad performances is probably the best measure in the long run. What follows are the questions of how we can help an athlete replicate this ideal state and how we can reduce or modify anxiety.

Making Competitive Anxiety Work for You

Anxiety is an anticipatory emotion, a future-oriented response to a perceived but vague threat that makes us feel powerless because we cannot protect ourselves from an uncertain and unpredictable event. The action tendencies of anxiety are escape and avoidance, which explains why anxious athletes often think, "I just want it to be over," or find the ultimate escape—injury.

The primary goals of interventions are to eliminate disproportionate fears and any maladaptive behaviors to avoid or prevent anxiety. The interventions can occur at a variety of points and should match the main symptoms. The athlete's distorted thoughts and images regarding the feared situation can be challenged through cognitive restructuring—that is, learning to identify emotional reasoning, meaning thinking about what we fear may happen, and substituting it with evidence-based reasoning. An athlete who starts worrying about failure can be reminded of all the times she has performed the skill correctly, the good practices and hard training that underlie her performance. Physical symptoms of anxiety can be countered with relaxation skills, and avoidance and escape can be addressed by increasing self-efficacy and challenging negative and unrealistic self-evaluation.

Perhaps the most important element in the treatment of anxiety is the knowledge of one's ideal state of arousal before and during athletic performances. When we make that determination, we set up the model we intend to replicate. This self-awareness is the actual goal of any intervention. Some athletes have no trouble describing their sensations, whereas others need help, such as labeling on a scale of 1 to 10 the level of tension they feel in different parts of the body. Ideally, this is a skill that is trained in practice so that athletes can learn to replicate their desired levels of tension and relaxation.

The second part of self-awareness is the capacity to discern where in the body the athlete feels the first signs of anxiety. Some notice it as stomach tightening, and others catch themselves clenching their jaws. Some get sleepy, and others have to go to the bathroom frequently. The sooner the intervention can be implemented, the easier it is. Once anxiety reaches a very high level, it is harder to regain balance. That is why most of the applied sport psychology texts suggest some form of a precompetition arousal check. Athletes should be able to determine whether they feel the correct level of tension or higher or lower. Ideally, this should be done when there is enough time to intervene, but not so far ahead of time that the level is likely to change by the time competition starts.

Because anxiety also has a major cognitive component, monitoring and self-awareness should include the athlete's thoughts or focus of attention. In long events or competitions, the optimal focus or thoughts are likely to change. Of special importance for cognitive changes are the pauses in between competition, such as set changes in tennis, in between innings in baseball, or in between jumps in track and field.

Develop a relaxation ritual   Relaxation training is the main modality of somatic intervention. All of the many types of relaxation are equally good, so find one the athlete will use. Relaxation is a skill that improves with training; but as with physical training, once the athlete no longer practices relaxation training, his or her ability level decreases rapidly. Relaxation must be learned in a quiet setting and practiced regularly before the athlete can be expected to apply it successfully in a stressful environment. Relaxation training is also a preventive

©Icon SMI

Understanding, identifying, and learning to regulate anxiety before competition are beneficial skills that athletes and coaches should add to their practice and training regimens.

intervention: The idea is to teach the athlete to take several mini-relaxation breaks during the day to avoid a big increase in muscle tension. One of the most effective methods is slow, deep breathing. Since most anxious people tend to breathe in a shallow manner because of tightness in chest muscles, teaching deep breathing provides noticeable, instant relief. If it is the only technique used, it is unlikely to last long enough. However, it is helpful for specific moments, such as before a putt in golf or before a free throw in basketball. Coaches should emphasize the notion of training the psychological skills: Like any skill, psychological skills do not improve after only one practice, nor should they be used in competition without sufficient practice time.

Progressive muscle relaxation (PMR) is a deep, total-body relaxation method that is effective in reducing physical anxiety and insomnia in the days before a competition. Of the many versions of PMR, one of the most effective is first tensing a muscle group and then relaxing it. The contrast between increased tension and relaxation improves awareness and facilitates learning. Deep relaxation is often accomplished with PMR, so it should not be used immediately before a competition. Other versions use peaceful, relaxing images to induce the same state.

Experts indicate that most people end up using their own particular combination of techniques to relax. Traditional methods used for clinical populations tend to be too time consuming for athletes, who are usually more in tune with their bodies than the general population. Lengthy methods are likely to bore them, which would result in lack of compliance. Some athletes may have trouble focusing and may need the help of a tape-recorded relaxation session to stay on task, while others do better with imagery-based relaxation rather than words. Finally, a sophisticated version of relaxation is offered by biofeedback (see chapter 4), which typically gives concrete information about the method's effect on heart rate, finger temperature, or breathing rate. Some athletes and coaches need physiological evidence of the effect of relaxation.

Another coping technique is *outward focus*, which consists of helping the athlete shift from excessive internal focus to specific events or items outside. Anxious athletes find it difficult to stop worrying, but they can learn to focus on something else for a while. Focusing on some aspect of the task tends to be most helpful. *Precompetition routines*, used and recommended by many athletes and coaches, accomplish this function.

Create a precompetition game plan   Even if an athlete's symptoms of anxiety are mainly somatic, the underlying cause tends to be the way in which he or she perceives the situation. The specific worries listed earlier, about the task, one's ability, or the consequences, need to be identified. The next step is to substitute the worries with helpful thoughts. The athlete's self-dialogue is a crucial element in the management of anxiety. If one starts thinking about everything that *can* go wrong, the list is huge because everything can, possibly, go wrong. The question to address is what is *likely* to happen (based on past evidence and knowledge). If an athlete had a bad performance at a certain meet, the next time she competes there she should keep in mind that this is a different time; she has the experience of the previous one, so she can avoid some of the problems. The process of switching the self-dialogue from defeating to helpful must be worked at in practice during the season so it can be used during the competitive season. In many instances, the athlete needs a "neutral" thought before he or she can transition from a negative one to a positive or helpful one. Switching to an external focus and using mindful breathing are some of the ways to make that transition smoother.

Practice competitive routines   Competitive routines, fine-tuned in minor competitions or competitive situations, offer the combination of brief elements or steps inducing physical and psychological readiness. These elements enable the athlete to avoid having to make more decisions at the time of competition, such as "What should I focus on?"

Again, let's get back to John's situation: He was so stressed out when he later sought help that he had a hard time focusing. We introduced deep relaxation training as a way to help decrease his physiological symptoms and improve his sleep. Relaxation training gave him some relief and also increased his self-confidence about coping with being nervous. The images and thoughts he had while thinking about playing were that he would be unable to control the ball and it would fly into the stands or the field. He was also very aware of people watching and imagined them commenting negatively on him and his abilities. He could not even play catch with his friends. He started a program of systematic desensitization, in which he would visualize some of the scenarios that caused him anxiety and then practice his relaxation until he could keep the images in his mind and remain relaxed. After he could do that a couple of times, he moved on to another image that was higher on the anxiety scale, and he would again practice relaxation while imagining it. He resumed his physical training and was asked to keep track of his improvements and to notice the number of negative comments he made to himself. To the next session, he brought a list of the negative comments he had made to himself, and we analyzed their accuracy, examining the evidence for or against them. Eventually we generated accurate, more helpful alternatives. He was then ready to start trying these skills in real life. We made a progression from playing catch with a friend to eventually training in front of other players and coaches. One of the things he also found helpful was to have meaningful routines that kept his attention focused on the task. He decided he needed to "fire" the coach he had in his head and replace him with a more helpful advisor. This scenario engaged his sense of humor and gave him a strong sense of control. After 10 weeks, he was ready to go back to playing.

Future Directions

Education of coaches and parents regarding skill development must be a focus of future interventions. Consistently critical feedback does not make all players stronger. Encouraging parents and coaches to be more accepting of mistakes as part of the progression of learning would help reduce the amount of pressure some athletes put on themselves. Sport psychologists have found that coaching style does not cause anxiety, but in vulnerable individuals it can facilitate it.

The technical advances of virtual reality also offer an intriguing scenario for the future, where athletes could be put into feared situations via virtual reality, and anxiety management, coping, and self-efficacy interventions could be implemented almost as in real life. Finally, psychological skills training will probably eventually be recognized as an essential element of training for all athletes, much as strength and conditioning training are now.

Anger: How to Moderate Hot Buttons

Mitch Abrams and Bruce Hale

In the 1993 NHL playoffs, Dale Hunter of the Washington Capitals blindsided an unsuspecting Pierre Turgeon seconds after Turgeon had scored what would turn out to be a game-winning goal for the Islanders, eliminating the Capitals from the Stanley Cup hunt. For Turgeon, the hit resulted in a third-degree shoulder separation and a concussion that would keep him out of play for two weeks; for Hunter, the result was a 21-game suspension, the longest in NHL history at the time.

On May 19, 1998, after giving up what would turn out to be the game-winning three-run home run to Bernie Williams, Armando Benitez drilled Tino Martinez right between the shoulder blades, leading to a bench-clearing brawl. And on August 24, 2003, football player Bill Romanowski seriously injured teammate and tight end Marcus Williams, breaking the orbital bone that protects his eye and possibly ending his career in a fight on a practice field. Williams claimed that Romanowski hit him while he was completely unprepared, having just finished a practice drill.

Angry outbursts on and off the courts and fields are regular occurrences in Western sports competition. Almost every day, the newspapers report another fight, assault, or shooting in which an athlete was involved. The intense "win-at-all-costs" philosophy that has pervaded sport at all levels gives permission to coaches and athletes to vent their anger on opponents, officials, fans, friends, and family. At the individual level, an angry, out-of-control athlete or coach cannot perform at their best during competition. After competition, the venting of uncontrolled angry impulses can lead to serious problems such as assaults, domestic violence, and even homicide.

To date, little in-depth research has measured and interpreted these reports of athlete violence, and until recently nothing has been done to organize systematic interventions and anger-management programs to help coaches and athletes deal with these problems. This chapter begins a long-needed effort to understand the emotion of anger in sport, identifying common problems associated with uncontrolled outbursts and ways to assess angry moods, and offering practical guidelines for the development of intervention and prevention programs for athletes and coaches.

Understanding the Aggressive Mind-Set

Anger and aggression have been primary areas of study for psychologists for more than a century, leading to the development of the famous frustration-aggression hypothesis in 1939. Simply put, this theory states that people are more likely to become aggressive and frustrated if they are unable to reach their goals. Because of the nature of competition, frustration is a fact of life that both athletes and coaches must face nearly constantly. Further research helped to define other factors that led to aggressive behavior; not surprisingly, one of them was being in a bad mood. Another theory, the completion hypothesis, suggests that whenever someone is in a negative mood state (which could be tired, irritable, sick, anxious, and so on), they are more likely to become aggressive.

Anger is not a necessary prerequisite for aggression; it can stem from different situations and emotions. But of all the emotions, anger is the most common precursor to aggression. It makes sense that if you're in a bad mood, you're more likely to get in a fight. Is it because you are always in a bad mood? For some people, the answer is yes, because they have a mind-set that makes them more likely to be put in a bad mood.

One such mind-set, called a "hostility bias," occurs when the way someone thinks leads him or her to perceive neutral stimuli as provocative. Let's say an athlete walks down the hall in high school and someone accidentally bumps into him. The athlete immediately believes it was deliberate and that he must respond to this provocation, so he yells at the other person or perhaps shoves him. This is an example of how an accident can quickly escalate to an altercation. Further, those with such a mind-set often believe that it is acceptable to use violence as a method to "solve the problem."

Why do some people develop a hostility bias? One major reason is the environment they are exposed to when their personality is being formed. People learn how to act by observing and practicing behaviors that they see their role models do. The social-learning theory explains that we acquire new behaviors by observing, copying, and perfecting skills that we see someone else enact. It is therefore not surprising that children often act in ways similar to their parents. Charles Barkley, ex-NBA great, was right when he said that professional athletes shouldn't replace parents as role models; however, he ignored the fact that they are indeed seen that way by youngsters. Coaches often spend more time with the young athletes than does anyone else apart from their parents. If they see that their coach handles anger by losing control and throwing chairs across a gymnasium, they will be more likely to imitate this behavior and act in similar ways when they become angry.

Outbursts of anger are often justified as a catharsis, or venting. The idea behind catharsis is that when you are overwhelmed or bubbling over with anger, you can release those emotions with a controlled violent act and feel better as a result. It is true; you do feel better when you punch a pillow when you are angry. The problem is that because you felt better after you

© Empics

Expressing anger can result in costly performance and personal consequences. Learning to self-manage feelings of anger is the key to controlling anger on the field and off.

punched something, you are more likely to use this strategy again. And what if you don't have a pillow available? What do you punch when the referee just made a bad call and is preparing to call the technical foul? Venting does take the edge off and make you feel better at the moment, but at what price? The price is the consequences you face when you use that strategy in an environment with no safe place in which to vent. Research shows that aggressive behavior does not reduce the likelihood of subsequent aggressive behavior; in fact, it sometimes increases its frequency and intensity. Expressing anger physically, even in a controlled way, is not a good self-management strategy to use or to teach athletes.

Terms Used in Describing Violence in Sport

When people discuss anger and aggression in sport they often seem to be speaking different languages. For the purpose of clarity, let's offer the following definitions.

First, anger is an emotion. It is a normal emotion that requires no judgment be made of it. It is neither good nor bad to be angry; it is as normal as being happy. Anger, in itself, is not observable to others. If you were furious at this moment, people would only be aware of it if you behaved in a way that displayed your emotions, such as gritting your teeth or yelling. The emotion itself, however, is the feeling that you have. Many other emotions, like hate, fear, frustration, and disappointment, can lead to anger. Your body responds to anger in much the same way as it responds to anxiety; the major difference between the two is in their associated thoughts. Anger may be associated with thoughts of confrontation, while anxiety-related thoughts often involve avoidance.

One of the premier researchers in the anger literature, Charles Spielberger, differentiates between "anger-in" and "anger-out." In anger-in, athletes either direct their anger at themselves or attempt to suppress it. Examples of this inward-directed anger include common acts such as kicking the dirt and cursing out loud after a mistake in a game. The athlete's performance may suffer since he or she is no longer concentrating on the competitive task at hand.

Anger-out is typically a physical or verbal affront to other people or convenient objects. These attacks are not always directed toward the provoker and may have serious game-ending or legal consequences. This aggressive behavior also often interferes with performance.

A classic example of extreme anger-out occurred in 1977 when Kermit Washington nearly killed Rudy Tomjanovich during an NBA game. He became angry after being consistently mauled and fouled during the game and finally retaliated at the first opponent he saw. In what later became known as "The Punch," Washington's right hand shattered several of the bones in Tomjanovich's face.

Aggression is the use of force to reach a goal. A typical example in basketball is swinging your elbows after a rebound to try to keep defenders from stealing the ball. This type of aggression may be a natural part of sport and the rules of the game usually allow it.

On the other hand, violence can occur in two forms in sport. *Incidental violence* involves physical contact and can be a normal part of contact sports, like a hard check or a heavy tackle. *Hostile violence*, which usually involves the intent to harm an opponent, can be either planned or spontaneous and has no place in sport. Spontaneous hostile violence is almost always associated with anger. While coaches may applaud a retaliatory check in hockey, it usually means the athlete is out of control and acting irrationally. Planned hostile violence evokes deeper concerns because it assumes that someone—management, coaches, or athletes—supports its use to achieve goals. As the violent behavior of hockey "goons" illustrates, it is almost always premeditated violence that's reinforced in the sport. Courts have recently been asked to consider such behavior criminal, with two of the more notable cases from the NHL including Marty McSorley striking Donald Brashear in the head from behind with his stick and Todd Bertuzzi punching Steve Moore, leaving him with a broken neck.

In sport, aggression without violence may be tolerated or even encouraged if it achieves competitive goals. But hostile violence is never acceptable, and athletes and coaches should try to minimize its occurrence. Using aggression appropriately while reducing hostile violence can optimize success in sport. Inability to do so is a sign of poor self-discipline.

When describing self-discipline, Bill Parcells, Dallas Cowboys coach and former Super Bowl champion with the Giants, exalts the ability to keep your poise when those around you are losing theirs:

> A lot of kids nowadays have grown up macho. They can't take a dirty look; they can't take a harsh word; and they definitely can't take a slap on the back of the head from some cheap-shot artist on the other team. But mature players will absorb these excesses in stride, even when they're out-and-out flagrant. I tell my players to put their emotions on hold, to stone-face their opponents. . . If you lose your cool, no matter what the provocation, you're giving the other side of the table a diagram on how to push your buttons.

Some sport psychologists have used the term "assertiveness" to refer to actions that reflect appropriate levels of performance intensity without any intention to harm. Assertive athletes, they say, are intense, confident, never give up, and constantly challenge themselves to reach optimal performance. The problem is that this definition deviates from what assertiveness truly is. To assert oneself is to insist on one's rights. In sport, you do not have the right to win; you must compete to win. It is a misuse of the word to explain that a tailback *assertively* found his way through three defensive players to score a touchdown. He did so aggressively. Therefore, assertiveness really is not the appropriate term for these types of action.

The Myth of the "Violent Athlete"

The regular reader of the sports section in newspapers may be forgiven for believing that athletes (specifically, male athletes) are more violent than non-athletes. Interestingly, the research on this topic is equivocal—there is little strong evidence that athletes are more violent than non-athletes in life outside the playing field. The main reason for this lack of clarity is that there are fundamental problems with the research.

Violence research regarding athletes has historically been based on results of self-report questionnaires that do not necessarily reflect the subject's emotions or behaviors accurately. Some studies show elevated anger levels in collegiate athletes compared to non-athletes, but the results are inconsistent. Further, people do not always answer these tests honestly, and making generalized conclusions about athletes can be misleading. Moreover, scoring high on an anger test does not translate reliably to a person's behavior.

Very often, criminal statistics are used to establish rates of violence among athletes, but this too is insufficient since a crime has to be reported in order to make the statistical record. Is being arrested adequate proof of violence, though? What if an athlete is arrested but inadequate evidence exists for charges to be pressed? Can we then conclude that the accused did or didn't commit a violent act? For these and many other reasons, violence in athletes is a difficult area to study.

The myth of the violent athlete is compounded by the media and the result of fame. In our society, sensational stories sell newspapers. It is not uncommon to see a story about an athlete on the back page of the newspaper or highlighted on the evening news, telling the tale of some less-than-savory behavior before any corroboration is done to confirm his involvement. Further, no one talks about the many athletes that never get involved with violence problems. Why? Because they don't sell newspapers.

The actual statistics on the number of athletes who commit acts of violence are limited. In Jeff Benedict and Don Yaeger's 1998 book, *Pros and Cons: The Criminals Who Play in the NFL*, they estimated that approximately 21 percent of the players in the NFL had been charged with a serious crime. They defined a "serious crime" as offenses ranging from driving under the influence to murder. Of those, 53 percent were for more traditionally violent crimes: assault, sex crimes, domestic violence, and murder. Interestingly, only 16 percent of those charged were convicted. The remainder either plea-bargained, were acquitted, or had their charges dropped. Further examination shows that of the 1,590 NFL players who played in the 1996–97 season, only 509 were researched regarding criminal history and of those, 109 were found to have been charged with a serious crime. Thus, the 21 percent figure reported was based on only one-third of the total NFL population. However, if you look at the total population, only 7 percent (109) were found to have a criminal history. The point is that arrest statistics do not provide a clear picture of the problem.

There is a growing perception, partially fueled by the media, that athletes are at high risk of being accused of criminal behavior. Therefore, they need to be even more cautious and aware of their behavior because of the intense scrutiny they are under.

The Relationship Between Anger and Optimal Performance

Sport psychology research shows that anger does not enhance performance; neither is sport participation a convenient outlet for it. But many coaches and athletes still strive to create feelings of anger because they believe that angry players intimidate others and play better. Once anger has been generated in competition, however, no one seems to know the best ways to control and diffuse it during and after the game.

University of Wisconsin sport psychologist William P. Morgan's series of studies on the "iceberg profile" in champion athletes in the 1970s and 1980s showed that the mood states of elite athletes tended to include lower-than-average levels of anger. But because the Profile of Mood States questionnaire (POMS) measures states, not personality traits, and because these studies were correlational and not experimental, most researchers are not convinced that elite athletes perform better because they have lower anger levels than non-elite athletes or non-athletes.

According to research reviews by Yuri Hanin and others, high levels of anger can have deleterious effects on focus and concentration (especially anger-in), which is another problem for athletes who experience anger while competing.

All the research on performance-altering effects has examined aggressive behaviors. Except for early studies that crudely measured penalty minutes for aggression in ice hockey, research supports the hypothesis that aggression has an adverse effect on performance. Furthermore, study after study has shown that sport participation does not cathartically release anger or aggression; in fact, it prolongs both and can even lead to higher levels at the end of games and seasons. Unfortunately, these facts do not deter many coaches, who believe that angry players are more aroused and play better because they are within their "optimal zone of performance." There may be hope, however. The majority of applied sport psychologists today teach athletes and coaches to control their emotions responsibly; rarely do they attempt to raise the level of emotional outbursts.

Research that investigates anger management programs in sport is almost nonexistent. Psychologists and counselors in other therapeutic disciplines report success in controlling anger via awareness-training programs (if you are aware of it, you are less likely to vent it) and by role-playing methods (e.g., transferring anger control from simulated to real competitive situations). The use of such programs in sport settings is just beginning. Recently, a study of university soccer classes by John Brunelle of the University of Florida and his colleagues showed that the role-playing strategy produced more anger control than an awareness intervention and a nonintervention. These role-playing techniques seem intrinsically more viable for sport situations in which athletes and coaches are used to practicing skills before they implement them in competition. Most coaches already utilize a "transfer of training" practice philosophy by which they simulate gamelike situations and intensity to maximize the carry-over from training to games. Although more research is needed, role-playing seems to offer a natural means to implement anger-control training into practice and competition.

In summary, too little sound research exists on the relationship between anger and performance. Most of the reports that show that anger hurts performance are the indirect result of studies that examine arousal and anxiety effects on performance and of correlational studies that examine traits and behaviors associated with elite, successful performance. In sports such as weightlifting, football, boxing, and rugby, some anger may facilitate arousal or enhance an aggressive attitude, but no experimental data exists to support this assumption.

Far more data exists in the general anger and performance literature, which suggests that anger usually has a detrimental effect on performance. But from a scientific point of view, only limited generalizations to applied sport psychology are possible at present.

Identifying Your Anger Threshold

Coaches and athletes need some simple ways to identify individuals whose lack of anger-management skills leads to performance decrements and social problems. Athletes can learn to identify personal behavioral cues that indicate when they are losing control of their anger response. Nonverbal and verbal cues can be identified and dealt with through practice.

Warning Signs for Coaches

Someone who is experiencing problems with anger may have continuous angry, hostile thoughts, report feeling stressed and edgy or depressed and anxious, or focus on the object of their anger for long periods. Coaches need to be aware that athletes who have been under considerable stress for long periods and who may already have a high anxiety level are more likely to show anger.

Nonverbal cues that indicate a person is angry include a "stiff neck," body rigidity, growls, withdrawal from the anger object, shaking, twitching muscles, pacing and fidgeting, and showing aggression toward others or objects. Foul language directed at the object of anger or at themselves can also suggest out-of-control anger problems. Common behavioral cues to watch for include the tendency to use loud, impatient, quick responses to others; a change in posture where the athlete presents as ready to fight with chest out and eyes wide as if searching for a provocation; and unwillingness to listen to coaches and teammates about problem-solving that will facilitate sport-related goals.

Often you can identify your own anger by the way your body feels. Anger usually generates physical sensations such as a stiff jaw and neck, a hot feeling, a pounding heart, headaches, backache, tunnel vision, faster and more shallow breathing, burning and ringing ears, throbbing neck and head veins, and clenched fists. You can develop awareness of these signals by asking others to give you feedback on which symptoms you display or by keeping a record of thoughts and feelings during your last anger bout. A "hassle log," an index-card system in which you write down incidents that have made you angry, is a helpful tool. You can document how you felt, what you did in the situation, rate your performance, and develop plans to improve next time. Learning the ability to self-reflect is crucial if you are going to manage your emotions successfully and consistently.

Athletes can also predict situations that are likely to trigger anger by learning to be aware of situational cues that set off an anger response. Angry responses may accompany encounters with certain individuals, such as opposing players, disliked coaches and referees, ex-spouses, or former boyfriends or girlfriends.

Athletes may associate particular places with prior angry outbursts, such as arenas with vociferous fans or a playing field where a serious injury was sustained, and those places may continue to precipitate such responses. Specific parts of practice, such as disliked contact or fitness drills, boring rehabilitation exercises, or unproven training routines, might elicit anger over time.

Many athletes become so anxious, impatient with significant others, and aggressive in their responses in the days before a weekend competition that some family members avoid interaction with them. After games or practices, athletes who consume alcohol, drugs, or pain medications are more likely to become angry easily. Also, coaches should be aware that certain topics of discussion are almost certain to generate angry responses (e.g., demotion in playing time or to a lower team, criticism of past play, violations of team rules). In general, coaches should expect that frustrated athletes may become angry when they are losing, when several bad officiating calls have occurred, or when they are playing well below their ability.

A major problem for many athletes is retaliatory behavior. Once someone uses aggression toward him—especially if it is perceived as an attack or "outside of the rules"—the athlete may respond automatically with anger and hostile violence. Some research suggests that a player's perception of the opponent's hostile intent will determine whether he retaliates.

© Empics

Coaches can be proactive in teaching athletes self-management skills that enable them to deal with the natural experience of anger and frustration in sport without becoming hostile and violent. Coaches must hold athletes accountable for their behavior.

Athletes and their coaches must remember that sports violence, defined earlier as hostile behavior with goals that are inconsistent with those of competitive sport, is not tolerable in any sport situation, and coaches must immediately intervene to remove the offender from the competitive situation. Those who act violently must be held accountable by the coach or administrator according to team or personal rules on participation. Probably the single most powerful intervention is removing the athlete from competition participation. Coaches should also reinforce nonviolent alternatives and reward those who use them. The International Society of Sport Psychology in 1997 issued nine recommendations for curtailing aggression and violence in sport. The ideal response to hostile violence is proactive. The teaching of anger management skills is important for all athletes in improving behavior on and off the field. Implementing an intervention after a transgression occurs may help with damage control, but long-term goals to stop violence must provide athletes with skills to handle emotional and confrontational situations effectively. Such programs should be initiated early in the season or in the off-season as part of athlete conditioning, not in response to an incident of violence.

Measuring Anger in Sport

Little sport-specific research on anger has occurred in the past several decades and accordingly, no measures of anger in sport exist. Sport psychologists have borrowed, as they often do, previously validated questionnaires from general psychology and used them to measure anger in sport situations.

Few behavioral measures have been used to measure anger in sport. However, Brunelle and colleagues developed measures for ranking both provocations and anger responses during a study of anger management in soccer players, and several studies that examine aggression in sport (especially ice hockey) developed observational measures for calculating aggressive acts on the ice and used archival statistics on penalty minutes as measures of aggression.

In terms of self-report measures, the most common questionnaire used in sport studies to measure anger to date is Spielberger's State-Trait Anger Expression Inventory (STAXI), a 44-item inventory that measures anger intensity as a state or trait emotion and assesses the frequency of its expression. This inventory has been used in research that attempts to differentiate levels of athletic participation and evaluate the effects of anger-management programs.

One of the most commonly used measures of emotions in sport psychology research is the POMS, an easy-to-use self-report inventory that takes about 5 to 10 minutes to complete and has an anger subscale. It does not incorporate different dimensions of anger, nor does any correlational data link POMS and violent behavior, but its ease of use has made it the most frequently utilized inventory in anger research.

It is time for researchers to validate anger measures that are theory-based, multidimensional, and predictive of behavior. Brenda Light Bredemeier, co-director of the Mendelson Center for Sport, Character, and Culture at the University of Notre Dame, and colleagues have created several sport-specific measures of aggression (Bredemeier Athletic Aggression Inventory, Sport Aggression Inventory, and the Scale of Children's Action Tendencies), but these self-report tools assess aggressive intent, not anger or violence. Therefore, accurate observation by coaches and athletes can be the most valuable approach in assessing anger. Coaches must develop the observational skills needed to identify those athletes who are at risk for anger outbursts and negative consequences, and athletes need to learn self-awareness skills to become more aware of their emotions and those of people around them.

Strategies for Cooling the Boiling Point

Most athletes have experienced bad results subsequent to "losing it," and many coaches have realized too late that they needed to check their anger when pleading a case to an official. Anger-management is a life skill that can benefit athletes and coaches on and off the court. Resistance to providing anger-management training to athletes stems from two misconceptions:

1. Athletes are healthy, so they don't have problems with emotions.
2. Anger is necessary for sport success, and removal of it will hinder an athlete's performance.

Athletes are just as likely to experience anger-related problems as anyone else and are perhaps exposed to frustration more often than normal. As we have seen, anger probably does not help performance and in many cases seems to hurt it. The following sections provide information about ways in which athletes, coaches, and administrators can promote anger management in sport settings.

The first step in anger management is learning to accurately label emotions. One might expect that athletes would be proficient at labeling emotions because they have high levels of kinesthetic awareness, but no research supports this idea. In fact, some experts argue that the "macho" culture of competitive sports makes it difficult for many athletes to admit to experiencing negative emotions such as anxiety or anger.

A commonly used intervention to promote emotional labeling is the "hassle log," in which, as mentioned earlier in the chapter, athletes write down critical details about anger-inducing situations, including precipitating events, contributing factors, thoughts and emotions evoked, their response, the consequences of their choices, and a self-evaluation of how they handled themselves. The log allows them to monitor their patterns of anger and response and track their progress in dealing with anger-related problems. Figure 6.1 details a sample hassle log.

Name _____

Date _____

Mor _____ Aft _____ Eve _____

Where were you?

     Class _____ Gym _____

     Locker room _____ Outside/on-campus _____

     Home _____ Dining _____

     Off-campus _____ Home _____

     Other _____

What happened?

     Somebody teased me. _____

     Somebody took something of mine. _____

     Somebody told me to do something. _____

     Somebody was doing something I didn't like. _____

     Somebody started fighting with me. _____

     I did something wrong. _____

     Other _____

Who was that somebody?

     Another teammate _____ Teacher _____

     Coach _____ Parent _____

     Sibling _____ Other adult _____

     Other _____

What did you do?

     Hit back _____ Told supervising adult _____

     Ran away _____ Walked away calmly _____

     Yelled _____ Talked it out _____

     Cried _____ Told a peer _____

     Ignored it _____ Broke something _____

     Was restrained _____

     Other _____

How did you handle yourself?

1	2	3	4	5
Poorly	Not so well	Okay	Good	Great

How angry were you?

1	2	3	4	5
Burning mad	Really angry	Moderately angry	Mildly angry	Not angry at all

Figure 6.1 Hassle log.

Physiological Interventions

Central to the experience of emotion is the accompanying physiological arousal. The principal physiological signs of anger include an increase in heart rate, breathing rate, perspiration, muscle tension, and the urge to urinate. A direct method of lowering anger levels is learning to moderate this physiological arousal.

Commonly used interventions for lowering the arousal associated with anger include relaxation exercises such as diaphragmatic breathing, progressive muscle relaxation, and imagery and visualization. Diaphragmatic breathing is a widely used relaxation exercise in which the client focuses on consciously slowing down his or her breathing rate. This is partially achieved by focusing on the process of breathing. To begin, the athlete is advised to place his or her hand on his or her abdomen at the level of the diaphragm, immediately below the bottom of the sternum. During inhalation, the diaphragm should pull down and out, as if a balloon were being inflated in the abdomen. Exhalation should be slow and steady. A sequence of instructions might include the following: "Placing your hand on your abdomen, take a slow, full, deep breath. Hold it for a count of three, and then slowly exhale. Repeat this process." Deep breathing slows the heart and respiratory rates.

Relax   Progressive muscle relaxation trains the athlete to improve muscular control by tightening and then relaxing the muscles systematically. When first learning the skill, athletes are taught to tighten each muscle group, hold it to the point of discomfort, and then relax. They are directed to focus on the difference between tension and relaxation and to pay particular attention to the fact that they are in control of how their body feels. In the future, they will be able to relax themselves when they get too tense. If they can become aware of the anger-generated tension in their neck and shoulders, for example, then they can also learn to disperse it by using muscle-relaxation strategies.

One of the telltale cues of oncoming anger is a postural response: a stiffening of the neck and jaw, leaning of the upper body toward the object of the anger, and a tightened brow and clenched fists. Once they can recognize this response in themselves, athletes can practice keeping distance between themselves and the anger object and using muscle relaxation to maintain a more relaxed posture. By taking a few deep breaths, straightening up, and releasing to a relaxed posture, they can head off an angry outburst.

Imagine   Imagery has been documented as effectively promoting relaxation in a number of studies. A common approach is to teach athletes to imagine themselves in a peaceful setting, such as a tranquil beach or mountain setting. Then they are instructed to pay attention to relaxing sensations such as the warmth of the hot sand on their feet, the cool breeze on their skin, or the sounds of the birds in the distance. By imagining themselves in a peaceful place, they can learn to quickly deactivate the arousal response of anger.

Listen to music Many athletes know that music can serve as a very powerful mood modifier. Some use it to psych themselves up before a competition. Whether it is the escalating beats or vibrating bass, music can be invigorating. Similarly, it can be used to calm them down and regain balance. Some athletes use nature sounds or classical music to "quiet themselves down" and reduce potential anger caused by a frustrating competition or practice.

Once they become proficient in arousal-management skills, athletes can practice using them while being exposed to sport-related stressors. This concept, *stress inoculation training*, has been used by therapists for more than 20 years. Imagery and visualization exercises help the athlete plan and use effective coping responses in response to stressful situations.

Reevaluate Your Thinking

Endemic in people with anger problems are cognitive distortions and erroneous thinking patterns that make problem solving nearly impossible. Before one can focus on how to solve problems, these obstacles must be overcome.

Any behavior (B), no matter how simple or complex, has antecedents (A) and consequences (C). This idea of the ABCs of behavior is critical to understanding how to change behavior.

"Antecedents" refers to the things that immediately precede a behavior; they are useful in predicting outcomes and implementing interventions. Each of us has certain "irritability points," called *triggers*, that annoy or provoke us. If we can train athletes to identify these triggers, then they can select an intervention that will de-escalate the situation before they engage in the undesirable behavior, not unlike the young athlete in the story following.

Adam

A high school quarterback, Adam, is in his senior year and wants to be the star player. He believes that in order to gain that recognition, he needs to break records in passing yards and touchdowns. So every time he hears that a running play is called, he believes he will miss an opportunity to be successful. He gets angry and reluctantly runs the play, but it puts him in a bad mood that progressively gets worse with every running play called. Logic goes out the window. He doesn't care that passing on every down would be predictable and unlikely to be successful. He starts having tantrums on the sidelines and loses his concentration to the point that when a passing play is called, he executes poorly. If Adam can recognize this trigger, as soon as he hears a running play is called he can consciously calm himself down by taking a few deep breaths, focusing on the win that he hopes for, and engage in positive self-talk that can shape his emotions.

Talk it out People often engage in self-talk that ranges from complimentary to disparaging. For example, when an athlete is angry, his self-talk often reflects this. By muttering to himself some select insults about his opponents, teammates, or coaches, his thoughts serve as a mirror for his moods. Self-talk also provides a running dialogue that one can use to work through a problem. Using the example of Adam again, he might be thinking, "How am I going to be All-State if I'm not allowed to throw the ball? This just stinks; they don't want me to succeed." Often the first step in gaining control of thoughts involves invoking some form of stopping them. When Adam realizes that he is spiraling into his negative thought pattern again, he should yell, "Stop!" inside his head or slap his thigh or snap his fingers to regain control.

The next step is to replace the negative thoughts with positive ones. Suppose Adam thought, "I know every time I hear them call a running play, I get angry. I should just relax and execute this play, just like practice. I know I am going to get my chance. If I stay calm, when the opportunity comes, I'll be able to take over this game."

Communicate One of the struggles that coaches face is how to shape an athlete's behavior by giving critical review and instruction, while doing it in a manner that the athlete can hear. Learning to tolerate criticism is difficult. At the crux of it, the recipient has to be able to identify the goal of the criticism, what value to place on it, and how to respond to it.

People tend to respond defensively to criticism, especially when they feel it is delivered as an insult, or worse, identifies a legitimate weakness that they don't want to acknowledge. If the criticism is an attack on character (not an assessment of skills or performance), the recipient has to resist the urge to respond impulsively and ask himself or herself what is motivating his or her response. If someone thinks you are a fool, why merit it with a response unless you are afraid that it might be true? In this sort of situation, the goal, one could hypothesize, was to "get a rise" out of the recipient. As such, it should receive minimal value; by not reinforcing it, it will surely disappear. The best response would be to ignore it, which is difficult when public reputation is at stake; athletes sometimes find themselves in a physical altercation in such situations.

Consider this scenario: Coach Standowski calls you into his office. He states that he notices that when running the floor on the fast break, too often you keep your head down and miss open passes that some of your teammates could have translated into scoring opportunities. He says, "The other girls on the team are getting frustrated but don't want to approach you because they know that you don't respond to criticism well. I am talking to you because this is something that we can change that will lead to more success for all of us."

While one person might understand that this is an opportunity to learn something from the coach and improve her game, another might hear it as the coach nitpicking and not giving her credit for the things she does well. If the young point guard's response is to yell at her coach, "Dammit, why don't you let me play my game? You know I can lead this team, you know I always get us points on the board—why do you criticize one little thing that I do?" how do you think she will be perceived by the coach and the team?

Now contrast the preceding scenario with this: a quiet knock on the coach's door while he is alone, and "Hey coach, can I talk to you for a minute? I just wanted to ask you if you could help me understand why you are focusing on one thing I do that I don't think hurts the team at all. I feel like you are bringing me down and just criticizing me. I think I can help this team win by playing my game, but you are focusing on something that no one else even notices. Can I ask why?"

The first scenario makes this player seem uncoachable, but in the other situation she is trying to understand the coach's position. Even if she doesn't agree, it is nonconfrontational and more fertile for a positive interaction.

Tone of voice, including volume, rate, and pitch, is an important aspect of communication. The content is obviously important as well, but research shows that more than half of all communication is nonverbal. Body language is critical. If you stand over someone and talk authoritatively as if you are more powerful than him or her, you are more likely to get a defensive or counteroffensive response. If you open a conversation in a nonthreatening but assertive manner (e.g., using "I" statements), you can speak your mind and get questions answered without causing a major conflict. "I like the intensity of your game but I am concerned that it gets away from you sometimes and stops you from taking it to the next level" is more effective than "What the hell is wrong with you? Don't you see that you get so amped that you take bad penalty after bad penalty? You make it impossible for us to win." The messages are similar, but the delivery is the difference. Poorly timed sarcasm can lead to your listener shutting you down.

A related concept is active listening. People are more responsive to you if they get the impression that you are interested in their point of view. Good communication is not just about talking; it is about listening too. Maintaining good eye contact, not interrupting, thinking about what the other person is saying, and remaining open-minded are behaviors that can help communication to grow.

Take a time-out   When anger boils up and you feel that you're losing control and might lash out physically, emotionally, or psychologically, leaving the situation is a smart move. A "time-out" offers an angry player or coach a chance to cool off, regain some physical and emotional control, and decide how to handle the situation differently.

Once you have developed awareness of your anger cues, you have enough control to decide to take a time-out. If you find yourself standing up, getting into someone else's face, and clenching fists, it's time to leave. Go out of the office or locker room if dealing with coaches or athletes. If on the competitive field of play, turn away from your assailant, retreat to your huddle, find a teammate to duck behind, head for the sideline, or call a time-out, literally. Walk off the arousal, do some deep breathing or relaxation exercises, or use some thought-stopping and positive self-talk. Don't do something else aggressive like punching the wall or kicking over the water bucket; try to calm down and get control again. Return when you feel you can handle the situation again; that is, when you're able to ignore the bad-mouthing and taunting, resist the temptation to hit back, and take up the conversation again in a calm and rational tone. Coaches should try to get players to realize when they need to take a time-out rather than always calling one for them. Part of the athletes' learning process is taking responsibility for changing their own angry behavior.

Problem solve   Some athletes, perhaps due to their exposure to violent role models while growing up, don't know how to solve problems in any way except by violence. This behavior emanates from the hostility bias described previously, which is the belief that "might is right" and that the way to solve problems is with violence. It becomes the default setting.

If an athlete is going to be successful in problem solving, he or she must substitute other interventions for aggressive behavior. Some professionals believe that people who have difficulty controlling their anger turn to violence because it is the only tool they have in their toolbox, and they go back to what they know. If that is the case, coaches and sport psychologists must provide these athletes with more tools that won't interfere with their future success.

Tackling a problem requires defining it first. For any given problem, the map to the solution can be drawn from asking "who, what, where, when, why, and how" questions. Once defined, you can see what the contributing factors are and where intervention may provide a solution.

When searching for solutions, examine as many as possible, then rank-order them according to probability of success. Try as many different suggestions as possible to optimize your chance for success. When one fails, ask why. When one succeeds, ask the same question. *Why* did this work? *What* can I learn from this to apply to different situations in the future?

Equally important is *who* can help, and *how?* No one can do everything by himself or herself. Finding people who can help you solve your problems and whose problems you can assist with enriches your interpersonal life and makes you much more effective in general.

Evaluate and modify   No person, athlete or not, can do things perfectly the first time and every time. Too many people criticize themselves instead of evaluating their performance honestly. This constant self-criticism often comes out as cursing oneself after a mistake in practice or game. It's not easy to change the person, but with effort, the behavior usually can be changed. If coaches notice that athletes are constantly berating themselves, they need to help them stop the negative self-talk, gain emotional control, and focus on positive thoughts again.

Coaches and athletes also need to remember that the process of evaluation and modification also includes celebration and reward for good effort, even if it's something as simple as buying a sprinter some ice cream after she runs her fastest mile. However you choose to do it, behaviorally it is crucial to reinforce your successes. How often do you set difficult-to-achieve goals, almost achieve them, and then sulk about your "failure" rather than your "near success"? At the very least, the effort needs to be reinforced.

Research consistently shows that setting difficult-to-achieve goals that take a great deal of time and energy to reach have lower success rates than those that are broken down into smaller, easier-to-achieve goals along the way. This allows for frequent self-reflection, modification (if needed), and reward for these smaller achievements, and may avoid the continued frustration from not achieving those ambitious goals that can lead to anger.

Exercise   Exercise is a wonderful anger-management strategy. One reason for its success is a phenomenon called "reciprocal inhibition," which means that two opposite states that cannot occur at the same time inhibit each other. To illustrate, an athlete cannot be physiologically raging at the same time that she is exhausted from an hour of vigorous exercise. Therefore, when athletes exercise, exert energy, and tire themselves out, they still may get annoyed about an issue and have the cognitive components of anger, but they cannot achieve the physiological escalation associated with intense anger states. Exercise is a natural response to feeling stressed and may be the best way to handle anger situations.

Implementing Anger-Management Training

Both players and coaches play integral parts in creating and maintaining an effective anger-management program. Let's look at these roles in a little more detail now.

Individual and Group Roles

There are pluses and minuses to both group and individual interventions for anger-management training. In individual sessions, athletes are often more comfortable disclosing problems that they may feel stigmatized by if they spoke about them in public. Privacy allows them to explore problems that may reach clinical proportions.

In group sessions, however, the athlete learns new skills in a comfortable context with his or her peers. Bouncing ideas off each other and discovering how others handled situations and progressed can promote contagious improvement. A team-building component is common in situations where the team learns as a group. Identification of interaction patterns becomes easy, and utilizing each other as tools to identify triggers or reminders to predict consequences can build and reinforce newly learned skills at a faster rate.

Brunelle and colleagues' research on anger management in soccer players suggests that some kinds of group interventions may be more viable than others. While they found that both anger-awareness programs and role-playing techniques (practicing alternative responses to anger in competitive situations) are effective ways of controlling anger, only role-playing participants continued to reduce anger scores over the duration of their study. It makes good sense that athletes, who are used to learning by doing in practice, should make better use of simulation-training interventions than simple knowledge. This initial finding offers potential to coaches and psychologists who may be responsible for planning workshops for student athletes.

Role of Coaches

Coaches have a tremendous positive impact that can help their charges succeed on or off the field for many years. Unfortunately, they also can have a huge negative impact on athletes' means of expressing and controlling emotion. Top professional and college coaches who curse and shove officials, throw chairs, berate and hit players, and get into physical violence with fans or spouses send the message that getting angry at people and acting aggressively as a result is OK, and a key to success. When coaches tell players to get mad at opposing players and beat them up, they also spread the idea that angry aggression is permissible and helps one succeed and obtain power. And when coaches fail to suspend players who have been involved in assaults and violent criminal behavior, they send the message that violence is an acceptable part of life.

Coaches, like professional players, are essential role models for young people. Their nurturing job requires that they not be aggressive and abusive to others. If they can't control their own behavior, all the team rules in the world will not control their players' behavior. If they have problems with anger management, they have a responsibility to resolve it even if it means seeking professional help. If they cannot handle the problem with repeated help, then they should find another profession.

Team rules and athletes' codes of conduct are a good starting point for laying down expectations of nonaggressive behavior and anger control. Athletes need to know the consequences of lack of control; athletic directors and coaches need to make sure these consequences are carried out evenly for all players, whether stars or benchwarmers.

Future Directions

Anger-management programs in sport are still in their infancy, and research must begin to evaluate those that are being implemented. Most programs today have been borrowed from applied psychology programs for domestic violence, youth violence, and abuse problems. The basic tenets of these programs should transfer to sport, but some techniques may be more effective than others in sport settings. Group programs need to involve both coaches and athletes, and a key to success in anger management among athletes is peer pressure and peer-based interventions. Individual counseling must incorporate successful cognitive-behavioral techniques that have already proved effective.

Recently, many professional teams, professional athletes' unions, and the NCAA have introduced anger-management workshops for athletes in an attempt to enhance awareness and understanding and reduce the number of violent acts that involve athletes. These programs provide a variety of educational materials to athletes and coaches and also involve athletes in role-playing skits and brainstorming alternative responses to anger. The efficacy of these workshops on outbursts of angry behavior has not been evaluated to date. Research needs to examine the causes of anger and aggression among athletes and test the usefulness of various types of intervention in anger control.

Much research needs to be done on the prevalence of anger-driven violence on and off the sport field to determine the extent of the problem and get beyond the headlines. Exploratory work will identify those personality types or individuals at risk for anger's negative effects. We need to develop sport-specific state and trait measures of anger and embark on qualitative research to better understand how anger benefits or detracts from performance. The NCAA, professional sport leagues and unions, and the government need to fund studies that will determine optimal interventions for athletes within and outside of the sport setting.

Awareness and once-a-year anger workshops are not the answer to violent behavior. Athletes must practice alternative modes of behavior under simulated competitive situations in order for the lesson to carry over to the playing field. Coaches must practice what they preach concerning anger behavior in practice and competitive situations and give athletes numerous opportunities to learn appropriate and effective alternative behaviors if they want those behaviors to be learned well. Athletes learn by doing, and only when they learn to recognize the signs of anger and redirect the arousal that accompanies it into effective strategies for performance will this problem improve.

Concentration: Focus Under Pressure

Clark Perry

Effective concentration enables athletes to apply appropriate attention to internal and external cues in the sporting arena. At any given time, our senses detect information from millions of sources: images through our eyes, aromas through our olfactory organs, sounds through our ears, pressure applied to our skin, the position of our body in space, and the myriad thoughts and emotions that flash through our brains. How do we filter out the information that is vital to success from that which is useless? This question has plagued cognitive scientists, sport psychologists, coaches, and athletes for decades—or in the case of Aristotle's and Plato's ponderings, for centuries.

The athlete who can focus on the task at hand and avoid distraction enjoys the greatest possibility of success. We all know examples of mentally tough athletes who have overcome adversity to produce remarkable results; for instance, professional athletes who use the loss of a loved one to spur them on to victory rather than allowing it to consume their emotional resources. Others succumb to the perceived pressure of the event, like the elite golfer who has led an entire tournament only to have the "train derail" as he tees off on the last hole. Perceptions of the competitive environment can either enhance or destroy the quest for excellence.

This chapter discusses what we know about the influences on concentration and aims to provide insight into the ways to train the mind to become a more effective distraction filter.

Maintaining Focus in the "Zone"

Aidan Moran, in his 1996 text *The Psychology of Concentration in Sport Performers*, referred to attention as the psychology of concentration. He considers the *attentional system* to be a bridge between perception, cognition, and action. This system has three key components: selectivity of processing (focused concentration), mental time-sharing of actions (coordination of skilled behavior), and regulation of alertness (arousal control). Most important, attention is a skill that can be developed through appropriate practice and instruction. Figure 7.1 details this attentional system.

Phrases like "I was totally in the zone out there," or "If we stay focused on our game plan we should be OK," and "I lost my concentration for only a second and that was the ball game," all imply the importance of understanding relevant cues in sport. But which cues are important varies among sports and the athletes who play them. Let's look at a sport like archery, where there are very few external (outside the body) cues that contribute positively to the result. The target is not moving. No opponents are there to tackle the archer as she prepares to shoot. As she draws back the bow, no referees blow a whistle to call a foul. The archer only needs to read the distance and the wind. Once she has accounted for these variables, she must put a complex set of internal actions into place. If her actions match the external demands, the result is an arrow in the center of the target. Ah, if it were only that easy! A third element must be controlled: the internal distractions. These cognitive and emotional stimuli can either contribute to or detract from athletic performance. The archer could start thinking about the consequences of her next shot. She might have noticed what her competitor has scored. She may become aware of the public's expectations, and on and on. The mind is an amazing thing: When you want to stop thinking and recognizing, paradoxically, it becomes even more attuned and aware. As a result, controlling internal distractions in self-paced sports like archery can be exceptionally difficult. Try not thinking of a purple, spotted elephant!

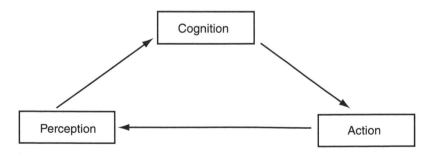

Figure 7.1 Moran's attentional system.

But what about sports in which the environmental elements are constantly changing? Sports such as soccer, football, basketball, baseball, and hockey all have a moving object that the athletes need to act on; at the same time, competitors try to prevent them from achieving that goal. There is arguably more information than it's possible to process, yet somehow the elite brain appropriately filters the distractions from the relevant cues. In basketball for example, the point guards bring the ball up the floor. They have to be aware of the call that the coach would like to have run, know the time on the clock, read their players, read the opponents, and control the dribble of the ball, all the while staying in control of their internal thoughts and emotions—and then execute the plan to perfection. Sounds impossible, yet elite athletes do it more often than not. They have mastered the ability to concentrate, or focus their attention on relevant cues.

Sports such as archery demand total concentration for success. One must learn to control both internal and external distractions to be on target.

Understanding Attention and Our Potential

How do we focus our attention on the relevant cues? We first need to understand more about this nebulous term "attention." Psychologists for centuries have struggled to derive a common understanding of its definition. The best explanation of the concept comes from the work of Bruce Abernethy of the University of Queensland, Australia. He extended the work of Michael Posner and S. J. Boies, who identified three major uses of the term "attention":

1. *Attention as alertness*, including concerns with the development and both short- and long-term maintenance of optimal sensitivity and readiness for responding.

2. *Attention as a limited capacity or resource*, as examined in studies of divided attention aimed at isolating capacity or resource limitation in information processing. That is, human systems have a limited amount of resources that can be used for processing information, and in studying attention, this limited capacity needs to be taken into consideration.

3. *Attention as selectivity*, as examined in studies of selective attention requiring the preferential processing of certain information in the face of competition from other sources of distraction.

In order to develop strategies to enhance effective attention, athletes, coaches, and sport psychologists should examine these conditions in more detail.

Attention As Alertness

Alertness and readiness depend on the emotional states of the athlete. Christopher Janelle's (University of Florida) review of the relationship between anxiety, arousal, and visual attention highlights the need to identify the underlying mechanisms responsible for attentional breakdown so that strategies can be developed in order to maximize performance. Not only is anxiety a cause of concern in performance decrement, it has also been shown to contribute to the occurrence of athletic injuries, because poor attentional control decreases the ability to react to risks in the competitive environment. As increases in anxiety occur, concurrent alterations to attention lead to (1) attentional narrowing, (2) conscious, controlled processing, (3) inefficiencies in attentional allocation, and (4) distraction by irrelevant or threatening cues.

First, let's discuss attentional narrowing. The attentional span, or width, of highly anxious people becomes restricted, and they miss important cues that would have contributed to a successful performance. In the point guard example discussed earlier, the fact that the game is close, he has just committed an error, or the fans are giving him a hard time all can cause him to experience a heightened state of anxiety. According to James A. Easterbrook and many recent researchers, this state could contribute to him having the ball stolen by an opponent, allowing the shot clock to expire, or missing a wide-open player under the basket. His attentional field may narrow, and his response might be "Sorry—I never saw him coming." Under normal levels of arousal, his attentional width would pick up those critical cues and he could react accordingly. This mistake may contribute to further anxiety and the continued downward spiral of attentional mistakes. The more the guard gets caught up in this vicious cycle, the more his attention changes direction as he becomes more focused on internal thoughts of failure.

Second, under high levels of anxiety there is a shift away from relatively automatic functioning to a more controlled, conscious processing, which has been shown to be associated with performance decrement. Brian Lewis and Darwyn Linder of Arizona State University studied the "choking under pressure" outcome of this downward-spiral phenomenon. They concluded that a self-focus model, in which increased pressure to perform may cause the athlete to focus attention on the process of performing at the expense of other relevant external cues, offered the best explanation. Once a task becomes automated, it no longer demands conscious attention. But as pressure to perform increases, it can cause the athlete to shift attention away from the relevant cues; it interferes with the previously automated behavior, and choking occurs. It is safe to say that at all stages of skill execution, from novice to elite, control of anxiety contributes to the best possible appraisal of the attentional field.

Third, inefficiency in attentional allocation contributes to performance that is less automatic and requires more effort. Studies over the past 30 years have revealed that these inefficiencies can be measured through an examination of a number of psychophysiological variables (e.g., muscular through electromyogram (EMG) and cognitive through electroencephalogram (EEG) and cortical event-related potential (ERP). In contrast, high-level performers are exceptionally efficient in their allocation of attention to the demands of the task.

As athletes become more anxious they experience not only an attentional shift in orientation but also changes in response time to relevant cues. As we've said, the fewer mistakes an athlete makes, the less likely he or she is to become anxious. To that end, important work by Joan Vickers and her team at the University of Calgary demonstrates the need to develop perceptual-training programs that could facilitate stress-resistant performance. They conducted studies examining "quiet eye" (QE), which is a period of time when the gaze is stable on spatial information that is critical to effective motor performance. A longer QE period has been shown to be more prominent in expert performances. As Vickers explains in response to a question about appropriate eye gaze in tennis:

> The location of QE in tennis is very early in ball flight. You should track the ball closely as it comes off your opponent's racquet and during the first part of its flight. It is true that as the ball is hit the gaze is located in front of the ball and not on it at contact. This is due to limitations in our ability to track fast objects. But more importantly, the flight of the ball has to be assessed early so the hitting action can be set up and organized correctly. The same sort of QE control is used in hitting a baseball, in playing table tennis, and similar skills.

Training programs designed to enhance visual control create more appropriate responses to attentional cues, thus counteracting the deleterious effects of anxiety.

And last, some researchers have proposed that athletes under high anxiety can become hyperdistracted and focus on the threat or irrelevant cues. Such distractions can cause the athlete to make mistakes, thereby contributing to the anxiety-mistake spiral.

In chapter 8, Shane Murphy discusses the use of imagery as a way to create the optimal emotional state to enhance attentional focus. In my experience, when athletes are aware of their optimal level of arousal for performance and are able to create and maintain it during competition, they increase the likelihood of optimizing their ideal attentional state in the process. As we've said, the cues that are important to success vary among sports and individuals, just as the levels of arousal required for optimal performance vary among athletes. Therefore, the interaction between arousal and attentional focus must be examined on an individual basis through extensive testing in varied conditions before an optimal level of arousal can be determined. A close examination of chapter 8 will provide immense insight into a greater understanding of the ideal performance state.

Attention As a Limited Capacity or Resource

Let's go back to the example of our point guard. When appropriately aroused and focused on relevant cues, he has a high level of basketball efficiency. He is able to process internal and external information flawlessly while expertly executing a complex motor skill. Remarkable. But could he do this from birth? There was a time when he could not walk. But that skill developed into running and dribbling a basketball, to shooting and passing, and eventually to running a whole offense. This development demonstrates the notion of limited information capacity and resources; that is, difficult tasks that are processed together have cumulative processing requirements. If those requirements exceed the capacity or resources of the individual, the processing of the relevant information will be incomplete or delayed, therefore causing a decrease in performance.

Abernethy argues that processing capacity is fixed, but the athlete may choose to apportion it to different tasks. This is similar to the way memory resources work in a computer. Complex tasks in a computer program require large amounts of random access memory (RAM), which allows the computer to process current information while still performing background operations. If the demands of the task exceed the capacity of the RAM, the operations are seriously slowed or halted completely, at which point we must either increase the RAM or partition the memory to accommodate the current challenges. Our minds handle complex informational challenges in a similar manner: If we devote attention or resources to inappropriate stimuli, we limit our ability to process the information that is vital to the success of the task.

Now let's examine two of the many tasks required of the elite-level basketball point guard: dribbling and recognizing developing offensive patterns. If the primary task of dribbling is difficult and requires a large percentage of his attentional resources, very little remains for the secondary task of identifying and responding to positional play. However, the elite player does not need to dedicate many attentional resources to dribbling; over time, with years of practice, the once-difficult skill has become more and more habitual, eventually becoming quite easy, as does skating to the elite ice hockey player. Greater resources can then be dedicated to the more complex tasks of passing and shooting, in both basketball and hockey. Performance decrements are generally greatest for anxious, untrained athletes who are performing two or more complex tasks simultaneously. Athletes who need to focus a large percentage of their energy on the primary task often exhibit "tunnel vision" in regard to secondary tasks that require a broad band of attention. As a consequence, errors often occur.

The understanding of limited capacity highlights the need for effective attentional switching. At any level of skill, as the athlete approaches the limits of attention, it would be advantageous to quickly "switch" attention from one stimulus to another. This time-sharing allows athletes to stay within their attentional boundaries while still meeting the demands of the task. Of course, switching attention, even momentarily, allows for mistakes in a dynamic environment. For example, as that point guard moves into the offensive end of the court and becomes more intent on hitting the open man with a pass, his lack of attention, even for a split second, to his defender can allow the opposing guard to steal the ball away from him and score. This is a common occurrence even in the highest level of professional basketball. The best players in the world cannot pay attention to everything all of the time; it's impossible, because we all have our limits of available resources. However, what those players do exceptionally well is (a) develop their skills so that they do not expend as much energy as their novice counterparts do on their execution, and (b) constantly switch their attention as they "make the rounds" of important internal and external stimuli.

Attention As Selectivity

Athletes are bombarded with continual information, from both inside and outside their bodies, every moment of the day. Which of these stimuli are important and which are distractions? In the process of *selective attention*, certain information is preferentially selected for attention while irrelevant information is ignored. Sport requires athletes to appreciate the demands of the competitive environment. The key to the development of athletic skill in this environment is an understanding of the unique nature of each sport: the rules, objective, strategy, opportunities, and constraints. Selective attention begins with an understanding of how to differentiate between the distractions and the relevant cues.

Abernethy has proposed a useful metaphor to aid the understanding of selective attention. In his "searchlight" metaphor, the intent of a searchlight's user is to focus the light on only what is important. When the light is focused inappropriately, errors occur. The following are three common errors:

1. Failing to focus all attention on the limited essential elements for task success. (The searchlight's beam is too broad.)

2. Being distracted from relevant information by irrelevant information. (The searchlight is pointed in the wrong direction.)

3. Being unable to divide attention among all the stimuli that need to be processed concurrently. (The searchlight's beam is too narrow, or the user is unable to move it rapidly enough from one spot to the next.)

The point guard who goes to the free-throw line processing general information about the score, the movements of the crowd behind the backboard, and the talk of the opposing team while trying to focus on the essential visual cues (the front of the rim and the rotation of the ball) is an example of the first error. His appraisal of the available information includes the relevant cues, but they become clouded by the distractions.

Golf provides us with a great opportunity to examine the second error. It is a sport that is generally played at each athlete's pace; there is ample time to rehearse each shot and create the optimal performance zone. The game has protocols that ensure that each player operates within a distraction-free environment, devoid of opponent interference, heckling fans, running clocks, or a dependence on teammates. Yet many people regard it as the most frustrating game. The player is generally in control of his or her destiny—why then do we continually find different players at the top of the leader board? Often the second error, *being distracted from relevant information by irrelevant information*, is the cause of the huge variations in performance. Most golfers have bought into the golf-course architect's evil plot to sabotage their confidence and self-esteem. The architects design courses that will challenge golfers' skills and create an artificial target called "par." The player's objective is to get as close to par, or the number that the architect has set for the course, as possible. Scoring anything above that number means that the player has failed; anything below it translates into success, especially in the eyes of the professional tour golfer. To make matters worse, the players don't wait until they have finished 18 holes to measure their level of success. They examine it after each hole and determine how well they are playing according to par. This constant examination of success is the trap that the architect has laid in conjunction with his evil twin, the television commentator. Watching the Masters, year after year, we are reminded that "this is a big putt, because it is to save par; miss it and the player will drop a shot," which implies that one shot is more important than another. At the end of the round, the total strokes accumulated are tallied and compared to either the previous number of strokes taken (in establishing a handicap) or to another player competing at the same time (tournament play). This total number of strokes is the determinant of success. Each stroke taken during the day is important in its own right, yet players who buy into the par scenario often allow internal distractions to influence their play. As the round progresses, they are reminded of how they are playing after each hole. If they score a bogey (1 over par) on one hole, they believe they will have to score a birdie (1 under par) on another to compensate. This can cause them to shift focus to irrelevant information, which can negatively influence shot and club selection, as well as changes in motor skill patterns. Then the trap has been successfully executed—captured, one innocent golfer! But if a player treats each shot as an isolated game with no history, he or she can regard it as the challenge of executing the near-perfect swing on a golf ball; all he or she has to do is hit it in the direction and distance predetermined by an accurate appraisal of the terrain. Simple!

The third error, *being unable to divide attention among all the stimuli that need to be processed concurrently*, is one that plagues novices, particularly in complex ball sports like rugby. The complexity, especially at the elite level, requires a high capacity for attention and accurate switching from cue to cue at the appropriate time. Novices have not yet learned the nuances of the game and, especially when under pressure, will focus on the perceived essentials of play and miss other aspects that are vital to success. This can contribute to the "choking" phenomenon discussed earlier. Athletes, especially those under pressure, naturally narrow their attentional field, believing that concentrating means honing in on what is required to successfully complete the task. But paradoxically, complex tasks require a broader, more relaxed appraisal of internal and external information. The identification of relevant cues is paramount to the successful execution of a motor skill. But what is relevant and what is irrelevant?

Now is a good time to examine distractions in greater depth. A distraction occurs when a competing stimuli interferes with or

© Reb Tringali/SportsChrome USA

Games such as golf allow players to constantly compare their performance to what is expected (par). Focusing on expectations instead of what is required to hit the best shot possible is a common concentration error that can lead to poor performance and "choking."

diverts attention away from a functional focus. It can come from internally generated thoughts and emotions or from the recognition of external sources of interference. So what causes athletes to become distracted, especially highly trained athletes who know the difference between relevant and irrelevant cues? Invariably, it's a shift of focus away from the task at hand to an appraisal of the potential outcome. Once we begin to "move our heads away from where our bodies are," we open ourselves to a multitude of devastating mistakes.

Moran examined distractions, both internal and external, in his seminal text *The Psychology of Concentration in Sport Performers* mentioned earlier in this chapter. He defines external distractions as environmental stimuli that divert an athlete's attention away from the intended direction. Typical external distractions are noise, gamesmanship, weather and playing conditions, and visual distractions.

Noise   Noise is broadly defined as any unwanted sound. Typically, sports are performed in arenas or stadiums designed to hold thousands of spectators who are encouraged to cheer for the home team, thus contributing to the home-field advantage. In NFL football, opposition quarterbacks often change from audible signal calling to body-movement calling at the line of scrimmage when the cheers of the home team's fans make it impossible for the opposition players to hear a call. The perception of the noise can be enough to distract the players and affect their ability to perform beyond the actual limitation of the noise itself. But noise distraction doesn't have to be at high amplitude. An archer or golfer could be put off by any sudden noise. Their competitive arena is exceptionally quiet; an expected calm precedes all shots taken. If their performance routines are not ingrained so that they can perform them with ease, the distraction of an unexpected noise could negatively affect their performance. Paradoxically, distraction can also result from the *absence* of noise. When cheering is usually present, its absence can be quite disconcerting. When a visiting team scores quickly on a home team it is said that they can often take the crowd out of the game. This "deathly silence" in a large stadium can foster self-doubt in the home team and create an inappropriate focus on such internal distractions.

Gamesmanship   Competitors have been known to use strategic behavioral plots in an effort to disrupt their opponents' concentration. I've witnessed elite swimmers draw a mouthful of water from the pool at the beginning of a race. Once they were introduced to the crowd, they would spit the water into a competitor's lane. Many competitors would get angry, and the unexpected emotion would be just the distractions the perpetrator hoped for. Swimmers who have control over their race strategies would see this ploy for what it is, have a quick laugh, and execute their plan. In another example, tennis players Jimmy Connors and John McEnroe were masters at creating external distractions through the temper tantrums they frequently exhibited during their illustrious careers. And Gary Payton, NBA point guard, was renowned for "trash talking" opposing players, especially rookies, to get them thinking beyond the essentials of their game.

Weather and playing conditions   The temperature, precipitation, wind, and light conditions all contribute to sport performances. Of course, these conditions are all part of the sporting environment and don't discriminate between players. It's true that some athletes are better in certain conditions than others, but often those who realize they don't perform well in the heat, or the wind, or the wet, exacerbate that limitation by focusing on it. Athletes who believe they can't perform are often right, as their perceptions become their reality.

Visual distractions   In most sports, vision is arguably the prime information receptor. We need sight to track the flight of a ball, locate competitors and teammates, and play within the boundaries of the field, just to name a few examples. Perceiving unexpected objects in our visual field can distract us from our anticipated response set. The distinction between *open* (dynamic, typically ball-based) and *closed* (stable, without interference from a changing environment) sports needs to be made. Open sports rely on the environment to contribute to the competitive drama. The uncertainty of the referees' calls, opponents' offensive and defensive strategies, freezing or wet conditions, and crowd involvement all play a part in our fascination with elite sport. The top-level athlete in open sports must be prepared for all circumstances. The best anticipate the circumstances before they occur and have a planned response to counteract the potential distraction. Closed sports, such as archery, bowling, golf, and swimming, have a clearly defined skill set that's required for success in those sports. Typically, planning for a changing environment does not factor into their training regime. Yet a bird flying unexpectedly close to a target just as the archer prepares to release may make the difference between a high and low score. In a real-world example, Olympic gold medalist Ian Thorpe was disqualified in the 2004 Australian Olympic trials when he false-started because he thought he heard a noise and prematurely fell into the pool. The other seven athletes could have easily followed him into the pool if they had allowed his movement to distract them from their start sequence. To their credit, they all stood fast and were able to successfully compete in that event.

Elite athletes today prepare for all possibilities, even the ridiculous, on the chance that it may occur at the most inopportune time. The Australian Institute of Sport (AIS) in Canberra, Australia, has established peculiar training methods in the lead-up to the Olympic Games to prepare athletes for potential distractions in the host countries. For example, in 1988, to prepare the hockey team for the challenges of Seoul, the AIS psychology department installed loudspeakers around the training field and played loud Korean drums throughout practice. Imagery can be used in much the same way to assist the athlete in handling any possible distractions.

Mastery over such internal distractions as thoughts, fears, and worry gets to the core of the attentional dilemma. In reality, there is *no* distraction until we recognize it internally. Just because our perceptual field (vision, hearing, smell, and touch) receives information about the external environment doesn't mean that the information is perceived and processed. If we go back to figure 7.1 on page 114, we see that the relationship between perception, cognition, and action defines the attentional system. The spectator sees the *action* of the interaction between an athlete's *perception* and the subsequent filtered *cognition*. Athletes must distinguish distraction from valuable performance cues, then utilize this information to enhance self-confidence, self-efficacy, and performance strategy. Often internal distractions are created as information from the external environment brings into question one's preparedness for competition. Becoming preoccupied with the realization of internal and external distractions contributes to the choking phenomenon discussed earlier. The more focus that goes to inappropriate information, the less is available to deal with vital cues.

Enhancing Attention for Competition

Models and theories mean nothing unless we can apply them to improve sport performance. Some interesting work by Gabrielle Wulf and her colleagues at the University of Nevada at Las Vegas has challenged the appropriate attentional focus for motor-skill development. In a number of studies since 1998, they have examined the results of sport performers' focus on their actions in completing a sporting task as compared to focusing their attention on the *effects* of the action. Much of the training in sport has traditionally encouraged athletes to focus on the actions required to perform sporting skills. For example, in teaching how to hit a tennis ball, the coach would tell players to focus on the movement of their arms in hitting the ball. However, recent findings from the research by Wulf's team support a shift to focus on the racket head as it moves. Golfers have improved their game when they focused on the motion of the club head in chip shots rather than the bend in the elbow or stiffness of the wrists. Wulf argues that focusing on the immediate effects of the action are more advantageous than the resultant effects of the shot (e.g., the flight of the ball or landing on the green). The research goes even farther to suggest that thinking about one's actions during movement execution is detrimental to performance. This is an important consideration, because coaches and teachers of sport often encourage athletes to *think* about what they are doing. For example, in speech, rather than focusing on the shape of the mouth in creating words, we focus on the intended effect of the words.

A focus on a movement's *effect* rather than the movement itself seems to allow the motor system to use automatic processes unconstrained by conscious control. The feedback provided by coaches should emphasize the *impact* of one's actions. The swimming coach should use video and biomechanical data to demonstrate where in the race the swimmer is making performance gains. Instead of insisting on "high-elbow" recovery as the focus, the emphasis is placed on the recognition that when the elbows are high there is a greater distance per stroke in the water. The attention is aimed on the *impact* of proper swimming mechanics, not on the technique itself. As stated earlier, the point guard does not *think* about what he has to do to dribble the basketball; it has become an automated process, and focus on that process would have deleterious effects.

Mihaly Csikszentmihalyi of the University of Chicago is a pioneer researcher in the concept of *flow* (see chapter 1 for more information on Csikszentmihalyi's flow concept). As he describes it, it is an experience so enjoyable that people will do it, even at great cost, for the sheer sake of doing it. External rewards become irrelevant; it is the *process* that is internally gratifying. Many elite athletes have experienced that magical moment when everything comes together. Michael Jordan, when asked how he thought up the amazing move that resulted in a spectacular dunk, often responded, "I don't know—it just happened!" Flow is an experience that happens to you, and paradoxically, the more you try to get into it, the more difficult it is. This occurrence is consistent with the results of other work that demonstrates that a self-focus actually takes an athlete farther away from automated performance. Csikszentmihalyi argues that we don't help people get into flow by trying to create it. It happens as a result of creating an environment that matches the skills of the athlete with the challenges of the task. When they are perfectly matched, the athlete can "read" the environment (internal and external) in such a way that all relevant information is absorbed and distracters are ignored, creating a space for excellence. When the skills or challenges become too great and the balance pulls the sporting experience to one side or the other, boredom or anxiety results. If coaches and athletes can anticipate the sporting environment, they can prepare for the challenges ahead through appropriate skill development. Athletes who have the skills to meet sporting challenges have described the experience as "effortless" and "exhilarating." They described having "all the time in the world to react to the situation," and that "the ball was the size of a watermelon."

Attentional control is the result of preparing for the competitive arena through the understanding of the sporting demands. Athletes need to have the skills, perceptual awareness, self-confidence, and emotional control to execute a performance that matches or exceeds those demands. The extreme challenge of marrying the relationship between the environment, the individual, and the requisite skill is what sport is all about and what keeps us coming back time and time again. Ask Michael Jordan, George Foreman, Roger Clemens, and Martina Navratilova how difficult it is to find similar experiences outside of sport, as they continued to pursue sporting excellence when most of their contemporaries had changed careers.

Future Directions

The advent of the 20th century was led by the teachings of James, Freud, and Pavlov, which set the foundation for our current theories of how our minds work. But as we begin the new millennium, there are fantastic revolutionary advances being made in our understanding of the operation of the brain thanks to computer-driven imaging techniques. Early psychologists could only hypothesize about the inner workings of the brain as it was a mysterious, inaccessible organ that was left to the probes of medical students after it had ceased to function. But today through various scanning techniques we are on the verge of unlocking the secrets that to date have forced us to make "best guesses" about the relationship between the mind and body.

Neuroscientists are beginning to gain insight to the field of cognitive science, the study of brain mechanisms responsible for moods, decisions, thoughts, and actions. Richard Restak, in his 2003 book *The New Brain*, claims that by following certain brain-based guidelines, anyone can achieve expert performance in sport, athletics, or academic pursuits. Regardless of whether Restak's predictions prove valid, what is clear is that modern science is helping us study the brain in "real time," which will certainly influence future directions in attention research.

Imagery: Inner Theater Becomes Reality

Shane Murphy

Imagery, or visualization, is the most important of the mental skills required for winning the mind game in sports. Yet it is also the most misunderstood. Perhaps because it can seem so real at times and yet is such a private experience, imagery is often viewed as mysterious or almost magical. In my work with athletes over the years I have seen no other mental skill so often misapplied or wasted. But I have also seen imagery used with tremendous effectiveness by many athletes who understood its power. Athletes need a clear guide to imagery in sport, one that explains what it is and how to use it. This chapter demystifies imagery so that we can learn how to use it in practical ways to successfully manage sport performance.

We know that nearly all athletes and coaches use imagery to help them train and compete. In a survey carried out with my colleagues Doug Jowdy and Shirley Durtschi, we found that 90 percent of the athletes and 94 percent of the coaches we asked at the Olympic Training Center in Colorado Springs used imagery in their sport. Twenty percent of the athletes used imagery every day, and another 40 percent used it three to five days a week. When asked why they used imagery, 80 percent of the athletes said they used it to prepare for competition, 48 percent used it to deal with errors in technique, 44 percent used it to learn new skills, and 40 percent used it for relaxation. When we asked about effectiveness, 97 percent of the athletes and 100 percent of the coaches agreed that imagery does enhance performance. Imagery is nearly universally viewed as an effective way to improve athletic performance.

The Imagery Advantage

Imagery comes in a myriad of forms and has been used in countless ways by athletes and coaches. Two examples illustrate some of the key components of imagery.

Rebecca

Rebecca is an Olympic hammer thrower who uses imagery during her careful preparation for every throw. First, she does some deep breathing to relax the muscles in her body. Then she closes her eyes and imagines the throw she wants to make. She tries to feel all the muscles in her legs, back, and arms that she will use in making the throw. As she feels this throw in her mind, she repeats a phrase to herself that reminds her what to focus on during it, such as "Slow builds power." This reminds her not to rush the throw. Rebecca ends her imagery by mentally "seeing" a good throw land well past those of her competitors. Then she opens her eyes and makes her way to the circle, ready to recreate the throw she has just made in her mind.

Rebecca's imagery shows us that imagery involves more than just seeing an action and a result. Athletes, especially, often *feel* their own involvement in their imagery, reporting sensations similar to the muscle movements they make when playing. Rebecca's imagery gives her confidence before a competition and also reminds her where her focus of attention should be during performance.

Bart

Bart is a competitive sailor who uses imagery to prepare for his races. The morning of a race, he checks the weather and the course layout, and in his mind he sails the course several times, imagining different possibilities. He sees his boat making its way around the course, imagines the tactics that his competitors might use, and devises his own strategies to respond to these moves by his opponents. His imagery seems to be different from Rebecca's because he is not as physically involved in the experience. Also, instead of imagining an ideal competition as Rebecca does, Bart uses much more planning and strategizing. But both athletes use past experiences to mentally prepare for an upcoming competition, and both create a mental picture of a possible future outcome. These elements are common to nearly all forms of imagery used by athletes.

Advances in neuroscience over the past 20 years have helped us understand what imagery is and which parts of the brain it involves. We now know that imagery is a mental process that uses many of the same pathways and areas in the brain as visual perception. The old phrase "I saw it in my mind's eye" is therefore at least partially correct, since when we imagine that we see something, such as a winning touchdown catch, we use some of the same parts of the brain that would be used if we actually saw it.

Imagery, however, is not exactly the same as vision; we can construct in our minds pictures and scenes that never occurred in reality, and we can foresee, or even rehearse, events that have not yet happened. Also, athletes are often active participants in their own images, using imagery not just to "see" an event but to "feel" it. For example, a skier might imagine that he is skiing a downhill run, going as fast as he can, and when he closes his eyes he can experience sensations similar to the feel of skis on snow, his legs bending and turning, and the cold of the wind and snow. Imagery sometimes seems so vivid that it's like an alternative form of experience; the athlete can almost believe that what he or she imagined actually happened. Dreams and daydreams have a lot in common with imagery. Athletes have told me that they have had dreams that were so lifelike that the next day they wondered if it had really happened. But we can't consciously control the images in dreams. This chapter focuses on the kinds of imagery that we experience when we are awake, not dreaming.

Terms Used in the Study of Imagery

Because imagery is a special kind of mental process, sport psychologists have been studying it for many years, and they have defined some of its important aspects. Let's take a look at some of those definitions.

Five senses and beyond   The very word "imagery" implies a picture that we see in our minds, but in fact we can use all five senses in creating mental imagery. We are able to imagine not only how things look, but also how they feel, taste, sound, and smell. Sport psychologists therefore talk about visual imagery, auditory imagery, tactile imagery, and so on. These are known as "modalities." In fact, one of the most important kinds of imagery used by most athletes is what we call kinesthetic imagery—the imagined feeling of movement of the body, as when a golfer imagines how his body will feel hitting a perfect drive right before he steps up to the shot.

Sport psychologists have found that the more kinds of imagery used by athletes, the more vivid the experience seems. An athlete who actually feels herself swing a bat, feels the ball hit the bat, hears the sound of bat on ball, and then sees the ball fly out of the park is likely to experience a more vivid image than someone who merely imagines seeing a home run.

Imagery perspective   Sport psychology researcher Michael Mahoney suggested in 1977 that there is an important difference between imagery in which we feel that we are "actually there" versus imagery in which we feel as if we are "just watching." He called the first kind internal and the latter external, and described them this way:

Athletes who learn to use a variety of imagery modalities such as hearing, touch, taste, and smell, as well as feeling their body in imagination (kinesthetic imagery), experience more vivid life-like imagery experiences.

In external imagery, a person views himself from the perspective of an external observer (much like in home movies). Internal imagery, on the other hand, requires an approximation of the real-life phenomenology such that the person actually imagines being inside his/her body and experiencing those sensations which might be expected in the actual situation (p. 137).

Mahoney studied Olympic gymnasts and found that those who qualified for the Olympics used more internal images than those who did not. He concluded that internal imagery is probably helpful for generating kinesthetic feedback and may lead to better performance results in many cases. I examine this idea later in the chapter.

More recently, sport psychologist Lew Hardy has suggested that we should keep separate the notions of imagery perspective (internal and external) and imagery modality (visual imagery, kinesthetic imagery, and so on). He proposes that imagery is most effective when it is kinesthetic, which can occur from either the internal or external perspectives. For example, research by Aidan Moran and Tadhg MacIntyre showed that some canoeists (about 25 percent) can "feel" the muscle movements involved in paddling when they imagine an external image—seeing themselves rowing, as if watching from the stands. Most other high-level canoeists need to imagine that they are sitting in the boat, paddling, in order to feel their muscles. Coaches and athletes should be aware that both approaches are a natural use of imagery. There is no strong evidence that any type of modality or imagery perspective is "better" than another.

Imagery ability   The final concept to clarify before moving on to a discussion of how imagery works is the assessment of imagery ability. It seems that almost everyone can generate imagery, but there are differences in how easily and effectively they can do so. Two important aspects of imagery ability are vividness and controllability. An image is said to be vivid if it is clear and resembles a real experience in some ways. One athlete, for example, tries to imagine successfully sinking a basketball free throw in the final seconds of a tied game, but she can't do so clearly. She reports that she can't "feel" the ball, can't "see" the net, or can't "hear" the crowd. We say that her imagery is not vivid. On the other hand, some athletes create vivid images that don't turn out the way they want. For example, another athlete can vividly imagine himself standing at the free-throw line and can easily feel the imaginary ball in his hands. But whenever he tries to imagine making a free throw, he sees the ball missing the net. We say that he has low controllability of his image.

Research by sport psychologists consistently shows that athletes tend to gain more performance benefits from using imagery that is vivid and controllable. An important question to consider is whether athletes who report low levels of imagery ability can learn to have more vivid, controllable images. I will examine this question toward the end of this chapter.

Imagery Uses in Training and Competition

Athletes and coaches of all levels speak about the power of imagery to improve their performance. Jack Nicklaus, for example, has said that he always tried to imagine his shot before he actually hit it—not merely imagining the feel of the shot but picturing the flight of the ball after impact and where it landed. He felt this was an important aspect of his success, giving him the confidence to swing freely when standing over the ball. And Gustav Weder, the great Swiss bobsled driver, talked about his use of the power of imagination at the Olympics in Lillehammer. He described how he used visualization to help him win a gold medal in the two-man event and a silver in the four-man event. A year before the Games, Weder traveled to Lillehammer to preview the Olympic bobsled course. He took more than 40 photos of the course, capturing every curve and straight on film and paying particular attention to the entrances and exits of each curve.

When he returned home, he laid out the entire course, photo by photo, on his living room floor. Each day, he sat in front of the photos and practiced driving the course for an hour. He mentally rehearsed, practicing every turn and challenge on that icy, steep slope. By the time Weder got to the Olympic Games, his knowledge of the course, gained through imaginary rehearsal, helped him master the challenges thrown at him. With his partner Donat Acklin, he won the gold medal for Switzerland.

But how does imagery affect athletic performance? How can something that takes place only in the mind, "between your ears" as we commonly say, actually make a difference on the court, on the slopes, or on the field? Psychological theories and sport psychology research suggest that there are several different reasons why imagery improves sport performance.

Mental Rehearsal

Imagery can affect athletic skill performance because it is a physical process. Although we often speak of imagery as being a mental process, this is misleading because it implies that mental processes are separate from physical ones. In fact, mental processes—thoughts, feelings, and images—all originate in the brain and often involve other parts of the body as well, such as the autonomic nervous system and the hormonal system. So "cognitive process" is perhaps a better term to describe imagery—meaning it is a physical process that occurs in the brain and nervous system.

But where in the brain does this cognitive process take place? Thanks to imaging techniques that have been developed in the past 20 years, scientists can now take pictures of the brain that show which areas are activated, or being used, during different cognitive activities. Using imaging techniques such as positron emission tomography (PET) scanning and functional magnetic resonance imaging (fMRI), neuroscientists can look at pictures of the brain of a person who is resting quietly and compare them to pictures taken when that person imagines eating a steak or running a 400-meter race. These pictures show that certain areas of the cerebral cortex are much more active when a person uses imagery than when he or she is resting. Although we still don't know how the neurons and neuronal pathways in the brain combine to create pictures that we "see" in our minds, we do know where these processes take place. The brain becomes very active when imagery is occurring. In his extensive research into the neural mechanisms for control of actions, Jean Decety of the University of Washington Center for Mind, Brain, and Learning has found that when someone imagines starting a movement, various areas of the brain become active, including the premotor cortex as the action is prepared, the prefrontal cortex as the action is initiated, and the cerebellum during the control of movement sequences that require a specific order.

Even more fascinating is the discovery that many of the same areas of the brain that are used during the process of visual perception are also used during visual imagery, which means that imagery shares some of the same brain processes and pathways with actual vision. In cognitive psychology, this realization has led to the theory of "functional equivalence"—the idea that visual images use the same parts of the brain as visual processing. Likewise, when someone imagines a physical activity, such as throwing a ball, some of the same areas of the brain are used as when that person actually throws a ball. This amazing scientific discovery goes a long way toward explaining why imagery has such an effect on performance.

Any athlete who has imagined being the star quarterback in the big championship game knows that imagery can cause some of the same experiences as real life; he is likely to experience the same butterflies in the stomach and sweaty palms that he would have if he were playing in that game. Sport psychologist Richard Suinn did a simple experiment to demonstrate this phenomenon more than 30 years ago. He placed electrodes on the muscles of elite skiers so that he could record muscle activity as he asked them to imagine different events. He found that when he asked the skiers to imagine skiing down a hill, the electrodes showed that many of their leg muscles became active. Although the subjects were lying down, their muscles were still being activated slightly due to the imagery. The timing of the muscle activity matched their descriptions of the courses they visualized.

The theory of functional equivalence has led to the idea that one of the ways in which motor skills and athletic performance are controlled is by the development of motor plans in the brain. Each specific skill, such as serving a tennis ball or making a free throw, is associated with a particular movement pattern located in pathways and neural networks in the brain. Every time the skill is performed, that pathway, or cognitive template, becomes stronger. One of the main roles that imagery plays in sport is to activate these cognitive templates when a specific skill is imagined.

This understanding also shows that the old research comparing physical and mental practice in learning skills was somewhat misguided. Mental practice is not purely mental; imagery activates the same cognitive templates in the brain that are used for athletic performance. Likewise, physical practice is not purely physical; as any athlete can tell you, all performance begins with an image. A boxer enters the ring picturing how he'll knock out his opponent; a baseball pitcher imagines the location and velocity of his next pitch; a gymnast feels his next tumble as he readies himself to begin it. Instead of studying generic "mental practice," sport psychology researchers today attempt to describe the specific images and cognitive processes they ask their subjects to use.

Motivation

Advances in cognitive neuroscience help us understand how imagery helps an athlete learn new skills and improve existing ones. But how does the cognitive model explain the role imagery plays in the life of a 13-year-old figure skater who wakes up at 4:00 A.M. every day and is practicing on the ice by 5:00 A.M., motivated by her images of one day representing her country in the Olympics? As Alan Paivio pointed out in 1985, imagery serves a motivational as well as a cognitive role in the brain. Imagery helps the athlete select goals and also helps fuel the motivation to achieve them. This motivational function of imagery was well described in a 1998 paper by Shelley Taylor and her colleagues from the University of California on the use of imagination as a means of self-regulation:

> . . . The term *imagination* may be used quite specifically to refer to the mental activities that people engage in when they want to get from a current point in time and place to a subsequent one, having accomplished something in between, such as going on a trip or writing a paper. An activity fundamental to this task is mental simulation. Mental simulation is the imitative representation of some event or series of events.

Imagery is closely related to goal setting because it aids in the selection of both direction and intensity of effort. Images of far-off goals bring them closer, and positive images may also serve as secondary reinforcers of effort and persistance.

Ego-oriented athletes tend to want to defeat specific opponents and be seen as winners. They will focus on images of winning specific competitions and bask in the imagined glory of their success. These images influence the direction of their goals—which competitions they enter, what results they want to achieve, and so on. Such imagery also helps fuel the intensity of effort they expend in pursuit of their goals. Repeated imagery of a desired result helps bridge the gap between a far-off outcome and present-day reality, seeming to bring the desired goal closer and motivating the athlete to work hard in order to achieve it.

The process is similar for task-oriented athletes, although the goals are different. These athletes are inclined to imagine themselves making constant progress, setting personal bests, and mastering difficult challenges. These images influence their choice of training programs, type of coach, and competitions that will help them judge their progress. They want to see that image of a better, improved athlete become a reality, which serves as motivation to work hard, seek critical feedback, and make necessary adjustments. So for both goal orientations, imagery serves a motivational function separate from the cognitive functions described previously. Later we will explore how to use the motivational function of imagery to help manage performance.

Confidence

Cognitive-behavioral therapists, who have long recognized the positive effects of imagery on self-confidence, have developed imagery strategies that encourage behavior changes. These imagery strategies, which ask clients to imagine more successful behaviors than they presently exhibit, include systematic desensitization, flooding, coping imagery, implosion, and covert modeling. Indeed, in his comprehensive theory of behavior change, psychologist Albert Bandura states that although successful performance is the greatest influence on confidence, vicarious experience—imagining success or watching someone else achieve success—is also a consistent source of confidence.

Imagery that depicts success and competence has been associated with greater self-confidence. For example, a 1998 research study by Nichola Callow at the

One of the reasons why imagery can be so effective in helping athletes play well is demonstrated in Callow's study of elite badminton players, who improved their confidence when they learned imaery techniques.

© Icon SMI

University of Wales examined an imagery intervention's effects on the confidence of three elite badminton players. A single-subject, multiple-baseline design was used. Once a week for 20 weeks, the players completed Vealey's State Sport Confidence Inventory prior to a match to establish a baseline for their sport confidence. The two-week, six-session intervention consisted of imagery associated with confidence, control, and successful management of challenging situations. The intervention increased sport confidence for two of the players and stabilized the other player's level of confidence.

Does imagery produce performance improvements because the athlete gains increased confidence from imagining success? It is still an open question. Several studies that showed that imagery can improve performance significantly found that the subjects' confidence did not change as their performance changed. Imagery may enhance confidence but it may also change behavior through other means.

Attention and Focus

Sport psychology researchers Deborah Feltz and Dan Landers proposed that mental practice of motor skills may facilitate the development of an "attentional set" for the athlete. They argue that mental practice helps athletes focus on the relevant aspects of performance, thus reducing the risk that attention will be directed toward irrelevant or distracting cues. They attribute the effectiveness of imagery to its effects on concentration.

One of the benefits of the cognitive template that develops when athletic skills are well learned is that athletes with good imagery skills may be better able to access information critical to successful task execution. A vivid image of a well-learned sport skill may enable an athlete to focus quickly and effectively on those elements needed for successful performance. Some researchers suggest that successful athletes learn their skills so well that they become automatic—because they perform the skills with little mental capacity, they do not have to expend a large amount of cognitive effort focusing on performance. Irish psychologist Moran suggests that ". . . researchers in sport psychology can benefit considerably from further collaboration with cognitive psychologists interested in the question of why practice leads to automaticity and improved performance of skills." However, he also states that evidence is insufficient to conclude that "visualization is a valid concentration strategy for athletes."

Emotional Shifts

Imagery also produces changes in emotions that can affect performance. As memorably demonstrated by the actor Adam Sandler in the comedy *The Waterboy*, images of frustration and ridicule can cause an angry emotional reaction. In the fictional movie plot, the waterboy's anger produced an amazing sport performance; however, in real life athletes have just as commonly experienced performance failure due to emotions generated by images of failure, embarrassment, or criticism.

Various kinds of imagery can produce emotional changes in athletes, as measured by self-report and by physiological measures. The effects of emotional imagery on performance, however, are unclear. In some studies, imagery produced anger and arousal but no increases in strength performance. In other studies, imagery reduced anxiety but the athletes showed no performance change. Although imagery is closely related to emotions, producing both cognitive and physiological changes, the relationship between imagery, emotions, and performance is complex and not yet well understood.

Personal Meaning

Every imagery experience has personal meaning to the individual that no one else can fully understand. The meaning of imagery is the least researched area of imagery study in sport psychology; few theorists have incorporated an understanding of it into their models. Yet it has the potential to affect the athlete every time he or she uses imagery.

The brain is largely organized through the process of association. Most of our learning and memories appear to be constructed via associational processes; that is, new memories or experiences are stored in the brain by associating them with existing concepts. Even the simplest experiences, such as hearing a song on the radio, often recall memories and feelings because our experiences (e.g., hearing the song) are stored in a web of interrelated memories and events (where we were when we first heard the song, the feelings we experienced when listening to the song with others, and so on). An important feature of imagery is that it tends to have more associations than other cognitive processes, which explains its effectiveness as a cognitive template for skilled performance and why it often has associations that were not expected or intended by the person imagining.

For example, psychologists have shown that people's memory for a list of unfamiliar words is much greater if they are asked to create an image of each word than if they are asked to speak the word aloud. The image creates more associations for learning the word than does saying the word. Similarly, a cognitive template for a movement pattern is likely to be better remembered during competition if it is imagery-based rather than offered as a set of verbal instructions. Although the many associations of images are a benefit when used to improve performance, they also make imagery more complex and difficult to understand and study.

One theorist who has considered this issue deeply is Akhter Ahsen, who proposed that a full understanding of imagery can be obtained only when three aspects of imagery are considered. His triple code model is a useful guide for anyone using imagery. Ahsen suggests that imagery experiences can be described in three ways: The *image* (I) is similar to a cognitive template—a set of sensations arising in the brain; the *somatic response* (S) is the set of physiological reactions that occur in response to the image; and the *meaning* (M) is the unique significance of the imagery to the individual. At the very least, this model suggests that sport psychologists and coaches who use imagery with athletes should always ask for feedback about each of the ISM aspects.

I realized the importance of obtaining this kind of feedback early in my career, when I was working with young figure skaters. One of my clients was a talented young skater who used a specific imagery routine to help him prepare for competitive performances. As he waited to step onto the ice for the start of his program, he would close his eyes and imagine a glowing ball of energy floating in front of him. He then took a deep breath and imagined the ball of energy moving inside his body, where it radiated a feeling of calm and energy. He would open his eyes and take that calm attitude and intense energy into his skating program. I thought a similar imagery routine might benefit a group of young skaters I was working with, so I wrote out a script similar to his and taught it to the skaters during one of our mental-skills training sessions. I suggested they practice this imagery and use it before their long program practices that week.

The puzzled looks on the faces of some of the youngsters prompted me to ask one of them what the imagery experience had been like for her. She described it as "seeing a tremendously bright ball of energy in front of me, so bright that it blinded me. I couldn't see, and when I tried to skate out onto the ice I crashed into the wall of the rink." I sat there stunned as the giggles of the other skaters subsided, and all I could think to do was to ask the next skater what he had imagined. He reported that the glowing energy ball "was sucked down into my stomach, and in there it exploded. I had a big hole in my tummy and I couldn't skate." I began to realize (I'm a quick learner!) that my imagery training hadn't gone as planned. The next skater said that in her imagery the energy ball became a helium-filled balloon, and when she took a deep breath it left her speaking in a high-pitched squeak, at which point she fell over laughing. As I continued around the circle, each skater reported a very different imagery experience, and the results were not what I had intended. Although the experience was embarrassing, it taught me a valuable lesson about asking for feedback whenever I use imagery training. Every athlete has a personal history, experiences, fears, and beliefs that color his or her interpretation of the imagery so that no two of them will have the same experience, even if the script is exactly the same.

In summary, imagery's combination of psychological processes enables it to change people's behavior, and in sport, to have a large role in managing performance. The cognitive function of imagery is critical—understanding imagery depends on knowledge about the way the brain functions—but imagery also influences motivation, confidence, emotions, and attention. Finally, each image has meaning specific to the individual, which determines the effect it will have on that person.

Imagery and Improved Performance Skills

As the examples of Rebecca and Bart showed earlier, athletes use many different types of imagery for a variety of purposes. Let's look at the main purposes of imagery use in sport.

Learning New Skills

Most of us can remember a time during the learning of a new sport skill, such as hitting a golf ball or riding a bicycle, when the necessary movements seemed painfully unfamiliar. I remember my first golf coach laboriously reminding me to turn at the hips, keep my head over the ball, and shift my weight as I struggled to learn how to execute a good golf swing. For a long time, it seemed as if the golf swing would remain a series of disjointed parts, performed with great effort and no fluidity. But with repeated practice, I could stand over the ball and "feel" the movements I needed to make to strike the ball cleanly; that moment marked a turning point in the development of my golf game. I had captured an image of what my swing should feel like and no longer had to rely on verbal reminders.

This kind of experience suggests that imagery is not only a useful approach for learning new athletic skills, but it is also probably necessary for skilled performance. Sport psychologists have studied what we call "mental practice" in great depth. As far back as the 1930s, researchers such as Howard Perry (1939) and Ron Sackett (1934) were studying the use of what they called "imaginary practice" or "symbolic rehearsal" in both the acquisition and retention of physical skills. Mental practice has proven to be an effective technique for improving performance, providing more benefits for cognitive tasks such as learning a maze than for primarily motor tasks such as balancing on a moving platform. Cognitive tasks are activities that require making plans ahead of time or coordinating several actions. When Bart makes a race strategy, it is clearly a cognitive task, but Rebecca's rehearsal of the proper timing of her hammer throw is a cognitive task also, despite its primarily physical nature.

That mental practice is an effective tool for improving many kinds of performance is not surprising if we recall that one of the major effects of imagery is to strengthen the cognitive templates in the brain that govern athletic skills. Thus, imagery is an important aspect of skill learning.

Retaining Skills Over Time

Once athletes have learned a skill, they face the challenge of maintaining it. Since an important part of any sport skill is the cognitive template for it, activating that template regularly will help maintain the skill. The regular rehearsal of learned skills, with the goal of retention, is another widely used imagery strategy among athletes.

A story that describes the skill-retention function of imagery is that of the American colonel held for several years as a prisoner of war. To relieve the tedium of his incarceration, he plays a round of golf in his mind, shot by shot, every day for the duration of his captivity. When finally released, he comes home and is invited to play at his home course, where he goes out and shoots par his first time out, despite having had no practice or play for several years. Research that demonstrates this function of imagery was done in 1985 by William Meacci and Ed Price, who studied young golfers learning to putt. Those who were taught to use an imagery-rehearsal strategy in addition to physical practice performed better than those who used imagery and visualization alone and those who only physically practiced. Interestingly, part of their visualization training was what they called "body rehearsal"—the learners made putting movements with their bodies but did not actually hit a ball. All learners were tested again after a period of time to measure retention of the skill, and all three groups (imagery rehearsal alone, physical practice alone, and the combined group) did better than a control group that received no training. Again, this finding supports the notion that imagery is effective in maintaining sport skills over time. I have often seen professional athletes use a similar rehearsal strategy.

Preperformance Rituals

Rebecca used imagery to help her achieve her best in the hammer throw, but she was neither learning the skill nor trying to maintain it. She believed that mental imagery immediately before performance helped her achieve her smoothest, best throw. Researchers have suggested that imagining a sport skill immediately prior to performance helps by "priming" the movement—that is, the cognitive template is readied and is immediately available for activation. As we discussed earlier, such preperformance rehearsal is also likely to benefit the athlete by increasing confidence and concentration.

Developing Strategies and Plans

When Bart prepares his race-day strategies, he is not interested in learning new skills or performing skills he knows well. His focus is on a more general aspect of competition that assumes he has the skills to carry out his plans. He uses imagery to develop a plan of attack, a strategy, that will help him make quick, effective decisions.

Researchers have found that using imagery for planning can help with rehearsing football plays, devising wrestling strategies, and planning entire canoe slalom races. In one study by Bob Rotella and his colleagues, successful skiers developed a visual image of the course after previewing it. In the time between inspecting the course and reaching the starting gate, they imagined and planned effective strategies for skiing the course. Less successful skiers, on the other hand, simply tried to maintain positive thoughts before racing.

A three-time Olympian I worked with gave me a good description of how he uses imagery to plan race strategy:

> It's as if I carry around a set of tapes in my mind. I play them occasionally, rehearsing different race strategies. Usually I imagine the race going the way I want—I set my pace and stick to it. But I have "problem" tapes I use as well—sometimes I imagine that a competitor has gone out very fast and I need to catch him. I use an image of me with a fishing pole, hooking him ahead of me and then reeling him in. I need to be flexible in races, able to adjust my strategy to whatever situation arises. Imagery helps me do that most effectively.

The great advantage of imagery for planning tactics and strategies is that it allows the athlete to try several approaches to the same problem in order to see which one makes the most sense or "feels" right. Some researchers suggest that the more experience an athlete has in a sport, the more useful imagery planning is.

Reducing Competitive Anxiety

Imagery has a long tradition of being used by psychologists to calm and relax anxious clients. Many sport psychologists have used imagery in a similar way to combat the negative effects of competitive anxiety on performance. The most direct use of imagery for anxiety reduction is to imagine a calm, peaceful scenario and allow the resulting physiological sensations to reduce the sympathetic nervous system arousal that accompanies anxiety (see chapter 5 for an explanation of the psychophysiology of anxiety). Many athletes use some variant of the "favorite place" or "safe spot" image, such as relaxing in a beach paradise, a peaceful meadow, or a favorite room. However, determining when to use such imagery to combat pregame jitters is critical. Using relaxing imagery in the days leading up to or even the night before an event is a good way to lessen the energy-draining effects of prolonged anxiety, but an athlete who becomes deeply relaxed immediately before a competitive performance risks being unable to re-energize in time to compete successfully. Trial-and-error experimentation is probably best for athletes who want to find out how they respond to relaxation before an event. I advise my clients not to try a new approach, such as an imagery program, during important competitions. It is best to gradually implement new mental skills during training and practice and to fine-tune and modify the approach during minor competitions.

Psyching Up

Sport psychologists Tony Shelton and Michael Mahoney worked with many weightlifters to determine which psychological methods they used to prepare for performance. They found that athletes referred to this preparation process as "psyching up," and that imagery was a commonly used method, along with positive self-talk, control of attention, and preparatory arousal. Fifty-four percent of the weightlifters studied used a combination of these techniques.

If imagery is to be used to increase arousal prior to performance, theory and research suggest that it include kinesthetic cues and images of physiological arousal. Heart rate, for example, increases during imagery of sports scenes when the instructions contain phrases such as "You feel your heart begin to pound" and "You feel butterflies in your stomach." However, athletes must be careful not to become *over*aroused. Imagery that makes them angry, for example, might increase arousal but might also distract them and make concentration on the crucial aspects of performance difficult. (Anger and its role in sport are discussed in detail in chapter 6.)

Stress Management

Imagery can be a useful way to prepare for stressful sport situations. An athlete preparing for an Olympic Games, for example, may never have experienced an actual Olympic competition, but through imagery he can visualize himself attending the opening ceremonies and competing in his event. The athlete imagines how he would feel in such a situation; if he feels anxious and stressed by the imagery, the real-life experience is likely to be similarly stressful. Imagery gives the athlete the opportunity to mentally rehearse effective coping strategies, such as deep breathing, muscle relaxation, positive self-talk, and changing the focus of concentration. Preparing to handle stressful situations in this way allows him to approach the situation with greater confidence and feel less stress during the event.

Enhancing Confidence

The interesting case of a young athlete, Jenny, illustrates the use of imagery to affect self-confidence. Jenny, a top-10-ranked national table tennis player, consulted me because she had a problem defeating higher-ranked opponents. Her lack of confidence when competing against these individuals, despite possessing the skills necessary to defeat them, translated into unusually poor performances against good players. My strategy was to ask Jenny to visualize defeating specific higher-rated opponents. I asked her to imagine as vividly as possible a match against each of them. She was to imagine playing well, see and feel herself executing the winning shots needed to gain victory and end each match in triumph, and then imagine how she would feel and how her opponent, coach, parents, and others would react. In keeping with Bandura's theory on behavior change, I wanted her experiences to be as vicariously realistic as possible in order to generate maximum increases in self-confidence. Within weeks, she had achieved first-time victories against several high-ranked opponents. She attributed her success to a newfound confidence generated by her imagery rehearsal.

Athletes can use imagery as a performance boost immediately before competition, like a diver who visualizes a perfect dive while standing on the springboard, or over a period of time as they build a better self-image, like a backup quarterback who uses imagery to rehearse what he would do if he had to step into the game and take over the team leadership.

Enhancing Motivation

Chapters 1 and 2 describe two common types of goals: result-focused (ego-based) and mastery-focused (task-based) goals. Let's examine how imagery can be used to achieve both types of goals.

Ego-oriented athletes tend to want to defeat specific opponents and be seen as winners. They will focus on images of winning specific competitions and bask in the imagined glory of their success. These images influence the direction of their goals—which competitions they enter, what results they want to achieve, and so on. Such imagery also helps fuel the intensity of effort they expend in pursuit of their goals. Repeated imagery of a desired result helps bridge the gap between a far-off outcome and present-day reality, seeming to bring the desired goal closer and motivating the athlete to work hard in order to achieve it.

Even ego-oriented athletes, however, may wish to increase their motivation using more task-oriented goals such as making constant progress, setting personal bests, and mastering difficult challenges. These images influence their choice of training programs, type of coach, and competitions that will help them judge their progress. They want to see that image of a better, improved athlete become a reality, which serves as motivation to work hard, seek critical feedback, and make necessary adjustments. Imagery can serve a powerful motivational function of helping athletes become more task oriented in order to be more successful.

Improving Concentration

Imagery can be a useful concentration strategy both for performance of discrete skills and for more global strategic approaches to competition. When used before performance, mental rehearsal of a skill can direct an athlete's attention to its most important elements. For example, a golfer working on a better hip turn and on keeping the club's swing plane parallel to the target line might imagine that he is swinging his club in a narrow room and must avoid hitting the wall. This image focuses his attention on the swing plane in an effective manner. In addition, he might feel the torque produced by his body turning against the resistance of his legs as the coiling of energy in a giant spring, to be unleashed on the downward swing. Good coaches use imagery in this fashion on a regular basis, seeking to connect the athlete's experience to the new skills by using powerful and involving imagery. Although evidence has not yet established that such imagery reliably produces improvement in concentration, the experiences of many coaches and athletes suggest that it does.

On a more global level, an athlete who needs to remember a complex series of maneuvers and tactics in a sport like sailing or skiing might benefit from imagined rehearsal of the key moments in the upcoming competition. Some snowboarders, for example, imagine the entire run on an alpine course, seeing and feeling themselves dealing with difficult turns, bad snow conditions, and giant moguls. They do this, in part, to remind themselves of how they should approach the course. Once rehearsed in imagination, athletes find it easier to replicate that approach when faced with the real challenge. Memory research shows that imagery does indeed lead to better memory than nearly all other learning approaches because of its ability to integrate the cognitive, physical, and emotional aspects of a performance in a single experience.

Rehabbing From Injury

Injured athletes can use imagery to maintain skills, motivation, and attention during the rehabilitation period. For example, a basketball player with an ACL injury who is unable to play for nine months can mentally rehearse basketball skills such as free throws, passing, and defending on a regular, if not daily, basis. No concrete research shows that using imagery results in an easier transition back to playing after rehab, but my experience with many athletes at the Olympic Training Center (OTC) suggests that it is effective. In addition to strengthening cognitive skill templates, imagery may increase the motivation of athletes. Increased motivation benefits the athlete if it leads to greater adherence to and effort in the rehab program.

Building Teamwork

One of the least-studied areas of imagery use is in building teamwork. Many coaches use imagery with their teams to make practice drills more interesting and to rehearse team goals and objectives. Because imagery is so personal, it is difficult to use in large group settings; however, it can be done effectively with appropriate communication and feedback. For example, I observed a soccer coach at the OTC using imagery with all the team members involved in a corner kick. He asked each player to imagine his own role in the execution of the play. The athletes were asked to signal the end of the play in their imagination by raising their hands, and remarkably, all hands were raised nearly in unison. And the length of the imaginary play corresponded closely with the actual length of the play on the field, which suggests that athletes with well-developed skills can use imagery to practice their timing and positional play in team settings. No doubt other beneficial uses of imagery for building team cohesion can be developed.

Improving Your Imagery Ability

Can training in imagery technique improve the vividness and controllability of the experience? Research with non-athletes suggests that it can, but this question needs more serious study with athletes. Psychologists report that the types of instructions that people are given and that paying attention to certain aspects of imagery can make the experience more realistic and powerful for the visualizer. In other words, the more you focus on how your body responds during the imagery, the more vivid the experience will be. The more you focus on the external aspects (what you see), the less powerful the image is likely to be in changing your behavior. The following exercises, which I use with my clients to help them develop confidence in their use of imagery, should help you improve the vividness and controllability of your imagery.

The first step in successful visualization is learning how to make your imagination as vivid and realistic as possible. The best way to do this is by involving all the senses. Let's begin by working on the basic five senses; however, other aspects of imagery must also be used to reach maximum benefit.

Sight　Athletes vary greatly in their ability to use visual stimuli in imaginary experiences. Some can see in vivid color, in three dimensions, and with great detail; others can imagine only the vaguest outlines, without color or detail. But all improve with practice.

To practice visual imagery, imagine an event in which you want to perform well. Try to see as many details as possible. Recreate it in your mind, using past experience as a guide. See the people in attendance, and imagine the colors and sights of the competition. Then put yourself into the image as if you were really there. You may already have done this by instinct. If you haven't, practice that now by imagining that you are walking around the event. What can you see as you look around you? What scenery are you seeing? Does this imagery event seem realistic? Keep practicing until you can imagine the experience in detail.

Hearing　The ability to "see" pictures in your mind is only part of the power of imagination. Elite athletes also make use of the other senses, which, for some athletes, are stronger and more vivid than sight.

Many people can hear sounds during an imagined experience. Try it now. Can you recall the voice of your coach prior to competition? Can you hear what he or she is saying? Notice the voice pattern, the rise and fall of the speech. Add other sounds to your imagery to make it more vivid. A tennis player, for example, might imagine the sound of the ball on the racket and her grunts of exertion as she chases down her opponent's shots.

Music can be a particularly powerful imagined experience. I worked with an archer who imagined listening to one of his favorite passages from a Beethoven symphony during breaks in the shooting. This music made him feel calm and strong.

Smell   The sense of smell tends to evoke strong memories. Can you remember a situation where the scents associated with that time or place were particularly vivid?

A professional baseball player I worked with always used images based on the sense of smell when he rehearsed pitching mechanics in his mind. The smell of newly cut grass, the tangy smell of tobacco juice, and the leathery smell of the glove all were used to make his mental picture particularly clear and vivid. "If I can't smell it," he used to say, "then I'm not really there."

Touch   Touch can trigger another rich source of memories. An elite swimmer I worked with would focus her concentration before performance with imagery that used the tactile sensations of the water as she dove into the pool at the race's start and then felt the water rushing past her as she swam powerfully down the lane. Are there opportunities in your sport to add the sense of touch to make your imagery more vivid (e.g. the feel of holding a racquet, or the impact of your opponent's body as you tackle them)?

Taste   Many athletes use the sense of taste to create more powerful imagery. Swimmers remember the taste of the chlorine in the water as they swim up and down the pool. A boxer I knew psyched himself up for fights by remembering the taste of blood in his mouth after a hard punch. I have worked with runners who prepare for a tough race by recalling the taste of salt as they sweat through the tough task of staying on pace. As you explore the power of your imagination, try enhancing the situations you create in your mind by using taste.

Now that we've covered the five basic senses, let's discuss perhaps the most important sense for athletes—the kinesthetic sense, or what we call the "feel" of sport skills.

Feel   Athletes tell me that recollecting the feelings they experience as their body moves through its performance is the most important part of any image they rehearse. Chuck, a professional golfer, went through a little ritual every time he hit the ball. After he took his stance and settled on his grip, he imagined the feel of a good shot with the club. Next, he would concentrate on making the same good swing as he hit the real ball. It took extra effort to do this every time, especially when he was hitting practice balls, but it made Chuck a very consistent golfer—and a very successful one.

Getting the feel of a race, competition, or even a particular move may involve actually moving around while imagining the event. Gold-medal-winning kayaker Norm Bellingham told me that he sits up and pretends he has a paddle in his hands as he rehearses the strategy of an upcoming race. Elite athletes place a great deal of emphasis on mastering their sport by getting the right "feel" for the skills they practice. In order to perform a move such as a vault or a dive under the pressure of competition, the athlete must know what a perfect vault or dive feels like. Then she knows exactly what she must do. When she goes out in competition, she attempts to perform the move exactly as she pictured it.

Emotions   The last component of imagery that makes it vivid is the emotional experience that accompanies it. Psychologist Peter Lang of the University of Florida argues that imagery loses its power to change behavior if the visualizer does not experience the physiological changes that occur as a result of the emotions felt during imagery.

A simple exercise can demonstrate the extra dimension that emotions add to imagery. First, remember a winning experience you have had recently. Use all five of your senses, as we practiced earlier, to recreate that picture in your mind as clearly as possible. Where were you? What was happening? Who was there? What sounds do you remember as part of that event? What were you doing after you won?

Now add the emotional content to this imagery. Remember how happy you felt. Focus on the excitement and allow yourself to experience it again. What sensations and changes do you notice in your body as you experience this joy? Does your heart pound in your chest? Do you feel extra energy? Are there butterflies in your stomach, or is it a different feeling entirely? Do you feel like crying because you are so happy? Allow yourself to experience those emotions for a moment or two more.

Before we continue, can I ask you a question? How do you feel right now? If you are like most of my clients, the feelings you generated in your imagery will stay with you in the present moment. You will notice that the physical sensations of the emotion remain even after you stop imagining the situation. This remarkable ability to create real emotions via imagery can help you learn to handle emotional and stressful situations successfully.

Think of your imagination as you would a muscle—say, your biceps. If you never give your biceps a workout, they'll end up flabby, out of shape. But if you use them often, they'll be in great condition. Your imagination works the same way. The more you use it, the stronger it will be when you need it.

Now that we have discussed how imagery works, how to use it in sports, and how to improve it, it is time to turn to an important aspect of mental-skills training: the measurement of imagery.

Evaluating Imagery and Its Effectiveness

Imagery assessment can help determine how much imagery ability an athlete has, how often he or she uses imagery, for what purposes, and how comfortable he or she is with it. An athlete who discovers he has strong imagery ability will want to use it to enhance performance. Those athletes who have low ability may need to improve it before they attempt to change behaviors via imagery. Also, imagery assessment can provide an objective measure of the progress of mental-skills training. Athletes or coaches who have invested time and energy in imagery training deserve access to methods of tracking changes in imagery use or ability. Finally, imagery assessment may help to target specific problems or challenges that an athlete needs to overcome in order to improve. Low imagery ability does not mean that an athlete cannot be successful in his or her chosen sport, but infrequent or incorrect use of imagery coupled with a specific problem, such as too much precompetition anxiety, may provide a starting point for change. For example, a snowboarder who immediately before competition has vivid images of falling and failing may experience anxiety as a result, and the accompanying tension and worry may inhibit high performance.

Imagery Assessments Methods

A great variety of imagery-assessment instruments have been developed over the past 40 years, but many of them are difficult to administer and score, making them unlikely to be of use to anyone but sport psychology researchers. Thus, you may read about research using the Vividness of Visual Imagery Questionnaire or Gordon's Test of Imagery Control, but these measures have little practical use in the modern world of sport. However, two recently developed instruments are much more useful. These are the Sport Imagery Questionnaire (SIQ) developed by Craig Hall and his colleagues, and the Multidimensional Mental Imagery Scale (MMIS), developed by Dianne Vella-Brodrick. Both scales have been impressively researched and are well suited to measuring imagery use by athletes.

The SIQ is a 27-item scale with five subscales measuring motivation-specific, motivation-general (arousal and mastery), cognitive-specific, and cognitive-general imagery. These five scales correspond to theoretically important dimensions of imagery identified by Hall and his colleagues. The MMIS is a 21-item questionnaire that yields scores on three subscales: general factors, sensory skills, and controllability. As we have seen, controllability is an important aspect of imagery ability, and sensory skills are highly related to the vividness of imagery. Both the SIQ and the MMIS are sophisticated psychological instruments that should be administered and scored only by trained personnel.

A third potentially useful instrument is the Test of Performance Strategies (TOPS), a mental-skills assessment device I developed with my colleagues Lew

Hardy and Pat Thomas. Imagery is one of the eight main mental skills measured by the TOPS, which has the added advantage that it measures imagery use separately for both practice and competition situations. It too is a specialized device that requires extensive sport psychology training in order to use it effectively. All three of these instruments are excellent ways to help assess imagery ability, track improvement in imagery use, and identify imagery-related performance problems.

For coaches and athletes who simply wish to measure imagery use on a regular basis, much in the same way they log physical training sessions, I suggest using the questions in figure 8.1. These questions are not part of a research-based psychological assessment, but they do provide an excellent starting point in measuring frequency and effectiveness of imagery. Any athlete or coach could use these or similar questions. In fact, many athletes I work with use them as part of their weekly training logs, tracking their progress over the course of a season.

To use the tool, begin with goal setting. Set specific goals for the use of imagery in your training sessions. On a 1-to-10 scale, rate how effective this imagery is in improving your training. (For example, you might use imagery to rehearse new skills or to stay motivated throughout a workout.) Keep weekly records of your training progress using imagery.

Next, set specific goals for your use of imagery in competitions. On a 1-to-10 scale, rate how effective it is in improving your competitive performance. (For example, you might use imagery to build confidence before an event or to help focus on your tactics.) Keep records of your progress using imagery in competitions.

Potential Problems in Imagery Use

Imagery is a complex process that is not always easy to use. The work of Ahsen suggests that an image's meaning significantly affects the outcome of imagery use and that it is not easy to predict how an individual athlete will respond to imagery training. Rob Woolfolk, Alan Budney, and I discovered that the types of images that are used can influence the direction of performance changes. We asked subjects in some studies to use negative imagery, that is, to imagine performance failure immediately prior to action. We consistently found that negative images resulted in poorer performance. Indeed, the negative effect of these images was sometimes stronger than the positive effects of appropriate imagery. In another series of studies, we looked at various types of emotional imagery used by athletes attempting a strength task. We found that relaxing images consistently hurt strength performance, and that angry emotional imagery made some athletes stronger but others weaker. The ones who improved their strength performance with anger imagery were those who responded the most physiologically, as measured by diastolic blood pressure.

Our research findings are supported by the reports of athletes who experienced images of failure or disaster immediately before competitions in which they performed badly. In the previously mentioned survey study at the OTC, we

Place a checkmark next to each of the following uses of imagery that you employ

Rehearsing my athletic skills   _____

Planning my strategy   _____

Staying calm   _____

Staying focused   _____

Building my confidence   _____

Psyching up   _____

Rehabbing an injury   _____

Managing pain   _____

Relaxing   _____

On a scale from 1 to 10, rate how vivid your imagery is for the following tasks. If you did not use imagery for the purpose listed, place a "0" in the box:

1	2	3	4	5	6	7	8	9	10
Not at all vivid				Somewhat vivid					Very vivid

Rehearsing my athletic skills   _____

Planning my strategy   _____

Staying calm   _____

Staying focused   _____

Building my confidence   _____

Psyching up   _____

Rehabbing an injury   _____

Managing pain   _____

Relaxing   _____

On a scale from 1 to 10, rate how controllable your imagery is for the following tasks. If you did not use imagery for the purpose listed, place a "0" in the box:

1	2	3	4	5	6	7	8	9	10
No control				Medium control					Excellent control

Rehearsing my athletic skills   _____

Planning my strategy   _____

Staying calm   _____

Staying focused   _____

Building my confidence   _____

Psyching up   _____

Rehabbing an injury   _____

Managing pain   _____

Relaxing   _____

Figure 8.1   Keeping track of athlete imagery.

found that 35 percent of the athletes and 25 percent of the coaches surveyed gave personal examples of imagery use that hurt performance. Athletes and coaches should carefully monitor the effects of implementing any imagery-training program, especially if the imagery is novel or is used in unfamiliar ways. They should keep track of practice and competition performance both before and after imagery training has begun and ensure that over time the performance changes are positive. Also, coaches should ask athletes individually what their imagery experience is like. Some who have a poor experience and are shy or do not want to disappoint their coaches may not tell them about their problems with imagery. Athletes need to hear loud and clear that everyone is different and that not everyone uses imagery in the same way. Some of the causes of problems in using imagery effectively are as follows.

Anxiety   Athletes who tend to become overexcited before competition may find that imagery of an upcoming event increases their anxiety beyond manageable levels. One athlete in the OTC survey reported that "[the imagery] got me so pumped up and excited that I couldn't do anything." Such athletes may need to first learn mental skills that help them reduce their anxiety. When working with such athletes, I suggest two practical steps. First, I instruct them not to imagine the competition immediately before performance. If they do begin to think about the upcoming event and feel their anxiety increasing, I have them switch to a rehearsed image that they find calming, such as picturing themselves in an everyday workout. Second, if they feel their anxiety increasing, they use relaxation skills we have practiced such as deep breathing and muscle relaxation (see chapter 5).

Distractibility   Athletes who have a difficult time controlling their attention at competitions may find that *what* they imagine is critical in helping or hurting their efforts to focus. Imagery that directs an athlete's focus to irrelevant factors may hurt performance. For example, a golfer who is leading the tournament with nine holes to play may become distracted and perform poorly if he starts entertaining images of hoisting the winner's trophy. Many athletes find that imagery rehearsal of their performance is more helpful than merely imagining a positive outcome of competition.

Lack of imagery control   Athletes who report control problems with their imagery may be prone to experiencing unwanted images (for example, of failure). Athletes and coaches should use care in employing imagery rehearsals when athletes lack confidence in their imagery.

Overconfidence   Athletes are often advised to imagine a perfect performance prior to competition. However, in some cases this might lead an athlete to overlook small details of preparation that might be necessary for superior performance. Another athlete in the OTC survey said, "Sometimes when I see myself being too good, then things don't go well. It's a cocky attitude that overcomes me."

Nearly all problems with imagery use can be overcome with care and a thoughtful approach. Experience suggests that a useful way to deal with negative or uncontrolled images is to replace them with a positive image or to change from an imagery-based approach to another mental skill, such as self-talk or relaxation. If an athlete has problems with sport imagery or a coach lacks confidence in using imagery or other mental skills with his athletes, then a good option is to consult a sport psychologist. Sport psychologists have had special training in the workings of the mind and most use imagery frequently in their work with athletes, so they are a good resource for those struggling with performance concerns. (For guidance on finding an appropriate consultant, see chapter 16.)

Future Directions

Two major developments are likely to shape the future of imagery use by athletes. First, advances in brain-imaging devices and processes will continue to expand our understanding of the brain's functioning during cognitive processes, including imagery. As scientists gain deeper knowledge of cognitive processes, psychological theories of imagery will advance. Sport psychologists will benefit from a better understanding of cognitive templates of motor functioning and how motor-skill development occurs. Athletes and coaches will benefit from sport psychologists who have a better understanding of the cognitive control processes of skilled athletic performance. Imagery-training programs and imagery use are likely to become more specifically targeted to take advantage of how the cognitive control system functions.

Second, athletes and coaches will continue to benefit from increasing access to the imagery knowledge base being developed by sport psychologists. In the past, many athletes used imagery because it felt natural or because a friend or coach taught them how to use it. But imagery use remained largely a trial-and-error process for most athletes. This chapter summarizes a large body of knowledge about sports imagery gained from research and application and outlines a comprehensive approach to using imagery to manage sport performance. As access improves, coaches and athletes will be in a better position to choose, develop, and apply an effective program to their specific sport situation and to understand the problems they might encounter. In the years ahead, imagery training will be widely used as a fundamental aspect of athletic skill development and competition preparation. And it will be closely integrated with physical training and practice—as it should be.

Interactive Skills

When dealing with people, it is important to remember that everyone does not see things from the same perspective. Understanding someone's viewpoint is the first step to effective coaching. Unfortunately, the perspective of others is too often overlooked.

Jack Gibson, all-time great rugby coach

What makes a great team great? Why is it that we so often see teams made up of great players beaten by average players who make up a great team? These are the issues covered in part III. Surely the most striking example of tremendous teamwork and coaching was the winning 1980 U.S. Olympic ice hockey team, whose story was the subject of the movie *Miracle*. The team of mostly collegiate players, including nine from the University of Minnesota, was clearly one of the least talented groups in the Olympics. In fact, coach Herb Brooks told his players before the competition, "Gentlemen, you don't have enough talent to win on talent alone." Yet this group of scrappy youngsters (average age of 22) went on to defy the odds and defeat their more heavily favored opponents, including the seemingly invincible team from the USSR in the semifinals, 4-3. Their story illustrates how good coaching, communication, and leadership can result in a team that transcends the individual pieces that constitute it.

No one understands the issues involved in leadership better than sport psychologist Jim Loehr, who has spent his career studying and putting into practice the principles that make a person mentally tough. Chapter 9 not only explains what makes great leadership happen but also shows coaches and athletes how to become more effective in that role. In chapter 10, "Teamwork: For the Good of the Whole," the team of Tracy L. Veach and Jerry R. May explain the dynamics of teamwork and show how to build an effective team, based on their years of experience with both Olympic sports and leading business groups. Speaking of great teams, the terrific team of Charles J. Hardy, Kevin L. Burke, and

R. Kelly Crace break down the fundamentals of exemplary coaching and provide tips on how to improve communication in chapter 11. If you do any coaching, at any level, chapter 11 is one you can't afford to miss.

Leadership: Full Engagement for Success

Jim Loehr

Jack Welch served as chairman and CEO of General Electric (GE) for 20 years, during which time he led GE to unprecedented success in the business world. When asked where he learned his extraordinary leadership skills, he credits both his mother and team sports as his two most important influences. The personal and interpersonal dynamics of competitive sport provide rich opportunities to develop leadership skills that are, in many ways, prerequisites for success in life. Competitive sport can be a powerful laboratory for teaching discipline, social skills, conflict resolution, responsibility, attention skills, adversity management, goal setting, and leadership. Leadership development is clearly one of the real benefits of sport participation. In community, elementary, high school, or collegiate programs, the opportunities for learning leadership skills are limitless. A foundational goal of all youth sport should be the healthy development of the athlete as a person, an important dimension of which is leadership.

Types of Leadership

The question of what enables people to inspire commitment, loyalty, confidence, and extraordinary performance in others is at the core of personal leadership. Among the countless definitions of leadership that exist both within and outside sport, a common theme is the positive impact that individuals can have on group dynamics relative to a team objective. Noel Tichy, renowned authority on leadership from the University of Michigan, defines leadersip as "crafting a new vision and aligning people to it in a way that they will want to attain it." Researchers Henry Tosi, John Rizzo, and Stephen Carroll define leadership as the interpersonal influence that occurs when one person gains compliance from another toward achieving organizationally desired goals. Similarly, Martin Chemers conceptualizes leadership as the process by which one individual guides a group toward a collective goal, action, or accomplishment.

Well-known leadership models that have been developed in the past decade focus attention on particular aspects of leadership and its development. Peter Drucker's model, articulated in his book *Managing for the Future*, asserts that the essence of effective leadership is achieving the desired performance outcome. Great leadership, he argues, involves setting goals, priorities, and standards around a clearly defined mission. Drucker places the highest value on measurable outcomes. In *Principle-Centered Leadership*, author Stephen Covey's model places values and ethics at the core of effectiveness. He argues that great leadership is principle driven and that great leaders' trust, integrity, and respect for others is the foundation for their effectiveness. For Warren Bennis, University of Southern California professor and leadership scholar, the central issue is managing adversity. He claims that the skills required to conquer adversity and emerge stronger and more committed during difficult times are the also those that make for extraordinary leadership. Emotional intelligence expert Dan Goleman agrees that managing mood (of the leader and those who are being led) is the prime consideration in effective leadership. For him, a leader's "emotional style" plays a central role in the success of any mission.

In 1999, Packianathan Chelladurai, a professor at Ohio State University, proposed a multidimensional model of leadership behavior focused on training and instruction, social support, positive feedback, democratic behavior, and automatic behavior. He argues that alignment of situational factors, leader's qualities, leadership styles, and follower's qualities determine leadership effectiveness. The greater the degree of alignment, the greater the degree of effectiveness.

Several core competencies consistently appear in the literature about leadership, and they cluster around four themes.

Theme 1: Spiritual leadership   Core spiritual competencies include the ability to clearly define the team mission, vision, and goals; to recruit commitment and energy (motivation) to the overall mission by aligning team and individual values; and to institute and enforce ethical standards and a code of conduct that govern both leader and team behavior.

Theme 2: Mental leadership   Core mental competencies include the ability to focus attention and think clearly and rationally under pressure; to organize and mentally prepare for challenges that lie ahead; to effectively manage time; and to act decisively from a reality-based perspective. Important also is the ability to recognize the impact of one's decisions and behavior on others (self-awareness).

Theme 3: Emotional leadership   Core emotional competencies include the ability to communicate effectively; to instill confidence, hope, and trust in teammates; to demonstrate empathy, humility, and compassion; and to instill in others a sense of challenge, opportunity, and excitement when facing adversity.

Theme 4: Physical leadership   Core physical competencies include the ability to behave in accordance with personal and team values, ethics, and code of conduct; to "walk one's talk" and, in doing so, demonstrate behavioral integrity; to be accountable and hold others accountable to clearly defined, measurable outcomes; and to define team success in concrete behavioral terms.

Full-Engagement Leadership

We can use an energy-management-based model of leadership to simplify and integrate the range of leadership competencies we've just identified. Energy is the capacity to do work; it is the means by which any mission becomes possible and is the most critical resource required for accomplishing any team objective. When the team is either unwilling or unable to invest energy in the mission, all progress ceases. Effective leaders are experts in mobilizing and focusing the energy resources of themselves and team members toward the team objective. In a real sense, great leaders are stewards of energy. They are highly skilled in recruiting the necessary quantity, quality, focus, and force (intensity) of energy required to complete the team objective. Fundamentally, leadership is about energy management.

To be effective, any leadership model based on energy must reflect its full scope and complexity. There are four distinct but related kinds of energy: physical, emotional, mental, and spiritual. Leadership can be defined as mobilizing, investing, and renewing all forms of energy in the service of the intended mission. When this happens, the individual or team is said to be fully engaged; that is, they are physically energized, emotionally connected, mentally focused, and spiritually aligned with the mission.

The forms of energy can be viewed hierarchically, as a pyramid, proceeding from the most fundamental, at the base, to the most important, at the top (see figure 9.1). The pyramid also follows developmental lines: We develop first physically, then emotionally and socially, then mentally and cognitively, and finally spiritually and morally.

Physical energy, the foundation for all energy, is typically associated with physical movement and behavior. It derives from food intake and is influenced by sleep, rest, and physical fitness. Physical energy represents the *quantity* of energy available.

Emotional energy is associated with feelings and emotions and refers to the *quality* of energy available. Low-quality emotional energy stems from negative

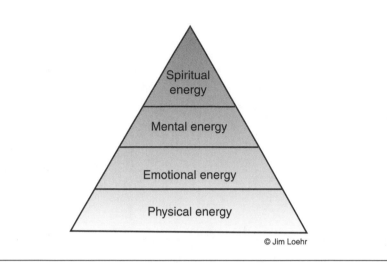

© Jim Loehr

Figure 9.1 Performance pyramid.

emotions such as fear, anger, and frustration. High-quality emotional energy stems from positive emotions such as hope, confidence, and excitement.

Mental energy is associated with higher-order functioning (cognition, perception, abstract thinking, creativity, self-awareness/self-regulation) and refers to

©Icon SMI

Spiritual energy such as passion, commitment, and persistence reflect the intensity needed to be a leader in the WNBA.

the *directional focus* of energy. And spiritual energy is associated with values and beliefs and refers to the *force*, or *intensity*, of the energy. Passion, commitment, and persistence all reflect intensity.

The dynamics of human energy correspond in many ways to the dynamics of light, or radiant energy, which also has quantity, quality, focus, and intensity. The similarities are not surprising since all energy has the sun as its source. Light energy from the sun is converted into human energy, which, in turn, is redirected back out into the world in the form of physical, emotional, mental, and spiritual work (see figure 9.2). Therefore, great leadership means mobilizing the greatest quantity (physical), the highest quality (emotional), the clearest focus (mental), and the greatest force (spiritual) of energy in the service of the mission. In sport, great leaders drive their team by engaging the body, heart, mind, and spirit of each athlete in the team mission (see figure 9.3).

Although development occurs from the base of the pyramid and proceeds upward, great leadership begins at the top and progresses downward. The fully engaged leader begins by articulating a clearly defined vision and mission, aligning individual and team values with the mission, and establishing a code of conduct. He or she then directs team members in how to think and focus their energy to maximize success by establishing priorities, confronting the truth, and designing solid mental-preparation routines. Moving down the pyramid, he or she helps team members summon the feelings and emotions that best serve the mission (e.g., hope, confidence). Finally, he or she helps team members behave appropriately, provides feedback on progress, holds team members accountable for their actions, and ensures that they have sufficient energy (e.g., they eat, sleep, and exercise properly) to successfully complete the mission.

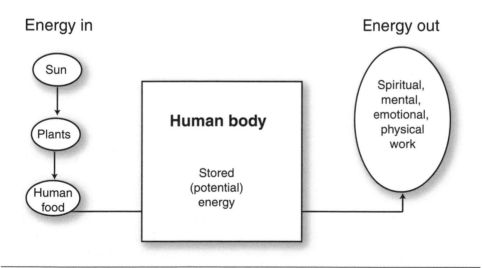

Figure 9.2 The origin and flow of energy.

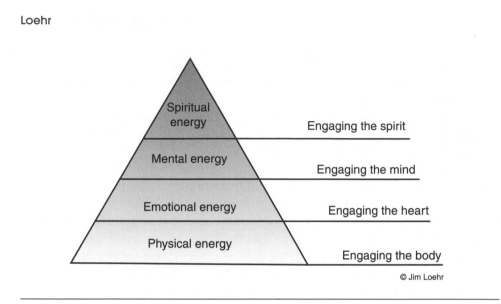

© Jim Loehr

Figure 9.3 Multidimensional engagement.

Ordinary vs. Extraordinary Leadership in Sport

Adversity is the true test of leadership. It is easy to lead under ideal conditions. Every individual or team crisis, hardship, disappointment, or setback is an opportunity to demonstrate and teach leadership principles. Teaching athletes how to remain fully engaged in spite of injuries, bad losses, excessive parental pressure, personality conflicts, and negative media is an important part of effective leadership. The crises of competitive sport can become powerful forces of disengagement and result in dramatic changes in the quantity, quality, focus, and force of energy invested by team members. All team members, regardless of the brilliance of their talent and skill, are ordinary people. No one is superhuman; everyone faces fears, doubts, and obstacles. So how do ordinary people become extraordinary leaders under extraordinary conditions?

Don Barr

Don Barr, coach of the University of South Florida tennis teams, witnessed an example of extraordinary leadership during the 1994-1995 season when two unthinkable tragedies occurred. Within the span of two months, a member of the team and the coach's son died. In a remarkable example of personal leadership, the team captain rallied the players to support the coach and his family in their grieving, pushed them to continue to work hard, and encouraged them to remain focused and positive despite the pain and confusion. Through his leadership, the deaths unified the team, deepening the character, compassion, commitment, and focus of each member. The team finished the season with a top-20 Division I national ranking.

Let's look at this example of extraordinary leadership in the context of the pyramid model. Leadership begins at the top of the pyramid; in the case of the University of South Florida's team captain, his spiritual leadership centered on his ability to use personal and team values as the starting point for making decisions and taking action during the crisis. Issues of character, compassion, strength, and commitment surfaced as rallying points for doing the right thing at the right time. Team members acted courageously because the captain's decisions stemmed from their values and beliefs. Extraordinary leadership from a spiritual perspective requires clarity of vision and mission, decision-making based on values and principles, alignment of team values with the intended mission, and a well-articulated code of conduct governing team behavior. In essence, the captain told his team, "This is how we are going to respond to each other and to the world in this crisis." Table 9.1 details spiritual leadership in the face of adversity by providing examples of both ordinary and extraordinary responses to such a potential setback.

Table 9.1 Spiritual Leadership in Adversity

Ordinary response	Extraordinary response
Lose clarity in both vision and values.	Continue to keep vision and values clear and vivid.
Make expedient-based decisions rather than value-based decisions and choices.	Make value-based decisions and choices.
Lose visibility of leader's character, honesty, and integrity.	Increase leader's strength of character, passion for the mission, commitment, and values.
Resist adhering to code of conduct and rules of engagement in order to gain a competitive advantage.	Adhere to team code of conduct regardless of competitive outcome.
Misalign personal values with those of the team and the leadership.	Align personal values with team's mission and code of conduct.

In terms of mental leadership, the captain kept the team focused and thinking clearly in spite of the shock and confusion surrounding the tragedies. He openly faced the truth about what happened, neither denying nor exaggerating it, and remained reality-based in his discussions about the events. Realizing that the events might disrupt the team's focus and concentration, he encouraged everyone to intensify their resolve to be mentally prepared and to show the coach and each other that if they worked together, they could get through this difficult time. He also encouraged them to help and support each other and the coach. One of the most important things the captain did was provide a logical, reality-based framework for managing the crisis—one that flowed directly from individual and team core values and vision. Table 9.2 details mental leadership in the face of adversity by providing examples of both ordinary and extraordinary responses to such a potential setback.

Table 9.2 Mental Leadership in Adversity

Ordinary response	Extraordinary response
Lose focus and concentration on the mission.	Continue to keep team members focused on what's important.
Increase mental confusion and disorganization.	Remain clear and logical in thinking in spite of the crisis.
Increase frequency of multitasking (not fully engaged in anything).	Resist multitasking on issues of real importance.
Distort the truth about what is actually happening (exaggerating or glossing over the truth).	Convey the truth about what's happening without distortion.
Fail to frame the crisis in a meaningful way.	Frame the crisis in a meaningful way, relative to the team's mission and to life in general.
Fail to connect the reality of what's happening to team member's core values.	Connect the reality of what's happening to the team member's core values.
Use crisis for justifying the anticipated failure of the team's mission.	Promote courageous action and individual sacrifice by logically linking the crisis with issues of character, personal growth, and the bigger picture of life.

The core issue in emotional leadership is helping team members recruit the feelings that best serve the team's mission, such as optimism, hope, and confidence, particularly during periods of adversity. By first linking the tragedy to their core values, helping them stay focused, and giving meaning to the tragedy relative to their values, the University of South Florida's team captain kept everyone from becoming engulfed in energy-debilitating feelings of fear, anger, and disillusionment.

Hidden within the turmoil and discomfort of nearly every adversity are opportunities for expanding team and individual emotional limits. For the University of South Florida tennis team, the crisis offered the members an opportunity to show extraordinary compassion and caring for the deceased team member's family as well as for the coach and his family. It also pushed them to find the courage to move forward with their lives and the team's mission. Pushed well beyond their emotional comfort zone, team members used the crisis to reflect on their own emotional limits and to achieve new levels of emotional depth and maturity. Table 9.3 details emotional leadership in the face of adversity by providing examples of both ordinary and extraordinary responses to such a potential setback.

The most important dynamic in physical leadership is taking action that protects the quantity of energy available and drives the mission-specific outcomes that define success. When adversity strikes, athletes' energy-supportive training routines often become disrupted. Healthy patterns of eating, sleeping, rest, and recovery are often abandoned, resulting in depleted energy reserves. When this happens, the mission becomes threatened. Adversity can cause athletes to lose

Table 9.3   Emotional Leadership in Adversity

Ordinary response	Extraordinary response
Shift into a survival, reactive mode.	Continue the flow of high positive energy in the form of optimism and hope.
Show or experience anger, fear, frustration, etc. (negative emotions)	Create the sense of challenge, opportunity, or adventure in the crisis.
Lose confidence in self or team members.	Sustain high levels of confidence in self and team members.
Become defensive, critical of others, impatient with team members.	Show caring, empathy, and trust in team members and everyone involved.
Allow adversity to turn team energy from positive to negative.	Help team members find constructive ways to express and deal emotionally with the loss.

their appetites completely or become obsessed with food; it can also disrupt sleep and rest cycles, heightening the risk of overtraining and injury.

Another important aspect of physical leadership is behavioral authenticity or integrity. When leaders "walk their talk"—when their actions are consistent with what they expect from others in the crisis—team members are much more likely to hear and follow the leader's message.

The University of South Florida team captain led with his behavior. He did what he expected others to do—trained hard; adhered to his eating, sleeping, and rest rituals; stayed focused and positive in practice and in matches (whether the coach was present or not); and showed empathy and compassion for everyone involved. Table 9.4 details physical leadership in the face of adversity by providing examples of both ordinary and extraordinary responses to such a potential setback.

So often, athletes abandon their training rituals when the demands of life or sport push them beyond their normal comfort limits. Those times are precisely

Table 9.4   Physical Leadership in Adversity

Ordinary response	Extraordinary response
Lose consideration managing one's own physical energy.	Recognize the importance of managing one's own physical energy.
Lose consideration helping others to manage their physical energy.	Recognize the importance of helping others manage their physical energy.
Fail to follow established routines for eating, sleeping, rest, and exercise.	Follow established routines for eating, sleeping, rest, and exercise.
Cause the quantity of energy available for investment to become steadily depleted.	Cause the quantity of energy available for investment to remain stable.
Fail to continue to provide concrete feedback on team's progress toward the goal.	Provide concrete feedback on team's progress toward the goal.
Fail to model what is expected of others (loss of behavioral integrity).	Show behavioral integrity by modeling what is expected of others.

when training rituals are most valuable. Routines of sleeping, eating, rest, and preparation bring order, rhythm, and control to whatever the athlete faces. Coaches who help athletes to understand why they should continue their training routines and help them adapt existing rituals to novel situations (such as international travel or extended road trips) maximize their team's energy availability.

Storytelling and Leadership

Fully engaged leaders are great storytellers who understand that the stories they tell about events that affect the team are often more important than the events themselves. In terms of energy management, storytelling is fundamental to good leadership. Different stories can be crafted from the same facts and can profoundly change individual and team energy dynamics. Stories can leave team members feeling inspired, challenged, and hopeful or frightened, frustrated, and discouraged. The wrong story can completely derail a team's mission.

As an example, let's look at the facts about the University of South Florida tennis team's situation:

- A member of the team died.
- The coach's son died in an accident.
- The team and the coach were devastated by the losses.
- Because of his son's death, Coach Barr was unable to attend many practices and some conference matches.
- Team members felt overwhelmed by the two events—they felt a mixture of deep sadness, confusion, and shock.
- The season was not canceled in spite of the two tragedies.

Stories 1 and 2 that follow show how different stories can be crafted from the same set of facts.

1. Two unthinkable tragedies have occurred that have devastated you as team members and the coach. The season will not be canceled, but the coach, as everyone understands, must tend to his family and be given time to heal and grieve. He will not be available for a number of team practices and conference matches. Do whatever you can to get through this and, should you be unable to play given the tragedies, let your conditioning coach know before any match. We recognize that many of you had great hopes for this season, but things occur in life that are simply out of our control. This is a very sad time. Do your best to get through it.

2. Two unthinkable tragedies have occurred that have devastated you as team members and the coach. The season will not be canceled, but the coach, as everyone understands, must tend to his family and be given time to heal and grieve. He will not be available for a number of team practices and conference matches. Life

events like these push us to the very edge of our capacity as human beings. They can cause us to reexamine and question nearly every part of our lives. In times like these, turn to your core values to guide you. Focus on the things that mean the most to you to find your way—family, compassion, kindness, faith, courage, and hope. If you turn to each other in this crisis and face these tragedies as a unit, neither you nor the season need to become lost. One of the most helpful things you can do for the coach is to continue to work hard, stay focused, and complete your mission as a team. What is needed here is great personal courage and leadership. The coach and this school need you to step up and continue to move forward. I need every one of you to pull together and become extraordinary leaders. It is in times like these that we build and reveal our character and strength as human beings. If we pull together, we will make it through this.

As human beings, we do not have direct contact with the world as it actually exists. The reality we experience is filtered by our senses, and once that reality is perceived, we give it meaning and interpretation. We build a story around the facts as we know them, and extraordinary leadership requires that the right story be told. Leaders should follow three rules of engagement for storytelling in adversity:

1. The story should reflect the leader's and the team's core values.
2. The story should represent the truth (facts) as fully as possible.
3. The story should leave those who are being led with a sense of hope.

Story 1 followed only the second rule of engagement, but story 2 followed all three rules. Reflect for a moment on which of the two stories you find more motivating and why. Think about your own storytelling habits. Recall a story you told when you faced a serious challenge or disappointment. Write it down, then review the three rules of storytelling and determine if it passed the test. How could it be improved?

Energy-Management Principles for Leaders

Human energy is a limited, finite resource; as a consequence, we must make difficult choices about how to invest that energy. Great leaders help team members mobilize the energy required for team success. The following 12 primary energy-management principles for leaders are derived from more than two decades of work in high-stress applications of sport, law enforcement, medicine, and business.

Principle 1: Growth follows energy investment Energy sustains and nourishes all life. Just as energy investment in exercise stimulates physical growth and development, so also does it produce emotional, mental, or spiritual growth. Team success requires skillful investment of energy by every team member, who choose who or what gets their life-giving energy. They can direct it toward specific muscles of the body to stimulate growth, or they can apply it toward building confidence and trust in one another, thereby stimulating emotional growth. The same applies to mental capacities such as preparation, visualization, or focus. When team members invest energy in team vision and values or in courage or integrity, they stimulate spiritual growth. Great leaders help team members make the right energy investments at the right time.

Principle 2: Growth ceases when energy investment ceases   If you cut off the energy supply to the biceps by putting the arm in a cast, the muscle begins to atrophy immediately. The same applies to confidence, mental focus, biomechanics, integrity, or honesty. Great leaders ensure that an adequate energy supply goes to actions, beliefs, and feelings that are vital to the success of the mission, including communication, rules of engagement, trust, physical fitness, strategy and tactics, or biomechanical fundamentals.

Principle 3: The best energy produces the most growth   It is not the amount of time team members invest that drives team success but rather the energy they bring to the time they have. Athletes can be present, showing up for practice or games, but not fully there in terms of their energy. Investing time without investing energy has little value. Time spent practicing, working out, or mentally preparing for competition is wasted without sufficient quantity, quality, focus, and force of energy.

Great leaders understand that the enemy of full engagement is multitasking. Multitasking means not being fully engaged in anything—or partially disengaged in everything. Whether watching television while doing homework, talking on a cell phone while driving, or thinking about personal problems during practice, the result is the same: reduced performance. The energy signal is split and its potential positive impact is compromised. Effective leaders help team members fully engage in anything that is significant to the team. This is why rituals that create clear boundaries for focusing energy can be so powerful. For example, in tennis, rituals like keeping the eyes on the strings of the racket between points or visualizing the flight of the ball to a target just prior to serving enhance appropriate energy focus.

Principle 4: Whatever receives energy gains strength   The more team members invest energy in anger, frustration, or jealousy, the more accessible, dominant, and powerful these feelings become. Athletes who complain, make excuses, or show impatience give these dynamics life. Just as investments in positive emotions stimulate positive growth, investments in negative or toxic emotions stimulate defensive growth. Great leaders help team members understand that the team's destiny, for better or worse, follows the path of their energy investments.

Principle 5: Four energy sources   The power of full engagement is the power of properly aligned and skillfully managed human energy (physical, emotional, mental, and spiritual). Without all four sources of energy, the success of the mission is compromised. When energy reserves are depleted or when individuals become engulfed in toxic emotions, lose focus, distort the truth, or can no longer connect the mission to their values, the team cannot perform to its potential. Great leaders integrate and align the four energy dynamics within every team member.

Principle 6: Balance energy investments with energy deposits   Both over-training (too much energy expenditure relative to recovery) and undertraining (too much recovery relative to energy expenditure) threaten the success of a mission. Periodization training allows skillful management of work–rest ratios. Full engagement requires cultivating a balance between the expenditure and recovery of all kinds of energy. Because human energy is a finite resource, it must be renewed intermittently (strategic disengagement). Examples of opportunities for strategic disengagement *during* competitive play include the between-point time in tennis, the between-shot time in golf, shift changes in hockey, inning changes in baseball, and changing from offense to defense in football. By reducing arousal through deep breathing, muscle relaxation, mental imagery, or positive self-talk routines, athletes can renew energy and prepare for the next dose of stress.

Outside competition, opportunities for strategic disengagement exist at all levels of the performance pyramid. The most important physical factors are sleep, rest, nutritional intake, and hydration. At the emotional level, strategic disengagement occurs when *relief* from feelings of pressure, anger, and frustration is achieved and feelings of joy, inner peace, and confidence are renewed. At the mental level, energy is recovered by changing focus to something entirely different (e.g., from thinking about sport to watching a movie or playing a video game). Spiritual strategic disengagement occurs by reconnecting to deep values and beliefs.

Great leaders understand the importance of energy renewal and recovery to the team's mission. They understand that without it, full engagement cannot be achieved.

Principle 7: Push beyond the comfort zone   We grow at all levels by expending energy beyond our ordinary limits and then recovering. Any form of energy expenditure that prompts discomfort has the potential to expand capacity. Just as growth in the biceps requires progressively greater workloads, the same principle applies emotionally, mentally, and spiritually. Increased emotional workloads might take the form of painful losses or hostile crowds. Pushing beyond normal limits mentally could mean concentrating with greater precision and intensity in spite of constant distractions. Spiritually, it might involve displaying character and sportsmanship in spite of an opponent's inflammatory comments.

Great leaders understand that discomfort is a prerequisite for growth. Every crisis can be used to expand team and individual capacity when managed properly.

Principle 8: Use positive rituals to manage energy   A ritual is a consciously acquired positive habit, fueled by deeply held values, that facilitates full engagement. Energy management is best achieved not through willpower and self-

167

discipline but through habits. Rituals encourage the entire team to do the right thing at the right time. They ensure that energy reserves will be adequate and that energy is directed toward what's most important to the success of the mission. Examples of positive rituals include precompetition, dietary and hydration, sleep and rest, concentration, preperformance, and self-reflection routines.

Great leaders encourage the team to build and adhere to rituals by modeling these behaviors in their own lives.

Principle 9: Energy is highly contagious   Every experienced coach has witnessed how a single team member's negative energy can quickly spread throughout a team. The adage "one bad apple can spoil the barrel" appears to have some validity when it comes to negative energy. Conversely, a team's energy dynamics can completely change for the better with the addition of high levels of positive energy. Some individuals display what might be termed "hypercarrier" potential for transmitting negative or positive energy.

Great leaders are quick to recognize hypercarriers, particularly in the case of negative energy, and take action to prevent the spread to other team members.

Principle 10: Negative energy outside the comfort zone   When adversity strikes, primitive survival instincts can quickly change energy from positive to negative. Events that can push team members outside their comfort level include injuries, bad losses, pressure about grades, relationship problems, a significant increase in training, or parental problems. The negative energy produced can, in some cases, spur them to take positive action to correct it. When the negative energy is carried back to the team, however, it is rarely constructive.

Great quarterbacks are great leaders who can turn negative energy into positive energy within the high-pressured environment of a time-out huddle.

Great leaders help team members create boundaries to contain their negative energy so that it does not contaminate the team. Implementing team rules of engagement can be particularly helpful.

Principle 11: Self-esteem deficiencies require energy Individuals who lack self-esteem can be very demanding on leaders and other team members in terms of energy investment. The attention they seek requires focused energy from others, presenting real energy-management challenges for coaches and teams. Ignoring their needs only intensifies the problem, and responding to them can be exhausting.

Great leaders recognize that those with low self-esteem create a potential energy drain on the team, and they work to ensure that energy investments in these athletes do not compromise the team's mission.

Principle 12: Repeated energy investment makes a difference Directed energy flow always has an effect, whether it is immediately visible or not. Repeated energy exposure produces cumulative effects. When highly positive people are put into an intensely negative team environment, a predictable contamination occurs over time, even in the strongest of individuals. When the forces of positive and negative energy collide, the one with the greatest force dominates.

Great leaders understand that the effects of positive and negative energy are ultimately played out on an individual basis. They also understand that the destructive forces of negative energy must be contained; if not, even the most positive athlete eventually becomes a casualty.

Regardless of age or sport, coaches can use the dynamics of athletic competition to teach leadership skills that translate directly into real life. The following strategies are examples of ways coaches can foster leadership and make leadership skills a priority:

- Begin every season by positioning leadership as a key objective of the team's overall mission.
- Explain in concrete terms how leadership is defined as the team establishes its rules of engagement with each other and the world outside.
- Establish that great leadership begins with values (individual and team) and extends to thoughts, feelings, and behavior.
- Make it clear why leadership is important to you as a coach. When leadership is an obvious high priority, team members start taking leadership issues seriously.
- Constantly encourage and reinforce team members to show leadership qualities: preparedness, loyalty, accountability, trust, resourcefulness, flexibility, and so on.
- Help athletes recognize "leadership moments" and use team crises or adversity to sharpen leadership skills.
- Provide concrete examples of what leadership means physically, emotionally, mentally, and spiritually.

- Provide athletes with numerous leadership opportunities, such as leading practice drills or warm-up and cool-down routines, or setting the pace in a two-mile run.

- Recognize leadership whether in practice, in games, or away from sport. Highlighting concrete daily examples of leadership is a highly effective learning strategy.

- Repeatedly give attention to issues of sportsmanship, character, honesty, and respect for others when opportunities present themselves. This establishes the central role that values play in your coaching.

- Make character and personal development more important than winning.

- Connect the hard work, sacrifices, and struggles team members are making for sport to the broader arena of life. Relate how the lessons of full engagement in sport will directly translate to full engagement in life.

Future Directions

Fully engaged leaders recognize that energy is their most precious resource and is the currency by which any mission becomes possible. Acknowledging this, they lead first and foremost with their own energy. They mobilize the greatest quantity, highest quality, clearest focus, and greatest force of energy within themselves and their teammates in support of the mission. Fully engaged leaders understand that at the heart of leadership is engagement, an acquired multidimensional energy state that enhances the full expression of talent and skill in themselves and in the team they lead. They also understand the difference between ordinary and extraordinary leadership. Extraordinary leadership begins with full engagement, which means one is physically energized, emotionally connected, mentally focused, and spiritually aligned with the mission. Extraordinary leadership is grounded in fundamental values and beliefs, which form the basis of the leader's rules of engagement and those of the team.

Competitive sport is a living laboratory for both effective leadership as well as providing countless opportunities to teach these dynamics to developing athletes. It is the hope that future sport science researchers will give special attention to exploring the value of sport for teaching critical leadership skills. The potential long-term value of an energy-based model of leadership in sport will ultimately be determined by sport science researchers. At the most basic level, human beings are dynamic energy systems. Energy is defined as the capacity to do work and every mission a leader is committed to requires work to achieve success. The possibility that leadership can be effectively characterized in terms of mobilizing, focusing, and renewing energy in the service of a specific mission holds considerable promise. The challenge ahead lies in creating energy-based leadership tools that do, in fact, result in deeper levels of commitment, passion, focus, hope, and resiliency by followers.

chapter 10

Teamwork: For the Good of the Whole

Tracy L. Veach and Jerry R. May

We are a species of social beings. We love sport and we love sport teams. We encourage our children to join in team sports at an early age and support these activities throughout our educational systems. We are fascinated with the duality of individual and team achievement in both work and sport teams, as participants and fans. Our pervading interest drives us, in this chapter, to look at team sport psychology and examine sport and business research that helps us understand the complexity of teams. In addition, we describe the sport-consultation process from our experiences working with different types of teams, from developmental to Olympic and professional-level sport. Finally, we describe effective team-intervention strategies and techniques gleaned from our experiences.

Good Teams vs. Great Teams

Astute, successful coaches intuitively recognize the importance of team dynamics in motivating and supporting their athletes to excel beyond the contributions of individual efforts. Descriptive terms such as "team spirit," "momentum," "winning attitude," and "team chemistry" are frequently used but not well understood.

Webster's defines teams and qualities of teams in a variety of ways. Interestingly, in the Collegiate edition, the first three definitions are about teams of animals! Only in the Universal Unabridged version do people take the forefront as a team: "a number of persons forming one of the sides in a game or contest." Perhaps a bit more useful is "team" as an adjective: "to put together in a coordinated ensemble . . . marked by devotion to teamwork rather than individual achievement." Teamwork is defined as "cooperative or coordinated effort on the part of a group of persons acting together as a team or in the interests of a common cause." The Collegiate edition provides a more explicit definition of teamwork: "work done by several associates with each doing a part but all subordinating personal prominence to the efficiency of the whole."

A team is far more than merely a group; *it's a coordinated ensemble that cooperates to achieve a common goal that overrides individual achievement.* Also, a dedication to teamwork does not necessarily diminish individual effort. Individual efforts are seen as necessary to teamwork, but they are not enough. Team members (as opposed to teammates) include not only the performing athletes but also coaches and other professionals who contribute to team development and performance. Even parents, although there are critical boundary issues to consider, can be considered an important part of the team.

Another concept to clarify is that of the team itself. Not all teams have the same quality of unity or "teamness." On a basketball team, a true team in the fullest sense of the word, all teammates are dependent on each other for the success of the team. No matter how many points an individual player scores, if his team scores fewer points than the other team, his performance, while perhaps outstanding as an individual, will not carry the day. Other sports, such as football, soccer, and volleyball, carry a similar degree of interdependence.

Ralph Vernacchia, a sport psychologist and professor at Western Washington State University, uses the term "individual team sports" to refer to teams for whom the cumulative performances of individual athletes determine team success, such as swimming, track and field, gymnastics, golf, skiing, and equestrian sports. For most of these types of teams, for which we use the shorter term "coacting teams," individual performance is a primary focus, and depending on the team and coach, team performance is an equal or sometimes secondary focus. At times, these coacting team players become true teams, for example, when sprinters or swimmers form a relay team. In this case, they are no longer individual performers who contribute to an abstract cumulative point total; they win or lose as a team.

We first observed the importance of building team support for individual athletes in what can now be called a coacting team, the U.S. ski team. Building team cohesion can have a strong effect on individual performance and may be an even more important factor for coacting teams than might appear at first glance. In this experience, team-building workshops were aimed at developing a high level of cohesiveness and support in response to concerns about teammate conflicts and interpersonal tensions. Group sessions were scheduled to identify the sources of these tensions, examine how they affected individual performance and team morale, and develop a consensus on conflict resolution or contain the tensions when resolution could not be achieved immediately. Athletic performance success is a complex result of many factors, often the least of which is the intervention of the sport consultant. In this case, however, the fact that most of the key members of the ski team agreed to support each other despite significant teammate issues through the Olympic Games was an important factor, one that contributed to the team achieving the best level of performance to that time.

In working with a West Coast equestrian team, we placed a strong emphasis on riders watching and providing positive feedback for each other in competitions. In subsequent group discussions, the riders commented that they felt a boost to their self-esteem and confidence because of this supportive behavior, since there was no benefit to the other riders for taking the time and effort to help them.

The characteristics of various types of teams have different implications for the athlete and coach. The individual athletes have varying views about their roles and responsibilities to the team and coach. The coach needs to tailor his or her approach to each athlete since the perception of success varies from individual to individual. Naturally, the individual and group coaching process will necessarily depend on the overall team goals. The complexity and richness of team sports challenge our understanding of the multiple, interdependent influences on team development and performance. The internal dynamics of the team itself add even greater complexity to the situation. In turn, individual athlete behaviors, in terms of leadership, attitudes, and performance, shape the dynamics of the team.

Understanding the Complexity of Teamwork

Fortunately, there is a growing body of research on team development, goal setting, and cohesiveness that can help us understand the complexity of teams.

Team Development

Regardless of the culture and history of a team, it first starts as simply a collection of individuals. Through continuing association, a collective identity begins to form, which is characterized by a shared sense of purpose and structured patterns of behavior, interaction, and communication. The evolution of the group into a team is characterized by a high level of task interdependence, a perceived common fate, a consensus that the group goal has precedence over individual goals, and a shared belief that the group output is more than the sum of the individual parts.

Each team is unique, even within the same sport. Team development principles must be understood and applied to each situation with sensitivity and attention to the particular features of the team, coaches, and athletes.

Paul Estabrooks and colleagues at Kansas State University have outlined several important principles in the complex process of transforming a group of individual athletes (and coaches) into a sports team:

1. Team goal-setting strategies. These are primary strategies to improve team function and performance used across a variety of team types, including skiing, swimming, basketball, soccer, and ice hockey. Although practitioners

include their own variations, the general components are quite consistent. In general, the approach involves the following:

- Initial clarification of the intervention strategy in terms of time, timing, and format
- Educational lectures, seminars, and workshops to outline the principles of individual and team interventions and their value to team success
- Working with group sessions to build team cohesion and communication by identifying, discussing, and achieving consensus on the relationship of individual and team goals
- Implementing follow-up sessions that address performance barriers identified by the team
- A feedback process to evaluate the effectiveness of the intervention and develop further intervention strategies

2. Interpersonal-relations approach. Here, the focus is on understanding personal and team values and how they affect team cohesion. An explicit effort is made to identify and develop effective strategies to improve mutual respect and communication between team members. Often qualitative and quantitative assessments are used to identify attributes such as independence, loyalty, and responsibility as they relate to team functioning and performance. In general, these approaches involve the following:

- Having athletes and coaches identify, describe, and discuss at least three important personal goals
- Having team members identify, describe, and discuss five or six major roles that take time and energy to fulfill
- Discussions of how team success will be determined and how this is related to the team values
- Brainstorming the team's strengths and challenges, with a focus on strategies to facilitate attainment of the team values
- Group meetings with coaches to identify their values and life roles
- Follow-up meetings between coaches and athletes to monitor, discuss, and adjust team-building activities

Team sessions that focus on both goal setting and clarification of values should be included. Moreover, since group dynamics are such an important part of team-building and performance, we invariably conduct sessions on stress management, interpersonal communication, and role-interpersonal conflict resolution. (See chapter 11 for information on communication in coaching.)

Another important consideration is determining who should direct team-development activities. In indirect consultation, the coach leads the team-development activities using a sport psychologist as a "coach" in learning and implementing psychosocial techniques; in direct consultation, the sport psychologist leads specific intervention activities.

Considerations such as resources and time guide the decisions about who will facilitate the interventions and how this process will unfold. There does not seem to be a simple answer to which is the best approach. Each team situation, with its unique mix of coaching styles and member dynamics, requires an individual decision. For example, when there is major conflict between players and coaching staff, it would likely be better for the sport consultant to facilitate initial and even subsequent sessions to resolve differences. Clarification of the issues in separate player and coaching sessions can reframe them into safer or less inflammatory terms. When the coach and staff are more interested in facilitating team-development activities, the sport consultant can observe, participate, and offer the coaching staff feedback and suggestions for improving the process. (See chapters 15 and 16 for roles and qualifications of sport consultants.)

Team Goals

Goal setting is clearly important for individual athletes, and it is an essential step in team building. Damon Burton and Sarah Naylor, who are research collaborators in sport performance at the University of Idaho and the U.S. Military Academy, respectively, reviewed more than 74 studies on the effectiveness of setting performance goals in athletes and non-athletes, finding that goal setting is part of virtually all coaching and that such efforts pay off in improved performance. Also, it is much more complicated than it first appears. Even with individual athletes, it is not a simple process of asking which goals they want to achieve. Issues of specificity, timing, context, immediacy, difficulty, and relation to other goals make the goal-setting process quite challenging. Added to this complexity are parental aspirations, coaching dreams, and multiple teammates whose goals, to varying degrees, may both compete with and complement the goals of all other teammates.

Table 10.1 summarizes the empirical support for different aspects of goal-setting and specifically for teams. Clearly, goal setting improves individual and team performances. In the "general goals" category, for example, of the 15 studies (both individual and teams), 11 showed strong support for goal setting. And of the 15 studies, the 3 studies that showed positive findings were specifically about teams. The remainder of table 10.1 shows strong but variable findings in other aspects of goal setting. The lack of support for goal proximity is surprising; we have found that setting immediate, short-term, and long-term goals is quite useful, as is having the coach and athletes take responsibility for generating individual and team goals. Perhaps the small number of studies and inclusion of ad hoc "teams" are part of the explanation for variable and weak findings in goal proximity. Consequently, having a clear plan for addressing the different aspects of goal setting and appreciating the issues surrounding individual and team goals is important.

Many team goals are important, including physical skill development, technical skill enhancement, team coordination, and fun, as well as competitive performance and winning. Coaches must involve all team members in clarifying the

Table 10.1 Relationship of Goal Setting to Performance Improvements in Groups and Teams

Goal attributes studied	All studies	Positive findings	Team studies	Positive findings
General goals	11/15	Strong support	3	Strong support
Goal difficulty	7/16	Moderate support	2	Strong–moderate support
Multiple goals	6/7	Strong support	2	Strong–moderate support
Goal proximity (short- and long-term goals)	3/8	Variable support	1	Weak support
Goal specificity	13/22	Moderate support	2	Moderate support
Goal collectivity (group goals)	2/2	Strong support	2	Strong support
Self-generated goals	1/7	Weak support	0	NA
Goal interventions (effectiveness)	4/5	Strong support	1	Moderate support
Goals and self-efficacy	NA	Strong support	0	NA

explicit and implicit goals and help the team reach maximum (though usually not complete) consensus.

In the case of youth teams, parents are important participants for the coach to consider. Parents provide social, economic, and personal support for their children as well as the team as a whole. Most coaches are familiar with the "pushy parent" phenomenon, in which parental motivations and goals override the child's interests and expectations in the sport. The coach can work to counter well-meaning but overly aggressive parents by meeting with them to clarify team goals and enlisting the support of other parents. In our experience, the support of other parents for goals of skill development, fun, and learning teamwork values can go far to convert the pushy parent. If not, then more direct measures or a referral to a sport consultant may help.

We also need to understand the apparent paradox of individual and team achievement. Teams are made up of individuals, after all, and bringing out the best individual development and performance while creating cohesiveness can be a challenge. As noted earlier, the effects of cohesiveness are surprisingly powerful and equally important for coacting and interactive teams.

Team Cohesiveness

A starting point for creating cohesiveness is clarifying and building consensus for the team vision, which should be created through team discussions. Bert Carron and his colleagues at the University of Western Ontario define cohesion as "a dynamic process that is reflected in the tendency for a group to stick together and remain united in the pursuit of its instrumental objectives or for the satisfaction of member affective needs." In other words, the team gets the job done and the team members feel supported and appreciated for their efforts. The following points summarize ways in which to create team cohesion:

- Focus on improving communication.
- Respect and celebrate differences.
- Use an inclusive process in developing team goals.
- Recognize outstanding role behaviors, particularly in the service of team performance.
- Create a vision of the team as greater than any individual.
- Establish a positive-feedback environment climate to maximize learning.
- Encourage fun activities outside routine practice drills.
- Set an example of giving of self to team efforts and self-sacrifice.
- Establish clear expectations regarding roles, hold everyone accountable, and know when to flex with exceptional situations.
- Teach the intellectual, emotional, and spiritual aspects of the sport in addition to the physical and behavioral components.

We have found that it is critical to focus on establishing clear role definitions and mutually understood interrelationships. Several components are important in this process:

- Role expectations: clarifying what each individual is responsible for doing on the team and how he or she thinks it should be done
- Role conception: what an individual thinks is his or her particular job on the team and how they have learned to do it
- Role acceptance: what an individual is willing to do and the extent of his or her acceptance of how others see their roles on the team
- Role behavior: what the athlete or coach actually does and says
- Role efficacy: how effective team members see other athletes and coaches in their roles on the team and in the organization

Some of the critical questions that can guide these discussions and the ensuing clarifications include the following:

- What does the team expect you to do in your job or playing assignment? What are your prescribed tasks, activities, and responsibilities?
- How do you see your job or playing assignment? What do you actually do and what are the discretionary aspects of your duties?
- What do you need from others on the team in order to do your job the way you would like to?
- What do you need to know about the other team members' jobs that would help you do your own role better?

Effective Coaches and Their Winning Teams

At a professional basketball game we attended, one of the star forwards was taking and missing a high percentage of shots in the first period of play. During an injury time-out called by the other team, the coach gently grabbed his player's arm and steered him into a quick consultation. Then he gestured for the other teammates to join the huddle. Although we were not privy to the conversation, when play resumed the improved performance confirmed the likely gist of the possible dialogue:

> Bill, your shot timing is off. It is time to shift to your great ball handling and passing to get the others shooting. Everyone, we need to connect with each other, find our rhythm, and pick up the pace, and the baskets will fall.

In this case, the player, who was masterful in setting up and crisply passing to his teammates, did so, and his teammates then picked up the scoring pace. In the heat of competitive encounters, athletes sometimes lose perspective about how they can best contribute to the team effort. The coach's role is to recognize these patterns and take quick, constructive action.

Coaches and their effectiveness are the most important factors in team development. The way the coach leads, teaches, and communicates greatly influences individual and team performance. Thelma Horn, a sport psychologist, researcher, and professor at the University of Miami, has extensively reviewed findings on coaching attributes that clearly show how coaching behaviors affect teams. For example, behaviors that lead to positive player outcomes in terms of satisfaction, motivation, cohesiveness, sense of competency, and a positive team climate include

- high frequencies of training and instructional behaviors with high support to athletes;
- more democratic leadership that fosters autonomy rather than rigid control;
- establishing a team climate of mastery or learning rather than only performance orientation; and
- high frequency of positive, supportive, and information-based feedback to athletes.

Bill Walsh, one of the most achievement-oriented and successful professional football coaches, strongly argues for using positive reinforcement rather than the big stick of criticism. He also notes the importance of sacrificing your ambitions for others'. He exhorts us, "Remember, praise is more valuable than blame."

Our experiences working with coaches and teams confirm the previously stated findings about coaching attributes, and we've come up with our own list of tips for effective coaching:

- Learn each athlete's individual learning style or preference.
- Coach to the style of your athlete (watch how much you impose your style).
- Provide unconditional support for the athlete (avoid hypercriticism, undue yelling).
- Be careful about unintentionally setting teammates against one another. You want them to work together.
- Support the concept of cooperation–competitiveness.
- Clarify the role of the individual team members and how they are to work together.
- Be a visionary for the team.
- Learn to deal with the pushy parent or the overly critical parent.
- Remember the development stage, needs, and characteristics of athletes.
- Have athletes behave respectfully to each other.
- Teach athletes to be friendly to each other. They do not have to be friends.
- Remember that males and females are different. Both can achieve at high levels.
- Teach the difference between aggressiveness and assertiveness.
- Look for overtraining and staleness of the team. More is not always better.
- Avoid favoritism.
- Deal with relationship tension. A team without conflict will be mediocre.
- Don't squelch it. Do teach the team how to resolve relationship tension.
- Hold people accountable; however, always point out more of what the team is doing well than what it is doing wrong.

Remember, no matter how serious the game is, we *play* sports. We play soccer, play football, play basketball. The word "play" must mean something—we do not say we *work* soccer.

Cooperation, Competition, and Conflict in Teams

The value of coaching that emphasizes cooperative or competitive orientations is vigorously debated. Coaches and other sport professionals frequently over-emphasize the competitive nature of sport; excessive focus on winning can be counterproductive to skill development and teamwork.

The principles of cooperation and competitiveness are not mutually exclusive alternatives that coaches must choose between in developing their teams. The athlete who is only cooperative is not able to appreciate or cope with the competitive realities of the sport. The athlete who is oriented only to competitiveness, who wants to win at all costs, limits his or her ability to reach his or her full potential. The drive to compete can be viewed as the striving for personal excellence and skill mastery rather than as beating someone else. Winning can be a goal, but it also can be an outcome of a focus on skill building, mastery, and cooperation.

We believe in combining the two concepts of cooperation and competition. Cooperative competitiveness is a seemingly paradoxical concept that, when implemented creatively, enhances skill development and team cohesion (see chapter 3). In practice, cooperativeness and competitiveness are part of a dynamic process in which one or the other may take the primary focus during the training cycle. The development of internal rather than only external competitive motivation is more useful in improving and mastering skills at a high level. As a counterpoint to learning competitive skills, children should also learn cooperative skills and cooperative play. If children or adults are taught only to cooperate, their skill development and success will be limited.

Over the years, we have worked with many individuals and teams on cooperative competitiveness. We encourage athletes to train and share their ideas and skills with their fellow teammates and competitors to facilitate mastery and teamwork at the highest level. However, it is true that on the day of competition the team that exhibits the highest level of skill mastery will excel over the other team; that is the nature of sport.

To some specific teams on the U.S. sailing team this concept seemed way out of the box. Sharing ideas and experiences is not often encouraged in sailing, but two of our best teams in one boat class decided it was a meaningful concept. They spent the next two years training and competing with one another and sharing ideas, techniques, and encouragement. Both teams became world-class performers. At the Olympic trials, only one team could win, and they knew that the winner would be a contender for a medal at the Games. They finished numbers one and two in the Olympic trials, and the winner went on to win a medal at the Olympics. The second-place team members were disappointed but had gained new confidence in their ability to compete at a world-class level. In fact, one of the second-place athletes went on to win a berth in the next Olympic sailing trials.

High-level cooperation and competition invariably involves conflict and stress. Managing relationship tension is an important task throughout the team-development process. Coaches often have a strong vision and plans for the team, and individual athletes have their own personal and professional goals, which are motivated by many different perspectives. Naturally, real and imagined differences will arise, especially with high-achievement-oriented athletes. Conflict and tensions are a natural part of high-performance team-building; what distinguishes successful teams is not the presence or absence of conflict but how relationship tensions are managed. Table 10.2 highlights some of the important factors in relationship tension.

In our workshops, the goal is to create a highly cohesive and cooperative team. When this goal is achieved, the result is respectful, friendly communication

Table 10.2 Understanding Team Relationship Tension

Factors increasing tension	Factors reducing tension
Negative communication: reduce self-esteem and stimulate defensive behaviors	Positive communication: increase self-esteem and cooperative behaviors through positive reinforcement
Judgmental criticism: judge tone of voice denoting authoritarian rather than authoritative expertise; focus on what's wrong rather that what's right	Seeking understanding: ask questions to clarify others' perception and understanding of issue ("what," "when," "where," "how" questions rather than "why" questions)
Acting superior: emphasize rank or status and its importance	Establishing equality: emphasize value of different roles and make person-to-person relationships equal and equitable
Rigid leadership: emphasize complete and inflexible plans that foster both mindless compliance and resistance	Flexible leadership: have clear goals and be open to modifications from others
Being self-centered: focus too much on own goals; act as if not concerned or interested in other's interests	Being other-centered: know own goals, but focus on what others are thinking and feeling about team tasks; emphasis on sharing rather than telling
One-sided communication: talk, instruct, teach—others only listen and do, you have all the important answers	Two-way communication: exchange with a balance between talking and listening for all; demonstrate you want to hear other opinions and ideas
Controlling: provide total structure and direct entire process to achieve goals	Problem solving: encourage others to fully participate and resist closure until all ideas, thoughts, and feelings have been expressed; validate decisions

and relations. Friendships often form, but they are not a necessary condition of high-functioning teams. In fact, high-performing athletes are often quite diverse in many characteristics and develop friendships outside the team. What distinguishes the high-performing team is the capacity to focus on team goals and not let individual and interpersonal barriers interfere with the larger aim.

The Link Between Teamwork and the Business World

Many research findings from business regarding leadership, team organization, and performance dynamics increase our understanding of sport and team development. Vision and leadership are concepts that cannot be overemphasized, but are often neglected.

In a review of effective leadership and personality, Dr. Robert Hogan, an international expert and principal of Hogan Assessment Systems, notes that

© Empics

Highly cohesive teams thrive on cooperation, communication, and mutual respect.

leadership is about persuasion, not domination. The view of the successful "captain of industry" as a hard-charging, iron-fisted, bottom-line-oriented entrepreneur is largely a myth. Such persons do exist and they can be pointed out to make this case; however, extensive empirical studies show that this type of person is not the norm.

In coaching clinics and consultations, we use the concept of emotional intelligence that was made popular by Harvard psychologist Daniel Goleman. Emotional intelligence is the ability to manage our relationships and ourselves effectively through self-awareness, self-management, social awareness, and social skills. Drawing on research involving a large, random sample of executives, Goleman relates their levels of emotional intelligence to six leadership styles that are distinguished by particular attributes and characteristics. These styles, which we have adapted from his article, are shown in table 10.3.

Research on leadership shows that although all styles can be successful, at least for the short-term, four—authoritative, affiliative, democratic, and coaching—are more effective than the other leadership types. In addition, different situations call for different leadership styles—one size does not fit all teams and situations. Consequently, coaches and other team leaders must learn to recognize their dominant or favorite style and develop alternative skills to use in meeting

Table 10.3 Leadership Styles and Characteristics

	Coercive	Authoritative*	Affiliative*	Democratic*	Pace-setting	Coaching*
Leader's style of interaction	Demands immediate compliance	Mobilizes people toward a vision	Creates harmony and builds emotional bonds	Forges consensus through participation	Sets high standards for performance	Develops people for the future
Identifying phrase	"Do what I tell you."	"Come with me."	"People come first."	"What do you think?"	"Do as I do, now."	"Try this."
Underlying emotional intelligence competencies	Drive to achieve, initiative, self-control	Self-confidence, empathy, change catalyst	Empathy, building relationships, communication	Collaboration, team leadership, communication	Conscientiousness, drive to achieve, initiative	Developing others, empathy, self-awareness
Overall impact on climate	Negative	Most positive	Positive	Positive	Negative	Positive
Benefits or use to the sports team	Crisis management, start a turnaround, problem athlete, coach, parent	When team changes require new vision, or a clear direction is needed	Healing rifts in team or motivating players during stressful times	Get buy-in, build consensus, encourage input from key personnel	Get quick results from highly motivated players and highly competent team units	Helping players and coaches improve performance or develop long-term skills

* Most effective leadership styles.

the changing needs of the team. Flexible leadership and the intellectual and emotional intelligence to recognize which type will achieve the desired outcome for the team is an essential part of coaching.

Building a Great Team

Given the great diversity in teams, coaching, and athletes, providing practical directions that have maximum application is a challenge in this brief chapter. The framework (MAPS) that follows illustrates the key principles and techniques for working with teams and can be adapted to various team sports.

Mission: philosophy or ideal that guides the team beyond the individual season, coach, or athlete. The mission helps guide specific process or outcome goals (e.g., achieving a high level of cohesion and communication, or winning a conference title or season). Goals can be broken down into long-term, intermediate, and short-term objectives.

Assessment: identification of team strengths and challenges. Careful assessment can indicate the resources, changes, and processes that will improve the potential of the team to achieve its goals.

Plan: team action steps that each member works at to improve individual and group efforts. Ideally, these steps have a high degree of consensus, with concrete actions, targeted behaviors, and specific timelines.

Systematic evaluation: periodic review of the entire "road map," looking at goals and objectives and assessment and resource needs. Implementation of the planned action steps will provide an empirical structure and process for reflection, review, and revisions.

Create a Mission

The foundation of team-building begins with formulating a consensus on a clear and concise mission statement, which describes what the team stands for, its values, and its commitment to excellence. A mission is not about scoring points, beating a competitor, or winning a trophy. With teams, this task is complex because the members all have individual ideas about what they are doing on the team and what the team purpose should be. With a clear mission statement in hand, the team can formulate specific goals and strategic objectives.

The creation of a mission statement and subsequent goals and objectives occurs through a dialogue between coaches and players. Although individual coaches can take the leadership role in this process, we strongly advocate for the presence of a sport psychology consultant who is knowledgeable about and experienced in group dynamics. An "outside" but knowledgeable facilitator is a powerful asset to the process, allowing the coach to actively listen to the team members while the consultant takes on the responsibility of ensuring that the dialogue is productive. This does not mean that the coach is passive; it is critical that he or she exerts strong leadership in supporting the *process* but not dictating the *outcomes*. The outcomes of the mission and goal-setting processes should be a product of the entire team.

A proven method for doing this work is in a retreat or workshop format, with a sport psychology consultant as the facilitator. We use the initial team session to inform all members about the critical aspects of developing team excellence, including relevant research findings on high-performing teams and the factors that will build success for the players and the team. This informative session begins to build group cohesion and establishes the credibility of the sport consultant.

Regularly Assess Team Qualities and Responsibilities

Regular assessment of team qualities that can positively or negatively affect team-building and performance is a critical part of creating excellence. Critical observations of team practice or competition—such as how players work together, communication, and adjustments to feedback from teammates and coaches—are a good place to start and can give a quick picture of the degree of team cohesiveness. Leadership styles in motivating players, giving instruction and feedback, and establishing team norms and values become evident by listening to coaching sessions. The functional and dysfunctional patterns that observation reveals over time can be discussed in workshops on how to improve team excellence.

Objective scales are also useful in increasing awareness of attributes that relate to improving team functioning. For example, we frequently use the Myers-Briggs Type Indicator (MBTI) as a way to foster individual awareness and the team's understanding and appreciation of personal styles and differences. The MBTI, available in a self-scoring version suitable for workshops, identifies preferences in interactive style, information processing, decision making, and implementing stratagies used in daily life. Discussing the value of individual differences can lead to greater appreciation of diversity as a strong contributor to excellence—and with understanding comes team cohesion and improved performance. Many individual assessment scales can be use creatively for this purpose; some are self-report questionnaires that can be used by anyone, while others require special training or licensure. Several scales have been specifically developed for use with teams:

- Leadership Scale of Sport (LSS): a 40-item, five-point scale that provides an assessment of leadership attributes
- Decision-style questionnaires: Case situations commonly faced by teams in which the athlete categorizes his or her coach on different dimensions
- Coaching Behavior Assessment System (CBAS): An observation scale adapted to a questionnaire that assesses both players' and coaches' perceptions and recall of the coaches' behavior (such as feedback or leadership style)
- Perceived Motivational Climate in Sport Questionnaire-2 (PMCSQ-2): Respondents indicate the degree to which the team climate is task involving (mastery oriented) or ego involving (performance oriented).
- The Group Environment Questionnaire (GEQ): A measure of cohesion in sport groups

Create a Motivational Action Plan

Another key step in team-building strategies is motivating team members to take specific action steps that will sustain the process. Neither individual nor group behaviors are easily changed. Establishing a commitment to take concrete steps to improve individual and team functioning is crucial to this process. As described in our discussion of cohesiveness, having team members define their values and clarify their roles is important; when sources of misunderstanding, miscommunication, and interpersonal conflict are uncovered early, they can be the focus of corrective plans.

Several ways to help teams develop action plans follow.

1. Open discussion and commitment. We often focus a discussion on individual action plans for improvement and how they relate to the team goals. In addition, a "buy-in," or commitment, to the team-focused action plan helps ensure follow-through. When team members attempt to clarify differences rather than merely make agreements of convenience, we say there is buy-in. Concrete language shifts from saying "but" to "and" often signify consensus.

2. Team goals. Team goals are those attributes that were identified as priorities in earlier discussions and assessments. For example, the goal of the basketball-team scenario with James as described on the following page could be to improve teammate communication by having meetings and encouraging each athlete to speak up about what is going well and what needs to improve. In this way, issues related to slumping performance can be discussed in a solution-oriented format. Discussion of individual goals can include brainstorming for solutions and an attempt to understand the role of individual efforts in the context of team communication and coordinated play. Team discussions can also address better coordination of individual skills and sharing of responsibilities to avoid overreliance on one or two "star" players.

3. Follow-up and feedback. It takes time for new behavioral patterns to become habits, and it takes time and discussions for athletes to fine-tune their efforts. Follow-up sessions provide an opportunity to reinforce and elaborate on successful efforts and instruct the group on those that did not work out as planned.

Evaluate Teamwork Through Constructive Feedback

Evaluating teams is a complex and challenging process. Constructive feedback is essential, yet difficult to achieve. Establishing a receptive climate for this feedback is essential to ensure that the team will hear the message and focus on improving rather than feeling defensive. Coaches need to validate the goals of athlete development and team improvement early in order to set the stage for trust and open communication. In addition to good communication skills, standardized objective assessments can reduce the perception that feedback is simply a personal negative opinion.

Ideally, the steps in the process of team building occur in a longitudinal, cyclical process. However, lack of time, resources, and other constraints may abbreviate the process, with the consultant working with the team for one or two sessions, followed by assistant coaches, trainers, and other local professionals stepping in as facilitators.

Take the following story of "James" as an example of these guidelines put to work through sport psychologists.

James

Recently, we worked with a collegiate basketball team at the request of the coach who had recruited "James," a 20-year-old transfer student in his junior year of college. He was a very high-performing junior college player, recruited with high expectations to improve the team's standing in the league. James started out well, quickly earning a starting forward spot, averaging 23 points per game for the first four games. However, as he improved, he became more of a focus of the opposition and began getting an increasing number of fouls. His free-throw percentages began to drop precipitously and his usual high percentage from the floor began to drop as well. He noticed that other teammates were slumping, but not as much as he was. They lost the next two games. He was even more introverted than usual, presenting a challenge for the coach as well as other players as to what to do. Several issues were obviously affecting James' performance. Our efforts were focused on the team, and trying to be all things to the team can present problems. In this case, we referred James for individual counseling to deal with the shyness, introversion, and social anxiety that contributed to his performance problems. In the meantime, we stayed focused at the team level, working to align individual goals to the team perspective. Because James made quick progress at the individual level, we were able to engage him, his teammates, and the coach in more open and constructive problem-solving about how to recover and move to even higher performance levels.

Another example is the U.S. parachute team. A psychologist who was working with the team on individual performance enhancement felt that a team consultation would be useful. The four athletes were performing at a high level in world competition but were not reaching their full potential. In addition to participating in weekly group discussions, each took a personality-type assessment in order to identify the styles of perception and decision making that each brought to the team. The significant differences we found were not surprising since three of the athletes were college-educated scientists and one was a blue-collar laborer. Intensive discussions clarified and resolved the barriers, allowing the team to move to a deeper level of understanding and respect for each other, which we believe led to more effective results from group imagery exercises. Imagery techniques (see chapter 8) are useful in team situations; however, they warrant greater preparation than with individuals, as well as awareness of group dynamics. Several months later, we heard that the team had achieved its goal of setting a new world record.

We have found that developing a long-term relationship with teams offers them the greatest benefit because it allows intervention methods to develop and change over time. We see this as well in business consulting, education, and counseling. One-time lectures give information, which is quickly forgotten unless it is reinforced by applying it to the sport. Comprehensive, long-term sport psychology can make a major contribution to team dynamics. There are no quick secrets to success. As one team member said, "You are not really an outsider; you are part of our team."

In summary, we offer a few reminders about essential behaviors for athletes, coaches, and parents that promote team-building.

For the athlete

- Understand your role in relation to those of your teammates.
- Understand your personal goals in the context of team goals.
- Take responsibility to communicate.
- Work toward cooperative competitiveness by focusing on the interdependency between individual growth, personal challenges, group support, and team achievement.
- Use your strengths to benefit the team, and let others use theirs.

For the coach

- Understand your own leadership style in terms of your strengths and blind spots.
- Listen to the views of athletes, assistant coaches, parents, and other team members.
- Provide clear, flexible leadership to accomplish team development, goals, and performance excellence.
- Build cohesiveness to improve both interactive and coactive teams.
- Recognize and maximize diversity and use it to build complementary strengths.
- Be open to leadership support from consultants, athletes, and other coaches.

For the parent

- Keep the child's interests, not yours, as the primary motivation for sport.
- Support the team as a way to help youth develop social cooperation as well as athletic skills.
- Participate in team activities but with good communication with your child. Remember that an increasing reliance on peers rather than parents is a marker of normal child development.
- Encourage fun and learning as part of team sports.
- Recognize that competition itself is not a negative attribute but that overemphasis on winning can be a major barrier.
- Offer adaptive support to the child, adolescent, or young adult, with the awareness of when to push, pull, or just be there.

All team members need to use common sense. However, as Voltaire noted, "The only problem with common sense is that it is so uncommon." Team members can help each other review their experiences and find their common sense.

Future Directions

Sport is here to stay, and all those involved are interested in doing better. Coaches are becoming more astute about psychological aspects of teams, and in the future, more teams at all levels will seek out professionals who can add value through team building, conflict resolution, supportive communication, evaluations, and feedback for improvement.

We expect to see evolutionary rather than revolutionary change. However, rapidly improving information about the physical, psychological, and social aspects of sport performance will increase the need for more sophisticated and comprehensive strategies for team development and performance—by all participants in the process. One area of breakthrough is in using technologies for virtual coaching. Sport consultants are already using these technologies in individual work with athletes and coaches, but the quantum jump will likely be in virtual group coaching. Here the consultant can extend the range and scope while at the same time providing more cost-effective services to teams, perhaps even through teleconsulting. This technology is already effective with relatively low-level methods, such as the telephone and email, but it is sure to become even more useful as telecommunications technologies mature and expand to provide widespread, easily accessed, and affordable service (e.g., video-conferencing, computer-supported group work).

Where will we be 10 years from now? Scientific knowledge and its relevance to individual tasks within team sports will be increasingly available to all. However, the process of implementing and integrating the relevant information will remain a complex, poorly understood, and professionally artful process. It will be the rare coach, athlete, or even consultant who has the time, energy, and expertise to handle all important team tasks. Therefore, coaches must develop resources within their own organizations to assist them and engage outside consultants when appropriate.

Coaching: An Effective Communication System

Charles J. Hardy, Kevin L. Burke, and R. Kelly Crace

I'm a teacher and a coach. I surround myself with other good teachers on my staff. And our whole approach to coaching revolves around teaching. Teaching is at the heart of my coaching style. If I teach them well, winning games will be the natural result. If my goal had to be only winning games, I wouldn't be a coach.

People learn how to think by communicating. So in our program, we not only employ an offensive system and a defensive system—we employ a communication system.

Mike Krzyzewski, Duke University men's basketball coach

The Essence of Coaching

The essence of coaching comes down to teaching and motivating. It is one of the few professions in which extremely hard work and commitment are devoted to a particular performance event in which others execute the performance. The performers have to learn from someone more knowledgeable than they are in order to grow and develop as athletes—hence, the necessity for teaching. They also have to have the right mind-set and emotional state to allow their talents to be unleashed; therefore, coaches need to know how to properly motivate them. If teaching and motivating are essential to coaching, then what could be more important to its success than effective communication? Yet coaches tend to communicate in a manner that is most natural for them, be it good or bad.

Effective coaches provide the vision the team will strive for and the instruction necessary to translate that vision into reality. If a team is to function effectively, coaches must communicate in a clear, honest, and direct manner. In addition, empathy, consistency, and responsiveness to player differences are critical to the development of successful coach–athlete relationships.

If a team is to be successful, its members must be able to communicate openly and honestly with the coaching staff and teammates about team functioning and the quality of interpersonal relationships. This is what Duke coach Mike Krzyzewski—"Coach K"—calls a communication system, and its development and maintenance are essential to any team's success. We have all known great coaches and talent-laden teams who have fallen short of their potential because of ineffective communication. This chapter focuses on the fundamentals of sending, receiving, and interpreting messages—building and maintaining an effective communication system. It is based on information consolidated from experts in the study of communication and coaches' responsibilities as teachers and motivators but is immediately applicable to any sport.

Successful coaches such as "Coach K" rely on a system of communication that is constantly under development and maintenance to ensure his team's success.

©Icon SMI

We have one favor to ask of our readers. We all have ingrained patterns of communicating that are difficult to change without hard work and perseverance. As you read this chapter, look for one or two strategies that have particular importance for you and work on those over the next year. If you try to incorporate too many of the strategies recommended here, you will come across as insincere and unnatural. Even more important, you may become overwhelmed and eventually abandon your efforts. Before you read on, honestly assess your communication style. What do you feel good about, and how would you like to improve? What have others said about your communication style? Ask those closest to you to identify one area of communication they would like to see you improve. Where does it rank in importance to you relative to other areas of self-improvement? To assist those of you who are coaches in this process, we have adapted a self-assessment scale developed by communications expert Lawrence Rosenfeld (see figure 11.1).

Communication Self-Evaluation Assessment

Think about how you communicate with others (i.e., athletes, assistant coaches, officials, media). How often do you find yourself engaging in the following behaviors? In the space provided, indicate whether you engage in the behavior:

1 = Almost always   2 = Usually   3 = Sometimes   4 = Seldom   5 = Almost never

_____ 1. I pay attention primarily to what an athlete is saying and give little attention to what he or she is doing.

_____ 2. I let an athlete's lack of organization get in the way of my listening.

_____ 3. I interrupt if I have something I want to say.

_____ 4. I stop listening when I think I understand the idea whether or not the reporter has finished.

_____ 5. I fail to repeat back what has been said before I react.

_____ 6. I give little verbal or nonverbal feedback to officials.

_____ 7. I pay attention only to the words, rather than to the words, tone, and pitch being used.

_____ 8. I let emotion-laden words make me angry.

_____ 9. If I consider the subject boring I stop paying attention.

_____ 10. I find myself unable to limit my criticism to my athletes' performance.

_____ 11. I find getting in the face of an official gets my point across.

_____ 12. I allow distractions to interfere with my concentration.

_____ 13. I do not recognize when I am too upset or tired to speak or listen.

_____ 14. I raise my voice when I want my athletes to pay attention to what I am saying.

_____ 15. I try to give advice when someone is telling me his or her problems.

Figure 11.1   Rosenfeld's self-assessment scale.

Adapted from Lawrence Rosenfeld

Reprinted, by permission, from Lawrence Rosenfeld and Larry Wilder, 1990, Communication fundamentals: Active listening, *Sport Psychology Training Bulletin, 1*(5):8.

Add your responses to the 15 items. This is your total communication self-evaluation score. The higher the score, the more effective are your communication skills. This instrument is based on the skills you need to possess to be a good communicator. The total number is less important than your responses to the separate items. Those items on which you gave yourself a rating of 1, 2, or 3 indicate areas in which you need to improve. While it is informative to evaluate yourself, we also encourage you to have assistant coaches and athletes evaluate you so that you can understand how others perceive you. Finally, we hope that a careful read of the information presented in this chapter will help you develop a plan of action to improve your communication skills.

Looks Can Be Deceiving

A couple of years ago, we had an interesting experience that exemplified the critical importance of effective communication and how things are not always what they seem. We were working with three teams concurrently that were struggling with different issues. Two were having performance-based problems, and one was preparing for the challenge of repeating a record-breaking year with a "new" team because of a high number of seniors graduating. The primary issues were not about communication but we were struck initially by the contrast between the coaches' communication styles and the responses of the teams. They were incongruent with what we expected. One coach was personable, involved, and positive in her technical communication with her team. Her team was having severe performance problems later identified to be closely connected to her communication style. Another coach was mild-mannered, even-tempered, and soft-spoken and rarely lost his temper with his team. Again, his communication style turned out to be a significant factor in the team's poor performances. Then there was the third coach. He was your stereotypical gruff, in-your-face, short-fused coach. We were certain that his communication style was going to be a problem. It was not. They had just come off their best season and the team was responding appropriately to the upcoming challenge of repeating with very few of the same players. They were loyal and responsive to him.

As we got to know the dynamics of the teams better, it became clear that each team was responding to another level of communication from their coach. What we were seeing and hearing initially was not what the teams were responding to. Not only that, it reminded us of one of the most critical links between communication and performance. We will come back to these three teams at the end of the chapter to review what was really going on and to clarify this important factor.

What Message Are You Sending?

You can communicate without motivating, but it is impossible to motivate without communicating.

John Thompson, former Georgetown University men's basketball coach

Communication involves sending, receiving, and interpreting messages through a variety of channels. When we interact with others, each message communicated has at least two types of components: informational and emotional. Depending on the person and the situation, these components can have different weights, which have dramatic effects on the communication process. Think about the last time you tried to communicate with your athletes during a break in a heated contest as opposed to communicating the same message during a practice session.

Although our main communication channels are vision and hearing, we also communicate through touch, taste, smell, and feel. The way a message is expressed affects how it is received and interpreted. We communicate verbally by writing or speaking and nonverbally by facial expressions, body language and positioning, symbolic gestures, and symbols. *How* coaches say something can be just as important as *what* they say. Coaches who are effective communicators use multiple channels to get their intended messages across.

Most people believe they communicate better than or as well as everyone else. Therefore, communication problems may remain because most individuals perceive them as someone else's fault or responsibility. Periodically, we hear coaches say that it is the team's responsibility to adapt to the coach's communication style, not vice versa.

It has been suggested that the foundation for effective communication in coaching is having credibility in the eyes of your athletes and developing trust and mutual respect. Trust is a two-way street that must be built brick by brick over time. Coaches who demonstrate, through their actions, honesty (can your athletes believe what you say?), integrity (are your actions consistent with your values and belief systems?), and openness (do you communicate in an open and honest manner?) earn the trust of their athletes. Their credibility is determined by the answers their athletes give to those three questions. Coaches who (1) establish open lines of communication; (2) act in an honest, fair, sincere, and consistent manner; (3) accept athletes for who they are as individuals; and (4) genuinely care about their athletes as people are seen as trustworthy and have developed and maintained an effective communication system.

Robert Kriegel and David Brandt, the authors of *Sacred Cows Make the Best Burgers*, state, "People don't care how much you know until they know how much you care." Caring is a rather soft concept that many in the tough business of athletics disparage as naive or silly. Caring is for preachers and sport psychologists, they say, not win–lose-driven athletic administrators and coaches.

However, coaches must invest in their athletes if they are to be successful. Communication systems must be built on the concept of caring if they are to be effective. But what are we talking about when we talk about the notion of caring? Are we delving into the touchy-feely world of hugs and I-love-yous? Hardly. Kriegel and Brandt argue that caring relationships are characterized by three factors: respect, empathy, and acknowledgment. An effective communication system must, therefore, make use of these three characteristics.

Communication is a complex process that requires skill and effort on the part of everyone involved. Unfortunately, the process often breaks down, usually because of mistakes by the person sending the message or the person receiving it, or both. Many attempts at communication fail because we cannot get a point across successfully to others. Multimedia communications expert Milo Frank suggests that we can enhance our communication skills by knowing how to get our point across effectively, precisely, and concisely. The basis of sending effective messages is determining "what," "who," and "how." "What" is the purpose of the communication—what do you want to communicate and why do you feel you need to communicate this to others?

Once you have determined your communication objective, you then need to identify whom you need to communicate with. You should know as much as possible about that person. The key here is to develop an understanding of and respect for the target of your communication. The adage of "know your audience" is worth remembering when trying to develop an effective message.

"How" refers to the approach you take in sending your message. Both verbal and nonverbal channels need to be employed. For example, if an athlete makes an outstanding play, the coach should show excitement through facial expressions and tone of voice while verbally complimenting the athlete's efforts. The message must capture the attention of the target person, have the appropriate facts and feelings, and empower the target to act or react to the message. An effective message allows the listener to "paint a picture" of what we are saying. The most effective messages are those that reach the heart—if you can inspire emotion in the listener, a behavior change will likely follow.

Failure to listen also contributes to poor communication. According to communication professors Lawrence Rosenfeld and Larry Wilder, we should strive for "level-one listening," or *effective listening*. An effective listener actively pays attention to main and supporting ideas and acknowledges, responds, and gives appropriate feedback. In other words, the listener shows concern about the content, intent, and feelings of the message.

Sport psychologist Mark Anshel developed a set of guidelines for coaches that he refers to as the 10 Commandments for Effective Communication. These are:

1. Thou shalt be *honest*.

2. Thou shalt *not* be *defensive*.

3. Thou shalt be *consistent*.

4. Thou shalt be *empathetic*.

5. Thou shalt *not* be *sarcastic*.

6. Thou shalt praise and criticize *behavior*, not personality.

7. Thou shalt respect the *integrity* of others.

8. Thou shalt use positive *nonverbal* cues.

9. Thou shalt *teach* skills.

10. Thou shalt *interact* consistently with all team members.

Excerpts from *Sport psychology*, 4th ed. By Mark H. Anshel. Copyright ©2003 Pearson Education, Inc. Reprinted by permission.

We've identified some of the principles of establishing an effective communication system. The subsequent sections describe how to facilitate these principles when sending and receiving messages.

Effective Message-Sending Systems

> Good communication is as stimulating as black coffee, and just as hard to sleep after.
>
> *Anne Spencer Morrow Lindbergh, American aviator,* North to the Orient

The following recommendations on how to effectively *send* messages come from our experiences in working with coaches and teams, and from the expertise of our colleagues Rainer Martens, Robert Weinberg, and Dan Gould.

Develop your message　Most of us think we know what we want to say; however, coaches often tell us that they have so much to say that they do not know where to start. Or worse yet, they blast their athletes with enough information to last a lifetime. You must determine what you want to communicate, and stick to it. Be careful not to employ hidden agendas (when the stated purpose and the real purpose of the message are not the same). These types of messages may cause mistrust and decrease the communication with the team.

Effectively communicated messages must not exceed the concentration and memory storage capacities of the listeners. Psychologist George Miller found that humans can hold five to nine items in their short-term memory banks. But as the stress of a situation increases—particularly during competition, when emotions and stress levels may be higher than normal—athletes' concentration capacities usually narrow, making it difficult to focus on multiple messages.

Athletes want to know what coaches are thinking while they are thinking it. You have seen their expressions as they look at coaches for cues about what they are thinking, which can significantly interfere with the athletes' concentration and decision-making. Immediate feedback is more effective and meaningful than delayed feedback, so when possible, coaches should deliver their message at the time they observe the behavior. In other words, when a player gives an outstanding effort, tell him or her so immediately rather than waiting until another day, by which time the window of opportunity for the message to have an effect may have closed. Of course, feedback needs to be timed so that strong emotions do not interfere with effective sending of the message or with it being heard in the manner intended.

Get in their heads   Communication is enhanced to the extent that coaches understand their athletes; that is, they should know as much as possible about the values, feelings, and unique situations of their athletes and fellow coaches. Coaches who show understanding lead athletes to believe that they care about them and appreciate what they bring to the team. Once athletes feel understood, appreciated, and cared about, communication is enhanced. In his book *The Seven Habits of Highly Effective People*, Stephen Covey refers to this as Habit 5: Seek first to understand, then to be understood. Before you attempt to offer a solution to a problem, give advice or criticism, or tell your side of the story, seek to understand the perspective of the athlete. When you can "get inside the head" of your athlete and understand his or her value system, interests, and goals, you open the door for effective communication and interdependence. Of course, it can take all your time to get to know all the players and coaches on an in-depth level, but do not let this reality cause you to take an "all or nothing" approach to getting to know your team. Rate yourself on how well you know your team on a 1-to-10 scale, then develop a plan to increase that understanding by 1 or 2 points. That creates a goal that is realistic without having to sacrifice other goals.

Tell the truth, directly and specifically   Having the courage to tell the truth greatly increases the trustworthiness and subsequent effectiveness of coaches with their teams. Telling the truth requires character, integrity, and a willingness to be open, direct, and specific in communicating. Coaches who "step up to the plate" and "square up" with athletes are respected and revered. They should provide direct communication to athletes so that there can be no doubt about performance expectations. In conflict situations, coaches must have the courage and skills to confront athletes so that the conflict can be resolved. The key here is to control emotions so that anger and hostility do not disrupt communication. Coaches often avoid this straightforward approach because they assume that athletes know what they expect or they do not want to hurt athletes' feelings. Credibility and trust are on the line here. Athletes have to know that what they hear from coaches is truthful. Those who hint around or work through a third party (e.g., an assistant coach, athletic trainer, or captain) may find that their trustworthiness is questioned. Once trust is broken, it is very difficult to restore. Remember, lies have long lives and create clogged internal arteries of communication that lead to active communication grapevines and powerful rumor mills.

In addition to openness, being direct and specific are critical components of being honest. Nothing is more frustrating to an athlete than for a coach to say something like, "You need to get your head into the game." While the coach may believe this covers what needs to be done, the vague message provides very limited information to the athlete about the problem or specific tasks to focus on. Something like this is more on the mark: "Focus on the cues the striker gives you. Watch her hips—if they are open, she is going to your left; if closed, to your right." Athletes need adequate and specific information in order to interpret a message correctly.

Interpersonal relationships grow and develop as the degree of mutual sharing of needs and feelings increases. It is truly OK to be human. Athletes respond to emotions. Messages that are attached to high emotional content tend to have great effects on the listeners. A word of caution, however: Do not overload the emotional component of the communication so that the informational component is not heard and understood. The key is to use emotions in communication to flavor the information. Be careful not to overdraw your emotional bank account with your athletes.

We are often asked how to determine when to communicate during times of strong emotions and when to wait. A good rule of thumb is to employ the "what else is true?" standard. Strong emotions tend to narrow our perception of the person evoking the emotion. If you did something to make me angry, in the intensity of that emotion I would see you only as the person who made me angry. Until I could see you in a broader framework (what else is true about you?), I would do best to refrain from communicating. However, immediate feedback is sometimes necessary, such as during a competition or practice, and we do not always have the luxury of waiting when we are emotional. But knowing that strong emotions prevent you from seeing everything that is true may temper how you respond. You may contract with yourself that whenever you are emotional but have to give feedback, you will speak only to the behavior, not the person. Of course, when possible, wait until you can see the full picture.

Use supportive language and empathy   If you want others to listen, build them up rather than tear them down. That means avoiding threats, sarcasm, negative comparisons, and judgmental statements. Using positive, supportive words and gestures will cause your athletes to want to talk and listen to you. If you pause and think before you speak, you can deliver all of your messages, including criticisms, in a positive and supportive way.

Empathy is the ability to think and feel another person's experience. It is the process of connecting to others' realities in order to understand not only what they are thinking and feeling but also how they got to this point. Although empathy begins with listening, messages that are empathetic can create powerful, resilient relationships within the team.

Coaches can deliver positive and supportive messages by acknowledging their athletes' efforts; unfortunately, they are much more likely to deliver criticism than praise and positive reinforcement. Negative feedback takes its toll over time. Athletes are loyal when they feel appreciated. Sometimes the most effective communication is to express pride in the athletes' effort or thank them for what they bring to the team. Kriegel and Brandt reported that 46 percent of the people who leave their jobs in the business world do so because they do not feel appreciated by their bosses. We suspect that many athletes choose to leave their teams because they too do not get the message that they are valued and appreciated by coaches. So make sure your communication acknowledges individual as well as team efforts, and deliver those messages frequently.

Using supportive and positive language also sends the message that you respect your athletes. Showing respect means treating athletes as human beings with value rather than as expendable entities. As the veteran baseball manager Sparky Anderson said, "Treat everybody as if they're somebody, because they are." Respect does not mean "smiles-at-all-times" coaching. If athletes perform poorly or make bad decisions, do not ignore it or accept it. On the contrary, showing respect means that you hold athletes accountable for their actions. You call them to task and point out the mistake, but never attack them. A rule of thumb is to demand excellence in terms of performance and be supportive of the athlete as a person. When you criticize performances rather than people, interpersonal relationships remain intact and defensiveness is minimized. When you attack an athlete as a person, you create deep animosity that sometimes cannot be repaired.

Model the message   In today's world there is a huge gap between knowing what to do and doing it. Indeed, an estimated 95 percent of managers today *say* the right thing, but only 5 percent actually *do* it—the "95/5 rule." Many coaches take actions that violate unwritten rules as well as their stated intentions. For example, they preach the importance of teamwork but only reward individuals who stand out from the team. Coaches' attitudes and actions must be consistent with their words; there is nothing that builds trust among the team more than a coach who consistently models his or her message. The power of personal example goes a long way in building trust and enhancing the communication process among teams.

Joe Erhmann is a former NFL All-Pro. He and his fellow coaches have developed a program called Building Men for Others, in which they use the sport of football to teach young men the important qualities of being a man. The cornerstone of their program is developing empathy—a sense of understanding, respect, and appreciation for each other that helps them develop and challenge each other to their potential. This program would fail if it were not for the coaches who consistently model empathy in all situations.

Nonverbal behaviors that communicate interest and attention include standing no more than a few feet from the other person, maintaining eye contact, making appropriate facial gestures, and keeping your bodies facing each other. It has been argued that 50 to 70 percent of all communication is nonverbal. That means athletes pay more attention to *how* coaches say what they say than *what* they actually say. The real key to influence is setting an example through behavior. This flows naturally from a person's character and values, not from who they say they are or who they want others to think they are.

One final word about modeling your message: Do it for yourself. The cornerstone of adult self-esteem is integrity, behaving congruently with an internalized set of values. We feel best about ourselves when we behave in ways that are consistent with what is meaningful and important to us; conversely, we feel worst about ourselves when our values and actions are out of sync. And we can never completely hide from that truth.

Three Rs: Repeat, repeat, repeat   If you want your athletes to hear what you say, say it once, twice, and a third time if necessary. Make sure you repeat the key elements, or "meat," of your communication often. The more a message is repeated, the more likely it is that the information will be remembered. When possible, tell them, show them, and then make them show you, so that you are comfortable that they have heard and understood your message.

Coaches often communicate intended philosophies, important points of focus, and motivational themes in the form of mottoes, slogans, and creeds. These are excellent ways to reinforce a message; however, they must not become invisible in the same way that the pictures in your house, which may have tremendous value, lose their salience over time. Go back to those mottoes from time to time to underscore why they are important, and periodically develop new slogans and mottoes that send the same message.

Watch body language   Coaches need to watch for verbal and nonverbal signs that the athletes they communicate with are receiving their messages. Body language is an excellent indicator, and it is also a good idea to check in periodically with questions such as, "How do you understand what I'm saying?" One of the best ways to verify whether a message has been received, however, is to ask athletes to explain what they heard. By putting the message into their own words, they reveal their level of understanding of the message.

Employ "the sandwich approach" when giving criticism   Coaches must analyze performance and provide criticism in a constructive and nonthreatening manner. As we have said before, that means critiquing behavior and coaching the person. Coaches who ridicule, demean, or put down an athlete create three problems: (1) They compromise the interpersonal relationship—athletes feel intimidated, hurt, and angry; (2) they cause athletes to become more self-aware and decrease their confidence levels—so that they second-guess themselves and lose the ability to trust themselves and their skills; and (3) they feed the "defensiveness monster"—athletes either immediately react in an emotional manner or psychologically disengage from the coach and the team. The result is that the communication system breaks down and performance suffers.

One extremely effective approach to delivering constructive criticisms involves what University of Washington psychologist Ron Smith and his colleagues have labeled "the sandwich approach." For example, in this technique, the coach, using the player's name, first begins with a positive statement, such as "Pat, good effort on getting in front of the ball." Next, the coach gives future-oriented instructions—he tells her what to do the next time she is in that situation: "When the ball is coming straight toward you, be sure to get your glove all the way down to the ground." Then he follows this instructive feedback with a positive or encouraging statement that describes how things will improve if his message is heard: "If you practice that, you will be able to consistently field balls at a variety of speeds and bounces." An alternative effective strategy is to follow the corrective instruction with a statement that gives general encouragement, such as "Pat, I really appreciate your consistently good attitude." Thus, the "meat" of the sandwich (future-oriented instruction) comes between the "bread slices" (positive and encouraging statements). The positive statements must be genuine and relate to the present situation. This strategy does not dilute constructive advice; instead it increases the likelihood that the message is received properly and that athletes view their interactions with the coach in a positive manner. It may take some practice in the beginning, but much time and energy is saved if the message is understood the first time. Another benefit of the sandwich approach is that it allows coaches to correct mistakes in a positive, productive manner that causes athletes to focus on what to do the *next time* they are in that sport situation, rather than dwelling on their mistakes. Remember, the key is to communicate in a way that increases the likelihood that the message is heard and acted on.

Great coaches are great listeners who employ simple stratagies such as active listening and reflection.

At times, a player is struggling so badly with his or her performance that it is difficult to find a "positive slice" to start with. Hint: Start with something that is the opposite of what is wrong. If technique is the problem, start with a positive statement about effort or perseverance. If poor effort is the problem, start with a positive statement about skills. If poor effort and poor technique are the problems, you can always start by speaking about the player's inherent value to the team.

Use more "ands" than "buts" When giving feedback, the use of "but" increases the chance that only half the message will be heard, and it will usually be the negative half. Even a message delivered in a positive manner will be received more negatively if you use "but" instead of "and." Replacing "but" with "and" fosters a clearer understanding of the message and greater motivation to work on the feedback. Why? Using the word "and" tends to result in both messages being heard. For example, "Nice steal, but you need to work on your transition pass." This message is typically heard and received as "You need to work on your transition pass." Inserting "and" results in both messages being heard: "I made a nice steal *and* I need to work on my transition passes." The positive comment serves as motivation to work on areas that need improvement.

Effective Message-Receiving Systems

It's not what you tell them—it's what they hear.

Red Auerbach, former Boston Celtics championship coach

Now let's focus on broadening the communication system to include active listening for optimal performance. The recommendations are based on our work with coaches and the research of two colleagues, Rosenfeld and Wilder, who are noted experts in interpersonal communication and listening.

Don't mistake hearing for listening Unfortunately, most people assume that normal hearing equals good listening. But, in fact, hearing and listening are not the same. Many of us get angry when the person we are talking to does not seem to get the point or even appear to be tracking the conversation. Some of the habits that interfere with effective listening are "pseudolistening" (appearing to listen without paying attention), stage-hogging (thinking of what you are going to say while the other person is speaking), selective listening (hearing only those parts of the message that interest you), insulated listening (forgetting completely a message you do not want to hear), and ambushing (listening only to collect information to use in attacking the speaker).

Get ready to listen Just as performing effectively in sport requires preparation, so does effective listening. There may be times, after an exhausting day, when you are talking with someone and find yourself thinking, "I do not have the energy for this conversation right now." Martens has emphasized the importance of anticipating conversations that may be draining (e.g., those involving confrontations and conflict resolution) and reserving them for when you have the necessary energy. In addition to practicing the fundamentals of effective listening, you may find it helpful to do some preparation so that you know more about the person. If you unexpectedly find yourself in a position when you need to listen to someone but know it will be draining, stall for a couple of minutes (shuffle a few papers on the desk or file something) to mindfully put aside what you have been doing and gather your energy to focus on the task at hand.

Use supportive behaviors as you listen *Effective* listening is *active* listening, which is accomplished by practicing supportive and confirming behaviors. Supportive behaviors communicate that the message is acknowledged, understood, and accepted. Attacking behaviors communicate the opposite message and curtail effective communication; their purpose is protection rather than the sharing of information.

Supportive language has several identifiable characteristics:

- It is descriptive, not evaluative, and emphasizes "I" language. The emphasis switches from judging the other's behavior—"You are being lazy today" (attacking)—to describing what you experience—"I am not seeing the same effort from you that I normally see" (supportive).

- It is spontaneous, not manipulative, and focuses on immediate thoughts and feelings. The emphasis switches from following a calculated plan—"We are going to have to do something about us remaining doubles partners" (attacking)—to communicating honestly in the here and now—"I am concerned about how we are playing as doubles partners today" (supportive).

- It is empathic, not indifferent, and focuses on accepting the other person's feelings by putting the speaker in the other person's place. The emphasis switches from treating the other person in a neutral and detached way—"I am not taking sides in your fight with the coach" (attacking)—to communicating understanding for how the other person feels—"I can see how angry you are with the coach" (supportive).

- It focuses on remaining open to new ideas, perspectives, and the possibility of change. The emphasis switches from attacking—"It is either my way or the highway"—to supportive conclusions—"My experience has shown this method to be effective. Let's try it first and see if it works. If this does not, we can try other alternatives."

As you can see from the preceding descriptions and examples, supportive behaviors do not have to mean agreement.

Use confirming behaviors as you listen Just as supportive behavior is best understood by contrasting it with its opposite (attacking behavior), confirming behavior is best understood by contrasting it with its opposite, disconfirming behavior. How would you feel in each of the following situations?

- Someone fails to acknowledge what you say either verbally or nonverbally.
- Someone consistently interrupts you.
- Someone responds to your comment with an irrelevant remark.
- When you ask a simple question or make a simple statement, someone responds with an impersonal monologue, such as, "Well, when I played the game, I . . . "
- Someone's comments are so unclear that you cannot determine their true meaning.

Disconfirming behaviors can curtail effective communication. Instead, let people know you are "with them" in the conversation and that you understand their message, even if you do not agree with them. You usually will have an opportunity to express your own opinion.

Appropriate verbal statements can demonstrate your understanding of what the other person or team says and how they feel. Two useful techniques are paraphrasing, or putting the other's thoughts in your own words, and reflecting, or identifying a feeling the other person is experiencing. Here is an example:

Player's statement: "I am so mad at myself right now. I cannot seem to get on base in crucial situations. I really feel I am letting the team down."

Coach's paraphrase and reflection: "You seem frustrated about not being able to help the team like you are used to doing."

The purpose of paraphrasing thoughts and reflecting feelings is to get a person to open up or keep a conversation going from their perspective. Doing so demonstrates that you are listening and opens the way to continued communication. These techniques encourage continued talking and expression while indicating to the other person that he or she is important to you. One word of caution: Try to avoid using the word "why" in your questions; it can imply a negative judgment of the other person and may be mistaken as an attacking statement.

Listen with flexibility   There is no single best listening strategy. Different situations require different strategies. Some athletes do not organize their ideas well; others do. Some athletes have to repeat major ideas to make sure they have grasped them. Some players give you time to think about what has been said; others just say what they have to say and do not seem concerned about understanding. Some intentionally use language to confuse and confound while others want their messages to be clear. You must learn to adapt to varying listening situations.

The world of sport requires that coaches extend their communication system beyond talking and listening to their athletes and staff. Because coaches spend quite a bit of time communicating with both sport officials and the media, we offer recommendations on how to extend a communication system to these situations.

Communicating With Sport Officials

The following recommendations stem largely from Kevin Burke's professional experience as a sport psychologist, as a college and high school basketball official for 23 years, and as a collegiate tennis coach.

Does it need to be said? The worst thing that can happen to an official is to lose concentration, which may happen when they experience high levels of stress. Criticizing (especially publicly), or "working," an official may cause him or her to feel stressed. Jerry West, a Hall of Fame NBA player, once said, "Arguing with officials simply breaks their concentration and may cause them to blow the next 10 calls in a row."

A common reason coaches give for ranting and raving at officials is to try to intimidate them (to get the calls to go their team's way). However, what may happen instead is that officials either lose their concentration (which is detrimental to performance) or retaliate by making calls against the coach. When a player or coach tries to "show up" an official, the official often makes a call against him or her to show that he or she will not be intimidated. Thus, attempting to intimidate officials has a better chance of causing errors or retaliation than it does of biasing the official toward the intimidator's team.

Coaches must be concerned with many facets of a contest, and many of them waste their energies harassing officials when their time could be better spent coaching. Many officials perceive coaches who constantly complain as either trying to cover up their inadequacies or as not doing their job. Therefore coaches must have effective, efficient communication with referees and umpires. Remember, effective communication involves making sure your messages are received by your target. Being effective means that your comments will be considered by and not negatively affect the official. Being efficient means that you get your point across to the officials more often yet spend less time in doing so.

When to say it To be more effective and efficient, you need to carefully "pick your spots." This means that the less frequent your attempts to get an official's attention are, the easier it is to do so. Then, when you do make statements to them, you will have a better chance of being heard. (Remember the parable of the boy who cried wolf?) The less that is said, the more is heard; officials tend to "tune out" coaches and players who constantly complain to, hassle, and confront them.

Get their attention If it needs to be said and you have picked your spot, you must then get the official's attention. Most officials are trained to pretend to ignore the coaches or not respond to them unless they get out of hand. So you have two choices: yell and gesture wildly at the officials, hoping they will consider what you are saying even though they are pretending to ignore you; or speak with them in a controlled and respectful manner. Keep in mind that some officials have a negative perception of a typical coach's behavior during competition, so by yelling and gesturing, you are simply fitting into that stereotype. The best way to grab and hold a referee's or umpire's attention is to act in a manner that is unexpected. Many officials will not talk with or consider what coaches say as long as they are acting inappropriately. Therefore, the best way to get your point across is to speak with them in a controlled manner.

What to say   The types of statements that coaches make are important also. Instead of attacking an official's decision with a personal judgment by saying something like "That was a terrible call!" try saying, "Please explain that call to me," which is less judgmental and offensive to an official. Both statements let the official know that you did not necessarily agree with the call, but the latter statement is likely to be more effective. When you make your point in a respectful manner, officials are more likely to respect what you have to say. Finally, after you have dealt with the situation, let it go and move on rather than arguing your point repeatedly.

Communicating With the Media

Communicating with the media can be a challenge for many coaches and athletes. Many times, comments made in jest are taken out of context and become the basis for conflict. The following tips will help coaches and athletes enhance their communication with the media.

Be prepared   We like to call this "setting the table." Before you speak with the media, make sure you have defined your objective; know what you want to say; and have a plan to state it simply and precisely. Often, preparation will allow you to take charge of the interview. Always prepare for the unexpected so that when it pops up you can calmly address the issue. These tips will help prevent your message from being misunderstood or misrepresented by the media.

Be professional   Remain calm and do your best to be sure you are accurately quoted. When possible, try to allow enough time to pass after the event so that you can engage the media without your emotions getting in the way of effective communication. If that is not possible, prepare a few comments before the competition that can be relied on regardless of your emotional state. Do not allow an interviewer to bait you, misinterpret your feelings, misstate the facts, or "put words in your mouth." Maintain your professionalism at all times, even if the media does not. Although the athletic world has been described as a subculture, complete with its own language, we encourage you to use words that the general public understands and to avoid profanity. Remember, you are a role model, and no one is impressed with a coach who loses his or her temper and delivers a profanity-laced tirade.

LTA—Listen, think, and then act   Make sure you listen to the question so that you can formulate an appropriate response. Do not let your emotions answer the question for you. Also remember the importance of being confidential when it comes to players' personal issues. If an athlete trusts you with a personal problem or if you have information that you were told in confidence, it is best for you not to comment on it to the media. If your athletes do not trust that what they have told you in confidence will not be shared with others, they will not tell you anything!

"We," not "I"   It has often been said that great coaches have the guts to take responsibility for their shortcomings and the wisdom to share the glory with their team. Saying "I," not "we," with the media can leave the wrong impression—that you do not value your team, and that only your opinion matters. "We" is an inclusive term, whereas "I" is exclusionary. "We" indicates a feeling of unity, and using such language builds loyalty and increases motivation and team morale.

Hit the target   Avoid generalities and get to the point. Use specific examples that clarify the issues. Remember, you may have a maximum of 30 seconds to get your point across. You can elaborate if needed and if requested to do so.

Be yourself   Be true to yourself. You know your strengths and your weaknesses. Play to your strengths and work on improving the challenge areas so that they will not cause you to stumble. If you are yourself, you will appear relaxed, confident, and comfortable. Relax and enjoy conversing with individuals who want to share your world. Realize that you are human, and that being human means not being perfect. You will be misquoted and misunderstood, but you will have other opportunities to communicate with the media.

Three Myths About Not Employing a Communication System

Coaches sometimes say that they need to communicate naturally—to think about how to communicate is insincere and comes across as fake. In addition, it is sometimes easier to offer excuses or reasons for not taking the time and energy to develop new skills. Below are examples of some of the excuses often given by coaches for not employing the principles of effective communication. The key is to be aware of the tendency to make excuses rather than roll up your sleeves and work toward enhancing your communication skills.

"I tell it like it is"   Telling the truth and conveying that you value honesty among your players are important to good communication, as is being yourself. However, coaches who boast of "telling it like it is" to their players and the media are using their behavior as an excuse to not devote energy to sending an effective message. They wear the fact that they have the guts to stand up and tell it like it is like a badge of honor. That is great, but have they taken the time to assess all of the information, examine their own emotional filters and biases, and think of the ramifications of their actions? In most cases, they are taking the easy way out. The easiest thing to do when one is angry is to communicate with anger, but that does not mean it is the correct thing to do in the role of teacher and motivator.

"I don't have the time or energy" Many coaches will try communication techniques such as the sandwich approach and abandon them because they take too much thought and effort. Think about that. Coaches constantly try to encourage athletes to persevere through the frustrating, draining learning curve so they can come out a better player on the other side. Making changes in one's communication style is also draining and frustrating during the learning curve, but perseverance results in the development of habits that will make you and your team optimally effective. The more you do it, the more automatic it becomes.

"It's too touchy-feely" Sometimes the principles of effective communication fly in the face of the image we have of what being a coach is all about. We often hear coaches defend their behavior with common clichés: "I'm just trying to toughen them up," "I am not going to coddle or spoil them," or "I am a coach, not their parent or intimate partner." These statements say much more about the coach than the coaching style. The claims that critical, demeaning, attacking messages serve a positive function in someone's work toward excellence; that delivering a message in a positive, supportive manner will result in negative development of one's character; and that coaches should not have an influential role in their athletes' lives simply do not hold up under scrutiny.

A favorite example of behavior that breaks the stereotypical mold is the pre-game exchange that occurs among Biff Poggi, Joe Erhmann, and their Maryland high school football team. Before each game they ask the team, "What is our job as coaches?" The team responds, "To love us." The coaches: "And what is your job?" The team: "To love each other." That's not something you hear in most football locker rooms! When Erhmann speaks at coaches' conferences about the Building Men for Others program, he is often questioned about that open expression of love and compassion for each other. However, the questioning ends when the team's continued status as a nationally ranked, powerhouse football program is revealed or when it becomes clear that taking the time to effectively communicate with empathy does not conflict with demanding excellence, commitment, and hard work. Erhmann, Poggi, and all the coaches on the Gilman football team realize the truth: that communicating with empathy and care fosters excellence, commitment, and hard work. This principle was the central theme in the movie *Remember the Titans*.

Back to the Beginning and the Bottom Line

At the beginning of the chapter, we referred to three coaches who presented a particular communication style on the surface; however, as we spent more time with their teams, it became evident that a different and more powerful message was being heard and responded to by the athletes on each team. The dynamics of these teams must be understood in the context of one fundamental principle of optimal performance. When individuals are in an *expressive* mind-set, they perform optimally. That is, they execute their tasks as if they were on automatic pilot, they play free, they openly take in relevant cues and act on them, and they focus on expressing their talents without fear. Conversely, when athletes are in an *evaluative* mind-set, they chronically monitor their behavior against some standard, make conclusions about their success or failure against that standard, and emotionally react to that conclusion. This mind-set places a ceiling on optimal performance and engrains a corruptive fear of failure. Playing with an expressive mind-set allows an athlete to monitor and correct faulty performances but without such a strong personal standard of success or failure. An evaluative mind-set is fine during practice sessions when the goal is to learn, stretch one's performance comfort zone, and break bad habits. But when it is game time, playing with an expressive mind-set must be the goal, and communication must facilitate and promote it.

With this fundamental principle in mind, let us go back to the three coaches. One coach was personable, involved, and positive in her technical communication with her team. Another coach was a mild-mannered, even-tempered, soft-spoken man who rarely lost his temper with his team. The third coach was a gruff, in-your-face, short-fused type. As it turned out, something very different was going on in each of their communication systems. In almost all of the communication by the first coach, she sent the message that everything was about her, not about her players. She used a very personable style to try to win the players' sense of duty to her, but then she manipulated those feelings to try to control the team. Poor performances and losses were met with cloaked statements that sent the actual message of "How could you do this to me, after all I've done for you?" and actions that were distant and neglectful. Good performances, though, were met with closeness and attention. Her players were so afraid of disappointing her and losing her "affection" that they became paralyzed by a fear of failure. They constantly watched her reactions and evaluated themselves. The result: performances that were far below their potential.

The second coach, on the other hand, was calm, even-tempered, and rarely yelled. He very rarely criticized the person, staying focused on behavior when he had to give constructive feedback. However, he believed that he should not be involved in his players' lives and did not see the need to understand their perspective. At one point, when we asked him how much he knew about his players, he responded, "I make it a point to know as little about my players as possible." There was very little message-receiving in his communication system. He viewed his role as imparting knowledge to his team, and he invested very little time in listening or trying to understand the team. The result: When it came time for the athletes to push their limits and reach for their potential, the first thing that came to their minds was "Why? For what?" They felt unappreciated, like expendable pawns on a chessboard that were there only to execute skills. They felt like they were being taken for granted and became unwilling to do the hard work of pushing through fear, adversity, and challenge.

Then there's the third coach, an old dinosaur kind of guy who could drive daggers through you with his stare. He demanded absolute commitment and devotion to excellence. He dogged his athletes and got in their faces when they did not push themselves. But something else was going on. We were surprised to discover that he was able to cite in-depth details about each player—not about their athletic ability but about them as individuals. He saw his role as teaching his athletes how to assess themselves, set goals, develop a plan to reach those goals, cope with adversity, and fight through fear. He taught them that it was OK to rely on each other and that in competition you should express yourself completely and have a blast doing it. He saw practices as an opportunity to build trust on an ever-broadening array of skills. During practices, he would push players to step out of their comfort zones, but before competitions he would encourage them to work with what they trusted. The adage "train for trust, then trust your training" was his theme. When he did get in their faces, his comments were always focused on behavior, not the person. He would end the feedback with a personal statement that revealed his philosophy: that by pushing ourselves to grow, to not be controlled by fear, and to allow others to help us, we become better people. The result: His players pushed themselves and each other in practice, expressed themselves in competition, and believed their existence on the team mattered to the coach and the others.

Just as in the example of the three coaches, all of us who have an influential role over others have a responsibility to take an honest assessment of our behavior and our beliefs from the standpoint of the preceding questions. If you see an area for improvement, try to find one or two tips from this chapter that could move you one step closer to where you want to be during the next season. Accept the energy and sacrifice that it will require, commit to it, and you will find that the return on your investment far outweighs any other investment of energy. Finally, if you can do one thing only to improve your communication system, make a commitment to never lose your curiosity about your players. Active curiosity fosters empathy and understanding. Your players will forgive every communication mistake you make if they know that you care about them enough to want to understand them and that you are pushing them to excel for their sake, not for yours.

Future Directions

> Feelings of worth can flourish only in an atmosphere where individual differences are appreciated, mistakes are tolerated, communication is open, and rules are flexible—the kind of atmosphere that is found in a nurturing family.
>
> *Virginia Satir, internationally acclaimed family therapist*

Effective communication systems are vital to the success of any team. The coach plays an important role in setting the table for the development and maintenance of such a system. The key to this process is investing in the athletes. Teams characterized by high levels of communication also have high levels of performance effectiveness. Developing and maintaining a communication system means focusing on both sending and receiving messages. Moreover, it means caring about athletes as both people and performers and having a system in place that allows for this concern to be communicated to every member of the team. Although much of this chapter focused on coach-athlete communication, the principles discussed are just as important and effective for athlete-coach and athlete-athlete communication. Thus, if you are an athlete, we suggest you reread this chapter and think about how the principles apply to enhancing your communication system.

In the future, communication will continue to be a fundamental aspect of team effectiveness, within and beyond the sport context. Future research into the dynamics of communication within sport and its impact on team productivity and team processes will be needed to provide effective and appropriate interventions. Moreover, the use of technological advances will greatly enhance the communication system and such advances will need to be applied and tested within the sport world. Finally, the impact of culture, language, and the globalization of sport will necessitate a broad and diverse approach to designing effective communication systems by both the researcher and the practitioner. We suspect that we have only scratched the surface of effective communication systems for coaches as well as athletes.

Potential Pitfalls

In 1993, the world's number-one women's tennis player, Monica Seles, was stabbed and badly injured during the changeover in a match by an assailant in Hamburg, Germany. In her autobiography, *Monica: From Fear to Victory*, she describes her rehabilitation from this shocking injury, and reveals that the hardest part was overcoming her emotional anguish. In this she was helped by her sport psychologist, Dr. Jerry May of Lake Tahoe, Nevada.

> I'd never been to a psychologist: walking into his office, I didn't know what to expect. I'm a strong person; he's not going to make me cry I thought as I sat down. [Her early attempts at counseling were unproductive. Nearly a year later she tried again.] This time, it was different. The first time I'd seen Dr. May I'd been in denial, certain that if I wished hard enough, trained long enough, flew far enough, the attack would disappear. In March 1994 I had come to realize that there was no escape. . . I spent two weeks in Tahoe going to therapy. At first I just cried, but slowly I began to open up to Dr. May, slowly I began to trust him. We started to talk about the last three months and how I'd succumbed to my depression and fears until they controlled me. . . Dr. May and I talked about my depression and he explained that I was experiencing post-traumatic stress disorder. All the shock, fear, depression and anxiety I'd tried to run away from had finally come to the surface. There were moments when I'd cry, and Dr. May would tell me that it was okay to feel the way I felt. To hear someone say that what I was going through was understandable, even normal, meant a lot to me. My life had lost its balance, and Dr. May was there to help me regain it.
>
> From Monica, *by Monica Seles with Nancy Ann Richardson,*
> *pp. 63, 126-128*

Not all injured athletes face the challenges in rehabilitation that confronted Seles. But all athletes know that their careers can end suddenly with one unlucky twist or hit. Injuries are just one of several issues that can tax an athlete's deepest emotional resources. One of the toughest issues I have to deal with as a sport psychologist is counseling athletes in sports where there is a widespread perception that many athletes use performance-enhancing drugs to gain an edge in competition. The problem doesn't come from the athletes who are using the drugs. If an athlete has decided to cut corners and cheat the system, there isn't much anyone can do to stop them. The big problem is working with athletes who *don't* want to take performance-enhancing drugs but who think that if they don't, they are doomed to losing. The public often gets the impression from the media that all athletes have a win-at-all costs mentality and are hell-bent to achieve victory at any price. But in truth, many of the athletes I know have a variety of good reasons for not taking performance-enhancing drugs, from concerns about their long-term health to a genuine desire to make competition a level playing field and to avoid bad moral choices. However, the pressure that these athletes can feel to give in and start doping can be enormous, especially when other athletes with suspicious histories take their starting job on a team or beat them out for a spot in the Olympic Games. It can take every bit of my skill as a counselor to help such athletes navigate the minefield of ethical and moral decisions that confront them, and I often get angry that athletes are ever placed in this precarious position in the first place.

Dealing with the widespread use of performance-enhancing drugs in modern sport is only one of the difficult issues that athletes face on a regular basis. Many other sport psychology books on the market ignore or gloss over these tough issues, but in *The Sport Psych Handbook* we want to help athletes and coaches deal with all the problems that they are likely to face in sport. Sport psychology is a holistic discipline that deals with the total life experience of the athlete. There is a lot of knowledge about such tough issues as injuries, eating disorders, and substance abuse that can be tremendously helpful to athletes and coaches. Each of the three chapters in part IV deals with the difficult problems of modern sport in a sensitive and helpful manner. In chapter 12, "Injuries: The Psychology of Recovery and Rehab," Charles Brown looks at the most common problem in sport-athletic injury and examines the emotional and psychological ramifications of being injured. He suggests effective mental strategies for dealing with rehabilitation. In chapter 13, "Eating Disorders: When Rations Become Irrational," Karen D. Cogan explains how the pressures of sport can contribute to a variety of weight-management problems and even eating disorders. Using her experiences as a counselor and a former competitive athlete, she suggests helpful strategies for dealing with an athlete suspected of having an eating disorder, and she describes the most effective treatment options available. No coach or parent can afford to miss this wonderful chapter. In chapter 14, "Substance Use: Chemical Roulette in Sport," Mark H. Anshel deals with the difficult issue posed by the use of performance-enhancing drugs in sport and suggests both individual and organization-based strategies for meeting this tough challenge.

chapter 12

Injuries: The Psychology of Recovery and Rehab

Charles Brown

Serious athletes come in two varieties: those who have been injured, and those who have not been injured *yet*. When a person constantly strives to push physical abilities to the limit, that limit occasionally will be exceeded and result in injury. When it does, the balance of elements in an athlete's life can change in a heartbeat. For example, see the following story on James.

James

James was on the way to a spectacular senior season with a major Division I basketball team when, during one of the best games of his career, his leg twisted as he came down from a towering rebound.

The roar of the home crowd hushed as he writhed in pain beneath the basket. In that single second, the balance of his life shifted. He had worked long and hard to prepare for his senior year, with hopes of a conference title for the team and professional career after graduation. As he headed to the hospital, the physical pain was nothing compared to the fear of having his dreams shattered and the uncertainty of whether he would be able to play again.

James was lucky. The MRI indicated only partial tears of two ligaments, neither of which required surgery. With proper rehabilitation, the doctors told him he should be able to play again in six to eight weeks. But would he be mentally ready to play by that time?

(continued)

(continued)

James was familiar with training hard and approached his rehabilitation with the same focus and intensity. He welcomed assistance and committed himself to improving his "mental game" while recovering. We began by having him learn rapid relaxation, which helped in a variety of situations. Whenever he found himself becoming nervous or fearful about his recovery, he would use centered breathing to help him relax and refocus on taking his rehabilitation one step at a time. In order to maintain his sense of timing, he attended every scrimmage with a specific goal: to watch the person playing his position and imagine what he would do in the same situation. Relaxation helped his focus and concentration while he observed the practices. It also helped intensify his imagery sessions, during which he mentally rehearsed plays using all of his senses—the pressure of boxing a player out from under the basket, the sound of sneakers on the hardwood court, and the taste of sweat on his lip. He broadened his imagery to include rehab sessions, incorporating images of himself successfully performing the exercises and the tendons and ligaments regenerating and becoming even stronger than before.

James is a success story. He missed 10 games but was able to finish out the season with the team. His physical rehabilitation was such that the final Cybex (strength) test before his return to play revealed that the injured leg was stronger than the uninjured one. After a six-week layoff, he needed only two days of practice before returning to play in competition. In his first game back, he played 18 minutes and scored 12 points and 5 rebounds. Before his injury, James was averaging 7.3 points and 8 rebounds per game; following the injury he averaged 9 points and 7.3 rebounds per game.

An estimated 17 million sports injuries occur each year in the United States alone. If you are a jogger, the chances are 1 in 3 that you will be injured during the upcoming year; if you are a habitual runner, the odds of a lower-extremity injury increase to 50 percent. Almost half of all collegiate football players in the United States lose playing time due to serious injuries. In a 1997 survey, 73 percent of all World Cup skiers had experienced a season-ending injury at some point in their careers. For women playing collegiate soccer or basketball, the odds are 1 in 10 that they will sustain an anterior cruciate ligament (ACL) injury during their careers (almost six times the predicted expectancy for male athletes in the same sports). Depending on the sport and level of play, women's probability of sustaining an ACL injury is two to ten times greater than their male counterparts. Aging baby boomers are attempting to stay physically active, which translates into higher injury rates. Between 1991 and 1998, sport-related emergency-room visits for persons aged 35 to 54 increased by 33 percent. And from 1990 to 1996, sports injuries among Americans *65 years or older* increased by 54 percent!

For the majority of athletes, injury produces an immediate imbalance in life. Some experience a general disruption in efforts toward health and fitness or a loss of the good feelings of health and accomplishment that come from regular exercise. For others, it means a loss of opportunity or livelihood. And at the very extreme, injuries may result in a permanent loss of physical ability or even death.

The impact of injury is far more than physical; it can jeopardize an athlete's confidence, self-esteem, and sense of identity. In a 1996 survey of certified athlete trainers, 47 percent believed that *every* athlete suffers negative psychological effects when injured. These include stress and anxiety, anger, treatment-compliance problems, depression, problems with concentration and attention, or exercise addiction.

As advances in medicine reduce the time required for physical healing, it becomes increasingly important that athletes address the mental aspects of injury rehabilitation. The "price" of injury is easy to see in the world of professional sports—the athlete is a financial investment that reaps benefits only when fully functional. But for the average person, injury takes a toll not only in terms of pain and suffering but also on self-esteem and quality of life. Constant or chronic pain can alter moods, disturb sleep, affect cognitive processes, and profoundly affect relationships.

Sport psychology has contributed to injury rehabilitation in several ways, which this chapter discusses. Some of the earliest efforts by sport psychologists involved prevention—identifying athletes who might be at greater risk of

For professional football players, like many other elite athletes, the impact of injury is far more than physical; it can jeopardize an athlete's confidence, self-esteem, and sense of identity.

being injured. In recent years, the focus has been on optimizing recovery, both in terms of speed (returning to play as soon as possible) and maintenance of performance levels. Some athletes actually perform *better* after an injury, and sport psychologists have sought to understand why and how this happens.

The Impact of Injury

The "old school" philosophy was simple: Physicians treated an injury as a biological problem and the athlete was expected to "tough it out." The mental and emotional aspects of injury were largely ignored. To make matters worse, many coaches treated injured athletes as though they were worthless, fueling their fears and desperation. During the 1970s, attitudes about injury began to change as physicians recognized that diet, exercise, and lifestyle—all behaviors rather than biological factors—had tremendous impact on illness and injury. The field of behavioral medicine emerged as psychologists applied behavioral techniques that had been designed to treat mental-health problems to medical disorders. Initially, behavioral medicine focused on lifestyle behaviors such as smoking, obesity, and exercise. Soon this broadened to helping people with pain management. Today, psychologists who work on behavioral-medicine teams treat a range of conditions, including asthma, diabetes, arthritis, and cancer. One of the major behavioral problems in medicine is *adherence*, or following a treatment plan as directed. Psychologists have made vital contributions in this area, which we will discuss later in this chapter.

Athletes at Risk

When sport psychologists first began addressing athletic injuries, the early research sought to identify athletes who were at risk of injury. After more than three decades of research, compelling evidence shows that a combination of conditions puts athletes at greater risk of injury: negative life stresses, an increase in daily hassles, previous injuries, and poor coping resources. These factors are mediated by an athlete's personality: The risk of injury increases if the athlete experiences competitive trait anxiety (routinely feels greater anxiety or tension in performance situations) or anger and aggression during competition.

How do these factors increase the chance of injury? The combination of stress history, poor coping resources, and personality factors results in what theorists call an *elevated stress response*. This involves increased muscle tension, increased distractibility, and a narrowing of attention so that the athlete is not as aware of or responsive to critical events or cues. Prolonged exposure to stress also changes the body's endocrine system, making a person more susceptible to illness and slowing down the healing process.

The impact of major life stresses such as the breakup of a relationship, death of a loved one, loss of a job, or moving to a new location is compelling at all levels of athletic competition. One study assessed the life stresses of players on the University of Washington football team, then tracked injuries during the subsequent season. Only 9 percent of the players with low life stresses experienced injuries that required missing either three days of practice or a game, compared to 50 percent of the players with high life stresses. In addition, an increase in daily hassles—minor problems and irritations that disrupt one's routine, such as being in a new setting, having transportation difficulties, or any annoying situations—appears to contribute to the likelihood of injury. The probability of injury also increases when a person has been previously injured, particularly if he or she returns to play before the injury is fully healed. Even if it is fully healed, the chance of reinjury increases if the athlete is not psychologically ready to return; in such cases, the athlete is likely to alter his or her technical performance by tensing unnecessary muscles in an effort to protect the injury (referred to as "bracing") or avoiding situations he or she considers threatening to the injury.

Athletes who have minimal coping resources (such as stress-management skills, healthy life habits, and social support) are more likely to be injured. The good news is that although many stresses cannot be controlled or eliminated, psychological coping resources can be improved and developed. One study with collegiate athletes found that when they were trained in progressive relaxation and imagery, injury rates decreased by 52 percent for swimmers and by 33 percent for football players.

Response to Injury and Rehab

As sport psychologists learned about athletes with injuries, it became obvious that there is more to dealing with an injury than simply "toughing it out." In this section, we explore efforts to understand the emotional reactions to injury.

Stage Model

Some believe that injured athletes go through a series of emotional responses that follow a predictable sequence of stages similar to those identified by Elisabeth Kübler-Ross in her work with individuals confronting death and dying. A person first experiences disbelief or denial at the onset of the illness or injury, followed by anger. The third stage involves bargaining, or an attempt to make a deal with God, such as "If you let me get better, I promise that I will do good deeds for the rest of my life!" That phase evolves into depression, which eventually progresses to acceptance and resignation. This theory of emotional stages was initially popular in sport psychology because it provided a framework for both the athlete and those associated with him or her to understand, accept, and support the responses following an injury. Rather than facing the traditional stoicism of "toughing it out," athletes were told that emotional turmoil was to be expected.

However, researchers discovered that not all athletes went through each stage in the predictable sequence and that the stages did not have particularly clear delineations. Skiers who experienced season-ending injuries rarely experienced denial; athletes who seemingly had progressed through the stages of anger and depression and were beginning to demonstrate acceptance would then experience more episodes of anger and frustration. Although it is helpful in many ways, the stage model does not account for variations in athletes' responses to injury.

Cognitive-Appraisal Model

More recently, the *cognitive-appraisal model* has guided our understanding of the response to injury. This model follows the growing emphasis within sport psychology on cognitive–affective theory, which states that emotional response is determined by the meaning, or appraisal, that a person attributes to an event. The advantage of this model is its ability to explain why some athletes respond differently to identical injuries and why a single athlete may respond differently to the same injury when it occurs in different contexts. For example, personality, past experience, and the context in which an injury occurs all influence a person's appraisal of an injury. For a seasoned athlete with a history of successful rehabilitation of minor injuries, encountering a sprain during the early part of the competitive season may elicit little emotional response. For someone who has never experienced an injury and is struggling to make the cut for the high school varsity team, the same sprain might be perceived as devastating and provoke a tremendous emotional reaction. A person's cognitive appraisal of a situation determines his or her emotional response, which then sets the stage for how he or she responds behaviorally. There is a reciprocal process throughout this model, in that a person's emotional response, behaviors, and the results of those behaviors influence ongoing and future cognitive appraisal.

Which model is accurate? A review of the research shows that both have valid features and both have flaws. Most of the initial efforts to understand injury response were guided by theory. During the late 1990s, sport psychologist Dan Gould and his colleagues gathered fact-based evidence on the emotional responses of athletes to injury. The study was unique in the level of participation and cooperation by elite athletes. Because of Gould's longtime association with the U.S. ski team and coaches, all of the top-20 alpine and freestyle skiers who experienced an injury that kept them off the slopes for three months or more participated. The nature of the sport also made it possible to clearly define whether a return after injury was successful, by comparing an athlete's world rankings before and after the injury. The study included in-depth interviews addressing the nature and extent of the person's injury, reactions to being injured, specific sources of stress, factors that facilitated recovery, coping strategies, important relationships, and recommendations for athletes with similar injuries.

These athletes' stories indicated that the primary stress following injury was psychological—they struggled with fears of losing their hopes and dreams, fears of reinjury, reminders of the crash, and worries of their eventual readiness to compete. The second most common stress reflected social concerns. These athletes went from training, traveling, and living in close quarters with the team to being isolated and feeling distant from coaches and teammates. The amount of attention and empathy that coaches and teammates gave an injured skier correlated with a successful recovery. Those who successfully recovered acknowledged the stress of isolation but had no complaints about the support and empathy they received, while unsuccessful skiers reported a lack of attention and empathy. Of all the skiers who did not return to the same or higher ranking after injury, half of them identified negative social relationships as a major stress. Other stresses were categorized as physical concerns (pain, concern about being reinjured), medical or rehabilitation concerns, financial concerns, and missed career opportunities.

Strategies for Coping With Injury

The insights from Gould's research, along with numerous other studies, have helped further our understanding of the coping strategies employed by athletes in addressing injury-related stress. Sport psychologists have attempted to categorize the infinite variety of coping behaviors that exist in response to a single situation; the two most widely accepted are problem-focused and emotion-focused coping strategies.

Efforts directed at managing or altering the problem that causes the stress are referred to as *problem-focused coping*. Examples include gathering information about the nature of an injury; learning about treatment options and resources; setting specific, measurable, action-oriented, reasonable, and time-oriented (SMART) goals for recovery; and adhering to a rehabilitation plan.

Emotion-focused strategies are directed at managing the emotions that are experienced as a result of the injury. These include many of the same skills that are used to achieve an optimal performance state: managing thoughts and emotions through self-talk and relaxation techniques, using imagery of being physically and mentally prepared, and self-soothing techniques. These strategies often involve dealing directly with the feelings associated with the injury—expressing emotions, seeking and using social support, being patient, and eventually accepting the injury.

In addition to problem-focused and emotion-focused coping, *distraction* or *avoidance strategies* are efforts to disengage and remove oneself, either mentally or physically, from the situation generating the stress. In Gould's study of skiers, several athletes used the time off from skiing to return to school, providing a sense of accomplishment as well as distraction from the stresses of skiing rehabilitation. Some athletes noted the importance of staying busy, regardless of the nature of the task; others found that a total change of scenery was an antidote for the stress of an injury. These distraction/avoidance efforts tend to be most effective in short-term situations in which the stress is likely to go away with time, such as when an injury occurs near the end of the competitive season and will heal with rest. An athlete can divert attention to a positive distraction while the injury heals, and then resume practice at the beginning of a new season. When the injury is likely to be long-term or when the athlete is expected to return to play during a competitive season, avoidance strategies may hinder recovery. These situations often have a window of opportunity for optimal physical rehabilitation; avoiding treatment at that time may limit the benefits. If an athlete is expected to return to play yet avoids the mental preparation required for successful rehabilitation, his efforts will be tentative at best, and the chance of reinjury is high.

Seek social support   Social support plays a critical role in the aftermath of an injury, especially with serious injuries. Social and family support is well documented in medical rehabilitation as being important to the rehabilitation process. In Gould's study of skiers who experienced season-ending injuries, the most frequently identified factor facilitating recovery was interpersonal resources (i.e., social support). A 2003 study of athletes who suffered spinal cord injuries identified social support as essential to the quality of life. For many athletes, friendships and social ties are interwoven with their identity as an athlete. Team members often live, work, and play together, establishing close-knit bonds. When injured athletes are removed from their support networks, the imbalance in their lives is often exacerbated.

An athlete may have been the center of all the team interactions, with coaches following and guiding her development, teammates relying on her, and being in the middle of all the team jokes and stories. With a sudden injury, she may be abruptly removed from this close-knit "family." While she struggles with when or if a return is possible, the team still plays. The vacated starting spot is an opportunity for someone else to move into the primary rotation. New jokes and social ties are formed in her absence. Even teammates who are genuinely concerned about the injured colleague may avoid her, fearing "bad karma" or confrontation with the possible dangers that they still need to face without fear.

Social support can be broadly categorized into four types: emotional, esteem, informational, and tangible. *Emotional support* is defined as "the ability to turn to others for comfort and security during times of stress, leading the person to feel that he or she is cared for by others." People show this in a variety of ways: by keeping in touch throughout the rehabilitation process, expressing concern, being a good listener, or providing moral support. The most important factor is simply conveying that others care and are there for the injured party. *Esteem support* includes efforts to build the injured person's sense of confidence and self-esteem. An example is reminding the person of her abilities, such as by saying, "You've got more mental toughness than anyone I know; if anybody can get back to play right away, I know you can." *Informational support* is data, advice, or guidance that helps someone deal with a stressor. Providing good information about the nature of an injury or what to expect during the rehabilitation process and offering feedback on progress and options are examples of this form of social support. Informational support can also be gained from rehabilitating with other injured athletes and by having access to previously injured athletes who can serve as models of successful rehabilitation. *Tangible support* is concrete assistance that helps a person cope with a stress, such as carrying an injured athlete's books to classes or providing financial assistance during the rehabilitation process.

Although social support is crucial to the rehabilitation process, all efforts to provide it are not necessarily beneficial. An individual's *perception* of support determines whether an action is helpful. Well-intended efforts may actually be experienced as a stress or intrusion. For example, a person might minimize the importance of an event, encourage a too-rapid return to play, criticize the treatment team (and thereby undermine confidence), or simply give poor advice. Several sport psychologists propose that matching support efforts with specific stressors is important. This undoubtedly will be an area of future research.

Several studies suggest that social support is particularly important during the first few weeks of a rehabilitation program, because it often helps establish the patient's confidence in the program. There also appear to be gender differences in placing value on social support. Injured female athletes tend to seek social support more than males. The support of coaches and athletic staff has a greater impact on female athletes' perceptions of stress and their abilities to successfully cope with the challenge of rehabilitation.

Set attainable goals   The manner in which a person approaches challenges and goals (see chapter 2) affects rehabilitation. Some athletes are inclined to judge their progress and achievements by comparing their efforts to those of other people. Such athletes are said to be *ego oriented* in approaching tasks because their sense of self-worth (ego) depends on demonstrating that they can outperform others. *Task-oriented* athletes focus more on internal standards and setting goals related to mastery, providing good effort, and steady improvement of ability regardless of the actions of others. Ego-oriented athletes will typically approach rehabilitation by finding someone with a similar injury and then attempting to outperform that person, such as by doing more repetitions or taking less time to recover. They are determined to beat the other person somehow, even to the detriment of their rehabilitation progress. They may begin the rehab process quite confidently, but then see that confidence erode if they cannot match the efforts of others in the rehab process, even if it is both unrealistic and inappropriate to perform at those levels. In contrast, task-oriented individuals use others as models of the rehabilitation process rather than as competition. They typically benefit from using the same mental skills that sport psychologists teach for peak performance: breaking the ultimate goal into small-step process goals and using their achievement as the foundation for regaining confidence. Knowing an athlete's orientation can be valuable for trainers who design rehabilitation programs, particularly when the process involves groups of injured athletes.

Commit to rehab   Adherence to a rehabilitation program is essential to an athlete's successful recovery. In spite of the apparent simplicity of this path to success, actual adherence rates range between 40 and 91 percent. Sport psychologists who work with injured athletes have a major interest in increasing adherence.

As noted earlier, social support is a significant factor in adhering to a treatment program. Research with cardiac patients indicates that a spouse's attitude toward a rehabilitation program is a better predictor of adherence than the patient's attitude. Early studies attempted to identify the predictors of adherence, but more recently researchers have been testing various theories that can guide and direct efforts of coaches, trainers, and athletes to increase adherence. In this section, we will discuss some of the most popular models in exercise research.

The *transtheoretical model of change* proposes that people who attempt to change a behavior (such as adhering to a rehabilitation program) progress through a series of stages. The goal of intervention is to help them progress from one stage to the next; strategies and techniques to facilitate this progression differ according to the stage. The key to successful adherence is matching intervention efforts with the stage of change. At the *precontemplation* stage, an injured athlete is not even considering change. By learning about the benefits of change, such as rapid return to play and the addition of new skills that will benefit an athletic career, the athlete progresses to the *contemplation* stage. He or she then moves to the *preparation* stage by learning what is involved in rehabilitation and how to do what is required. Anticipating possible difficulties and planning how best to tailor-fit efforts to the individual are helpful at this stage. When the athlete actually commits to the rehab program, the *action* stage begins. At this point, using behavioral principles of reinforcement is most effective. Charts that show specific target behaviors and offer rewards for successfully completing portions of the rehab process are useful strategies. As the athlete engages in the activities on a routine basis, the *maintenance* phase emerges. Here it is important to troubleshoot potential obstacles, incorporate social support for the new behaviors, and educate the athlete about the possible dangers of overtraining. Professionals dispute whether a sixth stage of change should be considered—the *relapse* stage. Opponents argue that planning for a relapse encourages it, while proponents say that in the real world, relapse is commonplace. When a person relapses, the cycle of stages starts over with the individual once again at the precontemplation stage, needing to become mindful of the benefits of change and then contemplating how to take action once again. By preparing in advance for a relapse and thinking of it as an expected step in the change process, people typically find it easier to resume their efforts and more rapidly return to the target behaviors of the action phase.

The *health belief model* proposes that adherence to a rehabilitation plan depends on two things: the athlete's perception of the severity of the injury and the balance of the benefits and costs of participating in the rehab program. According to this model, adherence can be maximized by educating the athlete about the nature of the injury, the rationale for rehabilitation, and the possible consequences of not completing the rehab as prescribed. Coaches and athletic trainers can structure rehab activities in ways that minimize the "cost" of rehabilitation. This may involve providing the services free of charge, but also scheduling physical therapy or other rehab elements at times and locations that minimize the inconvenience to the athlete.

The *protection motivation theory*, an extension of the health belief model, has received growing attention in recent years. It proposes that adherence is determined by (1) how severe the threat is to a person's health; (2) how susceptible one perceives himself or herself to be to that threat; (3) the perceived effectiveness of the proposed treatment plan; and (4) perceptions of self-efficacy, (i.e., the ability to carry out the treatment/rehabilitation plan). Of these four factors, belief in the effectiveness of the treatment program and the perceived ability to successfully perform the treatment are most influential in determining adherence. If an injured person believes that the treatment is not going to make any difference, or if the rehabilitation seems beyond his or her ability, dropout occurs.

Proven Methods for Effective Recovery

Of the numerous theories guiding injury rehabilitation, four strategies stand out in both research and practice: goal setting, relaxation training, thought management, and imagery. Each has specific applications for athletes and coaches.

Goal setting Effective *goal setting* has been consistently associated with effective, rapid recovery from injury. As noted earlier, research shows that goal orientation affects adherence to a treatment program, and subsequently, the degree of injury recovery. Goals that emphasize effort and steady improvement in ability are essential to effective rehabilitation and the restoring of confidence. Task-oriented people are naturally inclined to set goals that are *self-referred*, or relate to their own level of functioning. However, those who are inclined to compare themselves to others (ego oriented) still need to focus on the small self-referred tasks for rehabilitation success.

For example, Tracy and Joanne both experienced ACL surgery within a day of one another and began their rehabilitation at the same time. Joanne was task oriented; she readily approached rehabilitation by breaking her ultimate goal (returning to full play) into small-step goals: first increasing her range of motion, and then gradually and progressively increasing the strength of her leg. She set a schedule for performing her exercises, routinely evaluated her weekly progress, and adjusted her rehab program according to how well she had done in comparison to her previous range of motion and the amount of weight she could lift. She gained both confidence and a sense of accomplishment from knowing that she was working hard, keeping up with her program, and seeing progress week to week.

Tracy, on the other hand, tended to be ego oriented—from the moment she met Joanne, she approached rehabilitation like a competition. Tracy wanted to rehabilitate her leg more rapidly and better than Joanne, and used this comparison throughout her rehabilitation for her sense of accomplishment, confidence, and feedback. When Joanne's range of motion was 25 degrees, Tracy pushed herself to move her leg 26 degrees; when Joanne lifted 5 pounds, Tracy lifted 6. One week Tracy skipped her physical therapy on two days, and Joanne outperformed her on range of motion. Tracy was motivated by this loss and made certain that she adhered to the training schedule the following week. Her ego orientation was not a problem as long as she set task-oriented (and thus self-referred), small-step goals as the building blocks of her rehabilitation, and kept a long-range perspective. An ego orientation becomes dangerous when the comparison to others is repeatedly negative and the individual does not establish appropriate self-referred tasks or loses motivation altogether.

Imagery and relaxation   Imagery and relaxation also facilitate injury rehabilitation. In a well-controlled study of 30 people undergoing ACL reconstructive surgery, one-third of the group received 10 sessions of training in relaxation and guided imagery, one-third met in a group that provided support and encouragement and spent 10 to 15 minutes a day visualizing a peaceful scene, and the other one-third had physical therapy as usual with no special attention or training in mental skills. Those who practiced relaxation and guided imagery had significantly greater knee strength, less pain, and fewer fears of reinjury at the end of the rehabilitation program. In Gould's study of injured skiers, the routine use of imagery was correlated with successful recovery. None of the skiers specifically identified using relaxation techniques; however, "being patient and taking it slow"—a process that often requires the use of relaxation techniques—also made the difference between successful and unsuccessful rehabilitation.

Imagery can assist recovery in a number of ways. An athlete may use imagery of properly executed rehabilitation exercises to help develop skills and adherence. Mentally rehearsing timing or imagining a successful postrehabilitation competition can help maintain confidence. Although it may sound far-fetched, imagery can also speed the healing process; its impact was first documented in research with terminal cancer patients. Patients who routinely used healing imagery of their body fighting the cancer lived longer than those who did not use imagery, and in some cases there was a total remission of symptoms. In a 1991 study of athletes recovering from soft-tissue knee and ankle injuries, the routine practice of healing imagery was one of the factors that differentiated the fast-healing athletes (5 weeks or less) from the slow-healing athletes who required more than 16 weeks to return to play.

Relaxation can also facilitate injury recovery in a variety of ways: It can aid in managing the pain and stress that accompany injury and rehabilitation, facilitate the vividness of imagery, and is often an important part of managing emotions and facilitating positive thinking.

Positive self-talk *Positive self-talk* is another technique found to facilitate successful rehabilitation. For many athletes, an injury triggers a loss of confidence accompanied by a flood of catastrophic, negative thoughts: "My life is ruined . . . I'll never be able to play at the same level . . . this is the worst thing that could ever happen!" Stopping the downward spiral and countering the negative thoughts (the "stinkin' thinkin'") with positive ones is crucial to maintaining confidence, motivation, and hope: "The situation may be bad, but it's not the end of the world. Other people have come back from an injury like this, and so can I. I'm in great physical shape, mentally tough, and have better resources than most." In the previously mentioned study of athletes with knee and ankle injuries, the fast-healing group used positive self-talk. In the study of injured skiers, *every* skier who recovered successfully mentioned "managing emotions and thoughts" as a central coping strategy. Cognitive restructuring, or changing the way one perceives an injury, is a fundamental intervention of both the health belief model and protection motivation theory of injury rehabilitation.

Ultimate Success—The Treatment Team Approach

One of the most significant changes in recent years has been the recognition of the importance of a team approach in treating athletic injuries. Advances in this area have been guided primarily by successful practitioners in the field rather than by researchers in controlled settings. John Heil of the Lewis-Gale Clinic in Roanoke, Virginia, was one of the first sport psychologists to emphasize the importance of a multidisciplinary sports medicine team to successful recovery from injury. His book, *Psychology of Sport Injury*, was one of the first texts fully devoted to the mental and emotional aspects of sport injury. Heil advocates thinking of injury rehabilitation as a "sport performance challenge." With athletes constantly striving to push performance levels, injury is to be expected at times. When athletes adopt this perspective, an injury is no longer a catastrophe but merely another anticipated aspect of an athletic career. The sport psychologist builds on the skills that an athlete uses for peak performance on the playing field to optimize recovery in the training room. Rehabilitation skills become part of the repertoire of the serious athlete.

Surgeons throughout the world go to the Steadman-Hawkins Clinic in Vail, Colorado, to study the procedures of Dr. Richard Steadman because of his success in treating athletes and having them rapidly return to competition. Several features of Steadman's approach are noteworthy. First, the athlete is an active member of the treatment team; he or she is educated about the nature of the injury, treatment options, the phases of treatment, and expected challenges along the way. His or her input is part of the guiding process of the team and is integral to setting demanding yet attainable goals at each phase of treatment. Second, the focus on athletic identity is maintained throughout the rehabilitation process and is part of the framework of strategies. Since athletes are accustomed to daily exercise and intense physical activity, every effort is made to have the athlete engage in some form of aerobic activity immediately following surgery. If surgery was performed on a leg, the person may use a stationary hand-crank cycle machine; if on an arm, a stationary bicycle might be the equipment of choice. This immediate engagement in aerobic activity helps avoid the depression that is common after an injury. The athlete continues to be active, to have a daily boost of endorphins, and perceives the surgery as merely another step in the total athletic process.

The ideal treatment team comprises not only medical personnel, sport psychologists, and the athlete but also the coach, team trainer, and significant others in the athlete's life. The active support and involvement of the coach and team trainer helps facilitate the rehabilitation process, especially for female athletes. When an athlete has confidence in the team trainer, confidence and comfort in the rehabilitation facilities, and the support of the coach and significant others, self-confidence is more easily restored following an injury.

The scope of relevant parties included on a treatment team is continually evolving. A more holistic approach to treatment is often characterized as the biopsychosocial model. The "bio" refers to the biological aspects of treatment; the "psycho" acknowledges that thoughts and emotions are an integral part of recovery; and the "social" recognizes both the influence of personal relationships on coping with injury and the impact of the injury on significant relationships. However, a growing number of practitioners believe that a truly holistic perspective is based on a "biopsychosocial-*spiritual*" model. Serious injury or loss often challenges the foundations of one's spiritual beliefs; those who face it commonly ask, "Why me?" Asking this sort of question is not unusual, and coming up with answers that fit one's unique faith and belief in a higher power is often crucial to establishing a sense of meaning in life. Medical practitioners may be uncomfortable talking about spirituality and faith and are somtimes ill-equipped to do so. If the treatment team is not comfortable discussing issues of spirituality, a chaplain or person of faith can join the team to complete the holistic nature of recovery.

Final Tips for Avoiding Injury and Maximizing Recovery

How can we apply this new knowledge about the history and evolution of injury treatment, critical issues, and effective rehabilitation techniques to real-life situations? What can coaches, trainers, and athletes do to avoid injury when possible and maximize the recovery process when it does occur?

Avoiding Injury

As discussed earlier, the following factors predispose an athlete to injury:

- Negative life stresses
- Increase in daily hassles
- Previous injury
- Poor coping skills

Coaches and athlete can reduce the likelihood of injury in the following ways:

• Avoid introducing new, high-risk routines or engaging in high-risk situations during times of major life stresses. Coaches should know their athletes well and exercise judgment in these areas. For example, if a gymnast is going through the breakup of a significant relationship, steer clear of attempting new routines that have high elements of risk. A platform diver may want to practice the familiar repertoire rather than attempting new dives if his parents are in the process of divorcing. If a dancer who recently lost a coveted role due to a stress fracture wants to cycle as a means of recovery, cycling indoors on a trainer is far preferable to cycling on the road where the risk of accident and injury climbs.

• Provide or learn stress-management techniques as a preventative measure. Student athletes who learn such techniques are better able to cope with daily hassles; as a result, injury rates are reduced. Teams can minimize injury by attending workshops in stress management as part of freshman orientation (and by attending refresher courses each year). Athletes whose teams do not provide stress-management training should check with the counseling center to see if they can learn the techniques on their own.

• Address the psychological aspects of injury rehabilitation before returning to play. The restoration of confidence and comfort in performance situations is essential; without them, the chance of reinjury is high. For example, a basketball player who has physically rehabilitated an injured ankle but is not psychologically prepared to return to play may avoid putting full pressure on the foot, which disrupts the body's sense of flow and balance. Or a soccer player may brace herself in anticipation of being hit on her injured leg, with the resulting tension both hindering performance and increasing the chance of reinjury.

Coping With Injury

Injury is part of the process of being an athlete; expecting an injury-free career is unreasonable. By providing educational programs on dealing with injuries and establishing expectations of team support during the rehabilitation process, the coaching staff can dispel the myths that "injured athletes are worthless" or "you need to give 110 percent regardless of the pain." Injured athletes can focus on the task of rehabilitation with greater support and confidence, and the catastrophic reaction to injury can be reduced. The ultimate success of an athlete's career will be influenced by how well he or she copes with injuries and setbacks as opposed to expecting to avoid them altogether. Athletes should think of rehabilitation as an athletic challenge and approach it as they would any new skill or ability.

Use a team approach   Successful rehabilitation rarely occurs in isolation, so a team approach to dealing with injury should be adopted. Depending on the severity of the injury, the treatment team may include the athlete, team trainer, coach, teammates, and social support system; in more serious injuries, it may also include physicians, surgeons, nurses, physical therapists, sport psychologists, team chaplains, and family members. If you are an injured athlete, you are the one ultimately responsible for your recovery. The first order of business is to establish relationships with the members of the treatment team. It is important for you to let team members know about you, your concerns, your strengths, and your dreams. The time immediately following an injury is often extremely emotional and challenging. Look for someone on the team who understands, empathizes with, and accepts you—all essential for establishing a trusting, collaborative relationship. The wise athlete will mobilize all available resources to aid the process.

Coaches: Maintaining contact with injured athletes during the treatment and rehabilitation process facilitates effective recovery. Keep in contact by phone, letter, or e-mail if treatment requires that they be away from the team. You don't have to give advice or solve problems; what is most important is to communicate that you care and that you are there. Educate your players about the importance of support and how to show it. Make every effort to have athletes who are in rehab resume contact with the team as soon as feasible, even if they are not ready to return to play.

Trainers: An athlete's belief in the rehabilitation process depends on his or her confidence in the trainer's ability and his or her comfort level and confidence in the rehabilitation facilities. Maintain a clean, well-equipped facility that has easy access. Be professional and knowledgeable, and listen to the athlete's concerns. Often, the trainer is the team member who has the most insight and direct influence on the rehabilitation process. Be mindful of the athlete's psychological recovery as well as physical healing.

Teammates: Teammates can have tremendous impact on the rehabilitation process, but many athletes struggle with how to show support to an injured player. Even when an injury is not sport related, some players avoid contact due to superstition or because of their own discomfort in confronting injury, trauma, and change. Often they simply do not know what to do and fear they might say or do something that will make the situation worse. Coaches and trainers can alleviate fears by educating teams on the importance of showing support when others are in need. For example, before an automobile accident that disfigured his face, Sam thought of his teammates as his family—he spent almost every waking moment either working, studying, socializing, or rooming with others on the team. After the injury, he was dismayed that others openly avoided him. Sam's fears, depression, and rehabilitation efforts improved dramatically after two teammates dropped by his apartment and said, "We were thinking about you." They acknowledged the awkwardness of the situation and affirmed that

Coaches, trainers, and team-mates play tremendous roles in the success of injury rehabilitation.

©davidsandersphotos.com

they cared and were there for him. They listened as he shared what he had been through; there was no need for anything more.

Family members and significant others: With married athletes and those whose treatment and rehabilitation occur at home, family members and significant others should be involved as part of the treatment team. Just as athletic teammates need education about the injury and how best to provide support, family members do too. Often this is a challenging and emotionally charged process, since a young athlete may have just gone through the process of leaving home and establishing an independent identity. When an injury dictates that athletes return home, they may struggle with the loss of not only physical abilities but also their recently achieved independence. By including the family as part of the treatment team and helping them understand the "big picture," many of those difficulties can be avoided.

Seek information   If you are injured, learn everything you can about the injury—the nature of the injury, what to expect in the course of dealing with it, the goals and rationale for rehabilitation, the dangers and risks of various treatment options, and probable outcomes and expectations. Be a good consumer—don't be afraid to be a "squeaky wheel" by asking questions and getting second opinions. It is your body and your life. Don't assume that because a procedure is recommended by a physician it is always the best option. Write down questions for your treatment providers and write down their answers.

Return to aerobic activity as soon as possible   Work with your treatment team to implement some form of aerobic activity as soon as physically possible, while still protecting the injury and allowing it to heal. If you require surgery, discuss the surgeon's philosophy regarding aerobic exercise during recovery. Get more than one opinion, if necessary, until you have confidence in the surgeon and the proposed treatment and subsequent rehabilitation program.

Learn to differentiate between types of pain   Dealing with injury typically involves pain and discomfort. There is a fine yet absolutely essential difference between the discomfort of strenuous exertion, both on the playing field and in rehabilitation, and the pain of reinjuring damaged tissue.

Use time off from competition as an opportunity   If you are forced to withdraw from competition due to an injury, use the opportunity to address aspects of your life that may have been put on the back burner due to the demands of training. For example, when professional triathlete Karen Smyers had her Achilles tendon severed in a freak accident at her home, she knew it would be at least nine months before she could return to competition. She and her husband decided to use the time off as an opportunity to start a family. This can be your chance to go back to school or travel—to do whatever you have wanted to do but never had the time. If the downtime is relatively brief, use it as an opportunity to strengthen your mental skills. Become a smarter athlete by studying tapes, strategies, and training methods.

Learn skills to facilitate rehab   As we noted earlier in this chapter, there are several mental skills that facilitate and speed recovery from an injury. If you are not proficient in these skills, find resources for learning them—read books, consult with your trainer, check with a sport psychologist. If you already know the skills, apply them regularly and focus on improving your abilities even more.

• Goal setting: Effective goal setting is the cornerstone of rehabilitation. Begin by determining your baseline. Regardless of what you were capable of before the injury, determine what you can reasonably and safely do now. From that baseline, establish a ladder of small-step goals that will eventually result in your return to full ability. You may have been running a mile in less than 6 minutes two months ago, but last week you could walk only one city block before stopping in pain. Keep your focus on task-oriented goals that are based on improving your current level of functioning, regardless of what others are doing. Remember to evaluate your progress regularly and adjust your goals as needed. (Refer to chapter 2 for detailed information on goal setting.)

• Relaxation techniques: Relaxation can facilitate pain management, thought management, imagery, and the healing process. There are several variations of relaxation techniques, such as progressive relaxation, hypnosis, and centered breathing. In our example at the beginning of the chapter, James used self-hypnosis to facilitate his imagery work and centered breathing to calm himself whenever he started thinking that he might not successfully recover. (Refer to chapter 6 for information on relaxation training.)

• Imagery: Imagery is one of the most powerful tools that an athlete can use to facilitate the recovery process. Six months before the 2000 Olympic Games, U.S. platform diver Laura Wilkinson broke three bones in her foot during a practice session. For the next two months she was unable to dive, but she went to the pool every day as usual and *mentally rehearsed* each dive. Although she did not return to the diving platform until three weeks before the trials, she maintained her timing and confidence through the consistent use of imagery. She went on to qualify at the Olympic trials and subsequently won a gold medal in Sydney. Imagery can help adherence to a rehabilitation program as well as promote the actual healing of damaged tissue. James used the vicarious experience of imagery to help build his confidence about successfully returning to play after his injury.

• Thought management: By simply remembering to calm yourself and counter negative thoughts, you can stay more positive, focused, and relaxed during the rehabilitation process. It is common to have periods of doubt and fear when injured. It is important to be able to remind yourself, "This is not the end of the world—plenty of people have similar injuries and return stronger than ever. I'm going to be one of those people. I know that negative thinking will only make things worse. Instead, I'm going to focus on the possibilities."

Ensure confidence by returning to competition in gradual stages   In order to have confidence in your abilities and an optimal psychological recovery, it is important to gradually develop and test your physical abilities. By building on a series of successes, you will have trust in the recovered injury when it is time to return to full-speed competition. The first step is to be released from the treatment or rehabilitation program and authorized to return to play. Getting medical confirmation of recovery before undergoing the strain of play is crucial. Once you receive confirmation, your focus should be on the return of physical and technical abilities. This is a time for exercises and drills in order to regain the flexibility and strength needed for actual competition. Be sure to follow the principles of effective goal setting. As your physical abilities return, your focus can broaden to include the technical skills of your sport. Practice these skills in isolated, undemanding situations until they become second nature once again. Only after you can successfully perform the technical skills in drills should you gradually increase the intensity of situations in which you test your abilities, because during this phase the chance of reinjury is greatest. Continue in a stepwise progression until you are engaging in high-intensity training that mimics competition. Finally, you will be ready to return to full competition with the confidence that you have prepared well and tested the injury successfully in competition-like conditions.

When to seek a consultant   Most of the time, motivated athletes who work with knowledgeable coaches and trainers will deal effectively with injuries without need of outside consultation. However, when the emotional or psychological factors surrounding an injury require special attention and skills, the addition of a properly trained sport psychologist to the treatment team may be essential.

Eating disorders such as anorexia and bulimia can be life-threatening to the individual and wreak havoc on team members. Effective treatment requires addressing the psychological factors that underlie the person's distorted body image as well as coordinating the treatment team and support system to bring about change. Professionals who have clinical training in treating these conditions should be consulted.

If you have persistent, repetitive pain that does not respond to treatment as expected, or if there does not appear to be a physical basis for the pain, you may want to consult with a sport psychologist. The experience of pain is the brain's interpretation of messages from the central nervous system. There is a "gating system" that can open to let messages through to the brain or close to block them. Our emotions, thoughts, and beliefs influence this gating process and can affect when and how much pain we experience. For example, often an athlete will not experience pain during the intensity and focus of competition because the gate closes. Then after the game, pain suddenly seems to appear from nowhere. The process can work in reverse when certain emotions, such as depression and worry, open the gate wider and increase the experience of pain. In such cases, successful rehabilitation requires addressing the psychological and emotional aspects that affect the pain experience.

This chapter has focused on injuries that can be treated and successfully rehabilitated. Unfortunately, this is not the case with all injuries. Any time an injury results in permanent loss of ability or ends a person's career, special attention needs to be given to the psychological, emotional, and spiritual issues that accompany the loss. When an injury results in the death of an athlete, whether it occurred in the context of sport or in an unrelated setting, it affects the entire team and staff. This is a crucial time to have emotional, psychological, and spiritual resources available to help traverse the journey of dealing with tragedy.

Future Directions

During the past two decades, we have witnessed dramatic advances in our understanding of what is involved in rapidly and effectively treating athletic injuries. Effective treatment includes attending to the psychological aspects of the injury. In the next decade, we can anticipate that athletic practices will continue to evolve as our knowledge expands. Here are just some of the changes that we are likely to see.

Dealing with injury integrated as part of being an athlete   Because no serious athlete will ever be injury free, athletic programs and coaches will begin to include expectations and skills for coping with injury as part of their fundamentals. The ideal high school athletic program of the future will include stress-management training to reduce the likelihood of injury as well as injury-preparation programs to educate athletes on how to cope with injury and provide support to others. These are skills that can be used throughout life.

Greater specificity of mental skills on rehabilitation   Only recently have we started to discover how men and women differ in their experience of injury-associated stress and how they deal with those stresses. Hopefully future research will clarify what works best with which people and in which situations. As improvements in medicine decrease the time required for physical recovery, greater emphasis will be placed on the psychological aspects of recovery.

Proactive plans and resources for anticipating injury   As people become more accepting that injury is part of being an athlete, programs will become more proactive in anticipating and developing resources to deal with injury. Treatment teams will be established in advance and will include more of the athletes' natural support systems, as well as integrating resources for addressing the spiritual aspects of recovery and dealing with loss. Coaches and trainers will become better educated about how their behaviors affect and facilitate recovery. Athletic trainers will continue to be the front line in addressing both the physical and psychological aspects of recovery. Ultimately, trainers will instruct the injured athlete in key psychological skills such as goal setting, relaxation, imagery, and thought management.

Support and exit plans for career-ending injuries   Sports organizations will recognize the importance of providing services to assist those who are most severely affected by injury. Hospitals, rehabilitation centers, and organizations governing athletic participation are likely to lead the way in developing resources for those who must end their careers as a result of injury.

Greater emphasis on the aging athlete   As baby boomers continue to engage in sport as they age, we must address the rehabilitation needs of older adults. Caretakers will become better versed in how to incorporate family members into the treatment team. Since most of the research on athletic injuries has studied youth and young adults, the study of aging athletes is likely to be a fertile area for development.

Eating Disorders: When Rations Become Irrational

Karen D. Cogan

Healthy eating is a key factor in achieving peak athletic performance—that is common knowledge in the sport world. When nutrition is not at its peak due to disordered eating patterns, performance can be compromised, and more important, the overall health of the athlete is at risk. Documented cases of death due to overly restrictive dieting patterns and extreme weight-loss measures that lead to self-starvation indicate that disordered eating is a significant health risk and worthy of our attention.

The Impact of Disordered Eating

Unfortunately, restrictive dieting is not uncommon, especially in sports such as gymnastics in which weight and body appearance are central to performance. Behaviors such as severely limiting calories while increasing activity levels may seem like merely another way to maintain or lose weight, but they can be physically and emotionally damaging—and they become potentially life threatening when athletes get into patterns they are unable to discontinue on their own.

If you read any popular magazines or watch news shows, you are likely aware of the different types of eating problems that have gained national attention. Psychologists Laurie Mintz and Nancy Betz suggest viewing these eating issues on a continuum. On one end of the continuum are severe, diagnosed eating disorders. To be diagnosed with an eating disorder, a person must meet specific criteria, which are described in the next section. Only a small percentage of the population meets these criteria. On the other end of the continuum are individuals who have no symptoms of disordered eating. In the middle are those who demonstrate some characteristics of eating disorders, but not enough to warrant a diagnosis. We call this *disordered-eating behavior*, and just because it cannot be diagnosed does not mean it is an issue to ignore. These behaviors cause problems even if they do not meet the criteria. According to Mintz and Betz, some studies say more that than 60 percent of the population demonstrates some type of disordered-eating behavior.

In sport, we often view athletes as models of health. Ideally, they eat a balanced diet, and the right mix of nutrition allows their bodies to perform at their physical peak. If athletes gain or lose too much weight, then their performance is compromised, and we assume their goal is to regain the balance. But not all athletes attain this outwardly healthy appearance in a healthy way. When it comes to food and weight, athletes engage in a variety of unhealthy strategies to reach their goals. These behaviors can be harder to detect in athletes than in the general population because of the unique athletic environment. Some athletes will hide disordered-eating behavior behind a healthy eating facade. For instance, gymnasts will talk about eating healthy (cutting out virtually all the

© Empics

Athletes in artistic sports such as figure skating and gymnastics are prone to eating disorders due to the pressure of maintaining an attractive image combined with high-level artistic demand.

fat in their diet, eating only foods where the calorie content is clear, cutting out junk food to the point that there is very little they are "allowed" to eat), but they are actually severely restricting their food intake. Because coaches encourage healthy diets, they may not see this pattern as a problem. On the other hand, athletes can also get into the habit of eating too much and become overeaters. Because of their high caloric expenditures during training they can maintain a normal or slightly above-average weight even when eating more than they need. Thus, they can hide this pattern of eating out of habit or boredom or for comfort rather than sustenance.

Much of what has been written about eating disorders focuses on women because historically women have been more at risk to develop them. But men also struggle with eating disorders, and they should be monitored. Although they appear to be less at risk than women, male athletes face unique challenges to maintain certain weight requirements in the sport setting. The issues discussed in this chapter apply to both men and women.

Diagnosable Eating Disorders

Several types of eating disorders can plague athletes; the three diagnosable ones are outlined in the *Diagnostic and Statistical Manual of Mental Disorders IV-TR*.

Bulimia nervosa   *Bulimia nervosa* is characterized by a cycle of binge eating and purging. Binge eating involves eating huge quantities of food in one sitting, much more than most individuals would eat under similar circumstances. A binge is often followed by a sense of guilt, which then leads to purging through self-induced vomiting, fasting, misuse of laxatives, diuretics, or enemas, or excessive exercise. For a clinical diagnosis, binge/purge episodes must occur, on average, at least twice a week for three months.

Anorexia nervosa   *Anorexia nervosa* is characterized by a refusal to maintain a minimally normal body weight based on age and height, an intense fear of gaining weight, and a distorted perception of one's body shape and size. In women, amenorrhea (cessation of menstrual periods for three or more months or no menstrual periods by age 16) is also evident. There are two types of anorexia: restricting and binge-eating/purging. Restricting anorexics lose weight through severe dieting, fasting, and excessive exercise. Binge-eating/purging anorexics maintain a below-average weight and engage in binge eating, purging, or both. Some will not binge, but they purge even after eating small amounts of food because they perceive all eating as a binge.

Eating disorder, not otherwise specified   Sometimes people have most of the characteristics of an eating disorder, but not all. For instance, someone might have all the characteristics of anorexia but be of normal weight. Cases like this are still eating disorders, but they are categorized as "not otherwise specified" (NOS).

Nondiagnosable Eating Disorders

Athletes may also face the conditions that follow, which are not clinically diagnosable eating disorders but are related to disordered eating.

Overeating   Overeating involves bingeing without a purge cycle. Overeaters tend to be overweight; they eat even though they are not hungry because food helps them cope with emotions such as anger, loneliness, depression, and sadness. Overeating in athletes is difficult to detect because many of them need thousands of calories per day due to high metabolisms and intensive training schedules. These athletes' eating patterns may resemble overeating but are necessary to maintain health and fitness. Other athletes eat for emotional reasons rather than hunger, but they appear to be average or slightly above-average weight. If coaches do not observe athletes at meals or listen to their conversations about food, they may find it difficult to understand athletes' motivations for eating or to detect a problem that needs to be addressed. *Appearance alone is not an indicator of overeating.* Coaches cannot assume that an athlete is eating appropriately or is disorder free because she looks all right.

Female athlete triad   The American College of Sports Medicine and Kimberly Yeager and her colleagues have identified a condition called *female athlete triad.* It consists of three interrelated components: disordered eating, amenorrhea, and osteoporosis (bone loss). Disordered eating leads to a negative energy balance, which occurs when the amount of energy consumed is less than the amount of energy expended. Eventually the body interprets a negative energy balance as starvation and may shut down the body's reproductive capability by ceasing the menstrual cycle. The result is a decrease in estrogen and, consequently, amenorrhea. Decreases in estrogen and dietary intake of calcium (which occurs with restricting and lack of nutritional knowledge) signal the bones to release calcium to replace low calcium levels in the bloodstream. This may result in bone loss or formation of unhealthy bone. Many athletes think that how they eat now could not possibly produce osteoporosis until years into the future. Unfortunately, startling evidence shows that osteoporosis can occur in the early 20s. There are cases of 23-year-old athletes whose X rays indicate that their bones are equivalent to those of a 70-year-old woman.

Obligatory exercise   *Obligatory exercise* (also referred to as excessive or compulsive exercise) is physical activity that is extreme in frequency and duration that is done by people who are relatively resistant to change. These people are obsessed with maintaining an exercise program and will exercise even when injury, fatigue, or other personal demands persist. An example of an obligatory runner is a man who wakes up at 3:30 every morning to fit in a three-hour run and get to work by 8:00 A.M. He has to go to bed by 7:30 P.M. to maintain this schedule, so he misses out on many evening social activities. He refuses to alter his schedule or take days off from running to participate in other activities. Most obligatory exercisers prefer to exercise alone, maintain a rigid diet, are preoccupied with their bodies, and feel more control over their lives when they are engaged in their exercise regime. Obligatory exercisers display characteristics similar to those with eating disorders, which include compulsions and rituals, rigid diets, perfectionism, and control over their bodies. Also, male obligatory exercisers tend to use such regimens to attain fitness, while women use it to attain thinness.

Why Eating Disorders Develop

According to Mardie Burckes-Miller and David Black, three determinants explain the development of eating disorders: biogenetic factors, psychological factors, and sociological environmental factors. This chapter reviews biogenetic and psychological factors only briefly because athletes seem less vulnerable than non-athletes to their effects. Evidence suggests that athletes are superior physically and emotionally to non-athletes, presumably because of the intense selection process they must endure to get to the top. We will look more closely at the sociological factors, which are defined as the influence of the environment on human behavior.

Biogenetic factors   Researchers used to think that anorexia and bulimia occurred because of a malfunction in the pituitary gland. More recent research examines whether the biological abnormalities are the outcomes of starvation and disordered eating or if biology leads people to develop eating disorders. For instance, some researchers suggest that there is a genetic predisposition for eating disorders because individuals who have them have parents who demonstrated these behaviors. Other evidence suggests that bulimia is a variant of a depressive disorder, which also can be hereditary. There are no clear explanations yet regarding the cause and effect of biogenetic factors.

Psychological factors   Several psychological characteristics have been related to eating disorders. Personality characteristics such as perfectionism and obsessive-compulsive traits have been linked to disordered patterns. Athletes, especially in high-level sports, are often perfectionists, which sets them up for a possible eating disorder.

Some researchers view eating disorders as an addiction, similar to substance-abuse disorders, with food being the substance abused. Other researchers and clinicians view food as different from substances. An individual who has a problem with a drug or alcohol can abstain and not use it again, but someone who abstains from food is called an anorexic; abstinence from food is not an option. Rather, individuals with eating disorders must learn to live with food, using it in moderation. Regardless of whether eating disorders are viewed as an addiction, food can be used to cope with strong emotion or as a replacement for emotional expression. Other findings indicate that women who experience more stress are at greater risk for binge eating.

Environmental factors   The development of eating disorders in athletes seems to be most affected by the environment. All athletes, but women especially, may feel pressure to achieve a particular body type or weight that is consistent with their sport. Because of genetics and body size, some athletes find it impossible to achieve that ideal. Several sociological environmental factors contribute to these pressures, including:

- Culture: The preferred shape for women in Western cultures has shifted toward a thin, lean ideal even though the average American woman has become taller and heavier. Athletes face additional pressures concerning ideal body size, shape, and weight, especially for activities and sports that emphasize a small size or thin shape, such as dancing, figure skating, diving, gymnastics, and ballet.

- Media: The current emphasis in the media is on fitness and leanness. Pick up any magazine, especially women's magazines, and you will find articles and ads that refer to eating light and fat free or toning and losing weight. The media also presents athletes as ideal fitness models, and some athletes may feel that even *they* cannot live up to these standards.

- Roles of men and women: For women especially, there may be a conflict between behaving as a traditional female (feminine, pretty, someone who glistens rather than sweats) and what is expected as an athlete (strong, assertive, muscular). Women may feel conflicted about how their bodies are supposed to look. Should they achieve the societal standard or the sport standard? Consequently, they may be confused about how to eat.

- Community: Each sport has its community, some of which may predispose its athletes to eating disorders. A low weight may go unnoticed in an environment that rewards thin shape and low weight. Wrestling is an example of a unique community with its own standards and accepted behaviors.

- Peers: Peer pressure may contribute to eating disorders. Some teammates even teach each other unhealthy means of managing weight. This type of "mentoring" behavior is evident in sports such as gymnastics.

- Coaches and authority figures: Most coaches mean to be supportive of athletes, but inadvertent comments about an athlete's weight and physical appearance can contribute to the development of eating patterns. Other coaches overtly encourage unhealthy means of weight control with comments like, "Talk to Jennifer [a known bulimic] over there about how to control your weight."

- Family: Families can influence the development of eating disorders if weight, appearance, and weight loss are emphasized at home.

Athletes at Risk

The *Diagnostic and Statistical Manual of Mental Disorders (DSM)* reports that .5 percent of adolescent and young females in the general population can be diagnosed with anorexia nervosa. The rate of those who are subthreshold (do not meet all the criteria but have many of the symptoms) is believed to be higher. No rates are reported for males with anorexia. A prevalence rate of 1 to 3 percent for bulimia nervosa is reported for the general population of adolescent and young adult females, and one-tenth that rate, or less than 1 percent, is reported for males.

Athletes may be more at risk than most people for the development of eating disorders, especially those in sports in which weight or appearance are emphasized, such as gymnastics or wrestling. Research results have been mixed: Some studies report that athletes are more at risk and others report that they are less at risk. One survey of elite female Norwegian athletes by Jorunn Sundgot-Borgen indicated that 1.3 percent met the *DSM* criteria for anorexia nervosa and 8 percent met the criteria for bulimia nervosa. Another survey by Craig Johnson, the director of the Eating Disorders Clinic, and his colleagues indicated that of 1,445 American athletes, 9.2 percent of women and .01 percent of men have a "clinically significant" problem with bulimia and 2.85 percent of females and 0 percent of males have a "clinically significant" problem with anorexia. All these rates are higher than in the general population, suggesting that athletes may indeed be more at risk for developing eating disorders.

The previously stated prevalence rates are for studies across all sports, but the type of sport must be considered when assessing who is at risk. Sundgot-Borgen classified sports into six categories:

1. Endurance sports: The main training requirement is aerobic (cycling, rowing, speedskating, swimming).

2. Aesthetic sports: The outcome is based on the subjective evaluation of the competitive performance (gymnastics, diving, figure skating).

3. Weight-dependent sports: A specific weight is required to compete (wrestling, karate, judo).

4. Ball-game sports: A ball is exchanged among teammates (volleyball, basketball).

5. Power sports: The main component is strength training (discus, shot put, power lifting).

6. Technical sports: These sports did not fit into one of the other five categories (alpine skiing, golf, rifle shooting).

Only a few studies have examined athletes across sports and made comparisons between categories, so firm conclusions are difficult to draw. Initial results, however, suggest that some types of sports have a higher prevalence of eating disorders than the general population. Specifically, female aesthetic sport athletes (e.g., gymnasts, divers, synchronized swimmers) have a greater tendency toward anorexia than ball-game athletes or endurance athletes. These aesthetic sports involve subjective scoring systems that can, on some level, be affected by grace and body appearance. In males, both aesthetic and weight-dependent athletes had more symptoms of bulimia than endurance athletes. Wrestlers, for instance, are at risk due to the sport's use of weight categories and the athletes' desire to make weight in the lightest category possible.

Identifying Disordered Eating

Because athletes can be very secretive about disordered-eating behaviors, coaches and medical personnel find it challenging to detect these problems. Coaches must be very astute and attuned to the athletes' behaviors, because they are not likely to volunteer this information. Some signs of eating disorders are obvious, such as extremely low weight. But other signs, such as vomiting or using laxatives, are not always evident unless the athlete admits to engaging in them.

In addition, because of the intensity of their training, elite athletes often resemble non-athletes with eating disorders, and it may be difficult to tell if an athlete has an eating disorder or is just being a "good athlete." For instance, one of the diagnostic criteria for bulimia nervosa is excessive exercise as a means of purging. In addition, anorexics can use excessive training to maintain an unhealthy body weight. So is an athlete who trains extra hours exercising because of his dedication and commitment to improve? Or is the exercise a form of purging or maintaining a dangerously low weight?

Several other characteristics of high-level athletes also fit the criteria for disordered eating, including amenorrhea, denial of pain or injury, selfless commitment to the team, compliance with coaching instructions, perfectionist tendencies, and losing weight when instructed.

One of the biggest challenges for coaches is determining the motivations behind an athlete's excessive exercise. Having an open discussion is one approach, but don't expect an athlete with an eating disorder to be completely candid. Coaches need to keep a watchful eye on athletes who train excessively to ensure that they avoid eating disorders and physical overtraining. Coaches can begin by being aware of the characteristics that indicate eating disorders. The following signs can help coaches detect possible disordered-eating behavior:

- Repeatedly expressed concerns about being or feeling fat even when weight is below average (distorted body image)
- Fears of becoming obese that do not diminish even with weight loss
- Discomfort with compliments. For example, if the athlete hears, "You look nice," he or she might respond, "No I don't. I'm fat."
- Dichotomous thinking. The athlete views everything as either good or bad (nothing in the middle) and can't see choices
- Depressed mood
- Negative thoughts about self or guilt, especially after eating
- Avoidance of, or even disdain for, fat, protein, and dairy products

The following signs could indicate anorexia:

- Weight loss
- Extremely thin appearance
- Lanugo (fine, downy hair that grows in the facial area)
- Refusal to maintain a minimal normal weight consistent with sport, age, and height
- Denial that he or she is thin and talk of losing more weight
- Avoidance of eating with others
- Refusal to eat and stating, "I'm not hungry"
- Eating only tiny portions of meals and then possibly moving food around on plate
- Hair loss
- Complaints of being cold all the time

The following signs could indicate bulimia:

- Wide fluctuations in weight over short time spans. Bulimics can be normal weight, slightly overweight, or underweight, so weight fluctuations are better indicators than actual weight
- May wear baggy clothes to camouflage weight changes
- "Chipmunk cheeks" (swollen salivary glands)
- Sores on the back of the hands from purging
- Candy or laxative wrappers or excess food containers in the trash can
- Patterns of eating large quantities of food and then disappearing into the bathroom
- Bloodshot eyes, especially after trips to the bathroom

The following signs are things you might not see and would need to rely on the athlete's report for. Athletes typically will not tell you if you don't ask the right questions—even if you ask, they might not tell you. Sometimes they may not even be aware of these symptoms, and a medical evaluation would be necessary to detect them. Many of them can become severe physical and medical complications.

- Laxative abuse or dependence
- Diet-pill abuse or dependence
- Hair loss
- Brittle nails
- Diminished muscle mass
- Loss of menstrual periods (in women)

- Gastrointestinal problems including bleeding
- Tooth-enamel loss or tooth decay (e.g., stomach acid from vomiting damages teeth)
- Difficulty absorbing fat, protein, and calcium
- Tears in the esophagus
- Anemia
- Ulcers
- Cardiac complications
- Bone loss
- Dizziness or fainting
- Electrolyte imbalance
- Dehydration
- Heart arrhythmias

Rachel

Rachel is a 14-year-old, elite-level gymnast. She began taking gymnastics classes at the age of 5 and now trains at least 30 hours per week. Rachel never had a weight problem for most of her gymnastics career; she always had a muscular, lean physique. A few months ago, however, she began noticing that her body was filling out. She was still strong, but her body was becoming bulkier every day she looked in the mirror. To anyone else, Rachel would seem to be in excellent physical shape without any worries about her weight. But because Rachel is a gymnast and a perfectionist, she has different standards for herself. She was trying to decide if she should worry about a little extra weight, and then her coach commented that she seemed to be getting bigger and she might think about watching what she eats. That was the deal-breaker for her; it was time to diet. She thought the best solution was to essentially stop eating (or eat only minimally) until she lost the extra weight.

At first the weight came off quickly because she was not eating and still maintained the intensity of her workouts. She felt lighter and faster in the gym. After the first week with only minimal food she felt a little shaky, but she was not concerned. She felt proud of herself because now she was reaching her goal of losing weight. She began eating a little more for energy but limited herself to 1,000 calories per day. She found she felt full and uncomfortable if she tried to eat a normal meal, and then felt guilty. If she ate "too much," then she would not eat for the rest of the day. Her teammates and coach commented that she looked thinner, which only reinforced her dieting efforts. She thought if 1,000 calories a day worked, then 500 calories a day would work even better, and she steadily decreased her food intake. She stopped eating around her teammates, claiming that she was not hungry.

After a couple of months of this regimen, she was too tired to perform at her potential. In fact, now her coach was commenting that she seemed slow and lethargic. He was getting on her to speed up her movements, swing faster, and run harder. In fact, now he said she looked too thin. That was the compliment she was after! She didn't hear his other comment that she needed to eat more to have energy and speed. She was too far into the restricting mode and could not see that her diet plan had backfired.

If conditions like Rachel's are allowed to persist they can lead to death. Former U.S. gymnastics team member Christy Henrich developed anorexia and bulimia during her career and eventually died from multiple organ failure because of self-starvation. According to *International Gymnast* magazine, she weighed 95 pounds during her competitive peak but only 61 pounds when she died in 1994 at age 22. She even dropped below 50 pounds just before her death. Sadly, no one was aware of her eating disorder until it had taken such a firm grip on her that it was out of control.

Intervention Strategies

Much intervention focuses on what to do after an eating disorder has been detected, but the ideal approach is to prevent one from developing. Central to prevention are education and risk reduction that target both athletes and sport management personnel (e.g., coaches and trainers).

Education   On the surface, educating athletes about disordered-eating behaviors seems like the place to start; however, some educational efforts have been counterproductive. Instead of avoiding disordered-eating behaviors, athletes experiment with them in an attempt to lose weight. They may be more likely than the general population to use this information inappropriately because they tend to try anything to get that extra edge. The most helpful approach in educating athletes is to focus on health and performance rather than specific dieting or purging behaviors. Athletes are likely to pay attention to information about eating correctly if they realize that it can improve sport performance.

Athletes can benefit from nutritional information from a registered dietitian or nutritionist because they tend to adopt idiosyncratic, superstitious, or ritualistic eating patterns that are often based on myth or misinformation. A dietitian who has experience working with athletes and who is aware of the nutritional needs of athletes in various sports can redirect their efforts to healthy eating patterns.

Many athletes diet to reduce body fat, but they have little understanding of what the dieting process can do to their bodies. In general, diets are not effective. A discussion about how dieting can negatively affect training and competition may be more fruitful. The focus should be on healthy eating that fits the energy output of their sport, along with an explanation that performance can be enhanced by increasing physical fitness, strength, speed, and quickness and that decreases in these physical attributes can occur as a result of too much weight loss that is done too quickly or by unhealthy methods. Again, education from a nutritionist or exercise physiologist can be useful.

Education of sport management personnel is as important as educating athletes—perhaps more so. Sport management personnel have significant power with athletes and can have a role in placing athletes at greater or lesser risk for eating disorders. Generally, they need the same type of information as athletes do about nutrition, dieting and weight, and factors that affect performance. They also need information about eating disorders, warning signs, and female athletes' menstrual functioning. Most of them do not ask about menstrual functioning, probably due to discomfort about discussing such a personal thing or because of lack of knowledge. Tracking menstrual functioning can be a good indicator of health because as a woman's body fat decreases too much, her periods stop.

Risk-Reduction Strategies

Education is the first step, but coaches and sport management personnel can benefit from translating that into actions. The following are strategies for risk reduction.

- De-emphasize weight. The simplest way to de-emphasize weight is to refrain from weighing athletes. Weight monitoring by coaches is unnecessary and may even be detrimental in terms of athletes' achieving their ideal weight or fitness level. One study indicated that athletes were leaner and more fit after a year of having their body composition measured by a sports medicine professional rather than by their coaches. Coaches should keep the focus on physical conditioning and strength development as well as increasing mental toughness for performance.

- Eliminate group weigh-ins. Weigh-ins are potentially the most destructive form of monitoring. For athletes who are self-conscious about their weight, this type of public exposure can be degrading and embarrassing. If there is a legitimate reason for weigh-ins, the athletes should be weighed privately by a sport professional other than the coach. They should be made aware of the rationale for the weigh-ins as well.

- Eliminate unhealthy subculture aspects. Sometimes disordered eating and weight-loss patterns become accepted and even valued in a sport community. Wrestling is a good example of a sport in which the athletes seem proud to report their often unhealthy weight-loss methods. Coaches can play an important role by providing correct information about unhealthy weight-management strategies and communicating the serious consequences that can result from them.

- Treat each athlete individually, especially when dealing with weight. Weight is determined by a complex interaction of genetics and biological processes rather than willpower. Some athletes may try to achieve a shape and size that cannot be done in a healthy manner.

- Offer guidelines for appropriate weight loss. Directors of the Eating Disorders Program at Bloomington Hospital in Indiana, Ron Thompson and Roberta Sherman, recommend that athletes not be asked to diet. In reality, though, athletes will diet, so some helpful guidelines follow.

1. Consult a health care professional to determine whether the athlete is at risk for developing an eating disorder as a result of a weight-loss program. If the risk is minimal, then the weight-loss program can proceed. If there is risk, alternatives to dieting should be considered.
2. The athlete's weight should be higher than medically recommended so that he or she is actually overweight.
3. The athlete should agree with the decision to lose weight.
4. A dietitian should be responsible for determining the target weight and the eating plan.
5. The weight-loss program should be discontinued if any weight, eating, or psychological issues emerge.
6. The athlete's performance should be closely monitored to determine that performance improves with weight loss.

- Control the contagion effect. Athletic teams develop norms about eating, dieting, and losing weight that can become "contagious" or spread from one athlete to another through communication or observation. Unfortunately, we know more about how the contagion effect operates than how to prevent it. If sport personnel de-emphasize weight and thinness, perhaps athletes can adopt these attitudes, beliefs, and behaviors as well.

Prevention

Even with prevention, coaches will still encounter athletes with eating disorders and must know how to effectively work with them. Researchers and clinicians Shane Murphy and Bob Swoap, as well as Lionel Rosen and his colleagues, suggest the following ideas and recommendations:

1. The coach or staff person (e.g., trainer) who has the best rapport with the athlete should arrange a private meeting with him or her.

2. The tone of the meeting should be entirely positive and supportive. The staff member will want to express concern for the best interest of the individual (not just as an athlete).

3. Let's say you're the one meeting with the athlete. Start by expressing concern about how he or she might be feeling rather than focusing on the eating itself. For example, "It seems like you have been struggling lately. Is there something I can do to help?" or "You seem to be depressed [or anxious, upset, or whatever you have noticed]. What has been going on?" If he or she will confide in you, let him or her know that outside help is often required to heal from disordered eating. Then you can make a referral.

4. The athlete is more apt to follow up on a referral if it is made to a specific person. Give him or her the name of a professional to contact, preferably someone who has experience with athletes and eating disorders. A clinical sport psychologist is a good option, or a counselor in a college counseling center if the athlete is at a university. You can also find referral resources in the community or through insurance companies. The athlete has the best chance of getting to the appointment if it is made immediately, before he or she has a change of heart. If he or she is hesitant, you can recommend an assessment to determine if there is a problem. He or she might be more open to an assessment than to therapy.

5. If the athlete does not acknowledge difficulty with eating, you can address your concerns more directly. Indicate which signs led to your belief that there is a pattern of disordered eating. Be as nonpunitive as possible when outlining these concerns, and then allow him or her to respond.

6. Affirm that the athlete's role on the team will not be jeopardized by admitting to disordered-eating behavior and that his or her participation would only be affected if the behavior were to compromise his or her health or lead to injury.

7. Try to determine if the athlete feels the behavior is no longer under his or her control. (But realize that most believe they are in control and can stop at will unless they have seriously tried to curtail it and failed.)

8. If the athlete denies any disordered eating in the face of compelling evidence or if it seems that the pattern is very long-standing, consult a clinician with expertise in treating eating disorders. If the behaviors are not severe, you may choose to observe the athlete without requiring any treatment. It is best to avoid any power struggles because they will only exacerbate the eating difficulties.

9. If you continue to be concerned about behaviors you see, you can share your observations again with the athlete at a later date and suggest treatment again. If the patterns become too severe, the health of the athlete must take precedence over anything else and you may have to insist on treatment.

10. Athletes are more likely to benefit from treatment if they choose it themselves, but in many cases they refuse to seek it. If an athlete's health is severely compromised, you may need to make treatment mandatory as a condition of continued team membership. Also, you can institute a "no-play" option in which

his or her training or playing time is restricted if his or her eating behaviors become dangerous. You will want to rely on the advice of an eating-disorders professional in such cases.

11. Arrange for follow-up meetings with the athlete outside of practice time to determine progress. Realize that he or she may resist talking about these issues, but you won't want to focus on food anyhow. Instead, focus on how he or she feels and how he or she is managing any pressures. If he or she is seeing an eating-disorders specialist, you may also wish to contact that person for guidance.

There are things you should do when talking with athletes who may have eating disorders. The following points are things you should keep in mind:

- Learn more about eating disorders before talking with an athlete.
- Stress that you care and that you are approaching the athlete out of your concern for his or her well-being as a person and an athlete.
- Suggest seeking professional help and have some referral options ready. Offer support, but realize that ultimately the responsibility to get help rests with the athlete.
- Discuss feelings. Eating-disorder behaviors are not usually about food per se but are more about coping with intense emotions or pressures that an athlete might experience.
- Give encouragement. Tell the athlete "I have faith in your ability to fight this."

There are also things you should not do when talking with athletes who may have eating disorders. The following points are things you should keep in mind:

- Do not discuss weight, calories, or eating habits.
- Do not comment on appearance. Concern about weight loss may be heard as a compliment, and comments about weight gain may be interpreted as criticism.
- Do not get into a power struggle. You cannot force anyone to eat or stop throwing up.
- Do not expect instant results from counseling. Athletes in therapy may get worse before they get better as they tackle some difficult issues.

The issue of notifying parents about disordered eating can be complex. If an athlete is under 18, parents have a right to know about eating-disorder behaviors, and they are primarily responsible for arranging treatment. Legally, parents of athletes age 18 or older do not need to be informed; however, it may be in the athlete's best interest for parents to understand what their son or daughter is facing. Initially, allowing the athlete to choose with whom to share information about his or her eating disorder is best. However, if the disorder becomes serious, the coach may find it necessary to notify the parents. He or she should be honest and inform the athlete that he or she plans to do so. Most parents will want to help, but they can also be a part of the problem, so some athletes may be resistant to involving them. Again, coaches should seek the guidance of an eating-disorders specialist if there are any potential conflicts about informing the parents.

Treatment Options

Keep in mind that eating disorders are psychological in nature and have complex causes, including biological factors, self-esteem, emotional issues, and societal pressures. Sport rarely causes eating disorders, but being involved in sport can exacerbate them. Proper treatment requires the services of skilled professionals. In addition to the treatment modalities used for the general population, athletes also can benefit from a team-based approach that utilizes many professionals in the athletic environment. The coach's job is to refer an athlete for treatment, then leave the specifics of treatment to the professionals; however, being aware of various treatment types is helpful. A brief overview follows.

Individual interventions Generally, individual therapy is suggested for eating disorders. For the general population, most therapists recommend focusing on the person and how he or she copes with emotions rather than talking about food, diet, and weight, because doing so only reinforces an obsession with eating. Athletes may not be able to ignore the topics of diet and weight because of pressures to compete at a particular body weight. Therapists who work with athletes need to strike an appropriate balance between weight and food and personal issues.

Medication Antidepressant medications can be helpful in reducing disordered-eating behaviors. Athletes have a variety of reactions to taking them, from "I don't want to put any foreign substance into my body; I'll work this out on my own" to "I'm desperate—I'll try anything." Of course, the use of medication can have implications for drug testing, and athletes must consult medical professionals who know the guidelines for restricted drugs in their level of sport.

Group therapy Group therapy has proved effective in treating eating disorders as an adjunct to other therapies. A group setting provides athletes with support and a sense that they are not alone in dealing with eating issues. It also provides a forum for sharing information, interpersonal learning, instilling hope, and developing socialization techniques.

Family therapy Often, eating disorders are due to conflicts within the family and are a manifestation of these relationship dynamics. In such cases, family therapy is an option, which might involve the athletic "family" as well.

Treatment team Athletes often benefit from a treatment team composed of professionals who are knowledgeable about different components of eating disorders. Ideally, a treatment team consists of a sport psychologist or therapist, a dietitian or nutritionist, a trainer, and a physician. These professionals meet periodically to review an athlete's progress in recovering from an eating disorder and to coordinate treatment efforts. The athlete must be aware of who is involved in the treatment team and be willing to sign a release of information so that the team can share knowledge among its members. Generally, it is not recommended that coaches be part of the treatment team, but with the athlete's consent, a member of the treatment team should communicate to the coach any progress and changes in health status. Coaches need to implement any recommendations to restrict or return the athlete to training, so they must be apprised of the treatment team's findings.

Inpatient treatment The preceding interventions can be conducted on an outpatient basis; however, if eating disorders become severe and the medical risk to the athlete is great, hospitalization may be necessary. Signs that hospitalization should be considered include (but are not limited to) weight loss of more than 25 percent of ideal body weight, major depression, suicidal ideation, persistent substance abuse, medical complications (dehydration, gastrointestinal consequences), and failure of outpatient treatment. Athletes may resist hospitalization, but cooperation between them and their families, physicians, and coaches is important for treatment success.

Return to sport participation The goal of treating an eating disorder is to return the athlete to health and sport participation. Although a sport hiatus or no-play mandate may be necessary during treatment, with successful treatment athletes can, over time, regain previous performance levels. The process of reintroducing training depends on the individual and the severity of the eating disorder. Those decisions should be made with the guidance of the treatment team or eating-disorders specialist.

Future Directions

As athletes look for the edge in competitive sport, they will continue to grapple with issues about eating and body composition. Young girls, especially, in the current cultural climate may strive to attain bodies that are unrealistic for most of the population and even for the athletic population. Eating disorders will continue to range from minor disordered-eating patterns to life-threatening illnesses, and athletes are not immune. Many educational efforts are under way among athletes and coaches to minimize disordered-eating behavior before it gets out of control. These are effective on some level but have not been the preventative we have hoped for. Coaches can play a crucial role in de-emphasizing weight and helping athletes find and utilize adequate nutritional knowledge.

chapter 14

Substance Use: Chemical Roulette in Sport

Mark H. Anshel

The use of drugs and dietary supplements to enhance sport performance is not new. Starting with the Olympic Games in the third century B.C., Greek athletes tried to improve their performance by ingesting certain plants. Drugs were even given to racehorses during the Roman Empire. In the 1860s, swimmers and cyclists used chemical substances to enhance performance. The first fatality occurred in 1886 when an English cyclist, while racing in France, succumbed to a fatal dose of the stimulant trimethyl. American cyclists used strychnine in the 1904 Olympic Games, and another cyclist died during the 1952 Games in Helsinki due to an overdose of amphetamines.

Because of the combination of accusations of cheating and the illnesses and deaths of athletes in the 1950s, the International Olympic Committee (IOC) passed a resolution against "doping." Then, in 1967, the IOC established a medical commission to control drug use. But it was not until the 1976 Olympics in Montreal that penalties for drug use were implemented. Illegal drug use was rampant, with 2.9 percent of urine specimens testing positive. Two gold medalists and one silver medalist were disqualified. In 1983, the U.S. Olympic Committee (USOC) concluded that 20 years of education about drug use was ineffective in preventing abuse among competitors without the inclusion of drug testing. A USOC Drug Control Program was established that year, which included disciplinary action toward coaches, trainers, and physicians if they were found to aid or abet drug use. In more recent years, the combination of positive drug tests for Olympic Games medal winners, accusations of cheating by athletes and their coaches, and the deaths of high-profile athletes has resulted in an all-out effort to monitor drug use in sport. Not only Olympic athletes have turned to artificial means of performance enhancement—the use of drugs in professional sport is yet an additional challenge to sport administrators. The publicized deaths and high rates of heart disease and cancer among professional athletes lend further credence to the widespread use of banned substances in sport at the highest levels.

One particularly undesirable outcome of drug use, including steroids, by high-profile athletes is its influence on younger, less-skilled athletes. Steroid use is now ubiquitous in school systems, from college to middle school. Athletes of all ages want to become increasingly competitive and will do what their models and mentors do, including engaging in behaviors that are unhealthy and unethical. The use of steroids to gain a competitive advantage is widespread. Steroid use in middle schools has increased significantly, as the research of Chuck Yesalis has indicated. The primary influence on this age group is the well-known steroid habits of elite athletes.

This chapter will help you get a handle on the complex issues posed by the widespread use and availability of performance-enhancing drugs in sport. We examine the different types of drugs and their effects on mental processes, health, and sport performance. And I suggest ways in which coaches and sport administrators might regulate or eliminate drug use on their teams and in their organizations. I hope I can convince you that everyone who cares about sport needs to work on changing athletes' attitudes about the use of inappropriate substances.

Motives for Taking Performance-Enhancing Drugs

Before discussing how to prevent and limit the use of drugs in sport we must address the fundamental question of why skilled athletes who have trained for hundreds of hours and who are driven by a competitive spirit to test their talent against others and achieve extraordinary levels of competence would risk their health and future participation in sport by cheating. What are the motives for ingesting substances that are clearly against every sports organization's rules, deleterious to good health, and viewed unfavorably by coaches and parents? Why risk losing a future in sport by committing an act that goes against the fabric of fair play and proper ethical behavior? Although it may appear irrational to behave in a way that some may label dysfunctional, there are reasons (some may even consider them valid) for taking substances that are intended to provide a performance advantage—fair or unfair.

Competitiveness and Pressures for Success

Without question, elite athletes are under tremendous pressure to excel, meet the expectations of others (e.g., spectators, coaches, teammates, media, corporate sponsors), and remain competitive. If anabolic steroids favorably affect sport performance, then certain athletes will use any "tool" that gives them a competitive edge over their opponents. The decision of athletes to use steroids depends on the extent to which they can control the temptation to cheat and, instead, respond to the pressures of success with hard training, confidence, high-quality coaching, proper nutrition (including vitamin supplements), and social support from friends and family.

Self-Esteem

The problem of drug use in competitive sport has been widely studied, but literature that attempts to explain *why* athletes are willing to use these substances is scarce. Two related conceptual frameworks, often used interchangeably, that might answer this question are self-concept and self-esteem. *Self-concept* is the collection of ideas, or the picture, a person holds about oneself. *Self-esteem* is the evaluation one places on this picture. For example, an athlete can conclude that she considers her participation in sport an important part of her life, that she has demonstrated considerable competence as an athlete, and that she gets great satisfaction from her sport successes. A significant degree of her life satisfaction reflects the quality of her performance. Each of these points is a measure of her self-concept. Her evaluation of herself as an athlete comprises her self-esteem.

Sport is only one aspect of self-concept and self-esteem, however. These constructs are multidimensional. Researchers have identified seven forms of self-concept, each of which is evaluated independently by the individual: social, religious, work, knowledge (academic and intellectual), physique (physical), family, and sport. Each person gives the greatest attention and energy to the form of self-esteem that is the most satisfying and that he or she perceives as most important. This form best reflects the person's self-identity. Because self-esteem reflects the extent to which individuals value themselves, being successful in competitive sport is important to any skilled athlete. The perception of failure is painful, humiliating, and unacceptable. Success is the only viable outcome, even if it means cheating.

Of course, this is not healthy thinking. Any individual who identifies too strongly with only one form of self-concept, at the omission of others, is walking on thin ice. Success is never guaranteed, and the ability to cope effectively with failing to meet self-expectations is important to mental health. Nevertheless, unless athletes are able to separate performance outcomes from participation as a primary source of their self-esteem, the attraction to performance-enhancing drugs will likely persist. Failure to find reward and gratification in areas of life outside sport and to be able to deal effectively with disappointment in sport settings may lead to depression and other forms of self-destructive, often illegal, behavior.

Sport Deviance

Deviance is "any thought, action, or feeling that runs contrary to social standards or expectations". Deviance is about breaking rules. In sport, deviance can take positive (e.g., performing a skill in an unorthodox style) or negative forms (e.g., acting aggressively toward teammates, coaches, or spectators). A pitcher who throws toward the inside of the plate at the risk of hitting the batter, a form of instrumental aggression, is using positive deviance. However, the action is negative deviance if the pitcher consciously attempts to hit the batter.

Sport sociologist Jay Coakley developed the concept of positive deviance to explain why within a certain subculture, most of the members actually see a negative behavior, such as doping, a positive. Athletes will do virtually anything—legal or illegal, rational or irrational—to increase their chance of performance success. Athletes who take anabolic steroids to win are merely responding to the pressures that others place on them; therefore, their behavior is a form of positive sport deviance. Our highly competitive system creates the need for steroid use, which, in turn, justifies its use.

The literature about drug use in sport lists many other reasons for ingesting drugs, in addition to anabolic steroids, that are banned by national or international organizations. They include weight loss, boredom, low confidence, peer pressure, stress and anxiety, pain from injury, and experimentation. Athletes who are not "mentally tough" enough to cope with these pressures or mature enough to follow the rules or resist compromising their health will be victimized by their sport success. The next section examines the types and effects of these different substances.

Steve Bechler

On February 17, 2003, Steve Bechler, a rookie pitcher with the Baltimore Orioles baseball team, died unexpectedly after succumbing to heat stroke suffered during spring training. The leading contributor to death was his use of a drug supplement called ephedrine. *USA Today* reported the following: "The medical examiner cited several contributing factors, including Bechler's battle with a weight problem and use of a controversial ephedrine supplement, sold over the counter as a weight-loss aid and energy booster" (Mihoces, *USA Today*, February 21, 2003). Bechler had been taking a product called Xenadrine RFA-1, which includes ephedrine and caffeine and is identified on its label as a "clinically proven weight-loss catalyst." Ephedrine is a stimulant extracted from an Asian plant called ephedra that has the same effect as amphetamines. A supplement containing ephedrine, which is typically combined with a caffeine booster, is banned in the Olympics and college sports. The NFL and its players' union banned ephedra after the 2001 death of Minnesota Vikings tackle Korey Stringer at training camp.

Other athletes' deaths that have been linked to this drug include football players Rashidi Wheeler of Northwestern University and Devaughn Darling of Florida State University. This chapter addresses the reasons why athletes continue to ingest substances that are either banned by their sport or are known to pose a high health risk.

As New York Mets pitcher Mike Stanton claims, "I think it would be hard to tell a grown man that he can't take something an 18-year-old can still buy over the counter. We need to get all the facts and then make a decision about what happened."

The Language of Drug Use

An understanding of selected terms and concepts is important to a discussion of strategies for controlling drug use. The term "drug" means different things to different people, depending on its purpose. All drugs have the common characteristic of altering a physiological process, usually to treat, prevent, or diagnose disease. However, a drug that is classified as "performance enhancing" does not fit this definition. Instead, substances that are intended to affect the quality of movement are more compatible with the concept of "doping." Doping is defined by the IOC as "the administering or use of substances in any form alien to the body or physiological substances in abnormal amounts and with abnormal methods by healthy persons with the exclusive aim of attaining an artificial and unfair increase of performance in competition." The five doping categories that are banned from international competition are anabolic androgenic steroids, stimulants (including hallucinogens, or mind-altering drugs), narcotic analgesics, beta-adrenergic blockers, and diuretics. If you wish to read detailed information about steroids and their effects, I suggest the National Institute on Drug Abuse Research Report Series, sponsored by the National Institutes of Health.

Drug *use* is simply the taking of a drug for its intended purpose and in an appropriate amount, frequency, strength, and manner. Drug *misuse*, on the other hand, is "the taking of a substance for a purpose, but not in the appropriate amount, frequency, strength, or manner." Of greater concern, however, is drug *abuse*, defined by John Lombardo as "the deliberate use of a substance for other than its intended purpose, in a manner that can damage health or ability to function."

Drugs are categorized in various, often confusing, ways. For example, some drugs may be considered performance enhancing (e.g., anabolic steroids, stimulants, ergogenic aids), while others have a mind-altering effect, sometimes labeled by the common euphemism of "recreational" drugs or hallucinogens (e.g., marijuana, LSD, ecstasy). Drug use among competitive athletes includes both categories. The inappropriateness of their use for athletes as well as non-athletes is not debatable, so this overview includes only those drugs that are considered performance enhancing.

Ergogenic aids are illegal, nonsteroidal substances that are linked to improving sport performance. The term "ergogenic" means "an increase in the rate of work output," and it refers to any substance or technique that improves athletic performance beyond an athlete's natural ability and training. Performance-enhancing drugs, then, are one type of ergogenic aid.

Dr. Melvin Williams, emeritus professor at Old Dominion University in Norfolk, Virginia, and director of the Human Performance Laboratory and the Wellness Institute and Research Center, lists five categories of ergogenics in sport, including nutritional (such as vitamins and creatine), pharmacological (anabolic steroids), physiological (blood doping), psychological (mental skills), and biomechanical (sports equipment). While some ergogenic aids are legal and ethical (e.g., mental skills, updated equipment, and nutritional supplements), others have been banned by sports organizations (e.g., anabolic steroids, blood doping, creatine). See the "Notes" section at the end of this book for reviews of related literature on ergogenic aids by Mottram and Branch.

Blood doping   This technique, first discovered as a performance-enhancing technique by researchers in Finland and Sweden, is now banned due to its known advantages in improving aerobic endurance and slowing muscular fatigue by transporting additional red blood cells (and consequently oxygen) to muscles. Blood doping entails removing and storing about one liter of an athlete's blood one to two months before competition, then infusing it back into the athlete shortly before competition. In addition to being unethical by providing an unfair advantage, the practice is potentially fatal if the athlete accidentally receives the wrong (incompatible) blood. Another method of blood doping, which increases the secretion of red blood cells, is the ingestion of the hormone erythropoietin, or EPO.

Erythropoietin (EPO)   EPO is a hormone that is secreted by the kidneys in response to hypoxia (a lack of oxygen in the blood) and that stimulates production of red blood cells. EPO is used clinically to treat anemia in dialysis patients; however, world-class athletes have been known to ingest it, as the 1998 Tour de France cycling scandal showed us.

Any substance that promotes the circulation of red blood cell mass provides two advantages in cardiovascular endurance tasks (e.g., distance running) by enhancing the oxygen content of arterial blood and the body's ability to transport oxygen to exercising muscles. EPO reduces the onset of muscular fatigue, which provides an unfair advantage to distance runners, and also appears to improve regulation of internal body temperature, or thermoregulation. The American College of Sports Medicine (ACSM) considers blood doping unethical, and sports-governing bodies have banned its use.

Creatine   Creatine was popularized by former St. Louis Cardinal baseball player Mark McGwire, who admitted using it during his home-run-record-breaking 1998 season. Creatine is categorized as both a physiological and a nutritional sport ergogenic; however, its ergogenic effect on sport performance is not conclusive. It appears to improve muscular strength, but according to Williams creatine "is not a very important energy source for prolonged aerobic exercise." Creatine's effectiveness as an ergogenic aid has been supported more by laboratory studies than by field studies of aerobic performance.

Although creatine is banned by many professional sports, the IOC's Medical Commission has not yet restricted its use because it is considered a nutritional supplement. A survey of 115 professional sport teams about their policies on creatine use reported that only 21 teams voiced "official disapproval" about its use, while 16 other organizations approved of it and 24 teams actually provided it to their athletes. Opinion is similarly uneven in college sports.

Human growth hormone (HGH)   This hormone, banned by the IOC, is naturally secreted by the pituitary gland. Although recently it has been created by recent, more sophisticated DNA technology, it remains very expensive. Clinically, HGH is prescribed to overcome pituitary deficiency in children and to treat dwarfism by stimulating growth. In adults, it increases lean body mass and decreases fat mass. Although this anabolic outcome may appear to

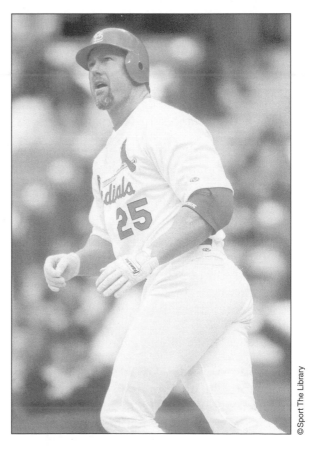

Mark McGwire admitted to using creatine during his home-run-breaking season. The verdict is still out on whether this nutritional supplement should be categorized as a performance-enhancing drug.

©Sport The Library

have an ergogenic effect on sport performance, similar increases in strength and lean body mass occur following resistance training with and without HGH supplementation. The effect of HGH on physical performance appears to be limited at best.

A related hormone that ostensibly has an ergogenic effect is gamma-hydroxybutyrate (GHB), which is also banned by the IOC. Although the body produces this substance naturally, too much can lead to distorted physical characteristics (e.g., "Frankenstein's syndrome") and death. GHB stimulates the release of HGH and can lead to a coma.

Caffeine   Caffeine, a central nervous system (CNS) stimulant, increases alertness and arousal, thereby preventing or overcoming mental and physical fatigue. These effects may improve forms of athletic performance that depend on heightened CNS activity. In excessive amounts, caffeine has prolonged endurance performance in high-intensity, short-duration exercise performed in a clinical setting, which would seem to create an unfair advantage in competitive sport. However, excessive caffeine may adversely affect thermoregulation due to its diuretic effect. Increased urination with insufficient water intake raises the internal body temperature, inducing premature fatigue and, at dangerous levels, heat-related illnesses. How much caffeine intake is too much? Before the 2003 annual IOC executive board meeting in Lausanne, Switzerland, moderate caffeine intake commensurate with less than 18 ounces of coffee was not prohibited. However, all levels of caffeine intake were removed from the list of banned drugs at the 2003 meeting. Specifically, "caffeine and pseudoephedrine, an ingredient in over-the-counter cold remedies such as Sudafed, were removed from the list of banned substances for international sports" (September 24, 2003,13C).

Beta-adrenergic blockers   Some sports, such as archery and pistol and rifle shooting, demand that the athlete remain calm and steady. Beta-blockers, used by many heart patients to reduce blood pressure, aid performance by slowing the heart rate and decreasing anxiety and other undesirable mood states. They decrease tremors and have an ergogenic effect for low-intensity, fine-motor tasks of precision such as shooting and archery. At the same time, they do not appear to impair performance of high-intensity, short-duration activities that require strength and anaerobic power. However, they do negatively affect high-intensity, longer-endurance tasks. In addition to the ethical dilemma of whether to use a substance to change normal physiological responses, beta-blockers have known dangerous side effects such as hypotension (low blood pressure), CNS disturbances, and impotence. Beta-adrenergic blocking agents are banned by the IOC.

Anabolic steroids   Unquestionably, the best-known and most widely used ergogenic aid used for the sole purpose of improving strength and power, anabolic steroids are synthetic derivatives of the male hormone testosterone. By increasing the male hormone androgen and reducing the female hormone estrogen, steroids stimulate a building-up (i.e., anabolic) process in the body for muscle growth and tissue repair. The result of this combination is the increase of masculine traits, even in females, including lowered vocal tone, increased facial and body hair, and interference with reproductive function. In addition, anabolic steroids expedite recovery from physical training, allowing for more intense workouts.

Do anabolic steroids enhance athletic performance, lending credence to the label "performance-enhancing drugs"? Not necessarily. First, the use of steroids alone will increase strength. However, using them in conjunction with training is likely to lead to enhanced muscular strength and power (although scientific literature reveals equivocal findings about this outcome). The best-case scenario in support of steroid use is more likely in sports in which strength, power, and total body speed are the primary components of desirable performance (e.g., swimming, weightlifting, contact sports, track and field, baseball). Steroids are far less likely to improve the performance of athletes in sports in which those qualities are not primary components (e.g., golf, bowling, archery, volleyball). One could also argue, however, that an athlete's mere *belief* that ingesting steroids will benefit performance might result in a behavioral response (e.g., a placebo effect, or self-fulfilling prophecy). In other words, expectations translate into performance outcomes that meet those expectations. Nevertheless, any possible benefits of steroid use have to be balanced with the costs.

The harmful effects of prolonged steroid use are extensive. When testosterone levels become too high, the hypothalamus in the brain starts to shut down the body processes that involve the hormone. These processes include, in men, stimulation and maintenance of the sex organs. In women, the development of masculine body characteristics is greater and more rapid than in men because of the limited natural production of testosterone in women. Both genders may experience temporary or permanent sterility. More ominously, prolonged heavy steroid users risk cancerous liver-cell tumors, high blood pressure (hypertension), premature heart disease, myocardial infarction (heart attack), stroke, and, when use is stopped, clinical depression. Adolescent abusers may suffer reduced bone growth due to premature fusion of the epiphyses (ends) of long bones. The result is permanently stunted growth.

Another undesirable effect of prolonged steroid use is heightened, uncontrolled aggression and temper, often referred to as "roid rage." This change in temperament is likely due to a marked increase in testosterone. Anabolic steroids increase the rate at which the body manufactures testosterone. Elevated levels of this hormone are associated with higher-than-normal rates of high-risk behaviors, such as drinking and driving, unsafe sex, nonuse of seat belts, suicidal behavior, and heightened aggression. Research in this area is very difficult to conduct and it is unclear how common these behavioral problems are in athletes using steroids.

Athletes may attempt to overcome these problems by taking "drug holidays" between periods of use by "pyramiding" or "stacking." Pyramiding consists of beginning with a low dose, then increasing the amount progressively until the maximum dose is reached, then tapering the dosage until the drug is completely withdrawn. Stacking consists of using numerous drugs and varying the dosage throughout the cycle. Athletes attempt to avoid detection by drug testers by cycling on and off these steroids, by using new, hard-to-detect steroids, and by using "masking agents" that covers up the tell-tale signs of steroids in the urine or blood.

Tetrahydrogestrinone (THG)   A recent steroid furor has erupted worldwide about a new drug, classified as an anabolic steroid, called THG. It is so new that the only way to read about it is through the popular media rather than in scientific journals and books. One reason for concern about this drug is that it is undetectable by the standard test given to athletes. According to the Associated Press in 2003, "THG's chemical components are similar to those of most banned steroids, but with an insidious twist: THG disintegrates during the standard testing process, fooling even the skilled doping detectives who hunt for steroids in urine samples." Potential U.S. Olympic team athletes have already tested positive for this drug. Alarmed at the potential problems of being unable to detect THG through regular drug testing, the USA Track and Field Association, the sport's national governing body, proposed an uncharacteristically harsh lifetime ban for a first THG steroid offense. In addition, U.S. senators Joseph Biden and Orrin Hatch introduced the Anabolic Steroid Control Act of 2003, which would ban THG, as well as another controversial substance, androstenedione, a building block for the creation of testosterone.

Pros and Cons of Legalized Drug Use

Should the decision whether to use anabolic steroids be left up to the athletes? Is it worth time and effort trying to control these banned substances? In his 1998 book, *Taking Sides: Clashing Views on Controversial Issues in Drugs and Society*, that examines controversial issues about drugs and society, Raymond Goldberg, professor at State University of New York-Courtland, presents articles that address both sides of this issue.

The Pro-Drug-Use Agenda

In Goldberg's book, Dr. Ellis Cashmore, professor of sport sociology at Staffordshire University in England, is strongly in favor of allowing athletes to use anabolic steroids because they are merely part of the athlete's array of aids and equipment that ostensibly enhance sport performance. He argues against the issue of unethical behavior and unfairness because competition is rarely fair.

Cashmore, whose original article appears in *New Statesman & Society*, contends that athletes recruit top coaches, nutritionists, and other specialists, and use state-of-the-art equipment. They consume a vast amount of vitamins and other chemicals that are not banned and whose side effects are unknown. Banning steroid use, especially if it is monitored by a physician, is not consistent with allowing the intake of other substances. Cashmore calls current antidrug policies as so "riven with hypocrisy, anomaly, and contradiction that the only course of action is to abandon them and let competitors decide whether they want to take substances that purportedly enhance their performance" (p. 283).

With respect to the "fair play" argument, Cashmore is, perhaps, somewhat less rational, speaking from a more personal, emotional perspective. He contends that "fair play and its antonym, cheating, are not preordained; they are products of how sports' governing organizations define them" (p. 283). He points out the lack of fairness associated with professional tennis players, who are born into well-off families and employ high-quality coaches at elite facilities, who compete against those players born in the ghetto who picked up their tennis skills in municipal parks and received minimal coaching. "Drugs," he says, "are no more artificial than the entourage of aides and physical equipment commonplace in contemporary sport . . ." (p. 284). From Cashmore's perspective, then, ingesting banned substances is merely one more way to gain an advantage over an opponent, even if the behavior constitutes cheating. Athletes who come from wealthy families already have an unfair advantage over more impoverished athletes; ingesting banned substances is just one more "advantage."

Cashmore's views are irresponsible. Rather than fostering a level playing field, allowing drug use in sport rewards competitors who are willing to compromise their health and who have the financial resources to do so. Where is the role of training, coaching, and skill development in sport success? How can adults allow younger athletes, who are habitually more likely to engage in high-risk behaviors and are less concerned with the potentially fatal consequences of prolonged drug use, to "do what it takes" to win? College admission is also highly competitive. Should we also allow high school seniors to cheat on their college entrance exams if they can get away with it?

Preventing individuals who are likely to engage in irrational, potentially harmful behaviors from doing so is called "limit-setting." Adults need to set limits on the inappropriate, self-destructive behaviors of people who are more concerned about short-term gain than long-term consequences (in this case, from taking banned substances). Sport administrators, coaches, and parents know better than to allow athletes to engage in high-risk behaviors and are therefore obligated to set strict guidelines and organizational policies about proper behaviors and the severe consequences of acting in a way that contradicts those behaviors (such as cheating). Antidoping rules serve a protective role.

The Case Against Drug Use in Sport

An article by reporter Joannie Schrof, that appeared in *U.S. News and World Report* (June 1, 1992), states the case against sanctioning steroid use in sport. She asserts that "athletes who take anabolic steroids are not fully aware of the potential adverse effects, and these athletes often use excessive quantities because they are under tremendous pressure to win" (p. 280). Her stance against steroid use also addresses a group that is often ignored in this argument: non-athletes who take steroids to improve their physical appearance. She asserts that "up to one-third of users are non-athletes who use these drugs to improve their physiques and self-images" (p. 280). Ironically, Schrof cites one claim in support of the decision *not* to regulate anabolic steroids that comes from the American Medical Association: Anabolic steroids have been used to improve growth and development, treat certain types of anemia, and expedite rehabilitation from certain injuries. Stricter regulations would impede individuals who would benefit from steroids from obtaining them. However, failure to generate and *enforce* a strict policy about steroid use might lead to unintentional misuse or purposeful abuse with serious medical consequences, which is exactly what happened in the ephedra-related death of Steve Bechler.

Controlling Drug Use in Sport

Coaches, and to a lesser extent, sport psychology consultants, must help athletes make wise choices about drug use. I believe that education, awareness, and communication with athletes are the keys to preventing and limiting drug abuse. Coaches who remain silent on this issue commit a sin of omission. The pressures to succeed in sport, especially at elite levels, are too great to expect athletes to regulate their own personal behavior. Short-term benefits prevail over long-term consequences. Influencing the thoughts, emotions, and actions of any person, athletes included, is extraordinarily challenging. This is why one must appeal to the athletes' passion and help them examine their values to determine what is important to them. I have adapted the work of James Loehr and Tony Schwartz and of Jack Groppel, who work mainly with businesspeople, about the use of values as a vehicle for making permanent change in behavior. I have generated a model based on this literature, which I refer to as the *disconnected values model* because it is based on the premise that people are more likely to change their behavior when they acknowledge the disconnect between their actions (negative habits) and their deepest values and beliefs.

The primary purpose of my model is to assist athletes in acknowledging that taking drugs, whether for performance-enhancing or recreational purposes, is a negative habit that has benefits but also dire costs and long-term consequences. What drives the model is the willingness of athletes to become aware of the disconnect, or contradiction, between their values and beliefs and their negative habits. For example, individuals who value close relationships, openness, friendship, genuineness, and concern for others yet fail to act toward others in a warm, open, and sensitive manner are out of sync with their values. Similarly, athletes who value competitiveness, integrity, fairness, health, honesty, and family, yet make a conscious decision to ingest substances that they know to be illegal, unhealthy, or against the rules are behaving inconsistently with their values. Athletes must decide whether this disconnect is acceptable. The ability to act in a way that is consistent with your deepest values and beliefs is referred to as expanding your spiritual capacity. The model, presented in figure 14.1, depicts the intervention stages.

The ultimate goal of the intervention model is to prevent or stop athletes from ingesting any substance that is banned, illegal, immoral, or unhealthy. This goal can only be achieved by changing their thought patterns, which in turn changes their behavior. We know that drug education programs have not been effective. Greater knowledge about the harmful effects of drugs, including anabolic steroid use, does not appear to affect the athletes' attitudes toward taking them. If attitudes about drug use are not strongly influenced by increased knowledge about harmful effects, that drug education *does not* influence drug-taking behaviors is hardly surprising. Therefore, future attempts to change the actions of athletes regarding ingesting anabolic steroids and other performance-enhancing drugs should address their spiritual capacity.

Loehr and Schwartz define spiritual capacity as "the connection to a deeply held set of values and to a purpose beyond our self-interest." Athletes who cheat by ingesting substances that they know are against the rules or illegal, and, therefore, risk their future participation in sport, demonstrate "limited spiritual capacity." People whose actions are self-serving and contradictory to their values and beliefs are being selfish and self-destructive; they are often driven by insecurity, low self-esteem, and unhappiness. The question now becomes how to assist athletes in acknowledging this disconnect, rediscovering their values, and creating the energy and commitment needed to act in a way that is consistent with their values—that is, to expand their spiritual capacity. Let's look at each component of the disconnected values model in greater depth.

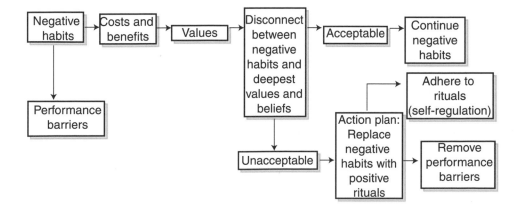

Figure 14.1 The change process in high-performance training.

Negative habits   The model begins with identifying thoughts, emotions, or behaviors that are consistent yet compromise health, energy, or performance, called negative habits. The athlete's choice to ingest substances that are illegal, contrary to policies of their sports organization or team, or that lead to poorer health, is a negative habit. Why do athletes persist in any negative habit that they know is bad for them? The reason is that there are some benefits to every negative habit that provide added incentive.

For example, the perceived benefits of taking substances that are purported to enhance performance appear greater than the costs (discussed later). The concept of positive sport deviance may even reinforce the benefits of ingesting performance-enhancing drugs. Nevertheless, drug use without a doctor's prescription or that is inconsistent with the rules of the sports organization is a negative habit—in all cases.

Benefits of negative habits   The next process in the model is to help athletes acknowledge the benefits of their negative habits. The benefits of taking anabolic steroids, for example, might include improved strength and power, higher self-expectations, more confidence, improved physical performance, and greater success in sports competition. There are perceived benefits to taking recreational drugs as well, including peer acceptance and approval, immediate pleasure, reduced tension and anxiety, more comfort in social settings, and "numbing out." Recognizing the perceived benefits of any negative habit is important because the athlete then acknowledges that he or she engages in this behavior for one or more plausible reasons and the *cost* of this same habit gains greater credibility. Acknowledging only the disadvantages of inappropriate behaviors without recognizing their advantages discredits the thought and decision-making processes that explain them. Respecting the athlete allows us to expect him or her to think rationally and to willingly change his or her behavior.

An athlete's use of substances that may enhance sport performance is driven by powerful motives. In some cases, athletes are even encouraged to take drugs by their coaches, sports organizations, and misinformed parents, either explicitly (e.g., they provide sources of drugs and the financial resources to obtain them) or implicitly (e.g., they fail to voice strong views against their use, set limits, or develop or enforce team/organization policies, and they ignore changes in the athlete's behaviors, emotions, or physical characteristics that suggest drug use).

Costs of negative habits   Central to the change process is an athlete's ability to detect the costs of negative habits. The use of hallucinogenic drugs is replete with costs to physical health, mental well-being, and sport performance. The costs of ingesting anabolic steroids, as we mentioned earlier, include removal from the sport if a drug test is positive, heightened levels of aggression, high blood pressure, reduced emotional control, and poorer information-processing capability.

Long-term consequences   The long-term consequences of drug-taking include poorer physical and mental health (most notably from heart disease and cancer), reduced level of sport performance, disconnection from others, and, if detected by authorities, disqualification from future participation in sport and a permanently tarnished image.

Long-term consequences of any negative habit are difficult for younger, relatively healthy individuals to recognize because the advantages of short-term benefits often seem to far outweigh them. Individuals differ in their ability to avoid short-term, impulsive behaviors that result in immediate benefits but poor long-term consequences. The tendency to want more immediate gratification is typical of those who possess poor "self-regulation" skills; that is, they are unable to initiate and persist at behaviors that encourage self-control. Researchers find that most people who are given a choice between a small, immediate reward or a large one that requires a period of waiting choose the former, especially children. With normal development, however, this tendency changes as planning behaviors emerge and longer-term, strategic forms of self-regulating behaviors develop. High, external sources of pressure that promote the short-term gains from taking performance-enhancing drugs can be difficult to resist for athletes who possess poor self-regulation skills and are consumed by immediate performance success. To them, the "benefits" outweigh the costs of long-term health consequences.

Another explanation for the difficulty of changing behavior based on long-term consequences is that athletes often suffer from the "Superman complex," also called the "Adonis complex," in which they feel impervious to the known harmful effects of drugs. These perceptions have been challenged by the publicized stories of high-profile athletes whose health has significantly deteriorated or who have died as a result of prolonged anabolic steroid use. The death of former Denver Broncos football player Lyle Alzado, who in 1989 died from liver cancer, is a highly publicized example of the Superman complex. Alzado and his doctors attributed his cancer to prolonged, extensive use of steroids and HGH. Alzado discussed his brain lymphoma and its likely causes in a *Sports Illustrated* article (July 8, 1991), titled "I'm Sick and I'm Scared," in an attempt to save other athletes from a similar fate. At the time, he was receiving chemotherapy and rapidly losing weight. Alzado, at only 42 years of age, soon lost the battle to beat his disease. Other anecdotal evidence of fatal long-term consequences from prolonged drug use among athletes abounds, including heart attacks in weightlifters in their twenties. HGH use can cause heart problems in adults, gigantism in prepubescent children, and impaired glucose uptake, possibly resulting in diabetes.

Values This stage is the heart of the model: the primary process by which change in thinking and acting occurs. Values represent a self-statement about what is important to an individual—the passion, purpose, and mission that ignites the energy needed to establish and meet goals and experience a high quality of life. According to speaker-consultant Jack Groppel, a value is "anything on which you place worth . . . whatever your value system is, you should emotionally connect to it." Examples of values for athletes might include commitment,

Long-term use of performance-enhancing drugs like HGH by elite athletes such as weight-lifters can cause heart attacks and even premature death.

character, fairness, competitiveness, perseverance, family, respect for others, loyalty, happiness, health, excellence, and compassion. At this stage, athletes select their most important values.

Disconnects between values and negative habits The model now requires deep and personal self-reflection to identify any incompatibilities between values and drug-taking behavior. This is called "walking the talk." Athletes who ingest steroids, yet feel passionate about values such as health, family, integrity, or fairness are behaving in a way that is disconnected with those values. One way to point out this inconsistency to an athlete is thus: "Joe, you say that maintaining good health is one of your most important values. Yet you admit to taking steroids, which you believe will improve your performance. You also acknowledge that steroids have health-related risks. There appears to be a 'disconnect,' or inconsistency, between the high value you place on your health and maintaining a habit that has serious health-related side effects. Would you agree?" Another example is to question the disconnect between an athlete's value of competitiveness or fairness and the use of banned substances that provide an unfair advantage.

Acceptable or unacceptable At this stage, athletes make a "final" decision about future actions. If they accept the contradiction between values and self-destructive habits (perhaps considering them the "price they must pay" for competing at elite levels in sport), they will continue their drug-taking. Until they no longer compete, become sick, or test positive, these athletes will continue to ingest these substances. However, if they conclude that this contradiction is not acceptable, they are likely to voluntarily stop taking the banned substances and, instead, rely on their training and ability to succeed at their highest level. Coaches and sport psychology consultants must provide as much support and encouragement during the decision-making process as possible.

Athletes must understand that all human beings have limitations, some of which are genetically determined. The goal of every athlete is to attempt to reach one's own inherited capacity through proper physical and mental training and nutrition; however, the extent to which we value ourselves, our self-esteem, must go beyond competence in sport. Although sport may be an important component of life, forces that go well beyond sport-related experiences define life satisfaction. As Alzado said before his premature death, "If I had known that I would be this sick now, I would have tried to make it in football on my own—naturally. Whoever is doing this stuff, if you stay on it too long or maybe if you get on it at all, you're going to get something bad from it. It is a wrong thing to do" (1991).

Roles in Drug-Use Prevention

The reasons why athletes ingest illegal substances that are deleterious to their health are psychologically based: low self-esteem; heightened fear of failure and chronic anxiety; inability to cope with stress and pressure; having unreasonably high performance goals and expectations, both self-imposed and external; and insecurity about their future in sport. Irrational thinking takes over, partly in response to the Superman complex. Athletes who fit that description do not feel constrained by the potentially harmful effects of drug use, despite their knowledge about these concerns. The combination of youth, health, fitness, and a high public profile forms a considerable obstacle to rational thinking about using steroids and ergogenic aids.

Sport Psychologists

What can sport psychology consultants do about this dilemma? Summaries of the approaches I've previously suggested, along with others provided by clinical sport psychologists Chris Carr and Shane Murphy, follow.

• Obtain support from coaches and the sports organization. Consultants must gain the trust of the coach and the organization that employs them, and they must carry out a policy that is consistent with that of the team or organization.

• Provide information. Sport psychology consultants should help educate team members about steroid use, including testing procedures, disciplinary outcomes if an athlete tests positive, and the medical and psychological effects of drug use. Because they discuss issues that are highly confidential with the athletes, they are often in the best position to help them resolve conflicts or uncertainty about decisions regarding the use of banned substances. Since consultants focus on building trust with each competitor and are not directly invested in performance outcomes, they should be viewed by athletes as highly credible. This credibility will be gained or lost based on the consultant's actions with individual athletes. Loss of credibility occurs if the consultant violates confidentiality, appears to be ignorant about steroid and doping issues in sport, is inaccessible, or acts for political reasons rather than focusing on the needs of the client.

• Communicate case history information to athletes. Many athletes are highly influenced by the personal stories of other athletes. Consultants may disclose information about the situations of other athletes that have been publicized by the media, or reveal the results of a published study or content from a newspaper or magazine article—perhaps providing photocopies of any published information about case histories to which the athletes can relate.

• Offer life-skills training to enhance and broaden sources of self-esteem. As mentioned earlier, self-esteem is multidimensional. It is a crucial part of people's confidence and quality of life because it helps them define the extent to which they value themselves and the source of that self-valuation. Typically, positive self-esteem is derived from the types of activities that we do best (i.e., perceived competence) and that we find most satisfying. Self-esteem should come from more than one source (e.g., sport, academic pursuits or knowledge, physical attributes, social supports). Sadly, the self-esteem of many athletes is derived from primarily one dimension: sport. This means that poor sport performance may inhibit life satisfaction and lower self-worth. To overcome this dilemma, many university programs now include life-development interventions conducted by sport psychology consultants or other professionals to assist athletes in dealing with the challenges posed by retirement from competitive sports. Such programs are designed to help athletes develop a healthy perspective about life along with inter- and intrapersonal skills, set reasonable yet challenging goals unrelated to sport, and cope with critical life events in a mature, effective manner. From this perspective, athletes must acknowledge "the big picture": the importance of leading a long, satisfying, healthy life after their sports competition days are over. The message to athletes is that abusing performance-enhancing drugs may have short-term benefits, but at great long-term cost.

• Enhance meaningfulness of the team role. Athletes who feel that their contribution to the team is minimal or unimportant are susceptible to the lure of high-risk behaviors. Either they are less likely to take competition seriously, and consequently, ingest hallucinogens (since they do not predict they will enter the contest anyway), or they feel pressure to improve and, therefore, take substances that will ostensibly improve their performance and result in more playing time. One way to combat this flawed thinking is to have each athlete acknowledge his or her unique contribution to the team, feel a sense of improvement, and associate hard training and skill improvement with more opportunities to participate. Teams must also recognize the contribution of "role players," that is, athletes who have a particular function in helping their team succeed. Examples include the substitute base runner in baseball ("pinch runner"), the defensive back in football who plays only on certain downs, and the nonstarting players whose job it is in practice to prepare the starting team. Covert messages that performance-enhancing drug-taking is an acceptable way to help the team must be eliminated.

• Teach coping skills. Sports competition is inherently stressful. Athletes need to learn effective ways—coping skills—to deal with the vast array of sport-related and other stressors they are exposed to. This is a role of the sport psychology consultant.

• Monitor the athletes' lifestyle activities. Many coaches "cop out" from responsibility for the behaviors of their players outside the game by claiming that such behaviors are beyond their control (or interest). Obviously, monitoring all aspects of an athlete's life that are unrelated to his or her team responsibilities is impossible and inappropriate. However, some athletes are susceptible to loneliness, feelings of isolation, discontent, experimentation, and curiosity, all of which could lead to behaviors that they would later regret. If counselors or consultants are available to athletes, then at least one person in the organization can take responsibility for helping them engage in a lifestyle that is healthy, safe, and legal. Networks of players who all commit to healthy lifestyle choices offer natural support groups to players who face stress. Peer approval is a strong attraction for anyone, especially during adolescence, and should be harnessed as a positive force if possible.

Coaches and Team Administrators

I have worked with an array of sports teams, players, and coaches over the years, and I have reached one conclusion relating to the use of performance-enhancing drugs: Coaches and the organizations who employ them are not doing nearly enough to address the problem. At the time of this writing, for example, even the death of a major league baseball player has resulted in only scant effort to regulate the use of substances that have potentially fatal consequences. Most coaches in professional sports want to win at almost any cost, and the temptation is high to utilize the latest drugs and ergogenic aids if the risks or consequences are perceived to be low. Many major league baseball coaches prefer not to know very much about their players' habits when away from the sport venue. In turn, many of their players do not support drug testing. This matter appears settled, since steroid testing is now an established policy supported by the Major League Baseball (MLB) Players Association. On an optimistic note, MLB now has a policy of monitoring and testing for steroid use among players. According to the *Times:* "In this first year (2003) of steroid testing under the collective bargaining agreement, the results will be used only to determine the percentage of players on major league rosters who test positive. Each team will receive an unannounced, anonymous testing this season, meaning that 1,200 players (on the 40-man rosters of the 30 major league teams) will be tested. If more than 5 percent—61 players or more—test positive, then program testing will begin next season." Amazingly, despite six months warning of the testing, 7 percent of MLB baseball players tested positive for steroids, and the new policy was triggered. The new policy will identify players who use steroids and provide counseling and monitoring for first-time offenders and disciplinary penalties if they test positive in additional tests. This chain of events reinforces the fact that only firmly established, written, and enforced policies about drug use that are endorsed by the sports organization and by each team will result in any serious attempt to regulate drug use in sport.

Why is it so important to generate team and organizational policies about the ramifications of drug use and to support these policies with severe consequences? Why, too, is it especially important to carry out disciplinary measures when athletes abuse the policy? The answers to these questions begin with the fact that the decision to use banned substances is not solely under the athlete's control. The pressure to succeed in sport—to be competitive—at a relatively rapid pace comes from different sources. In one study, I found that being competitive was the primary reason college football players ingested performance-enhancing drugs. The expectations of others are another source of pressure that fosters steroid use. The pressure of positive deviance can only be overcome by changing the entire culture of that sport or that team. It is not disrespectful to set limits on inappropriate behaviors.

Consider limit-setting another way. Children often want to eat only candy and fast food without regard to proper nutrition or weight control. Younger drivers want to go well beyond the speed limit to impress their peers, feel excitement, or simply to take risks. And athletes want to perform better and better in order to remain competitive and become successful. In most such situations, common sense prevails and we eliminate or at least regulate most behaviors that are considered inappropriate for proper health and well-being. However, common sense and emotional maturity do not always prevail. In addition, the values of some people do not include the honesty and integrity that prevents most of us from cheating and breaking laws, so to them, taking substances that provide an unfair advantage or are harmful to health is acceptable if the outcome results in a competitive edge. Strict rules and limit-setting protect these people from themselves, not unlike a parent who says no to a child's request to replace a meal with candy. In this way, coaches and sport administrators have a parenting role in looking after their athletes. Athletes need guidelines of appropriate behavior that will allow them to reach and maintain optimal performance while avoiding mistakes that arise from peer pressure and emotional immaturity. I recommend that the policy be in writing and distributed to each athlete; that parents of younger athletes be given a copy of the policy; that the policy be reviewed verbally by the team's head coach; and that it include the ramifications for breaking these rules. Some athletes will test these rules and the coach's willingness to carry out the ramifications of breaking them. Consequently, in order to effectively regulate behavior, these early attempts at testing drug policies must be met with firm, consistent responses. There may be casualties; players may be disciplined or even dismissed from the team in extreme cases. However, the testing period will soon end and the policy will become firmly entrenched on the team.

Sports Organizations

If the ingestion of banned substances is to be taken seriously by athletes, then the organization for whom they play or to whom their team is accountable at the local (e.g., school or community program), state, national (e.g., NCAA), or international levels (IOC) must establish, publicize, and enforce a substance abuse policy to which all team members must strictly adhere. If, for example, a team on the road requires athletes to be in their hotel rooms by 10:30 P.M., and the team captain is allowed to return to the hotel at 10:45 P.M. without disciplinary action, the athletes will not take the policy seriously. As I wrote in 1991, "A source of supervision outside the team is needed to implement policies and monitor actions to eliminate the need to cheat and endanger one's health" (Anshel, 165). A report from a 1989 conference on drugs in sport held in Australia concluded that governing organizations should perform at least three functions concerning drugs: (1) determine clear policies about ingesting banned substances, (2) provide funding for drug testing, educational programs, and counseling, and (3) protect athletes whose dependence on these substances is often beyond their control. In addition, rehabilitative strategies should be developed, at least for first-time abusers, rather than immediately dismissing the player from further sport participation.

The only way athletes will feel accountable for their agreement to abstain from ingesting banned substances is to be tested. Four general categories of testing have been identified: (1) testing of prospective team members, (2) testing for cause, perhaps after making observations about an athlete's appearance or behavior, (3) periodic preannounced testing that includes everyone, and (4) random testing, usually unannounced, which provides the greatest deterrence. Although a debate about the merits of each type of testing goes beyond the scope of this chapter, a testing program of some kind must be implemented. One reason for testing is to protect the athlete from peer pressure. Once a policy is in place, the athlete can respond to drug-using teammates by saying, "If I get caught using drugs, the league says I'll be suspended for the remainder of the season and the whole team will be hurt." The policy becomes a protective shield against the pressure to succumb to another person's (or group's) high-risk behavior.

Future Directions

What is the current state of anabolic steroid abuse in sport and where do we go from here? The news is uneven. On a pessimistic note, the April 2000 report from the National Institute on Drug Abuse (NIDA) reveals an increase in anabolic steroid use among adolescents in the United States and a decrease in the number of twelfth-graders who feel that taking these drugs causes "great risk." In addition, it indicates a surprising increase in steroid abuse among young women in recent years despite increased efforts to provide drug education programs about the potentially deleterious effects of steroids on health. This outcome lends credence to the very low correlation between athletes' knowledge about the effects of drug use and their attitudes toward their own use of these drugs. On a more optimistic note, however, the same NIDA report indicates that the incidence of new steroid abuse can be reduced by 50 percent when coaches and other team leaders (e.g., athletic trainers, strength coaches) discuss the potential effects of anabolic steroids and other illicit drugs on immediate sport performance, how to refuse offers of drugs, and how strength training and proper nutrition can help adolescents build their bodies without the use of steroids, through the Athletes Training and Learning to Avoid Steroids (ATLAS) program. In addition, every professional league in the United States and all the committees that represent U.S. Olympic teams have structured drug education and testing programs in place.

The ingestion of stimulants such as ephedra among competitive athletes is only the tip of the iceberg. Not unlike real icebergs, the danger is hidden under the surface, where it destroys the integrity of competitive sport and compromises the future health and well-being of currently healthy athletes. Athletes have a right to do everything in their power to compete successfully and perform at levels that exceed their current level. Winning, however, should not be at the expense of the athlete's physical health and psychological well-being. Sadly, when athletes define self-esteem by the quality of their sport performance, they become desperate to succeed at any price. Coaches, parents, sport administrators, physicians, and sport psychology consultants all have a role in helping athletes make rational and ethical choices about their actions. The future integrity of sport depends on it.

The Educated Consumer

Although this mental preparation seemed like a very logical area for us to tackle, it was not treated with quite the same urgency, or even seriousness, by our senior management. "Who needs a sport psychologist? We all know what we need to know. I've played plenty of sport. Sure, we need a physical fitness person for the crew, but why should we have anyone screwing around with our minds? We're all tough enough ourselves. We can handle it." I could sense [their attitude] very clearly: Maybe we have chosen the wrong person in John Bertrand. Maybe if he needs a headshrinker, there's something wrong with him. Perhaps he's just not tough enough.

John Bertrand, skipper of Australia II *in 1983, the first boat to beat the United States in the America's Cup in 132 years*

I have a lot of sympathy for the position that John Bertrand found himself in, having been there many times myself. Although there is no denying the critical role that mental and emotional factors play in deciding the outcome of competition, many athletes and coaches believe that they can handle mental preparation completely alone. Coaches who wouldn't dream of not having a trainer develop a strength-training program for their team nevertheless go into a season having given little thought to any systematic mental training. I believe there are two main reasons mental training tends to be overlooked in sport. First, most people believe that they know themselves better than anyone else. Many athletes and coaches genuinely believe that they already understand the mental factors that go into excellent performance. Second, the subject matter of sport psychology makes many people in the world of sport nervous. Athletes don't mind having their blood tested to determine oxygen-carrying capacity or having their muscles analyzed for speed and strength, but they often feel reluctant to discuss the personal issues that may prevent them from being fully focused and prepared in competition.

If you notice these attitudes in yourself, you need to overcome them. First, it is wrong to expect any athlete or coach today to understand the mental side of sports without extensive training. Even those of us in sport psychology find it difficult to keep up with the expanding knowledge base on brain functioning and the effect of the nervous system on sport performance. This knowledge can be critical in preparing for high-level competition. Second, although it is natural to feel reluctant or even embarrassed to discuss personal issues with an outsider, you can overcome these feelings if you find someone you can trust to work with. And the payoff from overcoming personal roadblocks, obstacles, and problems can be enormous.

The chapters in part V deal with implementing a successful and productive sport psychology program and finding a good sport psychologist, someone you can trust and develop an effective partnership with. In chapter 15, "Roles: The Sport Psychologist," sport psychologist Sean McCann offers many ideas for ways in which sport psychology can help you, whether you are just thinking about having someone give a talk about mental preparation at your local YMCA, or whether you are a world-class athlete preparing for major competitions. In chapter 16, "Qualifications: Education and Experience," Bradley Hack explains the modern field of sport psychology and describes what to look for in assessing a consultant's training, expertise, and approach to consulting. His chapter is an invaluable guide for anyone desiring to become an educated consumer of sport psychology services. In chapter 17, "Success in Sport Psych: Effective Sport Psychologists," David Tod and Mark Andersen describe the research on what makes sport psychology work and what makes for a good sport psychologist. They provide plenty of ideas on the qualities you should look for if you are ever in the market for a sport psychology consultant.

As a side note, Bertrand persevered and management allowed him to hire a sport psychology consultant, Laurie Hayden, who worked extensively on mental toughness with Bertrand and the crew leading up to the America's Cup regatta. Bertrand credits this psychological preparation as a key factor in his team's ultimate success. I wish you luck in putting together *your* mental training program, whatever your sporting goals happen to be. Have fun—and play smart!

chapter 15

Roles: The Sport Psychologist

Sean McCann

The nitty-gritty of the workings of sport psychology is a mystery to most coaches and athletes. This chapter focuses on the practical aspects of how sport psychologists work with athletes or teams and outlines the nature of their work. Current sport psychology practice focuses on enhancing performance—on helping good and great athletes attain more consistently strong performances through the partnership between coach, athlete, and sport psychologist. In order to understand how sport psychologists become part of a performance team of coaches and athletes, we will answer some underlying questions about the nature of their work.

What can athletes and coaches who choose to work with a sport psychology consultant expect from their time together?

- Professionalism and experience. Applied sport psychology has progressed a long way in the past 25 years. Although you will not find a sport psychologist in every town, the number of consultants around the world is growing. The U.S. Olympic Committee (USOC), for example, has 125 people on its Sport Psychology Registry, a listing of highly trained sport psychologists from all over the United States. The USOC looks at factors most potential clients would do well to consider, including graduate course work, supervised experience working with athletes, and experience with a variety of sports. The consultants on the registry all have a doctorate in psychology or sport psychology. Clients should be wary of "mental-training consultants" who do not have significant graduate education in psychology or supervised experience working with athletes.

- Agreement on key mental-performance factors. As sport psychology has become more established as a profession, its language has become more consistent, reflecting the common goals of mental-skills training. The chapters in this book reflect the most common issues faced by athletes and the most common approaches used by sport psychologists. Knowing that sport psychology consultants generally follow a similar "script" helps reduce the anxiety of coaches and athletes, who sometimes worry that the process will be "touchy-feely" or that they are in for discussions about their "inner child." Most athletes find that talking to a sport psychologist is as natural as talking to a coach. The major difference is that the work with sport psychologists focuses on the mental aspects of sport rather than the technical and physical aspects.

• Willingness to understand your sport. Like any area in applied psychology, sport psychology is only effective and useful if it recognizes the context in which the work is done. The sport environment is very specific, and each sport is different, with its own culture, rules (written and unwritten), and expectations. A sport psychology technique that works with figure skaters may or may not be useful with basketball players. Although many sport psychologists have worked with a variety of sports, it's possible that they have not worked with your specific sport before. If not, any good sport psychologist will take the time to learn about the specifics of your sport. In addition to obvious factors, such as basic rules, a sport psychologist needs to understand the subtle factors that lead to success for one athlete and failure for another.

• Good communication skills. Sport psychologists are sometimes hired by coaches and sometimes by individual athletes. When hired by a coach to work with some or all of the athletes on a team, sport psychologists develop a strategy to communicate effectively with both the athletes and the coaches. Typically, their communication with individual athletes on the team is confidential (for licensed psychologists, this may be a legal necessity), yet they also share general observations about the athletes with the coach and often suggest specific coaching strategies that will enhance the team's performance. This combination of confidentiality and communication can get complicated unless consultants discuss these issues with coaches and athletes before initiating any work. If there is full disclosure on how the process will work, then athletes know they can speak freely, coaches know that they will get useful feedback on their coaching, and all parties are aware that the sport psychologist may encourage coach and athlete to speak together more frequently and productively.

The Sport Psychologist at Work

As noted previously, sport psychologists work with athletes and coaches to build mental skills that will enhance certain facets of physical performance. The process of building mental skills works much like the process of building physical and technical skills in sport. Current skill levels are assessed in order to identify strengths and weaknesses. In some cases, the emphasis is on building on existing strengths; in others, new behaviors are suggested. Some athletes with specific problems such as recurrent injuries or substance abuse learn ways to overcome such obstacles.

Like technical and physical skill development, mental skills are introduced through demonstrations and discussion, practiced by means of specific drills, and enhanced through structured feedback. In psychological skills training (PST), these demonstrations, discussions, and drills can take place at practices or in the consultant's office. Of course, much of the process is "invisible"; the real change occurs inside the head of the athlete as he or she alters his or her thinking in an effort to change and improve his or her sport behavior.

The most inclusive term to accurately capture the broad variety of work that applied sport psychologists do is "consulting." As a consultant, the sport psychologist holds a unique position in a sports organization; consultants to any organization provide a new or more focused point of view that the internal organization cannot or does not provide itself. Consultants often have great influence on a team without being a part of it. Effective consultants build skills within the organizations they work with, eventually making themselves superfluous if they have done their job correctly.

Team Consulting

Frequently, a managing organization hires a sport psychologist to work with an entire team. In a typical first meeting, the sport psychologist introduces himself or herself to the team by giving an initial talk on sport psychology principles. After this presentation, he or she might meet with individual athletes to work on their specific performance challenges. He or she usually meets periodically with the whole team to discuss general issues of mental preparedness or specific issues for a particular competition. These team sessions can range from a didactic "how to" talk to an interactive session in which the consultant facilitates the discussion among athletes, coaches, or both. Examples of topics for these team talks include team chemistry, staying focused amid distractions, defining and accepting roles on the team, and general discussions on mental skills for the specific sport.

In a team-consulting situation, the training and competition schedule frequently affects the structure of the work. Consultation with a professional baseball team, for example, may focus on team education and other major initiatives during spring training, while the competitive season may require a consultant to travel with a team, meeting with individual athletes and coaches at the team hotel or in the clubhouse in the hours before a game. Extensive travel is a part of most team sports, and consultants may need to travel with the team to truly understand its needs.

Individual Consulting

In many cases, individual athletes are the focus of the consulting relationship. Sometimes the athlete initiates the consultation, and sometimes a team or a coach will make the initial contact. In individual-sport settings (sports in which only individual performances are scored, regardless of whether athletes train alone or as part of a group or team), consultation with individual athletes is the norm. In these relationships, the sport psychologist takes a great deal of time to understand the unique aspects of the athlete's performance "recipe," or those ingredients that contribute to a strong mental game for a particular person.

A typical individual sport psychology consultation involves: (1) a session or two to assess the strengths and weaknesses of the athlete, (2) building an action plan, with specific mental-skill development strategies, (3) assessment of the sport psychology intervention, based on results in training and competition, and (4) pre- and postcompetition sessions to develop specific mental strategies for a competition and then evaluate their effectiveness. The competition-related sessions may continue or the athlete may proceed with the planning and evaluation process independently.

In both team and individual consulting, an element critical to its success is the relationship between the sport psychologist and the coach. This can be more difficult to achieve with individual consultations unless the coaches are brought in at the beginning of the consultation process. In modern elite sport, an athlete often builds a support team composed of various experts. For example, at a recent Olympic Games, an athlete had built a personal support team of two technique coaches, a physical therapist, a chiropractor/masseuse, a sport psychologist, a significant other/manager, and an agent. In an ideal world, members of these support teams work well together and find ways to share information that affects others on the support team. In reality, these multiperson support teams have been known to undercut each other and become a distraction for the athlete. For this reason, at the USOC, the various support disciplines work hard to coordinate services and make sure the coach has the final say on all interventions.

The following stories from the Salt Lake City Olympic Games may provide a clearer picture of the kinds of team and individual consulting relationships that applied sport psychologists can have with coaches and athletes.

Mary

Mary, a sport psychology consultant hired by the U.S. Ski Association, has been working with this team for the last four years. Each year, she has come to more races with the team, sometimes spending weeks on the road with them—a difficult task since she also holds a full-time teaching position, but she manages. Since last year's World Championships, Mary has truly felt like part of the team. She attends team and coaches' meetings, goes to all training sessions, and schedules her meetings with individual athletes around the practice schedule. She shares a room with the physical therapist who travels with the team.

At the Olympics, all the staff and athletes share the same house. The coaches are under a great deal of stress, and they use Mary as a sounding board. Mary has some individual sessions with athletes, makes some brief comments in the team's daily meetings, and attends all training sessions. As the competition begins, she takes her usual position at the competition venue and finds that some of the athletes come to her before the event to check in on their mental state, just as they do at other competitions.

Joseph

Joseph, a psychologist in private practice who has an excellent reputation for working with athletes, has been working with Peter, an athlete on the national ski team, for three years. He has been to one competition, where he was introduced to Peter's coach and was given a credential so that he could see how Peter prepares for the event. Mostly, however, Peter and Joseph get together in the off-season, then stay in contact by e-mail and phone during the competition season. Joseph and Peter decided they would continue their email and phone contact during the Olympic Games, with scheduled appointments.

When Peter arrived at the Olympic village before the Games he was very anxious, so he sent an email to Joseph asking to move up their scheduled phone call. While they talked, Peter felt his anxiety decreasing as Joseph reminded him how they had anticipated these feelings. Peter decided to call once more, the evening before his main event. That evening, Joseph went through the mental checklist he and Peter had developed for competition. Then Peter asked, "Should we talk about anything else?" and Joseph asked, "Do we need to?" "No," Peter replied, "I'm ready. Thanks for your help."

As these two vignettes illustrate, sport psychology can be fully integrated with the work of a coach or be more independent of the coach and the team, keeping an individual focus. Both methods can be successful; they show that sport psychology approaches vary greatly depending on the needs of the team, the desires of the clients (coach and athlete), and the flexibility of the consultant. The following section illustrates the variety of performance roles that applied sport psychologists play in today's world.

Applying Sport Psychology to Performance

Applied sport psychology is not easy to pigeonhole. As is true for psychologists in general, the study of thinking and behavior can be applied in a variety of settings, with specific skills allowing special functions for various sport

The sport psychologist can play an important part in individual and team preparation and training—especially before important competitions like the Olympics or World Championships.

psychologists. The following examples of work in the field are not comprehensive but give a flavor of the diverse work of sport psychologists.

Sport neuropsychology Neuropsychology, the study of brain function through a variety of tests, has recently grown as an application of psychology to sport. With proven examples of the devastating impact of returning to play too early after a concussion, many NFL and NHL teams now do neuropsychological testing with their players. For example, when Joe, a four-year veteran of the NFL and the backbone of the defense of his team, made helmet-to-helmet contact with another player, his behavior changed. He began showing signs of a concussion, including difficulty focusing and a brief period in which he wasn't sure who he was playing against. After the game, the team physician called the team's neuropsychologist, who had done preseason baseline testing on all the players.

With this brief, computerized assessment on file, Dr. Keppel, the neuropsychologist, scheduled a follow-up assessment to see if the player's brain functioning was similar to the baseline level. If the tests showed that the effects of the concussion were still lingering, Dr. Keppel would do follow-up assessments until he determined it would be safe for Joe to play again. The tests showed that Joe should wait three weeks before returning to play. Given the millions of dollars the team has invested in Joe's continuing career, they held him back despite his desire to play. Dr. Keppel spent an hour with Joe, explaining the test results and counseling him on how best to manage his anxiety about not playing. (Even All-Pros can be replaced, and Joe hates to miss a start.)

Sport psychology assessment   Many professional teams use sport psychology consultants who have expertise in psychological assessment. To demonstrate why, consider the case of David, who is clearly the best player in the NBA draft and is coming out of college early.

As a college freshman, David was inconsistent, dominating some nights and disappearing on others. David has a horrible childhood history; drugs and violence killed two brothers and sent his biological dad to prison for life. David has a bit of a lisp and doesn't like talking, and he sometimes appears to be sulking during games. NBA teams are drooling over David's gifts, but they're uncertain about who this 19-year-old kid will turn out to be. Is he a sure thing or a time bomb?

While David is in town for a two-day tryout visit with one team, he spends three hours filling out a variety of personality, leadership, and behavioral history assessments. The sport psychology consultant reviews the data, which suggests that David is likely to struggle with the intense media pressure bound to affect a player with his talents. The coaching staff looks at this data in light of their plans to let some of their older stars go in order to rebuild the next year, and they decide that David would not do well as the only star on a young team. They decide to go with a college senior with slightly less talent but who has a consistent record of excelling under big-game pressures.

Team sport psychologist   Many professional teams use consultants to enhance team performance. Often, a team consultant's first job is to give a talk to the entire team, explaining the importance of sport psychology to high performance and offering confidential services to anyone who is committed to improving.

After this introduction, a number of players may schedule appointments to work on their mental game. Frequently, the media wants to talk to the psychologists about their work, but experienced consultants learn to answer all requests with the reply, "Sorry, but I don't talk about my work with my clients." Teams appreciate this discretion, and it can win over any team members who remain suspicious about whether confidentiality is a guarantee.

Team clinician   Frequently, sport psychologists' work with teams is primarily clinical. For example, administrators might notice that after a longer-than-expected layoff caused by minor knee surgery, a veteran star player has become despondent. After a very bad two weeks of little sleep, angry mood, and heavy drinking, he refuses to get out of bed one morning; the next day he starts drinking at 10:00 A.M. He admits to his wife that he isn't thinking right, and she insists that he talk to somebody. He talks to the team trainer, who refers him to a clinical psychologist who is on retainer with the team.

The psychologist has signed a confidentiality agreement, and he does not even disclose his relationship with the team. He has done a little work on performance enhancement with a few players who experienced performance slumps, but he mainly deals with athletes who face clinical issues. After one session, in which he learns of the athlete's family history of depression, his previous periods of depressive symptoms, and his current mood and cognitive changes, the psychologist believes that the athlete might be clinically depressed. He schedules two appointments, one a return visit with him, and one with a psychiatrist, to determine if the athlete might benefit from a trial of antidepressants.

Private consultation   In some sports, athletes have the resources to hire their own sport psychologists. Golf and tennis are two prominent examples. For example, a golfer with tremendous talent but a reputation for having one bad round every tournament might work with a sport psychologist to increase his steadiness under pressure.

Pro athletes, used to keeping their own counsel, are often amazed at how a good sport psychologist is able to describe exactly what goes on in their heads during times of stress. They may then be able to admit that their heads were swimming with destructive thoughts as the pressure increased. Most usefully, players may find that the consultant has a number of simple strategies to help them control their thinking and stick to a mental game plan no matter what happens on the course. Successful golfers who work with sport psychologists are fairly common on the pro tour.

Sport psychologists provide simple strategies and act as a sounding board to help athletes control their thinking and stick to a mental game plan no matter what happens on the course, court, or field.

The Sport Psychologist in the Field

The focus on the mental skills of athletes and coaches that is the basis of applied sport psychology has come to be called the psychological skills training (PST) approach. No matter which theoretical orientation a sport psychologist has, the first session or two with a team or athlete will include assessing strengths and weaknesses. This assessment may be formal, involving paper-and-pencil or computer-based tests of personality, mental skills, or other factors. Less-formal assessments consist of asking athletes to describe what they do when they are performing their best and worst in their sport. Assessment is the starting point for any intervention that focuses on building skills.

Although PST may involve some education, working with a sport psychologist on psychological skills is not like taking a course in school. First, no athlete has exactly the same needs. Even very young athletes differ a great deal in mental strengths and weaknesses, and older ones usually have a good idea of their needs. A second difference is that PST operates less like a tutorial and more like a partnership in which athlete and sport psychologist work together to find solutions. Sport psychologists who work with very successful elite athletes may feel as if they are the students and the world champion or Olympic medalist is the teacher, because the athletes have often tried many psychological-management strategies on their climb to the top. Nonetheless, the best athletes are often the ones who are most eager to find a new and better way to solve their sport challenges. Surprisingly, even they may have weak areas and seek help with specific mental skills, such as those described in chapters 5 through 8.

Athlete Performance Feedback

One advantage that sport psychologists enjoy over other types of psychology specialists is that they get rapid feedback on the effectiveness of their techniques and strategies when the athlete enters competition. For many of them, the competitive season is an opportunity to build and refine various mental-skill-building modules with the athletes they work with. Techniques might be developed in the precompetitive training phase, tried in competition-simulation practice sessions, and then modified based on success or failure. Once the competitive season begins, many athletes will check in with their sport psychologists in the week before a competition, then call or come back in to discuss how it went. This regular feedback is critical to solidifying mental skills or developing new ones.

Having a sport psychologist attend competitions is often useful for many coaches and athletes who otherwise would have a difficult time explaining the critical moments at a competition that might be important for a consultant to know about. In addition, sometimes sport psychologists cannot fully understand the mental demands of the sport until they see it. For these reasons, the best solution is to have the sport psychologist attend a number of practices and competitions. Sport psychologists who work for the USOC frequently travel with teams to competitions around the world, which provides an irreplaceable opportunity to build relationships, see the realities of international competition, and observe first-hand the responses of individual athletes and coaches to competitive pressure.

Clinical and Counseling Issues

Some sport psychology consultants have training in clinical and counseling psychology, which can be useful when an athlete or coach faces mental challenges that arise from areas outside sport. For example, a female teenage athlete may report that her perfectionism in sport is similar to her worries about food and that lately she is wondering if she has an eating disorder.

Research shows that extended relationships between athletes and sport psychologists frequently move back and forth between dealing with mental-skills and counseling issues. For a licensed sport psychologist, part of the job is looking at "the whole person" and determining which area to focus on at any point in a particular session. Of course, in the 20 minutes before a swim race, a consultant would rarely focus on the athlete's troubled relationship with a girlfriend, except to classify it as a distraction to be dealt with. On the other hand, he might raise the issue later that day, saying something like, "You mentioned your girlfriend this morning. Was that relationship on your mind before or during the race?" If the answer is yes, the consultant may decide to problem-solve about the relationship or the thinking about the relationship. Addressing the relationship (a counseling issue) might be the most critical performance intervention he could do before the next day's race.

Some coaches report that they want sport psychology to focus on sport, not on clinical issues, because they don't want the athletes to be distracted or softened by talk about non-sport concerns. Sport psychologists who have clinical training, including me, might argue that managing other life issues effectively results in an athlete who is much more mentally tough and ready to tackle the stress of competition. Even a hard-nosed, performance-oriented coach or athlete needs to be able to, for example, compartmentalize grief over the death of a loved one. This "clinical mental skill" of adapting to life challenges can be essential to a great performance at a big event.

Consultation Settings

As the preceding intervention examples show, sport psychology consultants today work with athletes on many different issues and in a variety of settings. There is no one "right" way for athletes or teams to work with a consultant—the timing, nature, and structure of such consultations should be dictated by the type of problem or issue being addressed. This section provides a brief look at common modes of service delivery in sport psychology across a range of settings.

Professional athletics Professional sports organizations were the pioneers in the application of sport psychology. The "founding father" of sport psychology in the United States, Coleman Roberts Griffith, was hired away from his academic job at the University of Illinois by the Wrigley family to work with the Chicago Cubs in the 1930s. Despite this early innovation, professional sport today has probably the least organized sport psychology programs in elite sport, perhaps because of the lack of a central site for overseeing such work. Although some sport psychologists do excellent work, a surprising number of teams use consultants with poor training and a lack of credentials. The result is the unsystematic application of nonmainstream programs, which unfortunately has hurt the credibility of the field in some areas.

College sport psychology programs   Sport psychology's presence on college campuses typically takes two forms. At some colleges, a university professor who has expertise in sport psychology begins working with a particular athlete or team, with some success, and the word spreads around campus. Without building a formal program, this in-house consultant ends up working with a number of teams. These relationships can evolve into paid programs of sport psychology support for particular teams and can last as long as the professor stays at the college. In a few cases, the success of these types of relationships has prompted athletic departments to formalize the program.

Formalized programs in sport psychology at colleges are generally housed either in the college's counseling center or, at least part-time, in the athletic department. Counseling-center-based programs may have one or two positions that are filled by psychologists with an interest and expertise in working with athletes. At times, these sport psychology specialists may work on general counseling issues that student athletes face (such as homesickness, substance abuse, mood disorders, eating disorders, and the stress of school and sports); at other times, they may work with athletes on PST to apply to their sport. Examples of programs developed by counseling-center-based psychologists include alcohol-abuse prevention programs, eating-disorder support groups for athletes, groups that focus on issues for minority athletes, team-building retreats, and academic support groups for athletes.

Sport psychology in private practice   In larger cities throughout the United States, the yellow pages include listings for sport psychologists or sport psychology consultants. Most of these people are licensed psychologists who have a private practice in some other area of psychology in addition to their work in sport psychology. The percentage of time that these individuals do sport psychology versus other work varies greatly. Typical clients for these individuals include local college sports teams, serious masters' athletes in sports such as swimming and tennis, gymnastics and figure skating clubs, and, frequently, golfers. The people who make a living doing only sport psychology private-practice work probably number fewer than 20 nationwide, although an exact count is hard to ascertain. On the other hand, those who do clinical work, consult with businesses or organizations, and also have a small number of athlete clients are much more common. Fee structures for work with businesses and in sport may differ. Consultants who structure their sport psychology business in this fashion probably number several hundred.

Sport psychology at the Olympic level   The USOC, the support organization for athletes and coaches on the U.S. Olympic teams, has had a full-time sport psychology staff since 1987. At the USOC, sport psychology is housed with the other "sport sciences" (physiology, biomechanics, engineering, performance technology, and strength and conditioning) as well as coaching, in the Coaching and Sport Sciences Division. At the time of this writing, the USOC employed four full-time sport psychologists, three at the Olympic Training Center in Colorado Springs and one at the ARCO Olympic Training Center in San Diego.

As the demand for sport psychology services has gone up over the past 10 years, the USOC Sport Psychology Department has moved from an initial balance between research, education, and applied service to an almost exclusively service-oriented model. As sport psychology has gradually become a more typical part of high-performance sports teams, the standards for service have gradually increased as well. Today at the USOC, a typical applied program for a national team includes the following:

- General education sessions
- Team-building
- Assessments of athlete strengths and weaknesses
- Regular individual appointments with athletes
- Creating relaxation CDs
- Creating individualized imagery CDs
- Individual mental-training manuals for all athletes
- Regular conversations with coaches (within the bounds of confidentiality) to suggest performance-enhancement strategies for the team or individuals
- Spending significant time at training sessions (3 to 20 hours per week)
- Spending significant time traveling with teams to competitions (5 to 50 days per year)
- Coordination with other support staff (e.g., sports medicine, physiology, strength and conditioning)
- Involvement in designing training plans for individual athletes
- Involvement in year-end evaluations
- Evaluations of sport psychology consultants by coaches and athletes each year
- Working with sports organizations and USOC staff to design comprehensive sport psychology coaching-education programs for coaches at all levels

Future Directions

The roles played by sport psychology consultants in the future will likely continue to expand in variety and scope. More and more frequently, sport psychologists will provide short-term focused applications, with longer-term follow-up. As PST becomes less exotic and more integrated into daily practices, sport psychology consultants may specialize in more unusual and challenging sport situations. The desire for a healthier and happier youth sport environment will result in more sport psychologists working with parent groups. Finally, at the elite level, more and more teams will continue today's trends and will regard sport psychology as necessary to continuing success in sport.

Qualifications: Education and Experience

Bradley Hack

Being an educated consumer in our society is a must these days. Everything from weight-loss products to get-rich quick schemes assault our attention through media and advertisements. Reliable information is needed to differentiate between the substance and the hype. The same holds true when choosing doctors or sport psychologists. The purpose of this chapter is to make you an educated consumer of sport psychology services. It explains the differences between sport psychology practitioners and, whether you are an athlete, coach, parent, administrator, or physician, helps you determine your needs for sport psychology services and find the right sport psychologist.

Differences Between Sport Psychologists and Sport Psychology Consultants

The variety of titles used by practitioners in sport today makes it difficult to know who is doing what. The need for regulation in the field of sport psychology in order to protect the public from those not qualified to provide certain services is growing. Public information is also needed regarding the qualifications of sport psychologists and the differences between various types of practitioners. In particular, two main types of practitioners provide sport psychology services, but most people use the title "sport psychologist" interchangeably to refer to both. These professionals can vary considerably in their training and their ability to work with certain problems that athletes face. Their titles are so similar, however, that most people think they do the same thing. I will detail the differences between the two types of practitioners, which may be tedious but is essential information for educated consumers. Although I point out general differences in education and training between the two groups, there are, of course, also individual differences between practitioners. Some sport psychologists are better at mental-skills coaching or counseling than others, just as some mental-skills coaches are better at mental-skills training than others. For example, some sport psychologists are better at conflict negotiation than others. Likewise, some mental-skills coaches are better at teaching emotional regulation than others.

To begin, we must break the title "sport psychologist" down into its component parts to fully understand exactly what the title conveys. First, in most states, the word "psychologist" signifies that the practitioner is licensed, which means that the state in which he or she practices has deemed him or her qualified to treat clinical problems, such as depression, anxiety, eating disorders, substance abuse, and adjustment disorders. Using the word "psychologist" in one's title without being licensed is illegal in most states.

Psychologists typically hold a PhD in clinical or counseling psychology and have been trained and supervised for an average of about six years beyond their undergraduate education. They are trained to understand the many aspects of psychological functioning, differences in personality types, psychopathology, and what constitutes healthy and dysfunctional modes of living. Psychologists are supervised extensively in providing effective therapy and counseling to individuals and groups. They are also trained to conduct psychological testing to assess, for example, a person's level of functioning, intelligence, and whether he or she has attention problems, learning disabilities, or neurological disorders

Using the word "sport" in front of "psychologist" indicates that a person has obtained additional specialized education and training, above and beyond the regular curriculum for clinical psychologists, in order to fully understand the various aspects of athletics, the science and specific culture of sport, and how to apply this knowledge to athletes, coaches, and parents. Because the field is still relatively young, unified standards are still being established. This means that consumers will find some variability in training and education from one sport psychologist to another. In general, though, the qualified practitioner will have taken numerous graduate level courses in sport psychology and the sport sciences, as well as had extensive supervision from other qualified sport psychologists when working with athletes.

Once qualified, sport psychologists can work with athletes who are experiencing problems in any of four categories of performance issues because they have been trained to use both mental-skills training (e.g., imagery, arousal management, or attention control) and psychological counseling to assist athletes. For example, sport psychologists might work with a defensive lineman in football who has become depressed and lost his motivation to practice, a cross-country runner whose times have slowed down because she has developed an eating disorder, or a baseball player who is having conflict with his coach.

They would also be qualified to work with an otherwise psychologically healthy diver who has a mental block that is preventing her from taking off from the diving board, or a basketball player who needs to improve his confidence at the foul line. Thus, sport psychologists are qualified to address on-court performance problems, whether they are due to personal problems or sport-specific issues.

While state law and the American Psychological Association's (APA) code of ethics currently define who can use the title of sport psychologist, in the past the title was also used by practitioners who helped athletes improve their performance by teaching them mental skills, such as relaxation strategies, goal-setting models, or visualization techniques. Using the title in this way, however, was

Sport psychologists help all kinds of athletes, from football linebackers to gymnasts, deal with a variety of issues such as concentration, communication, and injuries.

at times confusing to the public because it wasn't an accurate representation of the training and qualifications of some practitioners. The presence of the word "psychologist" implied that they were licensed, when in fact some were not—they had received education in sport psychology but had not been trained in counseling or the broader domains of psychology at the doctoral level. The use of the title "sport psychologist" was a semantic problem that arose because these practitioners were earning PhDs in sport psychology through physical education or exercise science departments, so naturally the title seemed logical. Most of these programs, however, were not designed for obtaining licensure as a psychologist. These practitioners were not governed by state licensing boards or the APA but instead represented a new group of unique professionals.

Today, these practitioners are more routinely called "sport psychology consultants," which seems like a reasonable alternative to using the title of "psychologist." Unfortunately, the use of the word "psychology" follows the same law for the use of the word "psychologist" in many states; thus, using the title "sport psychology consultant" would still be illegal unless they were licensed. So, for the purposes of this chapter and to avoid confusion, I will use the title "mental-skills coach" to refer to sport psychology consultants. I will also use the term "mental-skills training" to refer to the majority of work they do.

Mental-skills coaches are typically at the leading edge of sport psychology research and are often employed as professors in academic settings. They are experts at understanding the interplay of the various physical and mental processes that athletes experience as well as the social culture in which they reside. Mental-skills coaches also do applied work in mental-skills training with athletes, teams, and coaches. They are not typically trained to assess, diagnose, or counsel people who have adjustment or transition issues, anger problems, anxiety, depression, eating disorders, or substance abuse. Consequently, they typically teach psychological tools to improve performance but do not provide counseling, nor do they address performance decrements that arise from personal issues (as opposed to sport-specific issues). They are well trained in the development and interpretation of tests that measure specific sport psychology concepts but are not usually trained in general psychological assessment, such as testing for attention disorders, learning disabilities, personality disorders, or other psychopathology.

For example, mental-skills coaches might work with the diver and the basketball player in the preceding examples if their problems were sport-specific but would probably not work with the football player or the cross-country runner. If an athlete presents an issue that is "in between" these examples, whether the mental-skills coach should work with them is a fuzzy, gray area and boils down to an individual ethical decision. For example, a mental-skills coach might begin to work with a baseball player who becomes overly anxious before games and finds that it interferes with his performance. As they continue to work together, the mental-skills coach may find that the player is anxious on the field because he fears that his overly critical father will react negatively to a poor performance. Whether to continue working with the athlete or refer him to a sport psychologist is a decision based on the mental-skills coach's experience and training with this type of anxiety problem. This same adherence to ethics applies to sport psychologists. So, if a sport psychologist works with the baseball player in this example and finds instead that he is anxious due to conflict with a teammate, a mediation between the two players may be indicated. The sport psychologist may not be properly trained to conduct this intervention and might consider utilizing a mental-skills coach with mediation experience.

In an ideal world, if you contacted a sport psychologist or mental-skills coach, you would expect that either would have training in both psychological counseling and mental-skills coaching. In the real world, however, this is not always the case. As an educated consumer, you must find someone whom you can work with and who has the skills to help you solve your problem.

Deciding on a Practitioner

Now that you know the differences between the two types of sport psychology practitioners, it is time to find the right one for you. Before randomly making phone calls, you should do a self-assessment of your sport psychology needs. If you find it difficult to answer the questions by yourself, do the assessment with the help of your coach, parents, or trainer. An informal assessment follows.

"What's wrong with my game?" Think about the genesis of the problem. For example, "Is my concentration failing because I'm thinking about my problems with my girlfriend or because I am distracted by the crowd? Is the problem somewhere in between?"

"How do I want my performance or my life to be different as a result of my counseling with a sport psychologist?" This question helps to determine your goals before you ever step into a sport psychologist's office so that the work with him or her is more focused and efficient. Examples might include the following: "I want to be focused only on the pitcher for each at-bat," or "I want to learn skills to communicate more clearly with my teammates," or "I want to learn how to get along with my boyfriend and not fight all the time."

"What kind of help do I need?" Three options for help include mental-skills training to enhance performance, mental-skills training and psychological counseling when off-the-field issues affect performance on the field, and psychological counseling to work on more complicated performance and life issues. For example, ask yourself, "Would I benefit from learning new skills to block out the crowd, or do I need to talk with an objective person about how my relationship problems are affecting my concentration—or do I need a little of both?"

"How will I know when I'm done?" Answering this question establishes concrete expectations based on your goals, which helps you to evaluate when the counseling is complete. Examples might include "When I can consistently block out the crowd and other distractions and generate a deep focus on the pitcher during each at-bat" or "When I consistently remain calm and assert my thoughts clearly when arguing with my girlfriend or teammates."

The next step is to further refine your self-assessment by matching your concerns with one of the four categories of sport psychology problems. Of the four categories that follow, performance-development issues require training and experience in mental-skills coaching; performance-dysfunction problems typically require training and experience in both counseling and mental-skills coaching; and performance-impairment and performance-termination issues require training and experience in psychological counseling.

• Performance development: Athletes who need services in this category function well in most areas of their lives; their primary reason for seeing a sport psychologist is to improve athletic performance. This category could be referred to as "old-fashioned performance enhancement" and was how sport psychology was defined in the past. In this category the athlete's needs are not driven by off-the-field problems, such as academic difficulties, family conflict, maladjustment to new situations, conflict with coaches, or other behavioral problems. Consequently, mental-skills training to enhance performance is the intervention of choice, and psychological counseling would not be indicated. For example, an athlete with a performance-development issue would include a junior golfer who is well adjusted and has no clinical symptoms and no significant interpersonal problems, but needs help maintaining his concentration over 18 holes and recovering more quickly from errors.

• Performance dysfunction: Athletes with performance-dysfunction problems desire to improve their athletic performance, but their problems on the field are either due to internal psychological factors such as fear of failure, low frustration tolerance, or extreme perfectionism, or to off-the-field life events, such as a romantic breakup or family conflict. Often these athletes go to a sport psychologist because of their performance difficulties, not because of their personal issues; in fact, they may be unaware of the connection between personal issues and performance. The psychological barriers they experience not only affect their ability to perform but also their ability to cope with life's stressors. These athletes would benefit from both counseling and mental-skills training to help their functioning on and off the field. Examples include athletes with transitional problems, such as moving from high school to college or from starter to reserve, those experiencing strong emotional reactions to injury, poor coach–athlete relationships, or performance anxiety, or those grieving the death of a loved one.

• Performance impairment: Significant clinical problems such as depression, eating disorders, substance abuse, or panic attacks, which disrupt a major area of life, such as work, school, or interpersonal relationships, are likely to affect an athlete's performance. In these situations, psychotherapy is indicated and mental-skills training for performance enhancement is of secondary concern. An example is a college football player who is suffering from depression and finds it difficult to attend classes or make it to practice, has little motivation for football, and isolates himself from his friends.

• Performance termination: Unique issues are associated with the end of an athletic career. The termination may be due to a career-ending injury or may be a voluntary or involuntary retirement. Performance-enhancement skills are largely irrelevant given the termination of competitive performance. Issues faced by such athletes include grieving the loss of their identity, status, and perhaps income, as well as coping with potential changes in their relationships with friends and family. In these situations, psychological counseling is indicated.

Nikki

This true story was previously chronicled in the November 21, 2001, issue of *Sports Illustrated*. The athlete has consented to the inclusion of her experiences in this book in order to educate others about sport psychologists.

Nikki Teasley had all the talent in the world. She was the top high school player in the country and was supposed to bring championships to whichever college she attended. She was considered to be the female Magic Johnson: a 6-foot point guard whose passes never failed to dazzle and whose one-on-one moves embarrassed the top male players. But college basketball was a struggle. Her performances were good and occasionally great, but she wasn't living up to her potential. In her junior year, her teammates and coaches noticed that she was more and more withdrawn, irritable, and inconsistent on the court. One dark day in the middle of the season, she told her coach that she no longer wanted to be Nikki Teasley. She'd had enough of the hype and the pressure. She couldn't take it anymore and she wanted out of basketball; she wanted out of life.

Nikki's coach immediately sought help. She contacted a mental-skills coach who had done a routine assessment of Nikki in the past. The mental-skills coach, who had concluded from his assessment that Nikki couldn't handle pressure situations, said that her problems were out of his area of expertise. She then met with a middle-aged general psychologist who had some experience working with athletes, but Nikki didn't seem to connect with her because of their age difference. Her coach sought advice from their team physician. After an in-depth discussion of Nikki's needs and who might be a good fit for her, she was referred to me. We connected with each other right off the bat, and Nikki opened up a floodgate of thoughts and emotions that she had kept inside for years. She realized that these issues, combined with the pressure on the court, had proved to be too much for her coping skills, leaving her overwhelmed. Nikki's goals for counseling were to get her motivation back, improve her performance on the court, and enjoy the sport again. But she discovered that there were many life issues beyond basketball that she needed to learn how to handle before she could focus exclusively on her game.

During weekly counseling over the next two years, Nikki learned how to establish a broader array of coping strategies for life, as well as psychological skills for on the court. Her efforts paid off and she proved to herself that she could handle pressure situations. Nikki graduated from an outstanding university; she was the fifth player taken in the WNBA draft; she hit the winning shot as time expired for the WNBA Championship in her rookie year; and she was selected as the most valuable player of the All-Star game her second year in the league. Most important, she was happy again. Nikki's is a remarkable story that is not typical. Many factors contributed to her success, of which her work with me was only a small part. It highlights, however, how athletes can boost themselves back on track if there is a good match between the athlete and sport psychologist.

Finding a Sport Psychology Practitioner

Finding a sport psychologist or mental-skills coach is not as easy as it should be; there aren't a lot of them around and they can be difficult to locate. Most cities' phone books don't even include listings for sport psychologists or mental-skills coaches. There are some good options, however, if you are persistent and thorough.

Call your local university   Calling universities will often net useful results. You may need to call a few different departments to inquire whether there is a sport psychologist on staff. Calls to the counseling center and the exercise and sport science, sports medicine, psychology, or athletic departments may yield some leads. Ask if they have a sport psychologist or mental-skills coach on staff. If they don't, explain that you would like a referral to a sport psychologist and ask if they know of any in the community. If the administrative staffs in these departments are not able to answer your questions, ask for a faculty or staff person who might have the answers.

Surf the Internet   If you are Internet savvy, you will find that many Web sites have useful information regarding sport psychologists, though not all include names and phone numbers. For example, the American Psychological Association's Division of Exercise and Sport Psychology site, www.apa47.org, has useful information about sport psychology in general but does not have a sport psychologist locator service as of this writing. The Association for the Advancement of Applied Sport Psychology (AAASP) also has a helpful site, www.aaasponline.com, which includes a locator service for AAASP-certified mental-skills coaches. Some of the practitioners listed are sport psychologists and some are mental-skills coaches. Check to see whether they are licensed or not, depending on which type of practitioner will best meet your needs. You may also try using an Internet search engine. However, you must be wary of unqualified people who use Internet sites to promote themselves. It is always wise to check a practitioner's credentials.

Check with your state psychological association   Most practicing psychologists are members of their state psychological association and list their specialties with the association's referral network. Most of these organizations are relatively small and may not have a full-time administrative staff, so you may need to leave a message stating that you are looking for a sport psychologist.

Word of mouth   Often the most useful way to find a sport psychologist or mental-skills coach is by word of mouth. Ask other athletes, coaches, parents, administrators, athletic trainers, professors, sports medicine doctors, or primary-care physicians if they know of any sport practitioners in the area. If so, they may be able to tell you what the practitioners are like and whether they might be a good fit for your needs.

Evaluating a Prospective Practitioner

Before calling prospective sport psychologists or mental-skills coaches, prepare a list of questions so that you can interview them over the phone to determine if they are the right fit for you. Select a few practitioners to choose from; the more options you have, the more discerning you can be and the more likely it is that there will be a good fit. Give a brief synopsis of your concerns and answer any questions that they have. Then ask them about their credentials, experience, and how they work with people. The following suggested questions will help you get a feel for their style and qualifications:

1. "Whom do you typically work with (athlete versus non-athlete)? Which type of athletes (basketball, football, lacrosse, equestrian, and so on) do you have the most experience with? Which ages? Which level of competition (recreational, high school, collegiate, professional)? What percentage of them is male? Female?"

2. "Have you ever worked with an athlete in my sport?" (This answer does not have to be yes for the counseling experience to be effective, but it might help.)

3. "What type of degree do you have (PhD or master's)? From which type of department (psychology, kinesiology, physical education)? From which university?"

4. "Are you a licensed psychologist? For how long?"

5. "Are you a certified mental-skills coach or sport psychology consultant?" (You can check this with AAASP.)

6. "What can I expect from the initial interview? What about follow-up sessions? How long are the meetings?"

7. "How would you describe your style?"

8. "What is your fee? Do you accept insurance?"

Asking these questions may fluster or annoy some of the people you call. If this happens, I would suggest that you move on to the next name on your list. Remember that you are in control of whether to work with a particular practitioner, and you have every right to know the answers to the preceding questions.

One important question that you should ask about up front is the fee for services. Fees vary dramatically depending on the person's experience and the customary rate for services in your region. Typically, only a licensed sport psychologist is able to bill your insurance. Furthermore, the sport psychologist must be able to assign a mental-health diagnosis to the problem in order for the insurance company to even consider paying for part of the services. Examples of mental-health diagnoses are depression, panic attacks, eating disorders, and

It's important that the sport psychologist or mental-skills coach you choose has experience with or is interested in learning about and understanding your sport, whether it be lacrosse, kayaking or baseball.

©Sport The Library

substance abuse. Issues that fall under performance development or performance enhancement do not satisfy the criteria for a mental-health diagnosis and thus won't be reimbursed by your insurance company. This is not necessarily a bad thing, unless you are financially strapped. Getting an insurance company involved in your sport psychology counseling can feel intrusive and reduce the sense of confidentiality that you would have if you paid for services out-of-pocket. If you need financial help, you can ask the practitioner about payment plans or sliding-scale fees.

Determining the "Right" Practitioner

Once you have gotten all of the information you need over the phone, consider the following qualities in determining whether you have found the right sport psychologist for you.

Personality   Is there a personality match? Is this the type of practitioner you want to work with? Do you prefer a male or female? Someone who is younger or older? Someone who is laid back or more professional? Would you prefer a lot of opportunity to talk and express your thoughts and feelings? If so, you may prefer someone who is a patient listener or a bit more reserved. Do you want a lot of input and suggestions for concrete strategies? If so, you may prefer someone who is more directive and educative. Many athletes are used to being told what to do by their coaches and thus tend to prefer more active counseling to help them develop practical solutions. Share your preferences with the practitioners during the initial phone calls and discuss whether they can meet your needs. But keep in mind that a good counselor will help you to change, and that process might not always feel comfortable. Sometimes a counselor who can challenge you is the person you need.

Skill level Does this person have the skills to help you? Once you have figured out what your goals are, you will have a better idea of the skills that a sport psychologist needs in order to help you. Do you need primarily mental-skills coaching; do you have broader life issues that affect your performance; or do you need psychological counseling?

Experience Does this person have the right experience? Although all practitioners will have dealt with similar issues or even the same sport as yours, you need to decide if they have the experience and training to give you confidence in their work.

The First Session

Much of this information regarding the practitioner's style is difficult to glean over the phone, so the next step is setting up initial meetings with several candidates. Let them know that you are visiting a few practitioners to find the best fit. Again, if this offends them, they are not interested in you being an educated consumer, and I would suggest moving on.

During the first meeting, you may feel awkward telling a complete stranger about your thoughts, feelings, and problems, but this reaction is typical. Pay attention to whether you feel you are being heard; that is, whether you feel that they understand you and your concerns. Also attend to whether the practitioners convey a sense of warmth and are nonjudgmental. These qualities can help you feel more comfortable and safe in divulging your concerns. Finally, note whether they map out a logical plan to help you with your issues. If they pass these tests, then you have found a match. It may seem like a long and complicated process, but the results will likely be worth it. You will have the satisfaction of being a diligent and educated consumer of sport psychology services, and most important, of taking good care of yourself or your athletes.

Future Directions

As the field of sport psychology continues to evolve there is likely to be greater agreement on the necessary training and experience needed to develop practitioners in the short run and increasing numbers of practitioners as well as increasing areas of specialization among them in the long run. Both of these developments bode well for the consumer.

In the short run, the APA, which is the national organization for psychologists, is working on developing standard qualifications for sport psychologists. A division within the organization, APA Division 47, is devoted exclusively to exercise and sport psychology. The division has recently succeeded in getting the APA to officially recognize sport psychology as an area of specialty practice within the larger field of psychology. This recognition is the first step in establishing national standards for the field, and it sets the stage for the development of specific requirements to be credentialed as a sport psychologist. Although the specific criteria have yet to be agreed on, a more complete explanation of the latest status of sport psychology as a special area of practice can be found at www.apa47.org or www.aaasponline.org.

In the long run, it is easy to envision increasing specialization among sport psychologists, as so often happens in growing professions. The specialization may take the form of sport practitioners focusing on a certain aspect of mental-skills training, such as being a motivation coach or a relationship/communication skills coach. Perhaps collegiate or professional teams will employ different sport psychologists for specific purposes, such as mediating coach-athlete conflict, improving relationships between the athlete and the administration, and managing problems that arise within an athlete's family. Some sport psychologists already specialize by focusing exclusively on a single sport, such as hockey or track, and this trend will continue. It is also possible that coaches will retain their own sport psychologist to assist in handling team dynamics.

I believe that these types of specializations portend a boon for consumers as more talented people enter the profession and increase accessibility to services. Consumers will also have the confidence that their sport psychologist has met nationally accepted qualification standards and will be optimally helpful to them. Finally, it will enable consumers to specifically tailor their search to those specializing in their sport, position, event, or area of concern, and expedite the process of improving their satisfaction and their performance in their sport.

Success in Sport Psych: Effective Sport Psychologists

David Tod and Mark Andersen

Sport participants worldwide have found that sport psychologists have helped them prepare for competition; still, some athletes and coaches have had negative experiences. Although some consultants do help athletes, others may actually interfere with competitive preparation. Athletes and coaches who have had negative experiences with ineffective or incompetent consultants may believe that sport psychology cannot offer them any benefits; it usually takes only one bad experience to prejudice them against the field.

The perception that sport psychology has limited value might be partly influenced by the difficulty in separating applied sport psychology services from the individual providing the product. In other sport science disciplines, such as biomechanics and exercise physiology, consultants use objective measurement tools, which make it easier to separate the provider from the service. Because the sport psychologist is the primary intervention instrument, athletes and coaches might benefit from understanding the qualities that contribute to the effectiveness and competence of a consultant. This chapter describes the characteristics of effective sport psychologists as identified by researchers and presents guidelines for identifying competent practitioners.

Critical Issues for Effective Consultants

A great deal of research has examined the question of whether psychological skills can enhance sport performance, and it strongly supports the concept that physical sport skills can be improved by a variety of suitable psychological interventions.

Psychological skills, however, do not automatically improve performance; they need to be implemented carefully and judiciously, because some techniques are not suitable for some athletes or situations. To be helpful, psychological skills training needs to be applied in thoughtful and creative ways. Effective consultants realize that there is a difference between knowing that psychological skills can improve performance and being able to assist athletes in making productive use of those skills. Sport psychology intervention effectiveness must be evaluated in the following areas.

A foundation of techniques   One issue that surrounds consultant effectiveness concerns how sport psychologists help athletes use psychological skills such as goal setting, imagery, relaxation, and self-talk. These techniques are commonly described in applied sport psychology literature, yet helping athletes use them is not easy or straightforward. Sport psychology consultants who are capable of teaching psychological skills effectively can substantially contribute to athletes' mental preparation in their quest for optimal performance, development as sport participants, and increased sport and life satisfaction. In contrast, consultants who are unable to use psychological interventions optimally can distract athletes from their competitive preparation by misapplying techniques and wasting their time—and ultimately, compromising their attempts to achieve optimal performance.

Solid counseling skills   Athletes occasionally experience problems or crises that negatively affect their performance and quality of life. In coping with their lives, athletes may benefit from assistance beyond being taught sport psychology skills. Consultants who have solid counseling skills (e.g., active listening, empathic reflection) may help athletes feel safe in sharing sensitive personal information. Here's an example: A nationally ranked junior squash player approached a consultant to discuss her decision to stop playing competitively because she no longer had any motivation to play. Instead of using common motivational techniques, such as goal setting, the consultant talked with the player, exploring her competitive history in sport and the reasons why she lacked motivation. Toward the end of the session, the consultant reflected back his understanding of the athlete, who expressed gratitude that he had taken the time to let her talk. The underlying concern was not motivation after all but the difficulties the young athlete was having coping with the pressures placed on her by her coach to perform consistently. The consultant then helped the player identify strategies to cope with that pressure. This story illustrates how effective consultants do not make "snap" judgments and serve up an intervention; rather, they take the time to explore the surrounding issues and get the whole story.

Unbiased guidance   A third issue that surrounds consultant effectiveness concerns the various demands that athletes may face, including the pressure to perform consistently at an optimal level, take performance-enhancing drugs, make the most of a short playing career, deal with the media, play while injured, return from injury as quickly as possible, and sacrifice social time. Effective sport psychologists are comfortable discussing these concerns, are able to deal with their own reactions to them, and can focus on helping athletes determine the most beneficial coping strategies. The case of a young rugby union player provides an example of how effective consultants control their own reactions when assisting athletes. The player approached his sport psychologist for guidance: He had been offered a large contract to play overseas, but if he accepted he believed that he would end the prospect of representing his country at the international level. Although the consultant had an opinion on which option the player should take, she did not express her view but instead helped him consider the consequences of each choice by weighing the pros and cons. The consultant took an athlete-centered approach to help the individual make the best decision for him. The player expressed gratitude that the consultant had helped him clarify his own thoughts and feelings instead of telling him what to do. Effective consultants stay within their realms of expertise and help athletes draw on their own strengths and decision-making abilities.

Ineffective Sport Psychologists

The management team of a yachting crew was negotiating with the director of a university-based sport-science consulting business. They hoped that sport-science support would contribute to the sailors' preparation. Although keen to have nutrition, exercise physiology, and sports medicine consultants involved, the management team was not interested in the services of a sport psychologist, explaining that a sport psychologist who had been part of the support crew in a previous regatta had not been helpful. He had not offered practical or relevant techniques that the sailors could use, did not relate well to the team members, and had asked them to complete a lengthy questionnaire without explaining its relevance or providing useful feedback. The sailors believed that he was more interested in using them for personal research purposes and was not committed to helping them prepare for competition. Although the director of the sport-science consulting business detailed the types of services a sport psychologist could offer, the management team still decided not to include one.

Unfortunately, the preceding scenario and its various permutations are not uncommon. Poorly trained sport psychologists, or those with their own agendas, can leave trails of alienation behind them, whereas effective consultants build loyal followings. Applied sport psychology is a relatively new field of practice and does not have the long history of self-examination that one finds in clinical and counseling psychology. But "quacks" abound in most service-delivery fields, especially in professions that are seen as glamorous. The potential harm to both athletes and the profession caused by ineffective sport psychology services can be offset by understanding which qualities to look for in an effective consultant.

Characteristics of Proven Consultants

While the debate over training and service delivery was occurring in the late 1980s, researchers began to examine the qualities of effective sport psychology consultants. Initially, Terry Orlick and John Partington, sport psychologists working in Ottawa, Canada, examined the differences between effective and ineffective consultants as perceived by Canadian athletes, coaches, and sport psychologists from several Olympic sports. Since then, other sport psychology researchers have also examined the characteristics of effective consultants, and a number of common themes have emerged.

Effective sport psychologists have several key characteristics in common. They have highly developed relationship-building and associated interpersonal skills, including being likeable, trustworthy, empathetic, approachable, positive, and warm. Helpful consultants are people oriented, care about the athletes with whom they work, and are able to fit within a team environment. They also have excellent technical knowledge that they can apply to specific situations. Specifically, effective consultants excel in the following areas.

Relationship-building skills Interpersonal skills play an important role in service delivery because they help consultants develop solid working relationships with athletes. Many sport and mainstream psychology researchers and most practitioners consider a warm, trusting relationship to be a key determinant of successful therapeutic outcome. One aspect of this relationship is the working alliance: the ability of the psychologist and client to collaborate. This partnership consists of (1) a shared agreement on the goals of service, (2) a mutual understanding of the tasks each person will undertake to achieve the goals, and (3) a positive interpersonal bond between the two parties. The quality of this alliance reliably predicts the quality of outcome in psychotherapy, and the same might be expected in sport psychology counseling.

Technical competence Effective sport psychologists possess great technical expertise. Sport participants value consultants who can provide specific, practical, and concrete strategies. Effective consultants help athletes adapt psychological techniques to fit their personalities and the situations in which they need to use these skills. This ability to generate practical strategies most likely results from an understanding of the athlete, the psychological knowledge base, and the sport. Another component of technical competence is service-delivery style. Coaches and athletes like consultants who adopt an athlete-centered approach that identifies individual strengths, weaknesses, and needs. Effective consultants help athletes develop skills that enhance strengths, address weaknesses, and satisfy needs. Coaches should be wary of practitioners who do not adapt their interventions to the athletes' needs but instead offer a "one-size-fits-all" package. Canned programs are unlikely to help the majority of athletes and may be only moderately useful for a few.

Sometimes situational factors may undermine the effectiveness of sport psychologists' assistance. Sport participants perceive that practitioners are most helpful when they are able to have multiple one-to-one sessions with athletes, beginning several months before major competitions. Also, athletes report that intimidating or unapproachable coaches can impede consultants' helpfulness because they interfere with their attempts to develop relationships in which athletes feel comfortable sharing sensitive information.

Evaluating Consultant Effectiveness

Although conscientious consultants evaluate themselves and their service delivery, their influence on sport performance often cannot be assessed in an objective, quantitative manner. Statements like "This athlete's performance has improved 34 percent, and 79 percent of the improvement is directly attributable to sport psychology" could never be based on any valid or reliable measures. In addition, such claims are difficult to justify because sport performance is influenced by a large number of physiological, biomechanical, nutritional, social, and psychological factors that can vary from moment to moment. More commonly, consultants' effectiveness is evaluated subjectively: Do coaches and athletes perceive that the consultant has helped them improve?

Although enhanced sport performance is one important goal in the delivery of sport psychology services, another is satisfaction: Are athletes happy with their consultants? One indication that athletes are happy is their willingness to continue working with and paying their consultants. The following story of an exercise physiologist illustrates that the question of athlete satisfaction is starting to get a mention in other sport sciences.

An exercise physiologist met with colleagues from the same exercise physiology unit to discuss the group's mission. Suggestions included improving performance and increasing medal counts at the Olympics. The physiologist stood up and declared, "We offer a service aimed at helping athletes get better at their sport, but the final measure of all our efforts is whether the coaches and athletes are pleased with the service. Are they happy with how we have interacted with them? Are they happy with the information and suggestions we have offered? Performance outcome on any given day is mercurial, and even though performance improvements are definitely linked to happiness, the real measure of how we are doing our jobs is whether the athletes and coaches are happy with us and what we offer and want to come back." (Andersen 2002, p. 19)

Techniques of Excellent Consultants

The research described previously provides evidence that the sport psychologist is the primary consulting tool and the practitioner–athlete relationship is the main intervention. To be most effective in this capacity, excellent consultants work to build the following areas with their athletes.

Collaborative Relationships

Probably no other factor is more important in service delivery than the extent to which consultants and athletes form collaborative relationships. To help foster these relationships, effective consultants acknowledge that athletes are experts in their sports, invite them to share their knowledge and experience, and take time to learn about the sport from the athletes' perspectives. All other interventions occur within the context of this collaborative relationship. Athletes may not benefit from learning to use psychological skills without the rapport from strong working alliances. Rapport aids cosultants in eliciting frank histories that contribute to the understanding of athletes' needs and help determine useful interventions. The following story illustrates how the inability to establish a collaborative relationship may undermine a consultant's effectiveness.

A university-based consultant began working with a female student golfer. Although the psychologist had limited experience with golf, he decided to use a commercially available mental-skills training package. The athlete did not seem entirely comfortable with the system but agreed to try it the next day during a practice round. Several days later, the consultant contacted the client to find out if the system had helped. The golfer said that it had not helped her and had actually been confusing, and she declined to return for a second session with the consultant. The psychologist, who realized the importance of collaborating with the client to identify suitable interventions, decided that he would spend time with a golfer on the course if he ever used the system again. Effective consultants ensure that they have the full agreement of an athlete before embarking on any intervention.

A Working Alliance

Establishing a working alliance is not always straightforward or quick; it can take time depending on the characteristics of the individuals involved. Some degree of match between the personalities of the athlete and sport psychologist is essential. Also, the consultant has to have the skills to deal with the concerns of the athlete adequately. Currently, no foolproof criteria exist to help coaches and athletes determine whether a particular consultant is the correct person to employ. However, the following guidelines can help coaches and athletes make decisions about the suitability of particular consultants.

• Has the consultant tried to establish a collaborative relationship? Whether a consultant has helpful interpersonal skills is impossible to assess after a single session. If, however, after several sessions a relationship based on mutual trust is not developing, athletes may benefit from a referral to another consultant.

• Is the consultant willing to learn about the sport from the athletes' perspective? The value of learning about a sport from the athletes' perspective is revealed in the anecdote of a young consultant fresh out of graduate school who was asked to work with a rugby league team. The psychologist asked if he could participate in training one night because he had never played the game and wanted to experience the demands of preparation. The players took delight in helping the consultant experience the physical contact and fitness demands associated with the sport. In the weeks after this training session, several players told the psychologist that they were more comfortable talking to him because he had "gotten down and dirty" with them. The practitioner believed that he was able to suggest helpful specific interventions because he had a better idea of why they were needed. Although feedback from the players was positive in this example, some might view the practice of working out with the athletes as crossing professional boundaries. A one-time practice participation to gather information and experience the athletes' world would seem a valuable endeavor; however, if the sport psychologist were to work out regularly with the team, the blurring of boundaries that might result could threaten his effectiveness.

• Does the consultant have prior experience in the sport? Experience in a sport can help consultants understand athletes' perceptions, although sport psychologists need to be careful that they do not overstep their professional boundaries and offer coaching advice, especially if it conflicts with coaches' plans. The following anecdote illustrates the need for consultants to be careful when drawing on their prior experience in a sport. During a consultation with a javelin thrower, a sport psychologist inquired about the athlete's training regime, inadvertently mentioning some of the exercises he had done when he was competing. The athlete told the coach that the consultant had suggested that she change her training. The coach became upset and went to the sport psychologist to find out why he thought the coach's training plan was unsuitable. The practitioner explained that there had been a misunderstanding—he had not intended to imply that the athlete's training should be changed.

• Has the sport psychologist received certification or registration from a professional sport psychology organization? Certification or registration from a professional sport psychology organization, such as the Association for the Advancement of Applied Sport Psychology (AAASP), indicates that the individual has completed the necessary training and has the experience needed to be a competent practitioner. Registration or certification, however, is no guarantee that consultants will be effective, only that they have the needed competencies.

• Can the psychologist explain simply and clearly how the consulting process works? Sport psychologists consult with athletes in various ways. Effective practitioners can explain what they do and how they do it in ways that sport participants understand; psychobabble, or technical jargon, does not help the consumer and damages the reputation of the field. Sport psychologists who explain their approach clearly can assist athletes and coaches in making informed decisions. Coaches and athletes can also question practitioners about their consulting styles, their sport-specific experiences, and why their interventions might help. Sport psychologists who cannot give clear answers to these questions in everyday language might be unable to work with athletes in ways that they find helpful and may have trouble forming working alliances.

© Bongarts/SportsChrome USA

Effective sport psychology consultants not only have good training, extensive experience, and good credentials; they are great communicators who can take complex concepts and explain them clearly.

Keys to a Successful Sport Consultant–Athlete Relationship

Even excellent sport psychologists might prove to be unhelpful, because the behaviors and attitudes of coaches and athletes can influence effectiveness as much as the practitioners themselves. The following guidelines offer suggestions for extracting the most help from consultants.

Adopt a positive, realistic attitude toward sport psychology   For consultants to be helpful, coaches and athletes must believe that psychological interventions will contribute to improved performance. If athletes do not believe that the strategies will help, they might not practice and implement them as suggested. Coaches and athletes also need to be realistic; psychological interventions do not turn sub-elite performers into champions overnight.

Allow sufficient time for interventions to work   It takes time for comprehensive psychological skills training programs to be implemented and solidified. Orlick and Partington suggested that a minimum of one year of mental training was necessary to prepare for elite competition. Athletes may not always desire comprehensive psychological skills training programs; they may have specific issues that can be treated and resolved in less than a year. Regardless of the degree of involvement needed, athletes and coaches must allow sufficient time for interventions to work.

Acknowledge the influence of coaching   Coaches' attitudes toward sport psychology can greatly influence athletes' willingness to work with practitioners. Coaches who demonstrate a lack of support or make derogatory comments about sport psychology send the message to athletes that practitioners cannot help them, whereas their endorsements of sport psychologists can boost athletes' confidence in the process. Effective sport psychologists are usually happy to meet and work with coaches. Those who refuse to meet with coaches or prefer to work only with athletes might miss out on information that could enhance their effectiveness and can easily alienate coaches.

Define the consultant's role clearly   Both coaches and consultants realize that it is vital to clarify the sport psychologist's role. Coaches do not appreciate consultants who overstep their professional roles, and effective sport psychologists want to have a clear understanding of their responsibilities. A number of ethical and logistical issues associated with the sport psychologist's role, such as confidentiality, payment, and availability, need to be agreed on and understood by all parties involved as part of the foundation for a solid working alliance. Even though a sport psychogist might travel with a team, stay in the same hotel with the team, and have meals with their athletes, effective consultants maintain clear boundries in their work. We hope that sport psychology consultants are always friendly with their clients, but there is a difference between being friendly and being good friends or mates. Competant consultants are consistent in their interactions and do not confuse athletes by sending mixed messages such as "I'm your psychologist" one day and "I am your good friend" the next.

Future Directions

Although effective sport psychologists can assist coaches and athletes in meaningful ways, some purveyors of services have the aroma of snake oil about them and exaggerate the benefits that they can bestow. Because athletes often have limited resources, time, and financial support, they need to prioritize their efforts to perform at their best and achieve their goals. A poor choice of a sport psychologist can mean more than no benefit; it can mean wasted time and even performance decrements. On a more positive note, there are many university programs in sport psychology, both in exercise science and psychology departments, that are turning out fine practitioners. Now, more than ever, coaches and athletes have a wide choice of sport psychologists to choose from to meet their needs.

As the profession of sport psychology continues to develop, those consultants who will be most effective will be those who are able to empathize, communicate, and collaborate with athletes along with adapting interventions to suit athletes' needs in specific situations. The future of sport psychology as a profession looks promising. As sport psychologists move from narrow definitions of service (e.g., performance enhancement only) to more inclusive services (e.g., mental health of athletes, psychological well-being, rehabilitation), there will be a much broader spectrum of people to serve and issues to address.

A problem in the past has been the narrowness of sport psychology, especially with emphasis on elite athletes. Today, sport psychologists are trained in many interventions that have applications far beyond sport. Graduates are finding work in the allied areas of sports medicine, obesity treatment, exercise adherence, and cardiac rehabilitation as they market their skills more widely. This expansion of services can only help the field continue to be viable as one of the allied helping professions.

Notes

In order to make it easier for you to read more about the issues discussed in *The Sport Psych Handbook*, we have provided references for all the major sources and research articles mentioned in the book. If you wish to know more about a research area mentioned in a chapter, look up the page the research was mentioned on here, and you will find the reference for the research.

Scientific references follow a specific format so that scientists can communicate more easily with each other about their work. There are two main types of references: those published in scientific journals, and those published as books. Citations for research articles published in scientific journals include (in order) the person who wrote the research, the year the research was published, the title of the research article, the journal the research was published in, the volume number of the journal, and the page number(s) of the article. In contrast, citations for research described in a book include the person who wrote or edited the book, the title of the book, the year the book was published, and the city, state, and publisher of the book.

Chapter 1

p. 3   Triplett, N. (1898). The dynamogenic factors in pacemaking and competition. *American Journal of Psychology, 9*, 507-553.

Freud, S., & Starcley, J. (1964). *The complete psychological works of Sigmund Freud.* Oxford: Macmillan.

Skinner, B.F. (1965). *Science of human behavior.* New York: Free Press.

p. 5   McClelland, D. (1961). *The achieving society.* New York: Free Press.

Atkinson, J.W. (1974). The mainstream of achievement-oriented activity. In J.W. Atkinson & J.O. Raynor (Eds.), *Motivation and achievement* (pp. 13-41). New York: Halstead.

James, W. (1892, 1961). *Psychology: The briefer course.* Oxford: Harper.

Morgan, W.P. (1979). Prediction of performance in athletics. In P. Klavora & J.V. Daniel (Eds.), *Coach, athlete, and the sport psychologist* (pp. 173-186). Champaign, IL: Human Kinetics.

p. 6   Siedentop, D., & Rushall, B.S. (1972). *Development and control of behavior in sport and physical education.* Philadelphia: Lea and Febider.

p. 7   Deci, E.L. (1975). *Intrinsic motivation.* New York: Plenum Press.

Deci, E.L. (1971). Effects of externally mediated rewards on intrinsic motivation. *Journal of Personality and Social Psychology, 18*, 105-115.

p. 7   Vallerand, R.J. (1997). Toward a hierarchical model of intrinsic and extrinsic motivation. In M.P. Zanna (Ed.), *Advances in experimental social psychology*, 29, 271-360. New York: Academic Press.

p. 8   Bandura, A. (1997). *Self-efficacy: The exercise of control.* New York: W.H. Freeman.

p. 10   Nicholls, J. (1984). Conceptions of ability and achievement motivation. In R. Ames & C. Ames (Eds.), *Research on motivation in education: Student motivation,* 1, 39-73. New York: Academic Press.

            Duda, J.L. (1992). Motivation in sport settings: A goal perspective approach. In G.C. Roberts (Ed.), *Motivation in sport and exercise* (pp. 57-92). Champaign, IL: Human Kinetics.

            Ames, C. (1992). Achievement goals, motivational climate, and motivational processes. In G.C. Roberts (Ed.), *Motivation in sport and exercise* (pp. 161-176). Champaign, IL: Human Kinetics.

            Treasure, D.C. (1997). Perceptions of the motivational climate and elementary school children's cognitive and affective response. *Journal of Sport and Exercise Psychology, 19,* 278-290.

p. 11   Weiner, B. (1986). *An attributional theory of motivation and emotion.* New York: Springer-Verlag.

p. 13   Csikszentmihalyi, M. (1990). *Flow: The psychology of optimal experience.* New York: Harper and Row.

            Eliot, J.F. (1997). *Engagement.* Ann Arbor, MI: University Publishers.

p. 16   McAuley, E., Duncan, T.E., & Russell, D.W. (1992). Measuring causal attributions: The revised causal dimension scale (CDSII). *Personality and Social Psychology Bulletin, 19,* 566-573.

p. 17   Seligman, M.E.P. (1975). *Helplessness: On depression, development, and death.* San Francisco: W.H. Freeman.

            Seligman, M.E.P. (1991). *Learned optimism.* New York: Knopf.

p. 18   Healy, D. (1997). *The antidepressant era.* Cambridge, MA: Harvard University Press.

            Kaplan, H.R. (1987). Lottery winners: The myth and reality. *Journal of Gambling Behavior, 3*(3): 168-178.

Chapter 2

p. 19   Nicholls, J.G. (1989). *The competitive ethos and democratic education.* Cambridge, MA: Harvard University Press.

p. 22   Fry, M.D. (2001). The development of motivation in children. In G.C. Roberts (Ed.), *Advances in motivation in sport and exercise.* Champaign, IL: Human Kinetics.

            Duda, J.L. (2001). Goal perspective research in sport: Pushing some boundaries and clarifying some misunderstandings. In G.C. Roberts (Ed.), *Advances in motivation in sport and exercise.* Champaign, IL: Human Kinetics.

pp. 23-24   Ames, C. (1992). Achievement goals, motivational climate, and motivational processes. In G.C. Roberts (Ed.), *Motivation in sport and exercise.* Champaign, IL: Human Kinetics.

p. 25   Duda, J.L. (1992). Goal perspectives in sport. In G.C. Roberts (Ed.), *Motivation in sport and exercise*. Champaign, IL: Human Kinetics.

Duda, J.L., Chi, L., Newton, M.L., Walling, M.D., & Catley, D. (1995). Task and ego orientation and intrinsic motivation in sport. *International Journal of Sport Psychology, 26*, 40-63.

Hall, H.K., & Kerr, A.W. (1997). Motivational antecedents of precompetitive anxiety in youth sport. *The Sport Psychologist, 11*, 24-42.

Ntoumanis, N., Biddle, S.J.H., & Haddock, G. (1999). The mediating role of coping strategies on the relationship between achievement motivation and affect in sport. *Anxiety, Stress, and Coping, 12*, 299-327.

Hatzigeorgiadis, A., & Biddle, S. (1999). The effects of goal orientation and perceived competence on cognitive interference during tennis and snooker performance. *Journal of Sport Behavior, 22*, 479-501.

Cury, F., Biddle, S., Sarrazin, P., & Famose, J.P. (1997). Achievement goals and perceived ability predict investment in learning a sport task. *British Journal of Educational Psychology, 67*, 293-309.

p. 27   Thill, E.E., & Brunel, P.C. (1995). Ego-involvement and task-involvement: Related conceptions of ability, effort, and learning strategies among soccer players. *International Journal of Sport Psychology, 26*, 81-97.

Duda, J.L., Olson, L., & Templin, T. (1991). The relationship of task and ego orientation to sportsmanship attitudes and the perceived legitimacy of injurious acts. *Research Quarterly for Exercise and Sport, 62*, 79-87.

Dunn, J.G.H., & Dunn, J.C. (1999). Goal orientations, perceptions of aggression, and sportspersonship in elite youth male ice hockey players. *The Sport Psychologist, 13*, 183-200.

Kavussanu, M., & Roberts, G.C. (2001). Moral functioning in sport: An achievement goal perspective. *Journal of Sport and Exercise Psychology, 23*, 37-54.

p. 28   Duda, J.L., & Hom, M. (1993). Interdependencies between the perceived and self-reported goal orientations of young athletes and their parents. *Pediatric Exercise Science, 5*, 234-241.

Ebbeck, V., & Becker, S.L. (1994). Psychosocial predictors of goal orientations in youth soccer. *Research Quarterly for Exercise and Sport, 65*, 355-362.

Harwood, C.G., & Swain, A.B. (2001). The development and activation of achievement goals in tennis: I. Understanding the underlying factors. *The Sport Psychologist, 15*, 319-341.

p. 29   Harwood, C.G., & Swain, A.B. (2002). The development and activation of achievement goals in tennis: II. A player, parent and coach intervention. *The Sport Psychologist, 16*, 111-137.

Hodge, K., & Petlichkoff, L. (2000). Goal profiles in sport motivation: A cluster analysis. *Journal of Sport and Exercise Psychology, 22*, 256-272.

Harwood, C.G. (2002). Assessing achievement goals in sport: Caveats for consultants and a case for contextualization. *Journal of Applied Sport Psychology, 14*, 380-393.

Horn, T.S., & Hasbrook, C.A. (1987). Psychological characteristics and the criteria children use for self-evaluation. *Journal of Sport Psychology, 9*, 208-221.

Chapter 3

p. 38   Kellmann, M. (Ed.). (2002). *Enhancing recovery*. Champaign, IL: Human Kinetics.

p. 39   Ellis, A., & Harper, R. (1976). *A new guide to rational living*. North Hollywood, CA: Wilshire.

p. 40   Wooden's actions were studied in: Tharp, R., & Gallimore, R. (1976, January). What a coach can teach a teacher. *Psychology Today*, *9*, 74-78.

Kramer, J., & Shaap, D. (1968). *Instant replay: The Green Bay diary of Jerry Kramer*. New York: Signet.

p. 41   Robertson, S., & Botterill, C. (2000). Creating an Olympic success story. *Coaches Report*, *6*(3), 9-13.

Werthner, P., & Botterill, C. (2000). On sport psychology—team building. *Coaches Report*, *6*(4), 28-29.

p. 42   Riley, P. (1993). *The winner within: A life plan for team players*. New York: G.P. Putnam.

Newburg, D. Kimieck, J., Durand-Bush, N., & Doell, K. (2002). The role of resonance in performance excellence and life engagement. *Journal of Applied Sport Psychology*, *14*, 249-267.

p. 43   Baumeister, R., & Steinhilber, A. (1984). Paradoxical effects of supportive audiences on performance under pressure: The home field disadvantage on sports championships. *Journal of Personality and Social Psychology*, *43*, 85-93.

Brown, M. Cairns, K., & Botterill, C. (2001). The process of perspective: The art of living well in the world of elite sport. *Journal of Excellence*, *1*(5), 5-38.

p. 45   Garfield, C. (1986). *Peak performers: The new heroes of Amercian business*. New York: Avon Books.

p. 46   Maslow, A. (1962). *Toward a psychology of being*. Princeton, NJ: Van Nostrand.

Orlick, T. (1982). *The second co-operative sports and games book*. New York: Pantheon Books.

Vallerand, R. (1984). Emotion in sport. In W. Staub & J. Williams (Eds.), *Cognitive sport psychology* (pp. 65-78). Lansing, NY: Sport Science Associates.

Botterill, C. (1996). Emotional preparation for the Olympic Games. *Coaches Report*, *3*(1), 26-30.

Botterill, C., & Patrick, T. (2003). *Perspective: The key to life*. Winnipeg, Canada: Lifeskills.

p. 47   Botterill, C., & Patrick T. (2000). *A guide for sport parents*. Winnipeg, Canada: Sport Manitoba.

Chapter 4

p. 49   Counsilman, J.E., & Counsilman, B.E. (1990). No simple answers: Reduced training at a higher intensity may look like a better, faster way to success, but the answer is not that simple. *Swimming Technique*, *26*, 22-29.

DeHart, J. (1995). Taking DeHart way. *Swimming Technique*, *32*, 15-17.

p. 50   Morgan, W.P., Brown, D., Raglin, J., O'Connor, P., & Ellickson, J. (1987). Psychological monitoring of overtraining and staleness. *British Journal of Sports Medicine, 21,* 107-114.

Raglin, J., & Barzdukas, A. (Eds.). (1999). Overtraining in athletes: The challenge of prevention. *Health and Fitness Journal, 3,* 27-31.

Raglin, J.S., & Morgan, W.P. (1994). Development of a scale for use in monitoring training-induced distress in athletes. *International Journal of Sports Medicine, 15,* 84-88.

Samuelson, J., & Averbuch, G. (1995). *Joan Samuelson's running for women.* Emmaus, PA: Rodale Press.

p. 51   Coakley, J. (1992). Burnout among adolescent athletes: A personal failure or social problem? *Sociology of Sport Journal, 9,* 271-285.

Gould, D., Greenleaf, C., Dieffenbach, K., Chung, Y., & Peterson, K. (1999). *Positive and negative factors influencing U.S. Olympic athletes and coaches: Nagano games assessment.* Final grant report submitted to the U.S. Olympic Committee Sport Science and Technology Division. Colorado Springs, CO.

Gould, D., Guinan, D., Greenleaf, C., Medbery, R., Strickland, M., Lauer, L., Chung, Y., & Peterson, K. (1998). *Positive and negative factors influencing U.S. Olympic athletes and coaches: Atlanta games assessment.* Final grant report submitted to the U.S. Olympic Committee Sport Science and Technology Division. Colorado Springs, CO.

p. 53   Kellmann, M. (2002). *Enhancing recovery: Preventing underperformance in athletes.* Champaign, IL: Human Kinetics.

Gould, D., & Dieffenbach, K. (2002). Overtraining, underrecovery, and burnout in sport. In M. Kellman (Ed.), *Enhancing recovery: Preventing underperformance in athletes* (pp. 25-36). Champaign, IL: Human Kinetics.

Henschen, K. (2001). Athletic staleness and burnout: Diagnosis, prevention, and treatment. In J. Williams (Ed.), *Applied sport psychology: Personal growth to peak performance* (4th ed., pp. 328-337). Mountain View, CA: Mayfield.

Silva, J. (1990). An analysis of the training stress syndrome in competitive athletics. *Journal of Applied Sport Psychology, 2,* 5-20.

pp. 54-55   Bompa, T.O. (1993). *Theory and methodology of training.* Dubuque, IA: Kendall/Hunt.

Bompa, T.O. (2003). Understanding the periodization system. In T.O. Bompa (Ed.), *Serious strength training* (2nd ed.). Champaign, IL: Human Kinetics.

p. 55   Bompa, T.O. (1999). *Periodization: Theory and methodology of training* (4th ed.). Champaign, IL: Human Kinetics.

p. 59   Rusko, H.K., Harkonen, M., & Pakarinen, A. (1994). Overtraining effects on hormonal and autonomic regulation in young cross-country skiers. *Medicine and Science in Sports and Exercise, 26* (5), S64.

p. 60   Borg, G. (1998). *Borg's perceived exertion and pain scales.* Champaign, IL: Human Kinetics.

p. 61   Berger, B.G., & Motl, R.W. (2000). Exercise and mood: A selective review and synthesis of research employing the Profile of Mood States. *Journal of Applied Sport Psychology, 12,* 69-92.

LeUnes, A., & Burger, J. (2000). The Profile of Mood States research in sport and exercise psychology: Past, present, and future. *Journal of Applied Sport Psychology, 12,* 5-15.

p. 61   Martin, D.T., Andersen, M.B., & Gates, W. (2000). Using the Profile of Mood States (POMS) to monitor high-intensity training in cyclists: Group versus case studies. *Sport Psychologist, 14*, 138-156.

McNair, D.M., Lorr, M., & Droppleman, L.F. (1992). EdITS manual for the Profile of Mood States (Rev. ed.). San Diego: EdITS/Educational and Industrial Testing Service.

Morgan, W.P., Costill, D.L., Flynn, M.G., Raglin, J.S., & O'Connor, P. (1988). Mood disturbance following increased training in swimmers. *Medicine and Science in Sports and Exercise, 20*, 408-414.

Kellmann, M., & Kallus, K.W. (2001). *Recovery-stress questionnaire for athletes: User manual.* Champaign, IL: Human Kinetics.

p. 63   Kellmann, M., Botterill, C., & Wilson, C. (1999). Recovery Cue. Unpublished recovery-assessment instrument. Calgary, Canada: National Sport Centre.

p. 64   Kellmann, M., Patrick, T., Botterill, C., & Wilson, C. (2002). The Recovery Cue and its use in applied settings: Practical suggestions regarding assessment and monitoring of recovery. In M. Kellmann (Ed.), *Enhancing recovery: Preventing underperformance in athletes* (pp. 57-80). Champaign, IL: Human Kinetics.

p. 65   Kellmann, M. (2002). (For full citation see page 53).

pp. 65-66   Kentta, G., & Hassmen, P. (1998). Overtraining and recovery: A conceptual model. *Sports Medicine, 26*, 1-16.

Kreider, R.B., Frey, A.C., & O'Toole, M.L. (Eds.). (1998). *Overtraining in sport.* Champaign, IL: Human Kinetics.

The Physiology of Overtraining Resources

p. 59   Armstrong, L.E., & VanHeest, J.L. (2002). The unknown mechanism of the overtraining syndrome. *Sports Medicine, 32*, 185-209.

Foster, C. (1998). Monitoring training in athletes with reference to overtraining syndrome. *Medicine and Science in Sports and Exercise, 30*, 1164-1168.

Petitbois, C., Cazorla, G., Poortmans, J.R., & Deleris, G. (2002). Biochemical aspects of overtraining in endurance sports. *Sports Medicine, 32*, 867-878.

Urhausen, A., & Kindermann, W. (2002). Diagnosis of overtraining: What tools do we have? *Sports Medicine, 32*, 95-102.

Uusitalo, A.L.T. (2001). Overtraining: Making a difficult diagnosis and implementing targeted treatment. *Physician and Sportsmedicine, 29*, 35-50.

Relaxation Resources

p. 69   Anderson, B. (2003). *Stretching* (20th ed.). Bolinas, CA: Shelter.

Benson, H., & Klipper, M. (2000). *The relaxation response.* New York: Harper Torch.

Davis, M., McKay, M., & Eshelman, E.R. (2000). *The relaxation and stress reduction workbook* (5th ed.). Oakland, CA: New Harbinger Publishers.

Jacobson, E. (1974). *Progressive relaxation* (3rd ed.). Chicago, IL: University of Chicago Press.

Kabat-Zinn, J. (1994). *Wherever you go there you are: Mindfulness meditation in everyday life.* New York: Hyperion.

Chapter 5

p. 73   Barlow, D. (2002). *Anxiety and its disorders*. New York: Guilford Press.

p. 76   Barlow, D. (2002).(For complete citation see page 73).

p. 78   Spielberger, C. (1985). Anxiety, cognition and affect: A state-trait perspective. In A.H. Tuma & J.D. Maser (Eds.), *Anxiety and the anxiety disorders*. Hillsdale, NJ: Erlbaum.

p. 79   Scheier, M.F., Carver, C.S., & Matthews, K.A. (1983). Attentional factors in the perception of bodily states. In J.T. Cacioppo & R.E. Petty (Eds.), *Social psychophysiology: A sourcebook*. New York: Guilford Press.

Nideffer, R.M. (1989). Theoretical and practical relationships between attention, anxiety, and performance in sport. In D. Hackfort & C.D. Spielberger (Eds.), *Anxiety in sport: An international perspective*. New York: Hemisphere.

Pauli, S.M., Dengler, W., Wiedemann, G., Montoya, P., Flor, H., Birbaumer, N., & Buchkremer, G. (1997). Behavioral and neurophysiological evidence for altered processing of anxiety-related words in panic disorder. *Journal of Abnormal Psychology*, *106*, 213-220.

Borkovec, T.D., & Inz, J. (1990). The nature of worry in generalized anxiety disorder: A predominance of thought activity. *Behaviour Research and Therapy*, *28*, 153-158.

p. 80   Bull, S., Albinson, J.G., Shambrook, C. (1996). *The mental game plan: Getting psyched for sport*. Cheltenham, UK: Sports Dynamics.

Yerkes, R.M., & Dodson, J.D. (1908). The relationship of strength of stimulus to rapidity of habit formation. *Journal of Comparative Neurology and Psychology*, *18*, 459-482.

p. 81   Hanin, Y. (2000). *Emotions in sport*. Champaign, IL: Human Kinetics.

p. 82   Gould, D., Tuffey, S., Hardy, L., & Lochbaum, M. (1993). Multidimensional state anxiety and middle distance running performance: An exploratory examination of Hanin's (1980) zones of optimal functioning hypothesis. *Journal of Applied Sport Psychology*, *5*, 85-95.

p. 83   Kerr, J.H. (1989). Anxiety, arousal, and sport performance: An application of reversal theory. In D. Hackfort & C. Spielberger (Eds.), *Anxiety in sport: An international perspective*. New York: Hemisphere.

p. 84   Swain, A. & Jones, G. (1996). Explaining performance variance: The relative contribution of intensity and direction dimensions of competitive state anxiety. *Anxiety, Stress & Coping: An International Journal*, *9*, 1-18.

Hardy, L. (1990). A catastrophic model of performance in sport. In J.G. Jones & L. Hardy (Eds.), *Stress and performance in sport* (pp. 81-106). Chichester, England: Wiley.

p. 85   Woodman, T., & Hardy, L. (2001). A case study of organizational stress in elite sport. *Journal of Applied Sport Psychology*, *13*, 207-238.

Gould, D., Horn, T., & Spreeman, J. (1983). Sources of stress in junior elite wrestlers. *Journal of Sport Psychology*, *5*, 159-171.

Martens, R., Burton, D., Vealey, R.S., Bump, L.A., & Smith, D.E. (1990). Development and validation of the Competitive State Anxiety Inventory-2. In R. Martens, R.S. Vealey, & D. Burton (Eds.), *Competitive anxiety in sport* (pp. 119-126). Champaign, IL: Human Kinetics.

Chapter 6

p. 94   Abrams, M. (2003, October) Anger management for athletes: The nuts and bolts. Workshop sponsored by the Association for the Advancement of Applied Sport Psychology. Philadelphia, PA.

Dollard, J., Doob, L., Miller, N., Mowrer, O., & Sears, R. (1939). *Frustration and aggression.* New Haven, CT: Yale University Press.

Berkowitz, L. (1969). The frustration-aggression hypothesis revisited. In L. Berkowitz (Ed.), *Roots of aggression: A re-examination of the frustration-aggression hypothesis* (pp. 1-28). New York: Atherton Press.

Berkowitz, L. (1989). Frustration-aggression hypothesis: Examination and reformulation. *Psychological Bulletin, 106*(1), 59-73.

Feindler, E.L., & Guttman, J. (1993). Cognitive-behavioral anger control training for groups of adolescents: A treatment manual. In C.W. LeCroix (Ed.), *Handbook of child and adolescent treatment manuals.* New York: Lexington Books.

Dodge, K., Price, J., Bachorowski, J., & Newman, J. (1990). Hostile attributional biases of severely aggressive adolescents. *Journal of Abnormal Psychology, 99,* 385-392.

Kendall, P.C., Ronan, K.R., & Epps, J. (1989). Aggression in children/adolescents: Cognitive-behavioral treatment perspectives. In D. Pepler & K. Rubin (Eds.), *Development and treatment of childhood aggression.* Hillsdale, NJ: Erlbaum.

p. 95   Bandura, A. (1977). *Social learning theory.* Englewood Cliffs, NJ: Prentice Hall.

Tedeschi, J., & Felson, R. (1994). *Violence, aggression, and coercive actions.* Washington, DC: American Psychological Association.

p. 96   Spielberger, C.D., Reheiser, E.C., & Syderman, S.J. (1995). Measurement of the experience, expression and control of anger. In H. Kassinove (Ed.), *Anger disorders: Definitions, diagnosis, and treatment* (pp. 49-67). Washington, DC: Taylor and Francis.

p. 97   Parcells, B., & Coplon, J. (1995). *Finding a way to win: The principles of leadership, teamwork, and motivation.* New York: Doubleday.

Husman, B.F., & Silva, J.M. (1984). Aggression in sport: Definitional and theoretical considerations. In J.M. Silva & R.S. Weinberg (Eds.), *Psychological foundations of sport* (pp. 246-260). Champaign, IL: Human Kinetics.

Nation, J.R., & LeUnes, A.D. (1983). Personality characteristics of intercollegiate players as determined by position, classification, and redshirt status. *Journal of Sport Behavior, 6,* 92-102.

Newby, R.W., & Simpson, S. (1991). Personality profile of nonscholarship college football players. *Perceptual and Motor Skills, 73,* 1083-1089.

Simpson, S., & Newby, R.W. (1994). Scores on profile of mood states of college football players from nonscholarship and scholarship programs. *Perceptual and Motor Skills, 78,* 635-640.

p. 98   Abrams, M. (2002, August). The myth of violent male athletes. Paper presented as part of symposium titled, "Athletes: Sitting on Top of the World . . . Right?" Sponsored by the American Psychological Association's Annual Convention. Chicago, IL.

Benedict, J., & Yaeger, D. (1998). *Pros and cons: The criminals who play in the NFL.* New York: Warner Books.

Morgan, W.P. (1980). Tests of champions: The iceberg profile. *Psychology Today,* *14*(4), 92-102, 108.

p. 99   Gill, D. (2000). *Psychological dynamics of sport and exercise.* Champaign, IL: Human Kinetics.

Brunelle, J., Janelle, C., & Tennant, K. (1999). Controlling competitive anger among male soccer players. *Journal of Applied Sport Psychology, 11*(2), 283-297.

p. 102   Tenenbaum, G., Stewart, E., Singer, R., & Duda, J. (1997). Aggression and violence in sport: An ISSP position stand. *Sport Psychologist, 11,* 1-7.

Widmeyer, W.N., Bray, S.R., Dorsch, K.R., & McGuire, E.J. (2001). Explanations for the occurrence of aggression: Theories and research. In J.M. Silva & D.E. Stevens (Eds.), *Psychological foundations of sport* (pp. 352-379). Boston: Allyn & Bacon.

Spielberger, C.D. (1991). *Manual for the State-Trait Anger Expression Inventory.* Odessa, FL: Psychological Assessment Resources

p. 103   The tests of Bredemeier and others are discussed in: Stephens, D.E. (1998). Aggression. In J.L. Duda (Ed.), *Advances in sport and exercise psychology measurement* (pp. 277-292). Champaign, IL: Human Kinetics.

p. 106   Meichenbaum, D. (1977). *Cognitive-behavior modification: An integrative approach.* New York: Plenum Press.

p. 110   Wolpe, J. (1954). Reciprocal inhibition as the main basis of psychotherapeutic effects. *AMA Archives of Neurology and Psychiatry, 72,* 205-226.

Wolpe, J. (1958). *Psychotherapy by reciprocal inhibition.* Stanford, CA: Stanford University Press.

Wolpe, J. (1981). Reciprocal inhibition and therapeutic change. *Journal of Behavior Therapy and Experimental Psychiatry, 12,* 185-188.

Chapter 7

p. 113   Moran, A. (1996). *The psychology of concentration in sport performers: A cognitive analysis.* East Sussex, UK: Psychology Press.

p. 115   Abernethy, B. (2001). Attention. In R.N. Singer, H.A. Hausenblas, & C.M. Jannelle (Eds.), *Handbook of sport psychology* (2nd ed., pp. 53-85). New York: John Wiley & Sons.

Posner, M. I., & Boies, S. J. (1971). Components of attention. *Psychological Review, 78,* 391-408.

p. 116   Lewis, B.P., & Linder, D.E. (1997). Thinking about choking? Attentional processes and paradoxical performance. *Personality and Social Psychology Bulletin, 23*(9), 937-944.

Easterbrook, J.A. (1959). The effect of emotion on cue utilization and organization of behaviour. *Psychological Review, 66,* 183-201.

Janelle, C.M. (2002). Anxiety, arousal and visual attention : A mechanistic account of performance variability. *Journal of Sports Sciences, 20,* 237-251.

p. 117   Vickers is quoted on the following Web pages: http://pbs.org/saf/1206/hotline/hvickers.htm.

An example of relevant research is: Harle, S., & Vickers, J.N. (2001). Training quiet eye (QE) improves accuracy in the basketball free throw. *The Sport Psychologist, 15,* 289-305.

p. 124   Wulf, G., & McNevin, N.H. (2003). Simply distracting learners is not enough: More evidence for the learning benefits of an external focus of attention. *European Journal of Sport Science, 3*(5).

Wulf, G., McConnel, N., Gärtner, M., & Schwarz, A. (2002). Feedback and attentional focus: Enhancing the learning of sport skills through external-focus feedback. *Journal of Motor Behavior, 34*, 171-182.

p. 125   Restak, R. (2003). *The new brain*. New York: Rodale Books.

Chapter 8

p. 127   Jowdy, D.P., Murphy, S.M., & Durtschi, S. (1989). *An assessment of the use of imagery by elite athletes: Athlete, coach and psychologist perspectives.* Unpublished report to the United States Olympic Committee. Colorado Springs, CO.

p. 129   Farah, M., Peronnet, F., Gonon, M.A., & Giard, M.H. (1988). Electrophysiological evidence for a shared representational medium for visual images and visual precepts. *Journal of Experimental Psychology: General, 117*, 248-257.

Mahoney, M.J., & Avener, M. (1977). Psychology of the elite athlete: An exploratory study. *Cognitive Therapy and Research, 1*, 135-141.

p. 130   Hardy, L. (1997). Three myths about applied consultancy work. *Journal of Applied Sport Psychology, 9*, 277–294.

MacIntyre, T., Moran, A., & Jennings, D. (2002). Is controllability of imagery related to canoe-slalom performance? *Perceptual and Motor Skills, 94*, 1245-1250.

p. 132   Decety, J. (1996). Neural representations for action. *Reviews in the Neurosciences, 7*, 285-297.

Finke, R.A. (1989). *Principles of mental imagery*. Cambridge, MA: MIT Press.

p. 133   Suinn, R.M. (1980). Psychology and sports performance: Principles and applications. In R. Suinn (Ed.), *Psychology in sports: Methods and applications* (pp. 26-36). Minneapolis, MN: Burgess International.

Paivio, A. (1985). Cognitive and motivational functions of imagery in human performance. *Canadian Journal of Applied Sport Sciences, 10*, 22-28.

p. 134   Taylor, S.E., Pham, L.B., Rivkin, I.D., & Armor, D.A. (1998). Harnessing the imagination: Mental simulation, self-regulation, and coping. *American Psychologist, 53*, 429–439.

Bandura, A. (1977). Self-efficacy: Toward a unifying theory of behavioral change. *Psychological Review, 84*, 191-215.

pp. 134-135   Callow, N., Hardy, L., & Hall, C. (1997). The effect of a motivational-mastery imagery intervention on the sport performance of three elite badminton players. *Journal of Applied Sport Psychology, 10*, S135.

p. 135   Feltz, D.L., & Landers, D.M. (1983). The effects of mental practice on motor skill learning and performance: A meta-analysis. *Journal of Sport Psychology, 5*, 25–57.

p. 136   Moran, A. (1996). *The psychology of concentration in sport performers: A cognitive analysis*. East Sussex, UK: Psychology Press.

p. 137   Ahsen, A. (1984). ISM: The triple code model for imagery and psychophysiology. *Journal of Mental Imagery, 8*, 15–42.

p. 138   Sackett, R.S. (1934). The influences of symbolic rehearsal upon the retention of a maze habit. *Journal of General Psychology, 10*, 376-395.

Perry, H.M. (1939). The relative efficiency of actual and imaginary practice in five selected tasks. *Archives of Psychology, 34*, 5-75.

p. 139   Meacci, W.G., & Price, E.E. (1985). Acquisition and retention of golf putting skill through the relaxation, visualization and body rehearsal intervention. *Research Quarterly for Exercise and Sport, 56*, 176-179.

Mackay, D.G. (1981). The problem of rehearsal or mental practice. *Journal of Motor Behavior, 13*, 274-285.

p. 140   Fenker, R.M., & Lambiotte, J.G. (1987). A performance enhancement program for a college football team: One incredible season. *Sport Psychologist, 1*, 224-236.

Rotella, R.J., Gansneder, B., Ojala, D., & Billing, J. (1980). Cognitions and coping strategies of elite skiers: An exploratory study of young developing athletes. *Journal of Sport Psychology, 2*, 350–354.

p. 141   Shelton, T.O., & Mahoney, M.J. (1978). The content and effect of "psyching-up" strategies in weightlifters. *Cognitive Therapy and Research, 2*, 275-284.

Hecker, J.E., & Kaczor, L.M. (1988). Application of imagery theory to sport psychology: Some preliminary findings. *Journal of Sport Psychology, 10*, 363-373.

p. 146   Lang, P.J. (1977). Imagery in therapy: An information-processing analysis of fear. *Behavior Therapy, 8*, 862–886.

p. 147   Hall, C.R., Mack, D., Paivio, A., & Hausenblas, H.A. (1998). Imagery use by athletes: Development of the Sport Imagery Questionnaire. *International Journal of Sport Psychology, 29*, 73–89.

Vella-Brodrick, D.A. (1999). Development and psychometric evaluation of the Multidimensional Mental Imagery Scale. Unpublished doctoral dissertation. Melbourne, Australia: Monash University.

Thomas, P.R., Murphy, S.M., & Hardy, L. (1999). Test of performance strategies: Development and preliminary validation of a comprehensive measure of athletes' psychological skills. *Journal of Sport Sciences, 17*, 1-15.

Murphy, S.M., & Martin, K. (2002). Imagery in sports. In T. Horn (Ed.), *Advances in sport psychology* (2nd ed., pp. 405-439). Champaign, IL: Human Kinetics.

p. 148   Budney, A.J., & Woolfolk, R.L. (1990). Using the wrong image: An exploration of the adverse effects of imagery on performance. *Journal of Mental Imagery, 14*, 75–86.

Murphy, S.M., Woolfolk, R.L., & Budney, A.J. (1988). The effects of emotive imagery on strength performance. *Journal of Sport and Exercise Psychology, 10*, 334–345.

Chapter 9

p. 155   Welch, J. (2001, December). Personal histories. *Harvard Business Review, 34.*

p. 156   Tichy, N. (2003). *The cycle of leadership.* New York: Harper Collins.

Chelladurai, P. (1999). *Human resource management in sport and recreation.* Champaign, IL: Human Kinetics.

Covey, S.R. (1991). *Principle-centered leadership.* New York: Summit Books.

p. 156   Goleman, D., Boyatzis, R., & McKee, A. (2001, December). Primal leadership. *Harvard Business Review*, 42-51.

Drucker, P. (1992). Managing for the future: The 1990s and beyond. New York: Truman Talley Books.

Tosi, H., Rizzo, J., & Carroll, S. (1986). *Managing organizational behavior.* Marshfield, MA: Pitman.

pp. 156-157   Chemers, M. (1997). *An integrative theory of leadership.* Hillsdale, NJ: Erlbaum.

Collins, J. (2001). *Good to great.* New York: Harper Collins.

Loehr, J., & Schwartz, T. (2001, January). The making of a corporate athlete. *Harvard Business Review*, 120-128.

Zenger, J., & Folkman, J. (2002). *The extraordinary leader.* New York: McGraw-Hill.

p. 157   Loehr, J., & Schwartz, T. (2003). *The power of full engagement.* New York: Free Press.

pp. 165-166   Kellmann, M. (2002). *Enhancing recovery.* Champaign, IL: Human Kinetics.

Chapter 10

p. 172   Vernacchia, R. (2003). Working with individual team sports: The psychology of track and field. In R. Lidor & K.P. Henschen (Eds.), *The psychology of team sports.* Morgantown, WV: Fitness Information Technology.

May, J.R., & Veach, T.L. (1987). The U.S. alpine ski team psychology program: A proposed consultation model. In J.R. May & M.J. Asken (Eds.), *Sports psychology.* PMA Publishing.

pp. 173-174   Estabrooks, P.A., & Dennis, P.W. (2003). The principles of team building and their application to sport teams. In R. Lidor & K.P. Henschen (Eds.), *The psychology of team sports.* Morgantown, WV: Fitness Information Technology.

p. 175   Burton, D., & Naylor, S. (2002). The Jekyll/Hyde nature of goals: Revisiting and updating goal-setting in sport. In T.S. Horn (Ed.), *Advances in sport psychology* (2nd ed.). Champaign, IL: Human Kinetics.

pp. 176-177   Carron, A.V., Brawley, L.R., & Widmeyer, W.N. (1998). The measurement of cohesiveness in sport groups. In J.L. Duda (Ed.), *Advances in sport and exercise psychology measurement.* Morgantown, WV: Fitness Information Technology.

p. 177   Widmeyer, W.N., Brawley, L.R., & Carron, A.V. (2002). Group dynamics in sport. In T.S. Horn (Ed.), *Advances in sport psychology* (2nd ed.). Champaign, IL: Human Kinetics.

Carron, A.V., Michelle, M.C., Wheeler, J., & Stevens, D. (2002). Cohesion and performance in sport: A meta analysis. *Journal of Sport and Exercise Psychology, 24,* 168-188.

p. 178   Horn, T.S. (2002). Coaching effectiveness in the sport domain. In T.S. Horn (Ed.), *Advances in sport psychology* (2nd ed.). Champaign, IL: Human Kinetics.

Walsh, B. (1998). *Finding the winning edge.* Champaign, IL: Sports Publishing.

p. 181   Hogan, R., Curphy, G.J., & Hogan, J. (1994, June). What we know about leadership. *American Psychologist*, 493-503.

pp. 182-183   Goleman, D. (2000, March-April). Leadership that gets results *Harvard Business Review*, 79-90.

p. 185   Chelladurai, P., & Reimer, H.A. (1998). Measurement of leadership in sports. In J.L. Duda (Ed.), *Advances in sport and exercise psychology measurement*. Morgantown, WV: Fitness Information Technology.

Studies describing the measurement of cohesion in group sports, as well as the use of the Group Environment Questionnaire (GEQ) are discussed in: Carron, A.V., Brawley, L.R., & Widmeyer, W.N. (1998). The measurement of cohesiveness in sport groups (pp. 213-266). In J.L. Duda (Ed.), *Advances in sport and exercise psychology measurement*. Morgantown, WV: Fitness Information Technology.

Chapter 11

p. 191   Krzyzewski, M., & Phillips, D.T. (2001). *Leading with the heart*. New York: Warner Books.

p. 192   Yukelson, D. (2001). Communicating effectively. In J.M. Williams (Ed.), *Applied sport psychology: Personal growth to peak performance*. Mountain View, CA: Mayfield.

p. 193   Rosenfeld, L., & Wilder, L. (1990). Communication fundamentals: Active listening. In C.J. Hardy & R.K. Crace (Eds.), *Sport Psychology Training Bulletin*. *1*(5), 1-8.

p. 195   Kriegel, R., & Brandt, D. (1996). *Sacred cows make the best burgers*. New York: Warner Books.

p. 196   Frank, M.O. (1999). *How to get your point across in 30 seconds or less*. New York: Simon and Schuster.

pp. 196-197   Anshel, M. (1997). *Sport psychology: From theory to practice*. Scottsdale, AZ: Gorsuch Scarisbrick.

p. 197   Weinberg, R.S., & Gould, D. (2003). *Foundations of sport and exercise psychology* (4th ed.). Champaign, IL: Human Kinetics.

Martens, R. (1987). *Coaches guide to sport psychology*. Champaign, IL: Human Kinetics.

Miller, G. (1956). The magical number seven plus or minus two: Some limits on our capacity for processing information. *Psychological Review, 63*, 81-87.

p. 198   Covey, S.R., (1990). The 7 habits of highly effective people. New York: Simon and Schuster

p. 200   Marx, J. (2003). *Season of life: A football star, a ballboy, a journey to manhood*. Washington, DC: JAM Publishing.

pp. 200-201   Smith, R., Smoll, F.L., & Curtis, B. (1979). Coach effectiveness training: A cognitive-behavioral approach to enhancing relationship skills in youth sport coaches. *Journal of Sport Psychology, 1*, 59-75.

p. 203   Rosenfeld & Wilder. (1990). (For complete citation see page 193).

p. 206   Burke, K.L. (1991). Dealing with sport officials. In C.J. Hardy & R.K. Crace (Eds.), *Sport Psychology Training Bulletin*. *2*(6), 1-6.

p. 209   Marx, J. (2003). (For complete citation see page 200).

Chapter 12

p. 216   Booth, W. (1987). Arthritis Institutes tackles sport. *Science, 237,* 846-847.

Zemper, E.D. (1989). Injury rates in a national sample of college football teams. *Physician and Sportsmedicine, 17,* 100, 102, 105-108, 113.

Gould, D., Udry, E., Bridges, D., & Beck, L. (1997a). Stress sources encountered when rehabilitating from season-ending ski injuries. *Sport Psychologist, 11,* 361-378.

Arendt, E., & Dick, R. (1995). Knee injury patterns among men and women in collegiate basketball and soccer: NCAA data and review of literature. *American Journal of Sports Medicine, 23*(6), 694-701.

U.S. Consumer Product Safety Commission (2000, April). *Baby boomer sport injuries.* Web site: http://www.cpsc.gov/library/boomer.pdf.

Rutherford, Jr., G., & Schroeder, T.J.(2004). *Sports-related injuries to persons 65 years of age and older.* Retrieved June 14, 2004, from U.S. Consumer Product Safety Commission. Web site: www.cpsc.gov/cpscpub/pubs/grand/aging/injury65.pdf.

p. 217   Larson, G.A., Starkey, C., & Zaichkowsky, L.D. (1996). Psychological aspects of athletic injuries as perceived by athletic trainers. *Sport Psychologist, 10,* 37-47.

p. 218   Little, J.C. (1969). The athlete's neurosis: A deprivation crisis. *Acta Psychiatica Scandinavia, 45,* 187-197.

Bramwell, S.T., Marsuda, M., Wagner, N.N., & Holmes, T.H. (1975). Psychosocial factors in athletic injuries: Development and application of the Social and Athletic Readjustment Rating Scale (SARRS). *Journal of Human Stress, 1,* 6-20.

Kiecolt-Glaser, J.K. (1992). Norman Cousins Memorial Lecture 1998. Stress, personal relationships, and immune function: Health Implications. *Brain, Behavior, and Immunity, 13,* 61-72.

p. 219   Williams, J., & Anderson, M. (1998). Psychosocial antecedents of sport injury: Review and critique of the stress and injury model. *Journal of Applied Sport Psychology, 10,* 5-25.

Udry, E., Gould, D., Bridges, D., & Beck, L. (1997). Down but not out: Athlete responses to season-ending injuries. *Journal of Sport and Exercise Psychology, 19,* 229-248.

Davis, J.O. (1991). Sports injuries and stress management: An opportunity for research. *Sport Psychologist, 5,* 175-182.

p. 220   Hardy, L., Jones, G., & Gould, D. (1996). *Understanding psychological preparation for sport: Theory and practice of elite performers.* New York: Wiley.

Gould, D., Udry, E., Bridges, D., & Beck, L. (1997b). Coping with season-ending injuries. *Sport Psychologist, 11,* 379-399.

p. 221   Folkman, S., & Lazarus, A. (1980). An analysis of coping in a middle-aged community sample. *Journal of Health and Social Behavior, 21,* 219-239.

p. 222   Kelly, S.D., & Lambert, S.S. (1992). Family support in rehabilitation: A review of research, 1980-1990. *Rehabilitation Counseling Bulletin, 36,* 98-117.

Rees, T., Smith, B., & Sparkes, A. (2003). The influence of social support on the lived experiences of spinal cord injured sportsmen. *Sport Psychologist, 17,* 135-156.

Rees, T., & Hardy, L. (2000). An investigation of the social support experiences of high-level sports performers. *Sport Psychologist, 14*, 327-347.

Cutrona, C., & Russell, D. (1980). Type of social support and specific stress: Toward a theory of optimal matching. In B.R. Sarason, I.G. Sarason, & G.R. Pierce (Eds.), *Social support: An interactional view* (pp. 319-366). New York: Wiley.

p. 223   Magyar, M., & Duda, J. (2000). Confidence restoration following athletic injury. *Sport Psychologist, 14*, 372-390.

Billings, A.G., & Moos, S.R.H. (1981). Coping, stress, and social resources among adults with unipolar depression. *Journal of Personality and Social Psychology, 46*, 877-891.

Gould, D. et al. (1997b). (For complete citation see page 220).

p. 224   Brewer, B. (1998). Adherence to sport injury rehabilitation programs. *Journal of Applied Sport Psychology, 10*, 70-82.

Dishman, R.K. (Ed.). (1988). *Exercise adherence: Its impact on public health*. Champaign, IL: Human Kinetics.

Prochaska, J.O., DiClemente, C.C., & Norcross, J.C. (1992). In search of how people change. *American Psychologist, 47*, 1102-1114.

pp. 224-225   Rosenstock, I.M. (1966). Historical origins of the health belief model. *Health Education Monographs, 2*, 328-335.

p. 225   Prentice-Dunn, S., & Rogers, R.W. (1986). Protection motivation theory and preventative health: Beyond the health belief model. *Health Education Research, 1*, 153-161.

Brewer, B., Cornelius, A., Van Raalte, J., Sklar, J., Pohlman, M., Krushell, R., & Ditmar, T. (2003). Protection motivation theory and adherence to sport injury rehabilitation revisited. *Sport Psychologist, 17*, 95-103.

Gilbourne, D., & Taylor, A. (1998). From theory to practice: The integration of goal perspective theory and life development approaches within an injury-specific goal-setting program. *Journal of Applied Sport Psychology, 10*, 124-139.

Ievleva, L., & Orlick, T. (1991). Mental links to enhanced healing: An exploratory study. *Sport Psychologist, 5*, 25-40.

Weinberg, R., & Gould, D. (1995). *Foundations of sport and exercise psychology*. Champaign, IL: Human Kinetics.

Magyar, M., & Duda, J. (2000). (For complete citation see page 223).

p. 226   Cupal, D., & Brewer, B. (2001). Effects of relaxation and guided imagery on knee strength, reinjury anxiety, and pain following anterior cruciate ligament reconstruction. *Rehabilitation Psychology, 46*, 28-43.

Gould, D. et al. (1997b). (For complete citation see page 220).

Simonton, O.C., & Simonton, S.S. (1975). Belief systems and management of the emotional aspects of malignancy. *Journal of Transpersonal Psychology, 7*, 29-47.

Ievleva, L., & Orlick, T. (1991). (For complete citation see page 225).

p. 227   Ievleva, L., & Orlick, T. (1991). (For complete citation see page 225).

Gould, D. et al. (1997b). (For complete citation see page 220).

Heil, J. (1993). *The psychology of sport injury*. Champaign, IL: Human Kinetics.

pp. 227-228   Steadman, R. (1993). A physician's approach to the psychology of injury. In J. Heil (Ed.), *The psychology of sport injury*. Champaign, IL: Human Kinetics.

p. 228   Dishman, R.K. (1988). (For complete citation see page 224).

Oldridge, N.B., Donner, A.P., Buck, C.W., Jones, N.L., Andrew, G.M., Parker, J.O., Cunningham, D.A., Kavanagh, T., Rechnitzer, P.A., & Suton, J.R. (1983). Predictors of dropouts from cardiac exercise rehabilitation: Ontario exercise-heart collaborative study. *American Journal of Cardiology, 51*, 70-74.

Gould, D. et al. (1997b). (For complete citation see page 220).

Magyar, M., & Duda, J. (2000). (For complete citation see page 223).

Engel, G.L. (1977). The need for a new medical model: A challenge for bio-medicine. *Science, 196*(4286), 129-136.

Engel, G.L. (1992). How much longer must medicine's science be bound by a seventeenth-century worldview? *Psychotherapy and Psychosomatics, 57*, 3-16.

Griffith, J.L., & Griffith, M.E. (1994). *The body speaks: Therapeutic dialogues for mind-body problems.* New York: Basic Books.

King, D.E. (2000). *Faith, spirituality, and medicine: Toward the making of a healing practitioner.* Binghamton, NY: Haworth Pastoral Press.

McKee, D.D., & Chappel, J.N. (1992). Spirituality and medical practice. *Journal of Family Practice, 35*, 205-208.

Sulmasy, D.P. (2002). A biopsychosocial-spiritual model for the care of patients at the end of life. *Gerontologist, 42*, 24-33.

p. 233   Udry, E. (1998, March). The psychology of athletic injuries. Presentation at the University of North Carolina-Greensboro Sport Psychology Conference. Greensboro, NC.

p. 234   Melzack, R., & Wall, P. (1965). Pain mechanisms: A new theory. *Science, 150*, 171-179.

Vernacchia, R., Reardon, J., & Templin, D. (1997). Sudden death in sport: Managing the aftermath. *Sport Psychologist, 11*, 223-235.

Chapter 13

p. 237   Mintz, LB., & Betz, N.E. (1988). Prevalence and physical correlates of eating-disordered behaviors among undergraduate women. *Journal of Counseling Psychology, 35*, 463-471.

Ryan, J. (1995). *Little girls in pretty boxes: The making and breaking of elite gymnasts and figure skaters.* New York: Doubleday.

p. 239   American Psychiatric Association. (2000). Diagnostic and statistical manual of mental disorders: IV-TR (4th ed.). Washington, DC: Author.

p. 240   American College of Sports Medicine. (1997). ACSM position stand on the female athlete triad. *Medicine and Science in Sports and Exercise, 29*(5), i-ix.

Coen, S.P., & Ogles, B.M. (1993). Psychological characteristics of the obligatory runner: A critical examination of the anorexia analogue hypothesis. *Journal of Sport and Exercise Psychology, 15*, 338-354.

Willis, J.D., & Campbell, L.F. (1992). *Exercise psychology.* Champaign, IL: Human Kinetics.

Yates, A., Leehey, K., & Shisslak, C.M. (1983). Running: An analogue or anorexia? *New England Journal of Medicine, 308*, 251-255.

Yeager, K.K., Agostini, R., Nattiv, A., & Drinkwater, B. (1993). The female athlete triad: Disordered eating, amenorrhea, osteoporosis. *Medicine and Science in Sports and Exercise, 25,* 775-777.

p. 241   Burckes-Miller, M.E., & Black, D.R. (1991). College athletes and eating disorders: A theoretical context. In D.R. Black (Ed.), *Eating disorders among athletes: Theory, issues, and research.* Reston, VA: American Alliance for Health, Physical Education, Recreation, and Dance.

p. 242   American Psychiatric Association. (2000). (For complete citation see page 239).

Thompson, R.A., & Sherman, R.T. (1993). Reducing the risk of eating disorders in athletics. *Eating Disorders: The Journal of Treatment and Prevention, 1,* 65-78.

p. 243   Hausenblaus, H.A., & Carron, A.V. (1999). Eating disorder indices and athletes: An integration. *Journal of Sport and Exercise Psychology, 21,* 230-258.

Sundgot-Borgen, J. (1993). Prevalence of eating disorders in elite female athletes. *International Journal of Sport Nutrition, 3,* 29-40.

Sundgot-Borgen, J. (1994). Risk and trigger factors for the development of eating disorders in female elite athletes. *Medicine and Science in Sports and Exercise, 2,* 414-419.

Thompson, R.A., & Sherman, R.T. (1999). Athletes, athletic performance, and eating disorders: Healthier alternatives. *Journal of Social Issues, 55,* 317-337.

pp. 243-244   Hausenblaus, H.A., & Carron, A.V. (2002). Assessing eating disorder symptoms in sport groups: A critique with recommendations for future research. *International Sports Journal, 6*(1), 65-74.

p. 247   International Gymnast. (1994). Christy Henrich: 1972-94. 48-49.

Johnson, C., Powers, P.S., Dick, R. (1999). Athletes and eating disorders: The National Collegiate Athletic Association study. *International Journal of Eating Disorders, 26,* 179-188.

Thompson, R.A., & Sherman, R.T. (1993). (For complete citation see page 242).

p. 249   Rosen, L.W., McKeag, D.B., Hough, D.O., & Curley, V. (1986). Pathogenic weight-control behavior in female athletes. *Physician and Sportsmedicine, 14,* 79-86.

Swoap, R.A., & Murphy, S.M. (1995). Eating disorders and weight management in athletes. In S.M. Murphy (Ed.), *Sport psychology interventions.* Champaign, IL: Human Kinetics.

Thompson, R.A. (1987). Management of the athlete with an eating disorder: Implications for the sport management team. *Sport Psychologist, 1,* 114-126.

p. 252   Swoap, R.A., & Murphy, S.M. (1995). (For complete citation see page 249).

Yalom, I.D. (1985). *The theory and practice of group psychotherapy.* New York: Basic Books.

Chapter 14

p. 255   Prokop, L. (1970). The struggle against doping and its history. *Journal of Sportsmedicine and Physical Fitness, 10,* 45-48.

p. 256   Yesalis, C.E., & Cowart, V.S. (1998). *The steroids game.* Champaign, IL: Human Kinetics.

Notes

p. 257   Danish, S.J., Petitpas, A., & Hale, B.D. (1995). Psychological interventions: A life development model. In S.M. Murphy (Ed.), *Sport psychology interventions* (pp. 283-306). Champaign, IL: Human Kinetics.

Sonstroem, R.J. (1997). Physical activity and self-esteem. In W.P. Morgan (Ed.), *Physical activity and mental health* (pp. 127-143). Washington, DC: Taylor & Francis.

p. 258   Hughes, R., & Coakley, J.J. (1991). Positive deviance among athletes. *Sociology of Sport Journal, 8*, 307-325.

Leonard, W.M. (1998). *A sociological perspective of sport* (5th ed.). Boston: Allyn & Bacon.

p. 259   Chappel, J.N. (1987). Drug use and abuse in the athlete. In J.R. May & M.J. Asken (Eds.), *Sport psychology: The psychological health of the athlete* (pp. 187-211). New York: PMA Publishing.

Grollman, A.P. (2003, February 23). Senselessly, dangers of dietary drugs remain. *New York Times*, p. D7.

Lombardo, J. (1993). The efficacy and mechanisms of action of anabolic steroids. In C.E. Yesalis (Ed.), *Anabolic steroids in sport and exercise* (pp. 89-106). Champaign, IL: Human Kinetics.

Prokop, L. (1990). The history of doping. In J. Park (Ed.), *Proceedings of the international symposium on drug abuse in sport* (pp. 1-9). Seoul, Korea: Korean Institute of Science and Technology.

Mottram, D.R. (1999). Banned drugs in sport: Does the International Olympic Committee (IOC) list need updating? *Sports Medicine, 27*, 1-10.

Mottram, D.R., Reilly, T., & Chester, N. (1997). Doping in sport: The extent of the problem. In R. Reilly & M. Orne (Eds.), *The clinical pharmacology of sport and exercise* (pp. 3-12). Amsterdam: Excerpta Medica.

Sawka, M.N., Joyner, M.J., Miles, D.S., Roberson, R.J., Spriet, L.L., & Young, A.J. (1996). American College of Sports Medicine position stand: The use of blood doping as an ergogenic aid. *Medicine and Science in Sports and Exercise, 28*, i-viii.

p. 260   See: http://sportsillustrated.cnn.com/cycling/1998/tourdefrance/news/1998/07/22/financial_impact for a story about the 1998 Tour de France scandal.

pp. 260-261   Williams, M.H. (1998). *The ergogenics edge: Pushing the limits of sports performance*. Champaign, IL: Human Kinetics.

p. 261   Strauss, G., & Mihoces, G. (1998, June 4). Jury still out on creatine use. *USA Today*, pp. C1-C2.

Goldberg, R. (1998). *Taking sides: Clashing views on controversial issues in drugs and society* (3rd ed.). New York: McGraw-Hill.

For more information on the controversial issue of creatine use, visit: http://sportsillustrated.cnn.com/olympics/news/1998/12/14/olympics_creatine/ and http://sportsmedicine.about.com/library/weekly/aa042199.htm.

p. 262   The NIDA Web site can be obtained on the Internet: www.nida.nih.gov/ResearchReports/Steroids/anabolicsteroids3.html.

p. 263   Branch, J.D. (2002). Performance-enhancing drugs and ergogenic aids. In L.L. Mostofsky & L.D. Zaichkowsky (Eds.), *Medical and psychological aspects of sport and exercise* (pp. 55-71). Morgantown, WV: Fitness Information Technology.

Leccese, A.P. (1991). *Drugs and society: Behavioral medicines and abusable drugs*. Englewood Cliffs, NJ: Prentice Hall.

Schlaadt, R.G., & Shannon, P.T. (1994). *Drugs: Use, misuse, and abuse* (4th ed.). Englewood Cliffs, NJ: Prentice Hall.

p. 264 Goldberg, R. (1998). (For complete citation see page 261).

"Designer steroid" confounds scientists: Ignites sports scandal. (2003, October 24). *Daily News Journal*, p. A5.

Patrick, D. (2003, October 27). Recent steroid furor prompts two senators to propose crackdown. *USA Today*, p. 12C.

p. 266 Groppel, J. (2000). *The corporate athlete*. New York: Wiley.

Loehr, J., & Schwartz, T. (2003). *The power of full engagement*. New York: Free Press.

p. 267 Anshel, M.H., & Russell, K.G. (1997). Examining athletes' attitudes toward using anabolic steroids and their knowledge of the possible effects. *Journal of Drug Education, 27*, 121-145.

p. 269 Anshel, M.H. (1993). Psychology of drug use. In R.N. Singer, M. Murphey, & L.K. Tennant (Eds.), *Handbook of research on sport psychology* (pp. 851-876). New York: Macmillan.

Collins, G.B., Pippenger, C.E., & Janesz, J.W. (1984). Links in the chain: An approach to the treatment of drug abuse on a professional football team. *Cleveland Clinic Quarterly, 51*, 485-492.

Goldman, B., Bush, R., & Klatz, P. (1984). *Death in the locker room: Steroids and sports*. South Bend, IN: Icarus Press.

Pope, H., Phillips, K., & Olvardia, R. (2000). *The Adonis complex: The secret crisis of male body obsession*. New York: Free Press.

Branch, J.D. (2002). (For complete citation see page 263).

p. 271 Alzado, L. (1991, July 8). I'm sick and I'm scared. *Sports Illustrated, 75*(27), 21-24, 27.

Anshel, M.H. (2001). Drug abuse in sport: Causes and cures. In J.M. Williams (Ed.), *Applied sport psychology: Personal growth to peak performance* (4th ed.). Mountain View, CA: Mayfield.

Anshel, M.H. (1991b). Causes for drug abuse in sport: A survey of intercollegiate athletes. *Journal of Sport Behavior, 14*, 283-307.

Carr, C.M., & Murphy, S.M. (1995). Alcohol and drugs in sport. In S.M. Murphy (Ed.), *Sport psychology interventions* (pp. 283-306). Champaign, IL: Human Kinetics.

p. 273 Berkow, I. (2003, March 12). Plan to refuse steroid testing is exception, not rule. *New York Times*, p. C1.

p. 275 Anshel, M.H. (1991a). Cognitive-behavioral strategies for combating drug abuse in sport: Implications for coaches and sport psychology consultants. *Sport Psychologist, 5*, 152-166.

Anshel, M.H. (1990). Commentary of the National Drugs in Sport Conference, 1989: Treating the causes and symptoms. *Australian Journal of Medicine and Science in Sport, 22*, 49-56.

Schlaadt, R.G., & Shannon, P.T. (1994). (For complete citation see page 263).

p. 276 National Institute on Drug Abuse. (2000, April). *Research report*. National Institute of Health Publication Number 00-3721.

Chapter 15

p. 282   For a better theoretical understanding of the nature of consulting in sport psychology, see: Murphy, S. (1995). Introduction to sport psychology interventions. In S. Murphy (Ed.), *Sport psychology interventions*. Champaign, IL: Human Kinetics.

p. 286   For a good behind the scenes look at golf see Bob Rotella's book: Rotella, R. (1996). *Golf is not a game of perfect*. New York: Simon and Schuster.

p. 288   Two different views of the nature of sport psychology in professional sport are: Price, F., & Andersen, M. (2000). Into the maelstrom: A five-year relationship from college ball to the NFL. In M. Andersen (Ed.), *Doing sport psychology*. Champaign, IL: Human Kinetics. And: , Ravizza, K. (1990). Sport psychology consultations issues in professional baseball. *Sport Psychologist, 4,* 330-340.

p. 289   For a comprehensive look at the crossover from sport to business to performing arts, see: Kate Hays and Charlie Brown's recent book on the subject: Hays, K., & Brown, C. (2004) *You're on: Consulting for peak performance*. Washington, DC: American Psychological Association.

     For a better look at sport psychology in a college counseling setting, see: Greenspan, M., & Andersen, M. (1995). Providing psychological services to student athletes: A developmental psychological model. In S. Murphy (Ed.), *Sport psychology interventions*. Champaign, IL: Human Kinetics.

p. 290   For more detailed illustrations of psychology at the Olympic Games, Gould had written specifically about his work in 1998 with the ski team, and McCann has written about the work in general: Gould, D. (2001). Sport Psychology and the Nagano Olympic Games: The case of the U.S. Freestyle Ski Team. In G. Tenenbaum (Ed.), *The practice of sport psychology*. Morgantown, WV: Fitness Information Technology.

     McCann, S. (2000). Doing sport psychology at the really big show. In M. Andersen (Ed.), *Doing sport psychology*. Champaign, IL: Human Kinetics.

Chapter 16

p. 297   Gardner, F.L., & Moore, Z.E. (2004, March). The Multi-Level Classification System for Sport Psychology (MCS-SP): Toward a structured assessment and conceptualization of athlete-clients. *Sport Psychologist, 18*(1), 89-109.

Chapter 17

p. 306   Hardy, L., Jones, G., & Gould, D. (1996). *Understanding psychological preparation for sport: Theory and practice of elite performers*. Chichester, England: Wiley.

     Meyers, A.W., Whelan, J.P., & Murphy, S.M. (1996). Cognitive behavioral strategies in athletic performance enhancement. In M. Hersen, R.M. Eisler, & P.M. Miller (Eds.), *Progress in behavior modification* (pp. 137-164, Vol. 30). Pacific Grove, CA: Brooks/Cole.

     Weinberg, R.S., & Williams, J.M. (2001). Integrating and implementing a psychological skills training program. In J.M. Williams (Ed.), *Applied sport psychology:*

Personal growth to peak performance (4th ed., pp. 347-377). Mountain View, CA: Mayfield, 347-377.

p. 308   Orlick, T., & Partington, J. (1987). The sport psychology consultant: Analysis of critical components as viewed by Canadian Olympic athletes. *The Sport Psychologist, 1,* 4-17.

Partington, J., & Orlick, T. (1987). The sport psychology consultant evaluation form. *The Sport Psychologist, 1,* 309-317.

Partington, J., & Orlick, T. (1987). The sport psychology consultant: Olympic coaches' views. *The Sport Psychologist, 1,* 95-102.

Partington, J., & Orlick, T. (1991). An analysis of Olympic sport psychology consultants' best-ever consulting experiences. *The Sport Psychologist, 5,* 183-193.

Anderson, A., Miles, A., Robinson, P., & Mahoney, C. (2004). Evaluating the athlete's perception of the sport psychologist's effectiveness: What should we be assessing? *Psychology of Sport and Exercise, 5,* 255-277.

Gould, D., Murphy, S., Tammen, V., & May, J. (1991). An evaluation of U.S. Olympic sport psychology consultant effectiveness. *The Sport Psychologist, 5,* 111-127.

Lloyd, R.J., & Trudel, P. (1999). Verbal interactions between an eminent mental training consultant and elite level athletes: A case study. *The Sport Psychologist, 13,* 418-443.

Simons, J.P., & Andersen, M.B. (1995). The development of consulting practice in applied sport psychology: Some personal perspectives. *The Sport Psychologist, 9,* 449-468.

Weigand, D.A., Richardson, P.A., & Weinberg, R.S. (1999). A two-stage evaluation of a sport psychology internship. *Journal of Sport Behavior, 22,* 83-104.

Petitpas, A.J., Giges, B., & Danish, S.J. (1999). The sport psychologist–athlete relationship: Implications for training. *The Sport Psychologist, 13,* 344-357.

Bordin, E.S. (1994). Theory and research on the therapeutic working alliance: New directions. In A.O. Horvath & L.S. Greenberg (Eds.), *The working alliance: Theory, research, and practice* (pp. 13-37). Chichester, England: Wiley.

Martin, D.J., Garske, J.P., & Davis, M.K. (2000). Relation of the therapeutic alliance with outcome and other variables: A meta-analytic review. *Journal of Consulting and Clinical Psychology, 68,* 438-450.

p. 310   Andersen, M.B. (2002). *Doing sport psychology.* Champaign, IL: Human Kinetics.

Index

Note: The italicized *f* or *t* following a page number denotes a figure or table on that page. The italicized *ff or tt* following a page number denotes multiple figures or tables on that page

A

AAASP (Association for the Advancement of Applied Sport Psychology) xi, 300
Abernethy, Bruce 115, 118
ability, perceptions of 25-26
Abrams, Mitch 72
absence of noise 122
achievement goals 28-29
achievement goal theory 29t-31t
ACL injury 216, 225-226
action 114f
active listening 108
adolescent athletes. *See also* athletes; chapter scenarios; children
  ego orientation 28
  factors affecting performance 23
  need for support 34-35
  overtraining 51
  parental support 46
adversity 160, 162-164, 162t, 163tt
aerobic activity following injuries 232
aggression. *See also* anger; violence in sport
  and injury risks 218
  anger and 94
  in hockey players 4-5
  sport-specific measures of 103
Ahsen, Akhter 137, 148
AIS (Australian Institute of Sport) 123
alertness 115-116
Alzado, Lyle 269
ambushing 203
American College of Sports Medicine 240
American Medical Association 266
American Psychological Association (APA) xi, 295, 304
Ames, Carole 24
Anabolic Steroid Control Act (2003) 264
anabolic steroids 262-264
Andersen, Mark 278
Anderson, Sparky 200
anger. *See also* aggression; violence in sport
  controlling 99
  defined 96
  hassle log 100, 104f
  hostility bias 94-95
  injury risks resulting from 218
  management studies 102
  management through exercise 110

overarousal through imagery 141
physiological signs of 105
situational cues 100-101
time-outs for control 108-109
triggers 106
warning signs for coaches 100-102
anger-in 96
anger interventions 105-110
anger-management 103, 112
anger-management training 110-112
anger-out 96
anorexia nervosa 239, 243, 245
Anshel, Mark H. 196, 197, 213
anxiety. *See also* chapter scenarios
  cognitive 77, 79, 84
  competitive 140-141
  competitive trait 218
  defined 75
  direction 84
  effect on performance 80-85, 81f, 82ff
  ego orientation 26
  frequency 84
  imagery and 150
  intervention models 78
  making it work for you 87-88
  performance decrement and 116
  physical changes during 74-75
  physiological symptoms 77
  terms used to label 75-76
  threatening cues 79
APA (American Psychological Association) 295
Apter, Michael 83-84
archery 123
Aristotle 113
Armstrong, Lance 6
arousal
  defined 75
  reversal theory 83-84
assertiveness 97
assessment form, imagery 149f
assessments 29t-31t, 184-185
assessments, pencil-and-paper 61, 62t, 63-64, 63t, 87
Association for the Advancement of Applied Sport Psychology (AAASP) xi, 300
athlete preparedness, time course of 56ff
athletes. *See also* adolescent athletes; children; elite athletes; injured athletes
  achievement assessment 34

achievement-goal profiles 32
anger misconceptions of 103
assertive 97
at risk for injuries 218-219
college 9
coping with injury 228-236
coping with stress 26
ego-involved 20
goal preferences 22-23
individual motivational state 14-15
minimizing overtraining 69
myth of the violent athlete 97-98
perceptions of ability 25-26
task-involved 20
Athletes Training and Learning to Avoid Steroids (ATLAS) 276
ATLAS (Athletes Training and Learning to Avoid Steroids) 276
attention
  as alertness 115
  as a resource 116
  cognitive anxiety and 79
  selective 119
  term uses 115-116
attentional allocation 117
attentional control 125
attentional focus 124
attentional narrowing 116
attentional system 114, 114f, 123
attribution characteristics 11, 12t
Auch, Derrick 41
Auch, Susan 41
Auerbach, Red 6, 203
Australian Institute of Sport (AIS) 123
autogenic relaxation 68
autogenics 68
automated performance 124-125
autonomy 8-9
avoidance 87-88
avoidance strategies 221-222

B

Balague, Gloria 72
Bandura, Albert 134
Barkley, Charles 95
Barlow, David H. 73
Barr, Don 160, 164
basketball 118-119, 187
Baumeister, Roy 43, 47
Bechler, Steve 258-259, 266
behavior
  ABCs of 106
  confirming 204-205

defined xii
goal setting xii
moral 27
retaliatory 101
behavioral cues 100
behavioral symptoms of anxiety 77
behaviors, nonverbal 200-201
being in the "zone" 13-14
beliefs, irrational 39
Benedict, Jeff 98
Benitez, Armando 93
Bennis, Warren 156
Bertrand, John 277, 278
Bertuzzi, Todd 96
beta-blockers 262
Betz, Nancy 237-238
Biden, Joseph 264
biofeedback 68-69
Black, David 241
Blair, Bonnie 41
Blalock, Jane 71
body language 201
Boies, S.J. 115
Bompa, T.O. 55f
boredom 13
Borg's Rating of Perceived Exertion (RPE) 60
Botterill, Cal 2, 38f
Branch, J.D. 260
Brandt, David 195, 200
Brashear, Donald 96
Bredemeier, Brenda Light 103
Brooks, Herb 153
Brown, Charles 213
Brown, Matt 43
Brunelle, John 99, 111
Budney, Alan 148
Building Men for Others program 200, 209
bulimia nervosa 239, 243, 245
Bull, Stephen J. 80
Burckes-Miller, Mardie 241
Burke, Kevin 206
burnout 53

C
caffeine 262
California Task Force to Promote Self-Esteem and Personal and Social Responsibility Toward a State of Esteem vii
Callow, Nichola 134-135
canoeists 130-131
caring 195-196
Carr, Chris 271
Carroll, Stephen 156
Carron, Bert 176
Cashmore, Ellis 264-265
Casual Dimension Scales 16
catastrophe theory 84-85
catharsis 95
CBAS (Coaching Behavior Assessment System) 185
chapter scenarios
anxiety 74
eating disorders 246-247
effective communication 194
ego 21

ethical dilemmas 41
imagery 127
injuries 215-216
irritability points 106
leadership 160
overtraining 51-52
overtraining and injuries 58
performance-enhancing drugs 258-259
sense of purpose 8
sport psychologists 282-283, 299, 307
teamwork 187
Chelladurai, Packianathan 156
Chemers, Martin 156
children. See also adolescent athletes; athletes
anxiety disorders 78
coaches influence on achievement goals 24
cognitive abilities 23
irrational beliefs 39
overtraining 51
choking 72
choking phenomenon 121
Clemens, Roger 125
closed sport 123
coaches
achievement-goal athlete profile 32
anger warning signs in players 100-102
as role models 67, 111
children's achievement goals and 24
communication with game officials 206-207
communication with players 107-108
effective communication skills 208-209
minimizing overtraining 69
periodization errors 54-57
postgame observations for athletes 35
"pushy parent" phenomenon 176
recovery strategies 66-67
role in drug-use prevention 273-274
role of 111
teaching emotional management 46
techniques using achievement goal theory 29t-31t
coaching
role of the coach 191-192
tips for effective 178-179
Coaching Behavior Assessment System (CBAS) 185
coaching behaviors 178
coacting teams 172
Coakley, Jay 51, 258
Cogan, Karen D. 213
cognition xii, 114f
cognitive activities 132-133
cognitive anxiety 84
cognitive-appraisal model 220

cognitive-behavioral psychology xii
cognitive science 125
cognitive tasks 138-139
cognitive variables 117
cohesion, defined 176-177
collective belief 47-48
college athletes 9
comfort zone, pushing beyond 167
communicating with the media 207-208
communication. See also feedback
channels 195
effective 196-197
objective 196
self-evaluation assessment 193f
skills 35, 107-108
with players 192
competence in teen athletes 28
competition
ethical dilemmas 41
pressure of 37-38
win-win perspective 43-44
competitive anxiety 140-141
Competitive Performance Mentality (CPM) 33-34
competitive pressure 38-39, 38f
competitive routines 90-91
Competitive State Anxiety Inventory-2 (CSAI-2) 85-87, 86f
competitive trait anxiety 218
completion hypothesis 94
concentration 121, 142-143
confidence 8-9, 134-135
confidence building 141-142
confirming behavior 204-205
Connors, Jimmy 122
consciousness 13-14
constructive criticism strategy 201-203
contract, sport-involvement 36
cooperation 179-180
coping with injury 228-236
Courtney, Bryce xi
Covey, Stephen 198
CPM (Competitive Performance Mentality) 33-34
creatine 260-261
credibility 198
criminal statistics 98
criticism, giving 201-202
CSAI-2 (Competitive State Anxiety Inventory-2) 85-87, 86f
Csikszentmihalyi, Mihaly 13, 17, 124-125
cues
attentional bias toward 79
behavioral 100
relevant 115

D
Decety, Jean 132
decision-style questionnaires 185
depression 228
Diagnostic and Statistical Manual Of Mental Disorders IV-TR 239, 242-243
directed energy flow 169

Index

disconnected values model 266-267, 267f
disordered-eating behavior 238, 244-245
distance running 58
distractibility 150
distractions 114, 120-124
distraction strategies 221
Doan, Catriona Le May 41-42
doping 259
drive theory 4
Drucker, Peter 156
drug use among athletes. *See* performance-enhancing drugs
Durtschi, Shirley 127

E
Easterbrook, James A. 116
eating disorders
    athletes at risk 242-243
    determinants of 241-242
    identifying 244-247
    intervention strategies 247-248
    not otherwise specified 239
    overview 237-238
    prevention 249-252
    risk-reduction strategies 248-249
    sports most affected by 243-244
    treatment options 252-253
effective communication 196-197
effective listening 196
ego-involved athletes 20-22, 134, 142
ego orientation
    adolescent athletes 28
    anxiety associated with 26
    characteristics of 10
    perceived ability 25
    suppressing the development of 27-28
elevated stress response 218
Eliot, John F. 2
elite athletes. *See also* athletes
    attributes of 45
    badminton players 134-135
    distractions 123
    iceberg profile 99
    motivation 12
    overtraining by runners 50-51
    Rusko orthostatic heart rate test 59-60
emotional distress 54
emotional energy 157-158
emotional fitness 38-39
emotional imagery 136
emotional intelligence 182-183, 183t
emotional labeling intervention 103, 104f
emotional leadership 157
emotional management 46
emotional support 222
emotional symptoms of anxiety 77
emotion-based performance 136
emotion-focused strategies 221-222

emotions 46, 146
empathy 199-200
energy
    directed flow 169
    directional focus of 159
    flow and origin of 159f
    multidimensional engagement 160f
    pyramid hierarchy of 157-158, 158f
    rituals to manage 167-168
energy-based leadership 157
energy-management principles for leaders 165-170
energy pyramid 158f
engagement, multidimensional 160f
Enhancing Recovery (Kellmann) 38f, 65
environment
    anxiety-generating 78
    role of in sport 123
environmental challenges 44
environmental stresses 54
equestrian team, West Coast 173
ergogenics in sport 260
Erhmann, Joe 200, 209
escape 87-88
esteem support 222
ethical dilemmas 41
exercise for anger management 110
exercise heart rate 60
exercises
    imagery xii, 34
    Newspaper Article 34
exertion, rating perceived 60
expressive mind-set 209-210
external distractions 121, 123
external imagery 130
extrinsic encouragement 8

F
failure, fear of 42
fatigue 38-39, 53, 59
fear
    defined 75
    irrational 43
    of failure 42
feedback. *See also* communication
    athlete performance 287-288
    immediate 197-198
    motivational 9
    negative 24
    postgame self-reflection 35
feel, sense of 145-146
Feltz, Deborah 135
female athlete triad 240
figure skaters 137-138
figure skating 71
fitness, emotional 38-39
fitness model 38f
flow 13-14, 38, 124
fMRI (functional magnetic resonance imaging) 132-133
focus 38, 121
focus, outward 90
football
    developing empathy 200-201

motivation and research 6-7
NFL players charged with crimes 98
overtraining and injuries 58
Foreman, George 125
Frank, Milo 196
free will 6
frequency 84
Freud, Sigmund 4
frustration-aggression hypothesis 94
functional equivalence 133
functional magnetic resonance imaging (fMRI) 132-133

G
game challenge 33
gamesmanship 122
Garfield, Charles 44
genetics, mental 5
GEQ (Group Environment Questionnaire) 185
Gibson, Jack 153
global challenges 44
goal orientations 9, 23
goals. *See also* achievement goals
    attainable for rehabilitation 223
    basing success on 19-20
    factors influencing tennis players 28-29
    research on achievement goals 28-29
    self-challenge 34
goal setting xii, 40
goal-setting strategies 173-175
Goldberg, Raymond 264
Goleman, Daniel 156
golfers
    distraction 120
    imagery-rehearsal strategy 139
    immediate effect of actions 124
Gordon's Test of Imagery Control 147
Gould, Dan 51, 197, 220-222
Griffith, Coleman Roberts vii, xi
Groppel, Jack 266, 270
Group Environment Questionnaire (GEQ) 185
guided imagery 68

H
Hack, Bradley 278
Hale, Bruce 72
Hall, Craig 147
Hanin, Yuri 81
Hardy, Lew 130, 147-148
Harwood, Chris 2
hassle log 100, 103, 104f
Hatch, Orrin 264
Hayden, Laurie 278
health belief model 224-225
hearing, imagery experiences of 144-145
heart rate
    imagery effect on 141
    resting 59-60
heart rate monitors 69

Heil, John 227
Henrich, Christy 247
HGH (human growth hormone) 261-262
hockey
    aggression among players 4-5
    imagery to handle distractions 123
    National junior team 47-48
    penalty minutes for aggression 99
Hogan, Robert 181-182
Horn, Thelma 178
hostile violence 96-97
hostility bias 94
Hull, C.L. 4
human emotions, seven basic 46
human growth hormone (HGH) 261-262
hypercompetitiveness 47

I
iceberg profile studies 99
ice hockey 82f, 153
imagery. See also chapter scenarios
    assessment form 149f
    canoeists use of 130-131
    concentration improvement through 142-143
    consultants 151
    control problems with 150
    effects on self-confidence 134-135
    exercises xii, 34
    feedback 130
    for anger control 105
    for race strategy 140
    for performance improvement 131-132
    guided 68
    mastery over distractions 123
    mental practice 135-136
    motivational function of 133-134
    overview 127
    potential problems in 148-151
    psyching up 141
    skill-retention function of 139
    terms 129-130
imagery ability 131, 144-146
imagery and relaxation 226-227
imagery assessments 147-148, 149f
imagery perspective 129-130
imaginary practice 138-139
imagination 134
individual differences 15
individual team sports 172
Individual Zones of Optimal Functioning (IZOF) 81-83, 82ff
informational support 222-223
information processing 119-120
injured athletes
    emotional responses 219-220
    setting attainable goals for rehabilitation 223
    social support for 222
injuries
    athletes at risk 218-219

effective recovery 225-227
    impact of 218
    rehabilitation through imagery 143
injury avoidance 228-229
insecurity 40
instinct theory 4
insulated listening 203
internal distractions 114, 123
International Gymnast (magazine) 247
International Society of Sport Psychology (ISSP) xi
interpersonal-relations approach to team development 174-175
interpersonal relationships 199
interventions 64, 87-88, 224
in the "zone" 13-14
intrinsic feelings 8
intrinsic motivation 7, 39-40
inverted-U hypothesis 80-81, 81f, 85
irrational beliefs 39
irritability points 106
ISSP (International Society of Sport Psychology) xi
IZOF (Individual Zones of Optimal Functioning) 81-83, 82ff

J
Jackson, Phil 6
James, William 5
Janelle, Christopher 116
Johnson, Craig 243
Johnson, Magic 43
Jordon, Michael 23, 124, 125
Jowdy, Doug 127

K
Kellmann, Michael 38f, 53, 65
Kerr, John 83
kinesthetic imagery 129
Kriegal, Robert 195, 200
Krzyzewski, Mike 191-192
Kübler-Ross, Elisabeth 219

L
Landers, Dan 135
Landry, Tom 6
language, characteristics of supportive 204
language logbook 35
language, use of supportive 199-200
law of use and disuse 49
leadership. See also chapter scenarios
    adversity 160, 162-164, 162t, 163tt
    characteristics 182-183, 183t
    defined 155-156
    energy-management principles for leaders 165-170
    four themes of 156-157
    models 156
    multidimensional engagement 160f
    storytelling and 164-165
    teaching skills in 169-170

team behavior 161, 161t
Leadership Scale of Sport (LSS) 185
learned optimism 17-18
Lewis, Brian 116
limited information capacity 118
Lindbergh, Anne Spencer Morrow 197
Linder, Darwyn 116
listening, active 108, 203
listening, effective 196
listening, selective 203
listen with flexibility 205
locus of causality 7, 11, 12t
locus of control 11, 12t
Loehr, James 153, 266-267
logbook page example 62f, 63f
Lombardi, Vince 40
Lombardo, John 259
LSS (Leadership Scale of Sport) 185

M
MacIntyre, Tadhg 130
Mahoney, Michael 129-130, 141
Managing for the Future (Drucker) 156
Mandela, Nelson 48
MAPS, defined 183-184
marathon training 49-50
Martens, Rainer 197
Martinez, Tino 93
May, Jerry 213
MBTI (Myers-Briggs Type Indicator) 185
McCann, Sean 278
McEnroe, John 122
McGwire, Mark 260
McSorley, Marty 96
Meacci, William 139
memory 143
mental energy 158
mental genetics 5
mental leadership 156-157, 161, 162t
mental practice 133, 135-136
mental training trends 277-278
message-receiving systems 203-205
message-sending systems, effective 197-198
Miller, George 197
Mintz, Laurie 237-238
Miracle (movie) 153
mission statement 184
MMIS (Multidimensional Mental Imagery Scale) 147
modalities 129
models
    catastrophe, to sport performance 84-85
    cognitive-appraisal model 220
    energy-management-based 157
    health belief model 224-225
    leadership 156
    self-focus 116-117
    Spielberger's State-Trait model 78

models *(continued)*
  time course of athlete prepared-
    ness 56*ff*
  total fitness 38*f*
  transtheoretical model of change
    224
Monica: From Fear to Victory (Seles)
  213
monitoring training intensity 60
mood modifiers 105-106
Moore, Steve 96
moral behaviors 27
Moran, Aidan 114, 114*f*, 121,
  130, 136
Moran's attentional system 114*f*
Morgan, William 61, 99
motivation. *See also* chapter sce-
    narios
  deterministic *versus* free will
    6-7
  extremes 9
  individual styles 14-15
  intrinsic 39-40
  research 6-7
  rewards 7
  strategies 16-17
  sustainable growth 18
  team motivator knowledge of
    teammates 15
motivational climate 9, 23-24
motivation psychology 3-4
motivators 5
motor-skill development 124
motor skills 135
Mottram, D.R. 260
multidimensional engagement
  160*f*
Multidimensional Mental Imagery
  Scale (MMIS) 147
Murphy, Shane 117, 249, 271
muscular variables 117
music to control anger 106
Myers-Briggs Type Indicator
  (MBTI) 185

N
National Hockey League. *See also*
  NHL
National Institute on Drug Abuse
  (NIDA) 276
National Institute on Drug Abuse
  Research Report Series 259
Navratilova, Martina 125
NCAA, anger-management work-
  shops 112
need achievement 5
negative energy 168-169
neuropsychology 284-285
neuroscience, advances in 127-
  128, 133
Newburg, Doug 42
NFL. *See also* football
NHL
  criminal behavior 96-97
  players 8, 93
  playoff injuries 93
Nicholls, John 19
Nicklaus, Jack 131

NIDA (National Institute on Drug
  Abuse) 276
noise 122
nonverbal cues 100
nuclear war 45

O
objective scales 185
obligatory exercise 240
Olympic games
  Albertville France (1992) 71
  Australian Olympic trials (2004)
    123
  Canadian speed-skating (1998)
    41
  Salt Lake City (2002) xiv, 42
  swimming training loads (1972)
    49
Olympic sports
  bobsled 131-132
  ice hockey 153
  ski team 172-173
Olympic Training Center (OTC)
  49, 127
open sports 123
optimum experience 17
Orlick, Terry 308, 312
OTC (Olympic Training Center)
  49, 127
outcomes 11
outward focus 90
overconfidence 150
overeating 240
overtraining
  assessing 52-53
  effects of 50-52
  individuality 57-59
  minimizing 69
  periodization 54-57
  symptoms 57-60, 57*f*
Overtraining (Botterill; Wilson)
  38*f*

P
pain 232
Paivio, Alan 133
Parcells, Bill 97
Partington, John 308, 312
Pavlov 125
Payton, Gary 122
pencil-and-paper assessments 61,
  62*t*, 63-64, 63*t*, 87
pep talk, pregame 14
Perceived Motivational Climate
  in Sport Questionnaire-2
  (PMCSQ-2) 185
perception 114*f*
perception of support 223
Perceptions of Success Questionnaire (POSQ) 32
perfection 39
performance
  automated 124-125
  based on emotions 136
performance-altering effects,
  research on 99
performance-enhancing drugs. *See
  also* chapter scenarios

  legalized drug use, pros and cons
    of 264-266
  long-term consequences 268-
    269
  motives for taking 256-258
  overview 255-256
  roles in drug-use prevention
    271-276
  sports organizations account-
    ability for 275
  terms and concepts 259-264
performance evaluating 109-110
performance pyramid 158*f*
performance stagnation 49
performers, elite. *See also* elite
  athletes
periodization 54-57, 55*f*
*Periodization Theory and Methodology
  of Training* (Bompa) 55*f*
Perry, Clark 72
Perry, Howard 138
perspective 43-44
Petersen, Kirsten 2
PET (positron emission tomography) 132-133
physical energy 157
physiological signs of anger 105
Plato 113
playing conditions and weather
  122
PMCSQ-2 (Perceived Motivational
  Climate in Sport Question-
  naire-2) 185
PMR (progressive muscle relaxation) 89
Poggi, Biff 209
POMS (Profile of Mood States) 61,
  87, 99, 102
positron emission tomography
  (PET) 132-133
Posner, Michael 115
POSQ (Perceptions of Success
  Questionnaire) 32
practice, mental 133, 135-136
pregame pep talk 14
preparation ethic 45
preperformance rehearsal 139
Price, Ed 139
Principle-Centered Leadership (Covey)
  156
problem-focused coping 221
problem solving 109
process goal setting 40
processing capacity 118
Profile of Mood States (POMS) 61,
  87, 99, 102
progressive muscle relaxation
  (PMR) 89
progressive relaxation 68
Pros and Cons (Benedict, Yaeger)
  98
protection motivation theory 225
pseudolistening 203
pseudo team performers 47
PST (psychological skills training) 287
psychological skills training (PST)
  287

psychological symptoms of over-training 57f
psychologist. See also sport psychologists
psychology. See also sport psychology
    cognitive-behavioral xii
    motivation 3-4
Psychology and Athletics (Griffith) vii
Psychology of Coaching (Griffith) vii
Psychology of Sport Injury (Heil) 227
psychophysiological variables 117
"pushy parent" phenomenon 176
pyramid of success, Wooden's 40

Q
QE (quiet eye) 117
questionnaires, decision-style 185
quiet eye (QE) 117

R
race strategy using imagery 140
RAM (random access memory) 118
random access memory (RAM) 118
rating of perceived exertion 60
reciprocal inhibition 110
recovery strategies 63-67
Recovery-Stress Questionnaire for Athletes (REST-Q) 61-63
recovery techniques 67-68
rehabilitation
    health belief model 224-225
    skills to facilitate 232-233
    team approach to 230-231
    the treatment team 227-228
reinforcement theory 5
relationships, interpersonal 199
relaxation 67-68
    autogenic 68
    for injury recovery 226-227
    progressive 68
    to control anger 105
relaxation training 88-89
Remember the Titans (movie) 209
Resonance (Newburg) 42
Restak, Richard 125
resting heart rate 59-60
REST-Q (Recovery-Stress Questionnaire for Athletes) 61-63
retaliatory behavior 101
reversals 83
reversal theory 83-84
rewards
    external 124
    to improve motivation 7
Richardson, Nancy Ann 213
Riley, Pat 42
rituals 167-168
rivalries 41
Rizzo, John 156
role models
    athletes 95
    behavior of 22-23

coaches as 67, 111
    pressure placed on children 23
role-playing strategy 99
Romanowski, Bill 93
Rosenfeld, Lawrence 193f, 196
Rosen, Lionel 249
Rotella, Bob 140
RPE (Borg's Rating of Perceived Exertion) 60
Ruettiger, Rudy 6
running, distance 58
Rusko orthostatic heart rate test 59-60

S
Sackett, Ron 138
Sacred Cows Make the Best Burgers (Kriegel; Brandt) 195-196
Samuelson, Joan Benoit 49
Sandler, Adam 136
Satir, Virginia 211
Schrof, Joannie 265-266
Schwartz, Tony 266-267
Science and Practice of Strength Training (Zatiorsky) 56ff
science, cognitive 125
searchlight metaphor 119
selective attention 119
selective listening 203
selectivity, attention as 116
Seles, Monica 213
self-acceptance 40, 46
self-challenge 33. See also goals
self-confidence 134-135
self-efficacy 8-9
self-esteem 40, 169, 257
self-focus model 116-117
self-talk 106-107. See also imagery
Seligman, Martin 17
sense of mission 45
sense of purpose 8-9
Shelton, Tony 141
Sherman, Roberta 249
shift of focus 121
Shula, Don 1
Siedentop, Daryl 6-7
sight, imagery experiences of 144
SIQ, (Sport Imagery Questionnaire) 147
situational cues 100-101
skiers
    injuries 216, 220-221
    selected emotions in 82f
    use of imagery 128
Skinner, B.F. 4
smell, sense of 145
Smith, Ron 201
Smyers, Karen 232
soccer
    anger management in players 102
    imagery to build teamwork 143-144
    study of university classes 99
social comparison 9-10
social facilitation 4
somatic anxiety 84
speed-skating 41

Spielberger, Charles 78, 96, 102
spiritual leadership 156, 161t
Spitz, Mark 49
spontaneous hostile violence 96-97
sport
    anger-management programs 111-112
    as big business xii
    controlling drug use in 266-271
    global priorities and 47
    open/closed 123
    role of the environment in 123
Sport Imagery Questionnaire (SIQ) 147
sport injuries 93
sport-involvement contract 36
sport performance challenge 227
sport psychologists. See also chapter scenarios
    applying to performance 283-284
    at the Olympic level 290
    certification xiii, 311
    characteristics of proven 308-309
    clinical and counseling issues 288
    consultant-athlete relationship 312-313
    consultation settings 288-289
    critical issues for 305-307
    deciding on a practitioner 296-299
    evaluating a prospective practitioner 301-303
    in the field 287-290
    markers of effective 18
    options for locating 300
    overview 279-281
    role in drug-use prevention 271-273
    team/individual consulting 281-282
    techniques 309-310
    titles used by practitioners 293-296
sport psychology
    advancements in xi, 13
    cognitive 5-6
    defining themes xi-xii
    holistic approach xiv
    problems 297-298
    relevancy of xiv-xv
    scientific approach xiii-xiv
Sport Psychology (Anshel) 197
sport psychology consultants. See also sport psychologists
sports. See also Olympic sports
Sports Illustrated 269, 299
sports injuries
    overview 215-218
stability 11, 12t
stage-hogging 203
Stanley Cup 8, 93
Stanton, Mike 259
State-Trait Anger Expression Inventory (STAXI) 102

STAXI (State-Trait Anger Expression Inventory) 102
Steadman, Richard 227
Steinhilber, Andrew 43
steroids, anabolic 262-264
storytelling and leadership 164-165
strategic disengagement 167
strategies, goal-setting 173-175
strategy, role-playing 99
stress
    defined 75
    nontraining 54
stress management 68, 141
Stringer, Korey 258-259
success
    athlete's perception of 19-20
    attributions 12
    shortcuts and gimmicks xii
    Wooden's pyramid of 40
Sundgot-Borgen, Jorunn 243
support, tangible 223
supportive language characteristics 204
sustainability 8, 44
sustainable growth 18
sustained motivation 9
Swain, Austin 28
swimmers and gamesmanship 122
swimmers, impact of proper mechanics on 124
Swoap, Bob 249
symbolic rehearsal 138-139

T
table tennis 141-142
Taking Sides (Goldberg) 264
tangible support 222
Task and Ego Orientation in Sport Questionnaire (TEOSQ) 32
task-involved athletes 20, 134
task orientation
    commitment to practice 26-27
    overview 22-23
    task-mastery 9
tasks, cognitive 138-139
taste, sense of 145
Taylor, Scott 46
Taylor, Shelley 133-134
team-building 47-48, 185-186
team-building behaviors 188-189
team cohesion 172-173
team cohesiveness 176-177
team development, interpersonal-relationship approach to 174-175
team effort 178
team goals 175-176, 176*t*, 186
team interrelationships 177
team quality assessment 184-185
team relationship tension 181*t*
team sports, individual 172

teamwork 143-144, 171-172
teen athletes. *See also* adolescent athletes
tennis, chapter scenario on 160
tennis players
    factors influencing achievement goals 28-29
    gamesmanship 122
    immediate effect of actions 124
    visual control training programs for 117
TEOSQ (Task and Ego Orientation in Sport Questionnaire) 32
Test of Performance Strategies (TOPS) 147-148
tetrahydrogestrinone (THG) 264
The Mental Game Plan (Bull) 80
The New Brain (Restak) 125
The Power of One (Courtney) xi
The Psychology of Concentration in Sport Performers (Moran) 114, 121
The Seven Habits of Highly Effective People (Covey) 198
The Waterboy (movie) 136
THG (tetrahydrogestrinone) 264
Thomas, Pat 148
Thompson, John 195
Thompson, Ron 249
Thorpe, Ian 123
thought management 233
Tichy, Noel 155
time-outs for anger control 108-109
time-sharing 119
Tod, David 278
Tomjanovich, Rudy 96
TOPS (Test of Performance Strategies) 147-148
Torre, Joe 6
Tosi, Henry 156
total fitness model 38*f*
touch, sense of 145
training. *See also* overtraining
    loads 49
    monitoring intensity 60-64, 62*f*, 63*f*
    periodization 54-57, 55*f*
    questionnaire 62*f*, 63*f*
    theory 54
training logs 60-61
training-program design 54-57, 55*f*, 56*ff*
transfer of training philosophy 99
transtheoretical model of change 224
treatment team, the 227-228
triggers 106
Triplett, Norman 3-4
trust 198
trustworthiness 198
tunnel vision 119
Turgeon, Pierre 93

U
USA Today 258
use and disuse, law of 49
U.S. News and World Report 265
U.S. Olympic Committee (USOC) 50-51, 51, 71
U.S. parachute team 187

V
Vealey's State Sport Confidence Inventory 135
Vella-Brodrick, Dianne 147
verbal statements, appropriate 205
Vernacchia, Ralph 172
Vickers, Joan 117
violence in sport. *See also* aggression; anger
    committed by athletes 98
    research on violent athletes 97-98
    terms used 95-97
visual control 117
visual distractions 122-124
Vividness of Visual Imagery Questionnaire 147
Voltaire 189

W
Walsh, Bill 178
Washington, Kermit 96
weather and playing conditions 122
Weder, Gustav 131-132
weightlifters 141
Weinberg, Robert 197
Weiner, Bernard 11
Welch, Jack 155
West Coast equestrian team 173
West, Jerry 206
Wheeler, Rashidi 259
Wilder, Larry 196
Wilkinson, Laura 233
Williams, Bernie 93
Williams, Marcus 93
Williams, Melvin 260
Wilson, Clare 38*f*
Wooden, John 40
Wooden's pyramid of success 40
Woolfolk, Rob 148
work ethic 45
worry 79
wrestling 51-52
Wulf, Gabrielle 124

Y
Yaeger, Don 98
Yesalis, Chuck 256

Z
Zatsiorsky, V.M. 56*ff*

About the Editor

Dr. Shane Murphy is one of the nation's leading sport psychologists, with expertise in performance excellence, competitiveness, and teamwork. He is currently assistant professor at Western Connecticut State University. Murphy served as a sport psychologist to the U.S. Olympic team at the 1988 Summer Games in Seoul, the U.S. Olympic team at the 1992 Winter Games in Albertville, and the 1996 U.S. slalom canoe and kayak teams in Atlanta. In addition, he was sport psychology consultant to the U.S. snowboard team from 1999 to 2002. For seven years he worked for the United States Olympic Committee (USOC) as head of its sport psychology department and later as the associate director of its sport science and technology division.

Murphy is a popular speaker and author of the best-selling book *The Achievement Zone: An 8-Step Guide to Peak Performance in All Arenas of Life*. He has appeared on many television and radio programs on ABC, CBS, MSNBC, CNN, and NPR. He also has had articles containing or referring to his work in *USA Today*, *The Washington Post*, *The New York Times*, *Newsweek*, and other major publications. He is a former president of the division of sport and exercise psychology of the American Psychological Association (APA) and is a fellow of the Association for the Advancement of Applied Sport Psychology (AAASP).

Murphy lives in Trumbull, Connecticut, with his wife, Annemarie, and two children, Bryan and Theresa.

About the Contibutors

Mitch Abrams, PsyD, is the president and founder of Learned Excellence for Athletes, a sport psychology consulting company; an adjunct faculty member of Fairleigh Dickinson University; and director of inpatient psychology at Northern State Prison in Newark, New Jersey. He specializes in developing programs for athletes to improve performance through emotion management. Abrams is a member of the American Psychological Association's (APA) division of exercise and sport psychology and the Association for the Advancement of Applied Sport Psychology (AAASP).

Mark B. Andersen, PhD, is an associate professor at the school of human movement, recreation, and performance at Victoria University in Melbourne, Australia. He specializes in supervision, injury, exercise, quality of life, and chronic disease. Andersen has worked with athletes from a wide range of sports, including Arizona State University Intercollegiate Athletics, Victorian Diving Association, and various other diving, swimming, track and field, wrestling, and golf teams. Andersen has been on the editorial boards of *The Sport Psychologist, Journal of Applied Sport Psychology,* and the *Journal of Sport and Exercise Psychology.*

Mark Anshel, PhD, is a professor at Middle Tennessee State University in the department of health, physical education, and recreation. His primary areas of research and writing have included coping with stressful events in sport and the use of steroids and other banned drugs among competitive athletes. He is a certified consultant for the Association for the Advancement of Applied Sport Psychology (AAASP).

Gloria Balague, PhD, directs the sport psychology services at the University of Illinois at Chicago Sports Medicine Center and Human Performance Lab. An internationally acclaimed sport psychology consultant and speaker, she most recently addressed the Sydney Olympic Scientific Congress in Australia. Balague is a member of the executive committee and president of the sport psychology division of the International Association of Applied Psychology.

Cal Botterill, PhD, is a health and performance psychology professor at the University of Winnipeg, Canada. He has served as a consultant to seven Canadian Olympic teams, five NHL hockey teams—including the 1994 Stanley Cup champion the New York Rangers—and numerous corporations such as Coca-Cola and Great-West Life Assurance Company. Cal has authored hundreds of articles, books, videos, and international presentations

Charles H. Brown, PhD, is director of FPS Performance, a Charlotte, North Carolina–based company specializing in performance enhancement of athletes, performing artists, and business professionals. He has worked with athletes at every level, specializing in the contextual factors that impact performance, athletes' relationships, and the work-life balance of elite performers. Brown is a consultant certified by the Association for the Advancement of Applied Sport Psychology (AAASP), a member of the United States Olympic Committee (USOC) sport psychology registry, and a member of the National Register of Health Service Providers in Psychology.

Kevin L. Burke, PhD, is an associate professor in the Jiann-Ping Hsu School of Public Health at Georgia Southern University. As a certified sport psychology consultant of the Association for the Advancement of Applied Sport Psychology (AAASP), Burke has advised professional, college, high school, and recreational athletes from various sports. He has also coauthored *Sport Psychology Library Series: Basketball* and *Tennis* and actively served on numerous journal editorial boards for journals and research committees within the field.

Karen D. Cogan, PhD, is a psychologist and assistant professor at the University of North Texas (UNT). She has been a consultant to the U.S. ski team at the Olympics, a staff psychologist with the Counseling and Testing Center at UNT, a faculty member of the Center for Sport Psychology, and author or coauthor of several publications, including *Sport Psychology Library: Gymnastics*. Cogan is a member of the Association for the Advancement of Applied Sport Psychology (AAASP) and the American Psychological Association (APA).

R. Kelly Crace, PhD, is the director of the counseling center and an adjunct associate professor in psychology at the College of William and Mary. He is a licensed psychologist and a certified sport psychology consultant. Crace is the codeveloper of the Life Values Inventory, an empirically-based values clarification survey. His research and consultation focus on values and transition as applied to both individual and organizational development

John F. Eliot, PhD, is the director of sport psychology in the department of kinesiology at Rice University in Houston, Texas, where his areas of specialization include performance enhancement, management consulting, and rehabilitation. Eliot has worked with a wide range of sports teams, including the Houston Astros, Philadelphia Eagles, San Antonio Spurs, and Chicago White Sox, along with numerous health care and business clients.

Bradley Hack, PhD, is the director of sport psychology for the department of athletics at the University of North Carolina at Chapel Hill. He is an executive committee member of the American Psychological Association's (APA) division of exercise and sport psychology. In 2003, he was appointed chairman of the division's Presidential Task Force to establish national standards for sport psychology training, education, and experience for sport psychologists.

Bruce D. Hale, PhD, is an associate professor of kinesiology at Penn State Berks-Lehigh Valley College in Reading, Pennsylvania. His areas of specialization include sport and exercise psychology and educational sport psychology. He is a fellow of the Association for the Advancement of Applied Sport Psychology (AAASP), and has been a performance-enhancement consultant to hundreds of college, professional, and elite national teams. Hale has worked with USA Wrestling, the British Biathlon, USRowing, TAC, and USA Rugby athletes

Charles J. Hardy, PhD, is the acting dean of the Jack N. Averitt college of graduate studies and a professor in the Jiann-Ping Hsu School of Public Health at Georgia Southern University. He is a past president of the Association for the Advancement of Applied Sport Psychology (AAASP). His primary area of research has been in social influence processes in exercise and sport. He has extensive consulting experience at the youth sport, high school, university, Olympic, and professional levels.

Chris Harwood, PhD, is a lecturer in applied sport psychology at Loughborough University, United Kingdom. He is a BASES-accredited and BOA-registered sport psychologist whose research focuses on achievement motivation in sport, social psychology of elite youth sport, and performance-enhancement interventions. Harwood received the Doctoral Dissertation Award from the Association for the Advancement of Applied Sport Psychology (AAASP) in 1998. Harwood has served as a consultant to the Nottingham Forest Soccer Club, the Lawn Tennis Association, English Cricket Board, the Football Association, and the Youth Sport Trust, plus a variety of other national governing bodies in UK sport.

Jim Loehr is the chairman and CEO of LGE Performance Systems, a training company specializing in performance enhancement for professionals and athletes. He is a member of the American Psychological Association (APA), the Association for the Advancement of Applied Sport Psychology (AAASP), and the American College of Sports Medicine (ACSM). Loehr has worked with a wide range of teams — the United States Tennis Association (USTA), Women's Tennis Association (WTA), International Tennis Federation (ITF), and Intercollegiate Tennis Association (ITA)—as well as professional athletes from the NBA, NFL, NHL, PGA, and LPGA; wrote 13 books; received numerous awards for his contributions in sport psychology; and contributes regularly to a wide variety of sports and business publications.

Jerry R. May, PhD, is a professor of psychiatry and behavioral sciences at the University of Nevada's school of medicine. He developed and implemented the first official sport psychology program for the United States Olympic Committee (USOC) and has worked with such teams as the U.S. alpine ski team (1980-92), U.S. National soccer team (1997-98), and the U.S. sailing team (1992-present), and athletes in sports ranging from soccer, golf, tennis, and basketball to skiing, sailing, biathlon, and powerlifting.

Sean C. McCann, PhD, is the head of the United States Olympic Committee (USOC) sport psychology department. He works directly with teams and coaches at the U.S. Olympic Training Center and has traveled with the last five Olympic teams as a sport psychologist. McCann writes extensively about sport psychology in a number of outlets, including refereed journals, book chapters, columns, brochures, and workbooks for Olympic athletes and coaches.

Clark Perry, PhD, is senior consultant psychologist at the Australian Institute of Sport in Canberra and managing director of PST Systems, a performance-enhancement and training company. He is a world leader in sport psychology, leadership, and team development, having worked closely with some of the world's best athletes as a member of four Olympic Games, three Commonwealth Games, eight World Championships, five Pan Pacific Swimming Championships, and four Super 12 Rugby Finals. Perry has served as senior psychologist to the Australian Olympic swim team, Australian Cycling, Triathlon Australia, Australian Baseball, ACT Brumbies, and the Australian Wallabies.

Kirsten Peterson, PhD is a member of the United States Olympic Committee's (USOC) sport psychology staff, providing counseling and performance-enhancement services to athletes and coaches of numerous Olympic, Paralympic, and Pan American sports. She has traveled as part of the USOC sport psychology staff for three Olympic teams. Peterson is a licensed psychologist, a member of the American Psychological Association (APA), and is a certified consultant through the Association for the Advancement of Applied Sport Psychology (AAASP).

David Tod is a PhD candidate at Victoria University in Melbourne, Australia, specializing in professional practice and performance enhancement. Tod has worked with the Northern Institute of the New Zealand Academy of Sport and with professional rugby unions and rugby league teams. He has also worked with athletes in numerous sports including international track and field, swimming, cricket, triathlon, cycling, and powerlifting.

Tracy L. Veach, EdD, is a professor of psychiatry and behavioral sciences and internal medicine at the University of Nevada's school of medicine. He works with individual athletes and teams in performance enhancement and integrative health. He has consulted with a wide range of athletes at high school, collegiate, and national team levels in football, basketball, swimming, track and field, and equestrian sports. Veach also served as a sport consultant to a world record–setting U.S. sports parachute team.